# Common Fields

## an environmental history of St. Louis

T0069120

# Common Fields
## an environmental history of St. Louis

### edited by Andrew Hurley

MISSOURI HISTORICAL SOCIETY PRESS • SAINT LOUIS

©1997 by the Missouri Historical Society Press
Published in the United States of America by the
Missouri Historical Society Press,
P.O. Box 11940, St. Louis, Missouri 63112-0040
5 4 3 2 1  01 00 99 98 97

Library of Congress Cataloging-in-Publication Data

Common fields : an environmental history of St. Louis /
    edited by Andrew Hurley.
          p.       cm.
    Includes index.
    ISBN 1-883982-16-2 (pbk. : alk. paper). –
    ISBN 1-883982-15-4 (cloth : alk. paper)
1. Saint Louis (Mo.)–Environmental conditions–History.
2. Sustainable development–Missouri–Saint Louis–History.
I. Hurley, Andrew, 1961-  .
GE155.M8C66 1997
304.2´09778´65–dc21

                                96-51155
                                     CIP

∞ This paper meets the requirements of the American National Standard for
Permanence of Paper for Printed Library Materials, Z39.48, 1984.

Designed by: Robyn Morgan
Cover image courtesy of Earth Observation Satellite Company, 1993.
Printed by: Fiedler Printing Company, St. Louis, Missouri

For my brother (thanks for the car)

# Contents

# Foreword

The thirteen essays in this volume document a struggle that has concerned residents of the Mississippi River valley for thousands of years: the struggle to define an acceptable balance between our activity and the quality of our physical environment. At its most basic level, it is a struggle about how we live—a struggle that has forced us to confront our impact on the land, on the air that we breathe, and on the waters that nearly surround us. As populations have grown, resource consumption increased, and technological changes abounded, the questions raised by this struggle have grown increasingly complex. How many "conveniences" are we willing or able to give up to conserve our resources? What kind of and how much technology do we "need" in order to live happily? Who should be responsible for bringing about the changes needed to preserve our land, our air, our water?

Environmental scholars use the term *environmental sustainability* to address such questions, for the issue they raise is, How can we adapt our living habits to sustain the world we inhabit, given its limitations? It is unassailably true that this planet is finite, that it can only support a limited population, especially when that population consumes vast quantities of resources and recycles only a small percentage of them. Some might point to technology as a solution to this problem, but technology can only stretch the margins; it modifies but does not invalidate the equation. Furthermore, technology has always had unanticipated adverse consequences, which often require even greater applications of technology for their amelioration.

It is only recently that we have begun to realize the inadequacies of technology for "stretching the margins" of our planet. Neither nineteenth-century historians nor historians of even fifty years ago formally studied the history of human interactions with the earth's ecosystems and the adverse impacts of human activity upon these systems. After all, to most people in the nineteenth century, the earth's resources appeared infinite. Developing countries, including the United States, were preoccupied with the use of technologies to more efficiently exploit resources. A better understanding of the environmental consequences of human behavior had to wait for the scientific work of ecologists and the research work of environmental historians.

Two principal events created the circumstances that focused the attention of both historians and scientists on ecological issues. The first was the rapid escalation of technological prowess. In the twentieth century, our technologies—particularly the automobile—have consumed the planet's resources at rates that were unimaginable only fifty years ago. For example, in 1950 world oil production was 518 million tons; by 1994, it had expanded more than fivefold, to 2,953 million tons.

In the same period, global natural gas production has soared from the equivalent of 180 million tons of oil to that of over 2,000 million tons. Not coincidentally, automobile production multiplied by a factor of more than four, from 8 million to 35 million vehicles a year.

The second factor was the population explosion. In less than fifty years, the human population has doubled, from 2.6 billion in 1950 to over 5.6 billion in the mid-1990s. This increase is more than the total increase in all the preceding eons of human life on this planet. Both rates of population growth and resource consumption are receiving deserved attention from all fields, for the burgeoning population and its attendant increase in resource consumption have accentuated national and global social and economic fissures. As production has increased, the benefits have accrued largely to the wealthy, while the costs have fallen largely to the poor. Never before has the chasm between rich and poor been so wide as it is now.

Environmental history is thus an excellent example of how historians have shifted their work from simply documenting and explaining past events to considering how those events inform the present and the future. Environmental historians are concerned with suggesting modified values and behaviors that will improve both our individual lives and the life of our planet.

The essays that follow are excellent examples of the new field of environmental history, but they are more than that. Each author examines the natural characteristics of our place and our relationships with each other as we have allocated both the benefits and costs of our exploitation of resources. Herein we discover local manifestations of global questions, such as what is acceptable environmental quality, and whether our definitions of justice require that all people who live here have an equal claim to live in a healthy environment.

While environmental problems are global, their resolution, as always, requires local action—changes in us. Fortunately, it is easier for humans to understand and respond to those problems that directly affect them. It is easier for us to comprehend and respond to the impacts of automobiles upon our people and our place, for example, than it is to respond to global repercussions of emissions pollution. We must care about our place first. Yet the same environmental ethics that are healthy for the St. Louis region will, we must hope, lead to insistence on a global ethic and global action.

The same ethic that can create an earth with a balance among people, resource consumption, and technological change may also assist in overcoming the pervasive isolation and ennui that confounds the human spirit as we approach the millennium. Many of the technologies that have accelerated our capacity to consume resources have also isolated us from each other, loosened our sense of attachment to place, lessened our sense of mutual obligation, and severed many of the ties that once bound us together as a community. On a typical day, we speed to work in automobiles with radios repeating weather forecasts and traffic reports, cram into parking garages and then into buildings with self-contained artificial environments, and repeat the process at the end of the day until finally we push the button that lowers the garage door. Then we watch electronically generated images on television, or even conduct "relationships" on-line.

Never, in this typical day, do we experience our community—those people with whom we share so much: this place, the air we breathe, our sewer system, our schools, our economy, our political system, our courts, and our future. No wonder we feel we have lost a sense of community, a sense of being inextricably linked to each other. This sense of isolation is heightened by the way we design our neighborhoods and houses and where we choose to build them. The ongoing process of suburbanization of our region is not a response to population growth; rather, it is an effort to escape from each other, to avoid each other's problems. We now have back decks, not front porches. The most prominent features of our homes are garages built for private automobiles. They face on streets, often without sidewalks, that lead to arterial roads that lead to interstates. We cannot walk to shopping, to church, to school, to the park, or to the library. We never even have to see each other. This arrangement wastes resources, devours farmland, creates air pollution, isolates us from each other and from the natural world, and, because it encourages isolation, undermines community and common purpose. A reexamination of our environmental past, the reexamination that is suggested by this book, may lead us to a healthier environmental future.

In her wonderful clarion call to environmental awareness, *Silent Spring*, Rachel Carson writes: "We stand now where two roads diverge. But unlike the roads in Robert Frost's familiar poem, they are not equally fair. The road we have long been traveling is deceptively easy, a smooth superhighway on which we progress with great speed, but at its end lies disaster. The other fork of the road—the one 'less traveled by'—offers our last, our only chance to reach a destination that assures the preservation of the earth." I hope that this volume encourages St. Louisans to pursue that road "less traveled by," for the essays that follow underscore the most profound conclusion of history: the values, decisions, and actions of one generation have obvious and critical consequences for all those yet to come. Our hubris has been the tendency to insist that the earth, and our place upon it, belongs only to us. History is both antidote and burden, for in it we find affirmation of our debt to those now gone, a debt that can only be repaid by leaving to unborn humans a planet and its people balanced and in harmony. It is only in this way that the survival of humanity will be assured.

Robert R. Archibald
President
Missouri Historical Society

# Common Fields

## an environmental history of St. Louis

# Common Fields

*An Introduction*

~

## *Andrew Hurley*

Until recently, the environment has not been a category of analysis in studying the history of our cities. Perhaps this is because we still conceive of our cities as entities divorced from the natural world. To experience nature we visit the countryside, read scientific magazines, or, most likely, watch nature shows on television. We take little notice of the water circulation cycles, food chains, temperature gradients, and other natural processes that both support and endanger life in our own backyards. Having established a false dichotomy between the urban and the natural, we find ourselves unprepared for many of the environmental consequences of our actions and ill equipped to address them.

This essay collection is a step toward better preparing citizens of St. Louis and students of urban and environmental history to grapple with the St. Louis region's natural environment and to consider the complex interaction between human and natural forces. The contributors address the relationship between urbanization and environmental change from a variety of disciplines and perspectives. Some of the essays that follow show how the natural environment has shaped human behavior; others emphasize the ways in which humans have modified the physical landscape in pursuit of particular social, economic, and political objectives. All attest to the fact that the physical environment is not simply an inert stage upon which human activity takes place, but rather an independent force that must be taken into account in any assessment of how our cities have changed over time and why they are in the condition we find them today.

The false dichotomy between the urban and the natural, so misleading in our analysis of cities, is exacerbated by a misguided impression that there exists a nature in wilderness that has somehow remained untouched by human history. In fact, human beings have shaped the physical environment in both its "natural" wilderness settings and in its urban context. When we think of pure wilderness, whether we imagine the sequoias in our national parks, the lakes and forests of the Missouri Ozarks, or even the survival of the gray wolf, we are projecting an idealized notion of what constitutes nature, seeing it as something pristine or separate from ourselves. We ignore that these plants, places, and animals have evolved in the context of human activity, if not through deliberate manipulation, then at least through the indirect effects of global ecological changes in which humans have exerted a role. More often than not it has been people living in cities who have been responsible for both constructing our idealized notions of nature and introducing the human element into it.

All of this is not to deny that urban societies have been responsive to particular features of their environmental surroundings. If city planners, policy makers, and property holders have not always appreciated the complex natural processes that support urban life, they have nonetheless constructed their cities and organized urban space in the context of a physical world not entirely of their own making. Most major cities are where they are because of environmental factors: snug harbors, breaking points along rivers, junctures of ecological zones, and so forth. Moreover, the spatial distribution of economic functions and population groups within cities have followed the physical contours of the landscape. It is no coincidence, for example, that in so many cities, the wealthiest districts are found on high ground where the air circulates rapidly, vistas are the most pleasing, and the ground is best protected from unforeseen floods. Likewise, factory districts often occupy land adjacent to rivers and harbors where manufacturers have enjoyed easy access to water for transportation, waste disposal, and power. To exclude this dynamic from the history of our cities is to miss much of the story.

Putting the environment back into the city, or at least into the history of the city, compels us to revise the familiar arrangement of events, settings, and actors. Traditionally, when constructing our urban histories, we have been drawn to milestones that spurred economic growth, generated civic pride, or influenced national or international developments. Most St. Louisans, for instance, are well informed about the 1904 World's Fair, the Gateway Arch, and the Lindbergh flight. Our historical celebrities, those for whom we name our streets, plazas, and stadiums, tend to be people who furthered the city's economic growth or contributed to its political maturity. In St. Louis, founder Pierre Laclede, bridge builder James B. Eads, and beer baron Adolphus Busch have been among the most prominent civic heroes.

The rise of social history over the past thirty years has expanded the cast of historical characters to throw light on the contributions that women, laborers, racial minorities, and poor people have made to urban society. In the process, the setting of historical studies has shifted from the corporate boardroom and legislative hall to the factory floor, neighborhood street, and tenement kitchen. The benefits accruing to St. Louis from this trend have included recent scholarship about ethnic communities in the nineteenth century, labor organizations in the 1870s and the 1930s, and the civil rights movement of the 1960s.[1] Rewriting history from the bottom up has necessitated a thoroughgoing revision of the way we understand our past and its key actors and processes. Moreover, our interpretations change when these previously ignored groups enter the picture. For example, the story of economic growth takes on a different cast when measured against the full array of costs imposed on workers, racial minorities, and others who suffered from a deteriorating quality of life.

As one might expect, reorganizing urban history around the theme of the physical landscape provides yet another set of criteria with which to assess our past: the salubrity of the environment, the sustainability of urban ecological systems, and the degree of equity involved as environmental transformations impinge on diverse social groups. An environmental history will, of necessity, bring different episodes and characters to center stage. Events that may have been considered of secondary importance—the Great Fire of 1849, the cholera epidemics of the mid-nineteenth century, the zoning plan of 1918, the smoke control initiatives of the 1930s—emerge as key turning points; characters that have received only passing mention in standard texts—sewer commissioner Robert Moore; sanitary engineer George Homan; smoke control architect Raymond Tucker; and Bill Sentner, champion of the Missouri Valley Authority plan—assume leading roles.

An environmental analysis of urbanization also forces us to readjust conventional spatial parameters. It makes little sense to restrict coverage to the city limits of St. Louis when the environmental transformations wrought by urban growth bear little correspondence to jurisdictional boundaries. Moreover, the vastly divergent settings that compose the metropolis form an integrated system that renders incomplete the study of only one part. Too many histories of St. Louis have turned a blind eye to the urban concentrations across the Mississippi River in Illinois, despite the fact that East St. Louis, Granite City, and the adjacent industrial suburbs have played an integral role in the growth of the metropolis. To correct that longstanding bias, this book considers the entire metropolitan area, covering both the Illinois and Missouri portions.

It is not enough, however, to stop at the borders of the metropolis. In *Nature's Metropolis*, a book which will remain a model for urban environmental history for years to come, William Cronon details the effects of urban growth on the hinterland of Chicago as it spurred the rise of commercial agriculture and the intensification of resource extraction.[2] In St. Louis as well, the environmental effects of urbanization reached far beyond the metropolitan area to the Ozark territory to the west, the lead and iron mining region to the south, and the woodlands and plains to the north. Hence, the geographical scope of the book comprises the St. Louis region, broadly defined.

Chronologically, the book ranges from the pre-Columbian settlements at Cahokia to the present day, but does not attempt to treat environmental change over the intervening years exhaustively or comprehensively. Rather, the authors, who are drawn from a variety of disciplines, including history, geography, archaeology, and architecture, explore selected aspects of the relationship between urbanization and the environment. Most of the essays, however, are set in the late nineteenth and early twentieth centuries, a time characterized by tremendous environmental change as St. Louis made the transition from a commercial river town to an industrial metropolis.

Walter Schroeder opens the book by outlining the basic geologic, climatologic, and biologic features of the region's natural landscape over several millennia. Situated at the juncture of three great river systems and various ecological zones, the St. Louis area presented human settlers with a unique set of opportunities that would guide future patterns of urban settlement. By describing a continuously evolving geography, the essay also serves as an important reminder that urban settlers placed their imprint on a landscape that was already very much in flux.

Cahokia was the first urban settlement to make its mark on that landscape. William Iseminger relies on archaeological evidence to trace the rise and fall of Cahokia in the context of the regional environment. The Mississippian culture that flourished there after A.D. 1000 benefited from a favorable climate and a rich resource base that facilitated maize agriculture, a wood-based architecture, and ceramic craft production. Its location at the confluence of three major river systems enabled the city to dominate a vast regional trade in marine shells, copper, and salt. Intensive cultivation and substantial environmental manipulation exacted a price, however. These factors, along with climatic changes, may have contributed to Cahokia's decline after A.D. 1200. In charting the fall of Cahokia, Iseminger warns of the dangers inherent in falling out of balance with a local ecosystem.

Centuries later, European exploration and settlement in the region signaled a new environmental era. Patricia Cleary demonstrates how an environmental analysis can serve as a basis for reconstructing the history of colonial race relations. Her essay examines the environmental assumptions and objectives of the French colonists, who established trading centers in territory already inhabited by numerous Indian societies that had very different environmental attitudes. The irreconcilability between the two cultures is exposed in the story of the dramatic encounter between French fur traders and Missouri Indians at St. Louis shortly after Pierre Laclede settled upon the site. By driving the Indians from the nascent community, Laclede ensured that St. Louis would develop in accordance with colonists' assumptions about the natural environment.

In the early years of the nineteenth century, St. Louis became a flourishing trading town largely as a result of river commerce. However, as Terry Norris describes in his essay, the era of the steamboat was also one of environmental devastation. An unprecedented demand for fuel stripped the forests of the Mississippi River valley of cottonwoods, pecans, hackberries, and oaks. Deforestation, in turn, caused significant river channel migration and the resulting destruction of numerous colonial settlements. Analyzing the decimation of these riverside villages through the use of archaeological remains, Norris demonstrates the catastrophic impact of environmental change on the lives of ordinary people who have been largely erased from the historical record.

While loggers and boatmen stripped the forests surrounding the city, construction crews laid down the physical infrastructure that would guide the contours of urban growth and affect the quality of life for ordinary citizens within the city limits. In his essay, Eric Sandweiss describes how existing features of the natural landscape and an evolving social geography conspired to deny south St. Louis residents the benefits of paved streets. Separated from the rest of the city by the Mill Creek valley and burdened with low property values, south St. Louis was deemed an inappropriate area for the investment of public funds. Instead, city officials lavished money on the elegant boulevards of the central corridor, thereby exacerbating the relative impoverishment of the city's south side neighborhoods.

Katharine Corbett carries this theme forward in her essay by showing how natural geography and class biases influenced the construction of the city's sewer system. Over the course of the nineteenth century, rapid population growth also presented the city with new problems of drainage and waste disposal. Garbage and storm water collected in the numerous sinkholes that pockmarked the city, creating a nuisance for citizens and applying a brake to further urban development. Sanitary engineers met this challenge by planning and building a sewer system that had become one of the nation's most advanced by the outbreak of the Civil War. Hampered by limited financial resources during the latter part of the nineteenth century, the engineers struggled to keep pace with urban expansion. Increasingly, public investment decisions were driven by the infrastructural needs of the city's most wealthy residential property holders.

Rapid internal growth and congestion exposed residents and property owners to new environmental dangers, including fire. Relying on the business records of a major fire insurance surveying company, Mark Tebeau explores how the insurance industry developed a systematic approach to fire danger in the years immediately following the Civil War. He argues that the economic assumptions framing understandings of fire risk were at the heart of the effort to reconceptualize urban space in the late nineteenth century. Indeed, by the twentieth century, formal guidelines were implemented to make the costs of at least one environmental hazard, fire, rational and predictable.

Both ethnicity and class figured into the city's response to manufacturing pollution, a topic I address in my essay. A widely held belief in the miasma theory of disease mobilized grassroots opposition to industries that generated noxious odors on the grounds that they endangered public health. Citizens were particularly repelled by offensive stenches generated by "nuisance industries," which included tanneries, slaughterhouses, and rendering plants. I argue that in adopting a quarantine approach to pollution abatement, public health officials started down a path toward zoning that would match differences in class, and by extension, ethnicity, with differences in environmental quality.

The theme of pollution control is also taken up by Craig Colten in the following chapter. Set in the industrial districts surrounding East St. Louis, this study explores the various legal mechanisms by which citizens sought redress against polluters in the first half of the twentieth century. Even though state regulatory agencies and courts professed a need to tolerate a certain degree of pollution in the effort to promote economic growth, they showed considerable sympathy for the victims of pollution. Local courts, in particular, were inclined to award damages to plaintiffs and to force corporations to abate offensive waste control practices.

One recourse available to well-to-do urbanites who were fed up with the congestion, noise, and grime of the city was to escape to the countryside. With the growth of railroad and automobile transportation in the late nineteenth and early twentieth centuries, St. Louisans ventured into the Ozark region, transforming it to conform to idealized notions of the pastoral. Jennifer Crets describes this process in her essay, paying particular attention to the ways vacationers sought to preserve both the amenities of urban life and the privileges of race and class in the creation of their rural retreats.

The twentieth century witnessed continuing efforts on the part of reformers, politicians, and technicians to improve environmental quality. Joel Tarr and Carl Zimring's essay on smoke abatement explains how, after many decades of failure, St. Louis had finally managed to rid its skies of dirty coal smoke by the 1940s. Tarr and Zimring attribute the city's success to the persistent efforts of women reformers to draw public attention to the issue and, above all, to Raymond Tucker, an engineer who devised an ingenious program that was technologically advanced, politically palatable, and easily enforceable. Tucker's achievement was significant because it not only provided relief to citizens of St. Louis, but also served as a model for air pollution control programs in other cities. Tarr and Zimring's discussion of how women's experiences as mothers and homemakers conditioned their understanding of the smoke problem demonstrates the utility of gender analysis in the study of popular environmental thought and activism.

Rosemary Feurer, on the other hand, calls our attention to the class-specific environmental vision of unionized blue collar workers during the 1940s. Although industrial workers have rarely been portrayed as active defenders of the environment, Feurer describes how St. Louis electrical workers spearheaded a grassroots political campaign to establish a regional planning authority in the Missouri River valley. Modeled on the Tennessee Valley Authority, the plan sought to democratize environmental planning and add a conservationist component to regional economic development. In the end, the coalition of workers, farmers, and small business interests was unable to wrest power from government bureaucrats and large power companies, with devastating environmental results.

Race and class necessarily loom large in any assessment of the social allocation of environmental costs in contemporary urban America. In St. Louis, two centuries of environmental manipulation produced a landscape that varies considerably from place to place, thereby providing widely divergent experiences with regard to quality of life for the more than two million inhabitants of the metropolis. In my conclusion, I use the examples of river flooding, rat proliferation, and toxic waste disposal to illuminate the historical roots of environmental inequality. The chapter emphasizes the role of both market forces and policy initiatives in the construction of an environmental regime that continues to discriminate against the poor and racial minorities.

Although this book makes no pretensions to being a comprehensive environmental history of St. Louis, taken together, the essays illuminate the major historical forces that produced the physical landscape which St. Louisans inhabit today. Three themes in particular emerge from the variety of topics and disciplinary approaches.

First, the essays document the insatiable human drive to control and impose order upon an unpredictable, unstable, and often recalcitrant environment. This endeavor has entailed dramatic manipulation of the physical landscape. Holes were dug to procure earth for building mounds, hills were leveled to fill the holes, and trash was piled high upon older trash to build new mounds. Meandering rivers were straightened into channels, streams were driven underground to function as sewers, and islands were flooded to become permanent waterways.

Few features of the natural landscape have been subject to more human manipulation than the Mississippi River. Over two centuries, engineers took a river that once stretched ten miles from shore to shore during periods of high flow and straightened it, narrowed it, and deepened it. In the interests of commerce, Old Man River has been surgically altered beyond the point where it would still be recognizable to the city's earliest settlers. Even far beyond rivers and municipal borders, the impact of urbanization was felt as fields were plowed under for agricultural production, resources were extracted from above and below ground to feed industrial furnaces and to furnish construction materials, and remote wilderness areas were transformed into residential subdivisions and vacation resorts.

Much of the human manipulation of the physical landscape has been directed toward making nature predictable, or at the least, insulating humans from the social and economic costs of an unpredictable nature. The goal of environmental predictability has been particularly crucial to those interested in making long-term investments in the city's physical infrastructure. Before sinking huge sums of capital into new factories, commercial facilities, and homes, private and public institutions required assurances that their investments would not be jeopardized by freakish weather, migrating river channels, or uncontrollable fires.

To cite one example not discussed in detail elsewhere in this volume, the city of St. Louis went to great lengths in the nineteenth century to ensure a constant flow of deep water in front of the downtown harbor. By the 1830s, the city had already expended considerable sums on levee construction and wharf improvements. But the viability of the central harbor was threatened by the accretion of an offshore sandbar and the concomitant movement of the main channel toward the Illinois side of the river. Over the next several decades, the city spent close to $900,000 to build and maintain a series of underwater dikes that permanently deflected the flow back to the Missouri side of the river. The engineering project also eliminated two islands situated in the river by attaching them to the shoreline, one on the Illinois side, the other on the Missouri side, thereby providing unobstructed access to the harbor for a seven-mile stretch.[3]

In the case of fire protection, private initiatives were responsible for both new construction techniques that made fires less likely and insurance programs that provided financial compensation in the event of property loss. Twentieth-century zoning policies, an outgrowth of late nineteenth-century nuisance regulation, extended the concept of environmental predictability to all built structures, guiding different land uses to specified areas so that investors could anticipate the future character of any given place within the city.

Although the environmental imperatives of urban growth exacted a hefty toll in terms of destroyed natural habitats and the contamination of air and water supplies, the environmental history of St. Louis should not be viewed as a tale of uninterrupted declension. Several essays in this book detail the courageous efforts of individuals to buck dominant environmental trends by reordering civic priorities around aesthetic considerations and the improvement of public health. In this same vein, the establishment of botanical gardens and zoos should be viewed as efforts to restore some measure of biotic diversity in the urban setting, if only in selected areas.

Perhaps some readers will be surprised by the extent of grass-roots activism and political agitation on behalf of clean air, pure water, and a more rational management of natural resources well before the environmental movement of the 1960s. These activists and reformers may not have called themselves environmentalists; rather than operating in the context of "environmental" organizations, they were more likely to be members of civic organizations, ad hoc community groups, and labor unions. Certainly, the perceptions of public health and environmental ideals that informed their agendas were different than those of more recent vintage. Yet their achievements were nonetheless significant. Not only did they contribute to an improved quality of life for many St. Louisans, but in the construction of a sewer system in the 1850s and the implementation of a smoke control program in the 1930s, they also provided models that were emulated in other cities.

Although it is tempting to read the environmental history of St. Louis, or of any other city for that matter, as a procession of relentless human domination over nature, many of the essays collected here emphasize the enduring power of the natural environment to constrain human choices and to shape the precise contours of urban growth. The city's success as a commercial entrepôt was largely a result of its fortuitous location near the junction of three major inland rivers. The presence of the Mississippi River at the city's doorstep influenced various aspects of the town's development, including the layout of streets and the disposal of domestic wastes. Despite concerted efforts to tame the region's waterways, the rivers have continued to behave independently of human will, as the Great Flood of 1993 made clear.

The region's natural features are responsible for much of what has made St. Louis distinctive. Just as one could hardly describe San Francisco without reference to its hills and fog, or Los Angeles without mention of its balmy weather and photochemical smog, one cannot fully explain the physical appearance of St. Louis's parks, buildings, and streets without acknowledging the influence of the natural environment. Like other cities, St. Louis has imported massive quantities of energy and materials from elsewhere to sustain its population. But much of the physical world constructed by humans represents the manipulation of local resources: the abundant bituminous coal that was spewed into the atmosphere as particulate dust, the clay deposits that were transformed into the red brick so prevalent in St. Louis houses, and the limestone blocks used to pave streets and alleyways. This book highlights the debt that city building incurred to a physical landscape already in place and in flux before the first urban settlers arrived.

Finally, the essays highlight the fact that environmental change is a product of negotiation and conflict among readily identifiable social groups and interests. Rarely did all members of society agree upon a particular course of development. Industrialists clashed with reformers, suburbanites battled inner-city residents, and certain ethnic groups arrayed themselves against others as the city debated the use and allocation of its physical resources. Fault lines appeared most starkly when issues found their way into the realm of politics, as in the cases of nuisance regulation in the 1870s, smoke abatement in the 1930s, regional environmental planning in the 1940s, and rat control in the 1950s. Yet even when decisions regarding the environment were made without fanfare, careful analysis exposes the guiding hand of particular interests who often acted to benefit themselves at the expense of others.

The techniques and insights of social history are particularly relevant in analyzing a changing landscape. In St. Louis, for example, it is quite clear that the variables of class, race, gender, and ethnicity conditioned social responses to environmental change and provided a basis for distinctive environmental agendas. Hence, when women reformers advanced the cause of smoke control in the 1920s and 1930s, they did so in the context of their role as "municipal housekeepers." Industrial laborers, on the other hand, conceived of regional environmental planning in the 1940s as a means of linking conservation and job creation.

These groups did not always compete in a context of equality; environmental outcomes tended to reflect the power biases within society. As the essays on fire prevention, nuisance regulation, sewer construction, and flood control make clear, large corporations and privileged property holders enjoyed superior resources that enabled them to direct the contours of environmental change in ways that were self-serving. Moreover, at times, the financial costs of environmental reform fell disproportionately on the backs of those least able to pay. For example, low-income households could ill afford the steep rates for legislatively mandated smokeless fuel in the 1930s. Hence, equity considerations form an important component in analysis of the urban environment. As the book's final essay makes clear, severe inequities based on race and class still stand as a legacy of a socially-divided response to environmental change.

Although the essays in this volume focus on the St. Louis region, they are also relevant to those interested in the environmental history of other cities.[4] After all, the broad economic, technological, and political forces associated with major environmental transformations—industrialization, automobility, suburbanization, and dependence on federal policy initiatives—were not exclusive to St. Louis. If a particular migration sequence gave St. Louis a distinctive social configuration at any given time, the basic categories of class, race, gender, and ethnicity have nonetheless conditioned the social response to environmental change in cities throughout the United States. At the very least, the St. Louis version of environmental history can serve as a basis for comparison with other cities.

On the cusp of the twenty-first century, urban America finds itself suffocating under an avalanche of environmental dilemmas. One need only glance at daily newspapers or scan the television screen to appreciate the enormity of the environmental challenges confronting our cities. How do we keep our drinking water free from contamination? How do we go about cleaning the soil of toxic materials dumped indiscriminately by manufacturers over the past century? How do we contain the floods, hurricanes, and fires that attack recently developed property? How do we reconcile the lure of suburban living with the rising levels of pollution and energy consumption created by an automobile-reliant transportation system? How do we maintain a crumbling infrastructure in an era of dwindling financial resources? How do we best preserve what little open space remains in our congested cities? The list goes on.

History will not necessarily provide us with solutions, but it will surely enrich our understanding of the social forces that led us into these predicaments in the first place. Perhaps we can benefit from the wisdom or folly of preceding generations as they grappled with similar issues of resource scarcities, waste disposal, and natural disasters. There is much at stake. For while we remain divided over our environmental priorities, and while defend our environmental prerogatives even at the expense of our neighbors, the air, water, and land that comprise the St. Louis region are our "common fields"— shared resources whose use and management impinge upon us all. As residents of the metropolis, we rely on these shared resources for our sustenance just as the colonial founders of St. Louis relied on their common fields to provide for their basic needs. And just as the common fields plowed and cultivated by the early French settlers laid a basis for the subsequent physical growth of the city—the way streets were laid, the way property was apportioned—the care we take with our common fields will determine the type of city we bequeath to future generations. At the very least, this environmental history may provide us with a different perspective on our cities, one that may help us work in concert with rather than in opposition to the natural processes that bind human beings to the physical environments they inhabit.

# Environmental Setting
# of the St. Louis Region

*Walter Schroeder*

The present environment of the St. Louis region is the cumulative creation of thousands, if not millions, of years of natural processes operating in the region. These processes—geologic, hydrologic, climatologic, biologic, pedologic—interact in complex ways. They affect landscape creation at different intensities at different times in history.

One way to make sense of this extraordinary complexity in the environmental history of St. Louis is to view the area as a zone of encounter between contrasting natural regions. First, on one side of St. Louis is the uplifted Ozark dome, bearing an array of metals, and on the other is the Illinois basin, a preserver of carbon fuels. The two contrasting resources are assembled at St. Louis. Second, part of the St. Louis region is a low-relief plain, the result of glaciation, while the other part is a hill country of narrow ridges and deep valleys that escaped all glaciation. Meltwater-carrying rivers and silt-laden winds tied these two parts together at St. Louis. Third, the St. Louis region extends on one side into the great grassland biome of the American Middle West, and on the other into a deciduous forest biome. The St. Louis region, influenced by the biological processes of both, is an intricate mosaic of biogeographical niches and a region rich in biological diversity.

Woven into the story of natural environmental change over time is human occupance of the region. Human participation in environmental processes began very long ago, but it is in the past century or two that it has been most pervasive. Humans have aggregated mineral resources at St. Louis; re-configured the topography; altered the air; changed water quantities, qualities, and distributions; and severely affected the soils, plants, and animals of the urban region. The growth of St. Louis is a story of how humans have responded to the opportunities granted and limits imposed by a complex, diverse, and powerful natural environment.

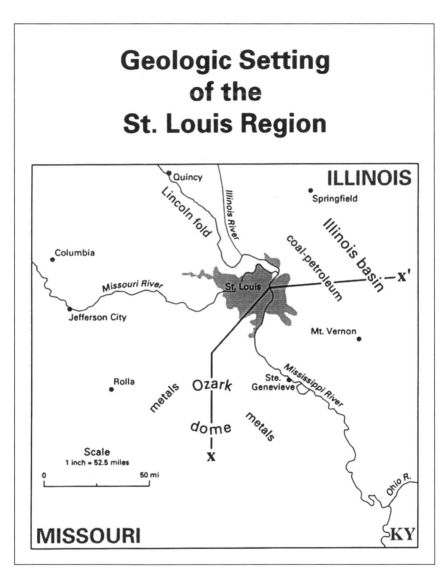

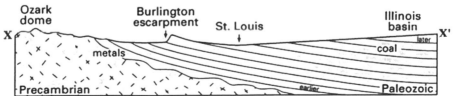

Figure 1. *Map by Walter Schroeder, Cartography by Adrianne Nold, Department of Geography, University of Missouri, Columbia.*

## Rocks and Mineral Resources

Tectonically, the St. Louis region lies between the Ozark uplift to the south-southwest, where rock strata have domed upward, and the Illinois basin to the east, where rock strata have subsided (figure 1). In the Ozarks some of the most ancient rocks of North America, those of Precambrian time dated at 1.5 billion years, are exposed at the surface, because so many strata that had buried them have been worn away. In the Illinois basin, however, much younger rocks of the late Paleozoic era, with an age of approximately 300,000,000 years, are at the surface. Subsidence of the basin has helped to preserve them. At St. Louis, between these two extremes, surface rocks are of the middle Paleozoic era of 320,000,000 to 440,000,000 years of age. The strata at St. Louis dip generally to the east northeast into the Illinois basin at an average rate of sixty feet per mile. For example, the formation known as the St. Peter sandstone is at the surface at Pacific, thirty-two miles southwest of St. Louis, where it has been mined for sand used in glass manufacturing. At the Arch in St. Louis, that formation plunges to sixteen hundred feet below the surface, and at Mascoutah, Illinois, twenty-three miles to the east, it lies three thousand feet below the surface. The dip, however, is not consistent, and minor structures reverse it locally. One place is in north St. Louis County, where the rocks of the Florissant dome or upwarp produced coal and petroleum and are used for underground gas storage. Another, larger-scale exception is the Lincoln fold, an anticline or upfold in the strata northwest of St. Louis in Lincoln and Pike Counties, where soluble rocks are at the surface and create a landscape strikingly representative of the Ozarks south of St. Louis.[1]

The east-northeast dip produces a succession of different formations at the surface, which, when mapped, show an arcuate, belted pattern (figure 2). Because the formations are of different resistances to weathering and erosion, the landscapes constructed on them vary. The more resistant form hilly belts, or eroded escarpments. The most prominent of these is the Burlington escarpment held up by the Mississippian-age Burlington formation composed primarily of limestone. Its arc swings from southern Warren County, Missouri, through far western St. Louis County and into eastern Jefferson and Ste. Genevieve Counties. Interstate 44 pierces these steep-sided hills in deep road cuts east of Pacific, and Interstate 55 pierces them in equally deep road cuts north of Herculaneum. In contrast, less resistant formations form lower-relief hills or even plains, like the soluble limestone strata which form the smooth and low-relief surface of St. Louis City itself. The courses of the Missouri and Mississippi Rivers at St. Louis precede the great glaciations in age and their courses may be associated with the belts of less resistant rock. The rivers have a generally arcuate location around northern and eastern flanks of the Ozark dome. Where the Missouri River cuts through the Burlington escarpment, between Labadie and

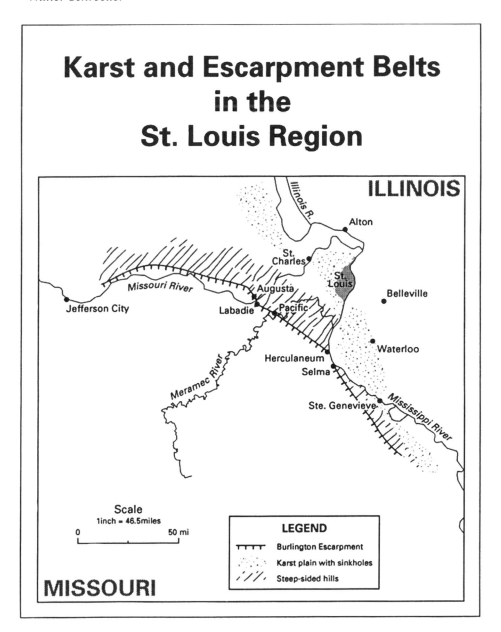

Figure 2. *Map by Walter Schroeder, Cartography by Adrianne Nold, Department of Geography, University of Missouri, Columbia.*

Augusta, its valley is noticeably narrowed and the river bluffs are higher and more perpendicular. The Mississippi River impinges onto the same escarpment, but never cuts completely through it between Kimmswick and Selma in Jefferson County. From the time of the French explorers, these bluffs have been described as exceptionally high, precipitous, pinnacled, and scenic. To the east of the Mississippi River, landscapes are less associated with bedrock types because of subsequent modification by glacial processes.[2]

The geographical pattern of these various rock types results in contrasting mineral resources on opposite sides of St. Louis and has major implications for the historic economic development of the city. The ancient rocks of the Ozarks to the south-southwest are a primary source for metals, including lead, iron, nickel, zinc, copper, cobalt, and silver. These metals provided the basis for the early and sustained growth of a prominent metal industry at St. Louis, beginning with lead in the early years of the nineteenth century and culminating in massive iron and steel works in the mid-twentieth century. St. Louis is the only metropolitan area in the United States that refines five primary metals (lead, zinc, copper, magnesium, and imported aluminum) in addition to maintaining iron and steel industries. The older rocks of the Ozarks also provide barite, used in the petroleum and chemical industries; granite, used for paving the St. Louis wharf and downtown streets in the nineteenth century as well as for dimension stone for buildings;[3] silica sand for glassmaking, including millions of bottles for St. Louis's large brewing industry;[4] and, until 1820 or so, salt from the Meramec River and the Saline south of Ste. Genevieve.[5] These rich and varied mineral resources of the Ozarks, especially iron and lead, were so prized by St. Louis industrialists and so difficult to reach by water that the first railroad projects proposed for St. Louis in the 1830s and built in the 1850s included a line directly to this great mineral district.[6]

In great contrast to the Ozark metals and minerals, the later Paleozoic rocks of the Illinois basin on the other side of St. Louis have provided fossil fuels to energize the industries, power the trains, and heat and electrify the homes. These important resources include coal, oil, and natural gas. Though the French discovered and mined exposed coal in the bluffs along the Missouri River in north St. Louis County well before 1800—a legacy preserved by the name of Charbonier Road—it is the large Illinois basin that has long been the primary energy source for St. Louis.[7] Train and barge loads of coal have arrived at St. Louis weekly if not daily for more than one hundred years to keep the city's economy functioning and life pleasant. Combustion of coal and gasoline, however, has had a negative side effect: it is largely responsible for an urban atmosphere of increased chemicals, particulates, and heat. Gasification of coals, common in the early years of the twentieth century, also introduced polychlorinated biphenyls, or PCBs, into the soils of St. Louis, some of which are considered toxic.

St. Louis lies, therefore, very conveniently at the geographical junction between metals and minerals to the southwest and the energy resources to process them to the east. Between these regions of contrasting mineral resources, where most of the St. Louis urban region is located, is an abundance of rock minerals necessary for constructing a large city. Chief of these is a thick succession of Paleozoic limestones and dolomites, or carbonate rocks. From them have come dimension stone used for foundations and other general construction purposes. More important, they provide cement and aggregate for concrete, which any city needs in abundance to create its "built environment." These minerals are as significant in modern society as the more glamourous metals and fuels. Physical St. Louis may be thought of as a transformation and reconstitution of natural limestone into streets and buildings. What used to be bedrock is now above the ground in human-created geometric forms. Huge quarries of rock withdrawal blemish the St. Louis region. The older ones in the heart of the city, dug as deep as eighty feet, were used as public dumping grounds for wastes through the end of the nineteenth century.[8] The largest ones in operation today are mostly out of public sight in river blufflands, where the useful limestones are most accessible and easiest to quarry.

Interbedded with the limestones and dolomites are shales and clays of mineable quality, including fire and pottery clays. One clay that figured prominently in St. Louis history crops out in several places, but is historically most notable just south of Forest Park and west of the Missouri Botanical Garden. This eminence, higher than the surrounding solution-lowered limestone terrain, is known as the Hill, an area occupied by Italians and other immigrants who found employment in the mines and clay-based factories of the neighborhood.[9]

All the carbonate rocks are soluble to different degrees. Over the quarter-billion years that they have been dissolving, they have produced a surface landscape of sinkholes and solution basins with a diminished number of streams and a subsurface landscape of caves, solution-widened joints and cracks, and enhanced groundwater movement. The solution-distinguished landscape, or karst, is part of a discontinuous belt identified with limestones that extend from Lincoln County, Missouri, through north St. Louis County, St. Louis City, south St. Louis County, Monroe County, Illinois, then back to the Missouri side at Ste. Genevieve (figure 2).

The largest limestone sink in the area, better termed a solution basin, was occupied by a marsh and shallow Chouteau's Pond, whose water level was maintained constant by an outlet dam constructed in the first years of St. Louis's existence. Chouteau's Pond received much of the surface runoff and subsurface drainage of the central city, so that, as the city spread and surrounded the pond, it became inexorably polluted and useless except as a wastewater sump. When railroads came to St. Louis in the 1850s, the fouled lake was drained, creating a large tract of land in the heart of the city suitable for acres of railroad yards, associated industries and warehousing, and a huge train station. It was partially filled in with as much as forty feet of dirt and rock excavated from downtown St. Louis when large buildings were erected during the closing decades of the nineteenth century.[10] The former Chouteau's Pond and the valley of Mill Creek that formerly led into it from the west are now a wide transportation and industrial corridor, dividing St. Louis into "north" and "south" to this day. In north St. Louis County, Spanish Lake is a well-known example of a water-filled, plugged sinkhole, once common throughout St. Louis City and County. The plugged sinkhole ponds behind the early village of St. Louis supplied the villagers with waterfowl and fish.[11]

Springs that drain the karst plain of its water via underground passageways were an early and valuable water supply. Like surface water, they suffered the fate of urban pollution early on. In fact, spring water issuing from caves at the base of the Mississippi River bluffs below Jefferson Barracks still runs dark at times.[12] Once polluted, the groundwater reservoir takes a very long time to regenerate.

Dozens of sinkholes per square mile may appear, where they have not been filled in and obliterated by urbanization. Some sinkholes are deep for their diameter, with steep sides exposing bedrock and occasionally offering a skylight to peer into the cave beneath. They have likely been formed by the collapse of rock into an underground void. Others are very broad and shallow depressions most noticeable after wet periods when water collects in them. They have likely been formed not by collapse but by the slow, ongoing solution of the calcium carbonate and its removal in the hard water that issues from cave springs. The Spanish land surveys at the end of the eighteenth century, done in French, mapped the sinkholes of the St. Louis region as *entonnoirs*, or funnels.[13] As the city grew in the 1830s, sinkholes as close to the river as Eighth Street were used for disposal of waste material of all kinds. Because they were so numerous and interconnected underground by passageways, the groundwater of the city became polluted from household wastes, dead animals, the manure of thousands of horses, and the waste products of industry and commerce. The seriousness of the groundwater problem and its geographical association with the occurrence and spread of cholera and other diseases led to the creation in the 1850s of sewer systems, each originally organized around a naturally interconnected assemblage of sinkholes, then finally integrated into larger sewer districts. The problems associated with building a city on karst terrain prompted St. Louis to create one of the earliest systems of wastewater collection through subsurface sewers in the nation. This civic effort ranks as one of the first large-scale, tax-supported efforts in St. Louis to correct a deteriorated environment.

The early problems with groundwater pollution also allegedly caused St. Louisans, once the city moved too far away from the Mississippi River to tote or wagon-haul water from it for domestic use, to turn to cisterns for water. Cisterns, it is thought, became a cultural practice in St. Louis and continued as a source for household water as the city spread into non-karst terrain and even after technology advanced to allow the drilling of wells deep into bedrock, far below the polluted-water zone. St. Louis still had about eight thousand shallow wells around 1890, but their water was so polluted that the city had condemned "thousands" by 1910.[14]

Associated with the sinkholes and springs of St. Louis's karst topography are numerous caves. In theory, they should be geographically coincident with sinkholes, even if their presence is not known due to lack of a surface entrance. Caves had an important function in the economic history of St. Louis. The rather constant air temperature of 55-60 degrees in the caves throughout both summer and winter provided a natural cool-storage facility for beer, cheese, and other products before refrigeration. The specific sites of many St. Louis breweries can be explained by the presence of large, accessible caves. St. Louisans used other caves for entertainment. For example, Cherokee Cave, at Thirteenth and Cherokee Streets, featured a beer hall and theater.[15] The long-gone natural bridge of north St. Louis City, which gave its name to Natural Bridge Road, an arterial road leading all the way to St. Charles, consisted of a narrow rock bridge at street level separating two adjacent, deep sinkholes, or "caves," in the vernacular.

The karst setting has presented still other problems for the city. Although the cavernous bedrock has not prevented the construction of tall buildings, nor has much abrupt subsidence been reported in the St. Louis area (no one soluble limestone stratum is very thick, hence the development of caves with high ceilings which collapse abruptly is inhibited), the construction of major highways has been affected. When Interstate 55 was being constructed through south St. Louis City, serious problems arose concerning the numerous voids in the bedrock underneath. To support the highway, some portions of the caves with thin roofs were collapsed and filled in, some cave corridors were enclosed with bulkheads and filled with grout, and water drainage in the caves had to be rerouted to prevent flooding and erosion of new channels.[16] In selected locations the placement of underground utilities—water, gas, and sewer pipes—has been affected by cavernous bedrock.

## Glaciation and Rivers

During the late Pleistocene Epoch, or the past one million years of earth history, continental glaciers overrode a large portion of the greater St. Louis region and utterly transformed it. This produced another regional

## Glaciations and Interglacials of the Later Pleistocene Epoch in the American Middle West

| Years Ago | Glaciation | Interglacial |
|---|---|---|
| last 10,000 years | | Holocene |
| 50,000-10,000 | Wisconsinan | |
| | | Sangamonian |
| 500,000-150,000 | Illinoian | |
| | | Yarmouthian |
| 2,000,000-1,000,000 | Pre-Illinoian (including Kansan and Nebraskan) | |

Table 1. *Graph by Walter Schroeder.*

environmental contrast between a glaciated terrain to the northwest, north, east, and southeast, and an unglaciated terrain in the southwest. St. Louis sits in the northeast apex of the unglaciated angle jutting into glaciated terrain (figure 3). The glacial history of the St. Louis region may be divided into four episodes: early pre-Illinoian glaciers (formerly divided between Nebraskan and Kansan glaciers); a later Illinoian glacier, and events after this ice left the St. Louis region; yet another ice intrusion, the Wisconsinan, which stayed well to the north of St. Louis but greatly affected the St. Louis region by its meltwaters; and a complex series of postglacial, or Holocene, events, much of which is recorded in the history of the region's rivers (table 1).

The pre-Illinoian glaciers moved into northern Missouri and into Illinois more than five hundred thousand years ago. There is still much to learn about these older glaciers, because the terrain they constructed in Illinois was overridden by later glaciers and thus partially destroyed and obscured; the terrain they constructed in Missouri has been radically altered by several hundred thousand years of surface water, wind, and gravity processes, which have removed much of the glacial material. The southern limit of the pre-Illinoian glaciers is imperfectly known. In general, it was just north of the Missouri River in eastern Missouri. One glacial lobe from the northwest reached well into St. Charles County, because ice-laid material, or till, is found as far east and south as the city of St. Charles. The glaciers may not have been thick enough at these southern margins to cover the land completely, for tracts of higher ground on the crest of the Lincoln fold in Lincoln and Pike Counties, Missouri, show no evidence of having been glaciated. Glacial motion has the general effect

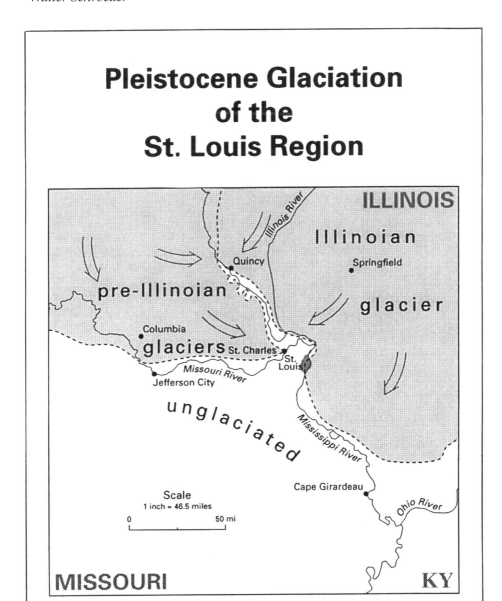

Figure 3. *Map by Walter Schroeder, Cartography by Adrianne Nold, Department of Geography, University of Missouri, Columbia.*

of smoothing out the landscape; subsequent water processes, however, created a fluvial landscape of low, rolling hills and wide valleys, especially along larger rivers like the Missouri and Cuivre. The till, where still present today, is thin in St. Charles, Warren, and Lincoln Counties, hardly ever more than fifty feet thick. After the retreat of the last pre-Illinoian glacier, soils developed on the till surface, followed by several mantlings of the surface by loess, or wind-deposited silt. Beneath the soils of today's surface, therefore, is a sequence of paleosols (buried soils) and loesses, the complex chronology of which is yet to be fully worked out. Material of the present surface is the result of soil and water processes of the past couple hundred thousand years rather than glacial processes.[17]

The Illinoian glacier, dating from 500,000 to 130,000 years ago, was restricted to its namesake state in the St. Louis region, crossing into Missouri probably only at St. Louis City, but possibly elsewhere. Nowhere did it intrude very far westward across the valley of the Mississippi River, which was already in existence. Because it is younger in age, the landscape it created shows more distinctly the effects of glaciation than the older glaciated landscape of northern Missouri. The upland surface of Illinois is, generally, much smoother and less dissected by postglacial streams. Flattish upland surfaces of great extent remain intact between the shallow valleys of postglacial streams; the monotonously flat upland followed by Interstate 55 in Madison County between Cahokia and Silver Creeks is one example. Smaller-scale glacial landscape features like low, narrow ridges of moraine that formed during a pause in the retreat of the glacier can still be distinguished in Illinois, whereas similar features have not yet been identified in the older glaciated terrain of Missouri, if ever they can be. The Illinoian till, in general, has thicknesses of from fifty to one hundred feet on the upland surfaces of Illinois in the St. Louis region, and exposures of bedrock beneath the till are much less common than in Missouri, even in the shallow stream valleys.

Where the Illinoian glacier crossed the Mississippi River at downtown St. Louis, it blocked the river's flow. Ice-dammed water backed up the Mississippi and Missouri valleys scores of miles and into their tributaries to create a huge lake. Sediments were deposited in it, especially in the tributary coves where sediment-laden stream water met the calm lake water. It is not known how or where the lake water got around the ice dam. Perhaps the depth of the water eventually forced the dam to give way. Possible drainageways for lake water around the ice are the shallow linear valley of the River des Peres and a north-south linear depression followed by the Union Pacific tracks from Kingshighway at Interstate 44 south to Carondelet. The bedrock floor of some of these drainageways is not much higher than the elevation of the present Mississippi River alluvial plain. In any event, the ice eventually left and the lake was drained. The rivers resumed their courses and have subsequently removed much of the sediment deposited in the glacial lakes. Remnants of the lake sediments remain as terraces tucked in tributary valleys behind the Mississippi and Missouri bluff lines, well above the floods of the contemporary rivers. The most spectacular remnant is the flat lake-clay surface at Lambert-St. Louis Airport. This former lake bed was still a poorly drained marsh when the French established the village of St. Ferdinand (Florissant) on its east side in 1785. The settlers found the wet prairie of the former lake bed to provide superb natural grazing for their cattle and horses. Subsurface drainage by storm sewers now conducts the water of the former wet prairie and Coldwater Creek out of sight beneath the airport's runways and on past Florissant.[18]

The Illinoian glacier began its retreat from the St. Louis region approximately 150,000 years ago. After a long interglacial period of 100,000 years during which more paleosols developed and more loess was deposited, another glacial episode occurred, the Wisconsinan. This ice cap, dating from 50,000 to 10,000 years ago, did not reach farther south than northern Illinois. Nevertheless, the St. Louis region was profoundly affected during the Wisconsinan event in two major ways. First, the ice caused the climate in the St. Louis region to cool significantly during the Wisconsinan time. Second, the Mississippi and Missouri Rivers served as the conduits for meltwater from this immense ice cap. Vast quantities came down the Missouri, but even more down the Mississippi and Illinois Rivers, which handled all the meltwater from emerging Lakes Superior, Michigan, and Huron due to the receding ice cap's coverage of all St. Lawrence River outlets to the Atlantic Ocean. Thus, the Mississippi River at St. Louis at that time had a drainage area much larger than that of today. It included the upper three Great Lakes and an even larger Lake Agassiz on the Minnesota-Dakota border that kept extending northward into Canada as the glacier continued its northward retreat. For thousands of years water from this melting ice cap flowed past St. Louis.[19]

With their larger volumes, the Mississippi, Illinois, and Missouri Rivers carried proportionately larger quantities of sediments, which water had easily dislodged from the loose, unvegetated surfaces of recently glaciated regions in the north. The effect at St. Louis was to aggrade, or build up with alluvial deposits, the three great river plains to higher elevations. The volume of water, at times stretching from bluff to bluff, eroded back the bluffs to create linear valley walls, if they were not already straight. By this aggradation process the glacial bedrock channels of the rivers were buried by alluvial gravels, sands, and silts up to thicknesses of one hundred feet and more. The bedrock channel of the Mississippi at St. Louis that was excavated during earlier glacial episodes lies deep below the present flood plain in the American Bottom three miles east of the present channel. Thus, during this period of aggradation, the Mississippi River shifted westward to its present location, which, curiously, is on top of a bedrock ledge. There it created a rapids, the Chain of Rocks.[20] The thick, coarse-sediment fill of these valleys forms a great natural reservoir of groundwater, accessible by very high-yielding wells (in contrast to lower-yielding wells from bedrock aquifers). Industries of the alluvial plains have taken advantage of this copious, clean, and easily accessible water supply to develop their own water supplies, mostly used for cooling during metal smelting and manufacturing processes.

Following the episode of alluvial aggradation came one of the reverse, alluvial degradation. The large rivers, having become much smaller in volume after the wastage of the glacier, had much less sediment and began eroding into their thick valley fill. Formerly wide channels with numerous bars and islands became narrower and more meandering as they migrated back and forth across the flood plain, impinging first on one valley wall, then on the other. By this process the surface of the alluvial plain across its entire width has been lowered up to twenty feet throughout its entire length. The large rivers, however, could not remove the glacial sediments that had backfilled into the tributary valleys in slackwater behind the bluff line. Thus, remnants of the higher, aggraded river plains remain at the mouths of these tributaries, giving testimony to the earlier episode of aggradation when the river plains were at a higher elevation. The original site of Herculaneum, both Moses Austin's 1809 townsite and the present-day location of a lead smelter, sits on one of these high alluvial terraces, beyond the reach of floods.[21]

Throughout the late Pleistocene, especially during its interglacials and in the time since the retreat of the last glacier, the American Midwest has been subjected to accelerated wind erosion and deposition of silts, some clays, and very fine sands, commonly called *dust.* Most of this wind-carried and wind-deposited silt, or loess, in the St. Louis region is dated as post-Wisconsinan. The thinking is that land laid bare by the retreat of glaciers, while still unvegetated or poorly vegetated, was subject to winds similar to those of contemporary deserts and other dry, unvegetated surfaces like bare croplands. Winds could have been stronger and more consistent in velocity and direction in waning glacial times due to high atmospheric pressure over the ice caps, which generated outward blowing winds; high pressure over the ice caps of Greenland and Antarctica generate such outward-blowing winds today. In this way, silt was wind-eroded over extensive surfaces, carried long distances, usually southward and eastward, and eventually deposited widespread over the land. It is generally agreed that all of the surface of the St. Louis region was mantled with at least a few feet of wind-borne loess during the few thousand years of the retreat of the Wisconsinan glacier and later. The loess blanketed the glacial till of the Illinoian uplands, the already dissected till plain of northeast Missouri, and even the unglaciated portions of the Ozarks in the St. Louis region.[22]

Long after the uplands to the north were revegetated and no longer serving as a source for wind-borne loess, the three great rivers carrying glacial meltwater—the Mississippi, Missouri, and Illinois—continued to be major sources of loess. The meltwaters they carried varied in volume seasonally. During summers, when the glacier was melting the fastest, rivers were the largest, overspreading their alluvial plains from bluff to bluff. During winters, however, the water volume was much less and the river sediments lay bare and exposed to strong winter winds. Vegetation, which would have protected the surface from wind erosion, could not get established on the bars and islands because it would be swept away during the next summer's flood. Thus, the river plains of the immediate St. Louis region continued to serve as a source for wind-blown silt while the distant glacier was melting. Silt was lifted up to the adjacent bluffs where trees and grass captured it and protected it from further wind erosion. The result is exceptionally thick loess deposits in the blufflands along these three major rivers in the St. Louis region, and only along them, because they alone served as carriers of glacial meltwater in the region. The loess thins rapidly a few miles from the river bluff crest, and the average size of its fine constituents also diminishes with distance. Loess is generally much thicker on the south and east sides of the valleys, because of prevailing north and west wind directions. Loess reaches thicknesses of more than forty feet at Collinsville, Illinois, and up to eighty feet in Calhoun County, Illinois, the narrow peninsula between the Illinois and Mississippi Rivers. The city of St. Charles is completely built on loess, and its famous Mamelles at East Point are twin loess mounds.[23]

Loess, in a natural state with vegetative cover, tends to resist wind and water erosion. However, once cut into by running water or plowing, it erodes very rapidly and in a distinctive vertical fashion, producing deep gullies or "canyons" in the blufflands. The gullying reported before 1800 by the French in their common fields behind St. Louis village was likely the rapid erosion of loess soils. The Missouri River bluffs at the Howard Bend waterworks near Chesterfield are rent with deep "canyons" in loess-mantled limestone as shown by the nearly perpendicular walls boxing in Hog Hollow Road. Loess has been washed to the base of slopes and bluffs on the sides of river bottoms where it collects into large colluvial aprons and alluvial fans. Illinois Highway 157, which follows the base of the bluff line on the eastern edge of the American Bottom, is largely built on redeposited loess. Loess is easily moved about by modern earth-moving equipment and has been leveled off in places like the bluff-top Chesterfield Mall in west St. Louis County and in urban developments in the Illinois blufflands from Alton to Columbia. Grading of streets in the bluff towns to provide less steep access between upland and riverside locations has involved the removal of vast quantities of loess. Indeed, the topography of blufflands in the St. Louis region has been more reconfigured by loess removal, both natural and human, than by any other process.

Soil formed in loess is wonderfully productive and rivals the alluvial soils of river bottoms without the latter's risk of being flooded. Its ease of plowing, natural fertility, and water-retaining property helped concentrate crop-raising pre-Columbian Indians of the St. Louis region on them and adjacent alluvial soils. They also attracted early Kentucky, Virginia, and Appalachian immigrants to the region, especially those who sought to grow tobacco. In a broader sense, loess soils of both the blufflands and across the upland plains in general have helped to make the American Midwest, including the St. Louis area, one of the world's great agricultural regions. Where the loess is more clayey, it can also be used for brickmaking. When the great mound on the north side of the village of St. Louis, at the present junction of North Broadway and Seventh Street, was razed, its loess was used to make bricks for a new market hall in the vicinity. In fact, so conveniently at hand was clayey loess to the early nineteenth century builders of St. Louis that the city became one of brick buildings (bricks were also made of other clays) rather than one of rock culled from the abundant limestone outcroppings all along the rivers, which were accessible but harder to work, or of timber, which was in short supply. Only a few of the early buildings of St. Louis were of native rock, and brick replaced the timber buildings of the French as they were demolished.[24]

During the past three thousand years of postglacial history, the intensity of climatic change has been less than during glaciations, but the great rivers continue to be the most dynamic natural agents of change in the surface environment of the St. Louis region. Longer-term, multiyear changes in river volume are more associated with climatic change that occurs in the immense drainage basins upstream from St. Louis, a surface area of 697,000 square miles. Change in river volume also has come from shorter-term climatic events, like "wet" and "dry" years. These climatic changes prompt responses in other components of the environment, such as cycles of river erosion and deposition and the drying and wetting of the bottomlands, which, in turn, create effects on plant and animal and human populations along the rivers. Great floods, prehistoric and historic, have brought immense energy to the channel and effected changes in the riverine environment, physical and biologic, that a hundred years of average flows could never accomplish. Understandably, the great rivers have been the focus of all human cultures in the region, and these various cultures developed different ways of adjusting to the dynamic fluvial system.

The steeper Missouri River (average gradient of one foot per mile) enables it to move coarse sediment, most of it as sand and gravel at the bottom of the channel. Because it drains a loess-mantled region of a marginally humid climate, it also carries a high suspended load of silts and clays in the water mass itself, giving the river its famous tawny color. These fines stay in the flow and pass on into the clearer waters of the Mississippi, where the two constituent flows maintain their separate identities for many miles past their junction, with the Missouri contribution staying on the St. Louis side; the French St. Louisans lifted muddier water on their bank than the French Cahokians across the channel. Sands and coarser materials moved by the Missouri River make up a disproportionate part of its flood plain materials—some fines are of course present—and Missouri River alluvium and soils have, in general, a coarse texture, allowing comparatively rapid drainage of flood waters and excessive rainwater. The Missouri bottoms, away from the channel proper, had a few natural lakes or perennial wetlands above St. Charles. In the St. Louis region they included, in historic times, Creve Coeur Lake in St. Louis County and Marais Croche and Marais Temps Clair in St. Charles County. The Missouri River channel, formed in relatively coarse sediments which erode easily and resist staying upright in banks, was broad and shallow, replete with numerous islands and bars, and shifted location continuously. It was a "western river." The Missouri channel, up to the mid-twentieth century, was approximately twice its present width, occupying thirty to fifty percent of the total valley width of two miles.[25] Very frequent lateral shifting of the channel caused impingement along the valley walls, removing rock debris at their base, and keeping them sharp and vertical.

Where the rivers have not impinged for some time, fallen rock debris and slope wash, unable to be removed by any other natural process, may have accumulated and obscured much of the rock face. The Mississippi River bluffs on the Illinois side from Pere Marquette State Park past the historic Piasa rock face to Alton were kept precipitous and free from rock debris because the river impinged against them. Below Alton, the bluffs are far from the river and lose their sheerness by being half buried in debris which they themselves produced. Quarrying for rock and blasting the bluff for a solid rock shelf for railroad tracks and highways also has removed fallen material and kept the rock face bold and, to many people, scenic. In this case, human scarification of the landscape is deemed aesthetically pleasing.

The Mississippi River above the Missouri River naturally has a gradient or drop of six inches per mile, half that of the Missouri, but because it also carries a coarse bed load of sand, it has to maintain a sufficient velocity in order to keep the heavy sand in motion. Therefore, the Mississippi's channel does not meander as the Missouri's does. If it did, it would further reduce its gradient, slow itself down, and be unable to transport the sand. The Mississippi carries much less suspended load since the loess region it drains is better vegetated and yields less silt. The flood plain is wetter than that of the Missouri, too. Much of it in St. Charles and Lincoln Counties, Missouri, has marshes or wet prairies and numerous tracts of open water.[26]

The lower Illinois River naturally has an incredibly low gradient of approximately one inch per mile, which is not much different from lake water.[27] Indians and French found the Illinois much easier to canoe upstream than the higher gradient and swifter Mississippi and Missouri Rivers. The Illinois valley had served as a major glacial drainageway from the north, including waters from Lake Michigan, and at times even served as the ancestral Mississippi. The geometry of both the Illinois River channel and valley was created under those past conditions and cannot be explained by the shrunken river today. It is a clear river, distinguished by its sandy channel and alluvial plain.

Below the junction of the three rivers, the united Mississippi combines features of all three. Its volume fluctuates, for example, most predictably according to the fluctuations of the Missouri, because that contributor has the greatest seasonal variations, though it contributes less than half of the water. In an average year, the natural, undammed Missouri carried six times more water in June than in January. The range in average monthly discharges of the other two contributors is much less, on the order of three to one. Below the junction the gradient of the united Mississippi is approximately three to four inches per mile, intermediate between the Illinois and the others. The united Mississippi lacks major meander bends in the St. Louis region, although Horseshoe Lake, the great abandoned channel or oxbow of the American Bottom, indicates great river loops of the not-too-distant past.[28]

The lakes and natural wetlands of the great river bottoms were, with good reason, associated with summer and autumnal fevers, especially malaria, by the European-Americans. They categorically considered these areas unhealthful for settlement, and those who did settle there were described as chronically sick and unable to do manual labor like those in the uplands. Riverine Indians, however, were thought to be immune by the arriving European-Americans; perhaps they had developed a partial immunity to mosquito-borne diseases. Those of African descent were also observed to be less susceptible than Caucasians—a partial immunity to malaria now associated with the sickle-cell trait of blood—and preferred for labor in the river bottoms in both Illinois as well as slave Missouri. But location on the bluffs above the river bottoms did not necessarily assure a nonmalarial environment. Even though it was not an easy task to tote military equipment up the bluff face, the U.S. military post of Jefferson Barracks was established on a bluff top south of St. Louis City in 1827, ostensibly because of its location high above the fever-ridden bottoms. Despite the choice of location, many a young soldier was introduced to western life, before being deployed in the real West, by a bout with malaria at Jefferson Barracks.[29] Much of the human occupance of the river bottoms before the twentieth century is thus a story of persistent efforts to drain them of their standing waters and wetlands because of the centuries-old fear of malaria. This once strongly held belief has now faded away after three malaria-free generations, and it is now public policy to prevent further wetland drainage and even to restore standing water and wetlands to these riverine environments. The most prominent example in the St. Louis region is the restoration of seventeen hundred acres of wetlands in extreme eastern St. Charles County as part of the federal project to construct the Melvin Price locks and dam at Alton, Illinois.[30] This restoration and preservation program would have been deemed irrational in the nineteenth century.

In the twentieth century, humans have thoroughly changed the nature of the large rivers and their alluvial bottoms in the St. Louis region through various engineering works. High earthen levees and concrete flood walls line the channels to protect adjacent flood plains from overbank flooding, but possibly not the highest floods. Confinement of river flow between levees during high-volume flows means that a higher water surface is necessary to move the same quantity of water downvalley than when water of the unleveed river could spread across the flood plain. Thus a higher water elevation is necessary to handle any given flow of flood magnitude. The floods of 1973, 1993, and 1995 may have been the same range of volume of water as the floods of 1795 and 1844, but they rose to higher elevations. Other factors, however, may offset this rise in water level. These include the effect of upstream flood-control reservoirs and the nature of the flood plain surface itself. For example, unleveed flood plains formerly had forests that restrained the flow of flood waters over them. These forests have now been replaced by croplands and open fields over which flood waters move more efficiently; the result is lower water elevations for a given volume of waters. Thus, the popular belief that the recent great floods of 1973, 1993, and 1995 were "man-made floods" due to levees is a misleading simplification, and possibly incorrect. Recent calculations show that if the meteorological events that caused the Great Flood of 1993 had occurred in the early 1800s, the crest stage at St. Louis likely would have been similar to the actual stages of 1993. Levees are certainly not the only way that humans have influenced the height of floods in the St. Louis region.

Other engineering works include different methods of bank stabilization, so that the large rivers no longer migrate laterally across the flood plain. Coincident with bank stabilization has been the use of dikes to narrow the channels, which makes the rivers use their own energy to keep their channels deep for better navigation without the expense of channel dredging. A narrower and deeper river is a faster river with more kinetic energy to erode the channel bottom. Sharp river bends have been straightened or rounded into smooth geometric arcs of circles so that larger and more cost-efficient barge tows can negotiate them. A very important early engineering work on the Mississippi River at St. Louis was the successful effort in the 1850s to keep the river channel from migrating away from the St. Louis waterfront and ending St. Louis's history as a river port. By 1817, a sand bar had formed along the waterfront and an island was quickly developing, both of which interfered with steamboat access to St. Louis. Dikes and wooden pilings were placed on the Illinois side in the 1830s to divert water to the St. Louis side. After twenty years of sustained effort, the project accomplished its goal of washing away both bar and island.[31] Other improvements for navigation on the Mississippi include the Chain of Rocks dam and diversion of river water through a bypass canal around those rapids. The Chain of Rocks dam is the lowermost of a series of twenty-seven low navigational dams (twenty-six of which have been completed) with locks upstream on the Mississippi. Above the Melvin Price locks and dam at Alton (number 26), therefore, the Mississippi River is basically dammed water with a lower water-surface gradient and less velocity and energy (except just below the dams) than in its natural state.

Though the average annual flow of the Missouri and Mississippi Rivers has not changed significantly from their natural states, except as would be expected from wetter and drier years, the timing of the flow during the year has. A main purpose of the large dams in the Mississippi-Missouri basin above St. Louis, especially on the Missouri River as far as Montana, is the regularization or evening of flow. To alleviate, if not prevent, floods, water is held back in reservoirs during higher flows in spring and early summer and released during lower flows in late summer or winter or as needed for navigation. Thus, St. Louisans now see rivers without anywhere near the large seasonal variations that occurred every year before the mid-twentieth century.

Management of the river has also changed the way humans use the flood plains. Levee construction fostered a sense of security, although perhaps falsely and foolishly held. Coupled with ever-increasing societal expectations of government or public assistance when flooding occurs, this sense of security encouraged more economic investment on the flood plains. In East St. Louis the process began in the late nineteenth century. At that time some districts were "protected" from floods by high railroad embankments, built primarily as bridge approaches, which also served as levees.[32] Flood plains have become a primary location for industries, warehousing, railroad yards, and other activities that require extensive tracts of flat land, as well as those activities tied to the rivers for shipping or water supply. In places, flood plains have also been used as primary dumping grounds for the wastes and derelict materials, some of them toxic, of a chemically and physically changing urban region. In this regard it should be noted that compared to a human engineering solution, the Great Flood of 1993 may have been a natural, efficient, and probably more harmless way to reduce the toxicity of those flood plain sites by floodwater removal and dilution of these materials. On the other hand, the dioxin-impregnated soil at Times Beach on the Meramec River was carefully placed on high mounds so that it could not be reached by flooding, which could move the dioxin downvalley. Instead, incineration will destroy the dioxin or dilute it by dispersion in the atmosphere.[33]

The smaller streams of the metropolitan area have had a different recent environmental history. Urbanization makes the surface relatively impermeable to rainfall by paving streets and parking lots, constructing buildings with impermeable roofs, and greatly compacting the soil of urban lawns, parks, and other open spaces. Impermeable surfaces cause the surface runoff from precipitation to move more rapidly to streams, some with concrete channels like the River des Peres, and into storm sewers, which are really the preurban rivers and creeks put underground and out of sight. The goal is to conduct runoff as fast as possible out of the urbanized area and, in effect, create a kind of "urban desert" deficient in surface water. The cumulative effect of the thousands of individual water engineering activities of homeowners, municipal street departments, and others has been to greatly increase the frequency and severity of flash floods and, conversely, to decrease streamflow, sometimes to nothing, in the periods between precipitation. This effect is the exact opposite of the regularization of annual flow of the large rivers.

To understand the human experience in the St. Louis region is to appreciate the role of its rivers. Historic Cahokia of the eleventh century was a Mississippi River settlement, both at its primary center in the American Bottom and in its "suburbs" in St. Louis City. Indians at European contact were concentrated along the rivers and interconnected by them. Their French-given names are the same as those of the rivers along which they lived: Missouri, Illinois, Kaskaskia, Osage. River systems originally organized the entire westering experience of the American nation as it passed through St. Louis. Most of the prerailroad westering funneled by river through St. Louis, including the nation's access to the commercial Santa Fe Trail and the western emigrant overland trails. In the mid-nineteenth century, St. Louis became the navigational fulcrum of the Mississippi River system.

Commodities brought upriver to St. Louis had to be sorted out there for redistribution on the three major upstream branches, and commodities coming downstream from those branches had to be grouped and assembled into large steamboats or barge tows for more efficient movement downriver. Below St. Louis ice has not normally been a factor in commercial navigation, but above, it causes winter closure of river shipping. Below St. Louis the river is wide and the bends large, permitting more efficient tows of barges, but above, the rivers are smaller with tighter bends, necessitating smaller steamboats and tows of barges, and hence requiring transfer at St. Louis. Below St. Louis the river is naturally large and deep enough to require little channel engineering, but above, the rivers were constantly in need of navigation improvements, whether by low navigation dams on the Mississippi or by timed water releases from upstream reservoirs on the Missouri. All these factors and others helped St. Louis become the navigational transshipment point and the commercial entrepôt for the Mississippi River system. St. Louis is the nation's largest inland river port, the country's largest metropolitan area founded on a river system and nurtured by it.

## *Biogeographical Change*

The climatic changes of the late Pleistocene and the Holocene, the past ten thousand years, produced not only a fluvial system of great variations and episodes of loess deposition, but also major changes in the regional biogeography (table 2). During the Wisconsinan glacial stage, even though the ice cap lay far to the north, the climate of the St. Louis region was very much cooler than now. A spruce-fir forest similar to that of the present upper Great Lakes region characterized the region. After that last ice cap had gone from the contiguous United States, approximately ten thousand years ago, the climate returned to warmer and increasingly drier conditions, the Hypsithermal, which prevailed from eight to five thousand years ago. During this time plant and animal species of the south and west expanded their ranges into the middle

| Holocene Climate Changes | | |
|---|---|---|
| 2000 AD | | warmer |
| 1850 AD | Little Ice Age | cooler |
| 1500 AD | | |
| 1200 AD | | warmer |
| 1000 AD | | |
| 500 AD | | |
| 2000 Years Ago | | |
| 3000 | Subboreal | cooler, wetter |
| 4000 | | |
| 5000 | | |
| 6000 | | |
| 7000 | Atlantic (Hypsithermal) | warmer, drier |
| 8000 | | |
| 9000 | Boreal | cooler, wetter |
| 10,000 | | |

Table 2. *Graph by Walter Schroeder.*

Mississippi valley, displacing some, but not all, of the existing cooler, moister species. The spruce-fir forest gave way to grasslands and deciduous trees. After another cooler period from five to two thousand years ago, the climate moderated to become similar to what it is today. During these years the warmer and drier species that had earlier invaded and prevailed were gradually replaced, but again not entirely, by others—most notably, a return of trees.[34]

Within the past several centuries, however, considerable shifts in climate and associated biogeography still have occurred, and within shorter cycles of change. It was warmer from A.D. 1000 to 1200, cooler during the "Little Ice Age" from A.D. 1450 to 1850, then warmer again from 1850 to 1940, after which the trend is not so clear. This latest warming is often attributed to an increase of atmospheric carbon dioxide from fuel combustion, yet the range of air temperature fluctuations before 1850 was greater than what has been observed since. The warming and cooling trends of the present century are well within the range that has naturally occurred. Therefore, it is unclear how much of the present observed change is due to natural causes and how much is human–induced.[35]

The migration of plants and animals into the St. Louis region, as changing climatic conditions favored first one kind then another, was not matched by a complete withdrawal or dying out when unsuitable climate conditions prevailed. Some species adapted to the changing climate, and some found distinctive ecological niches in which to survive. These ecological niches or microenvironments include cool, moist sinkholes that favor northern species and hot, dry, rocky glades that favor southwestern species. These are usually geographically isolated from others of a similar nature, and the result is restricted populations of relict species in small microenvironments. The Ozarks, including its reaches into the St. Louis metropolitan region, has been identified as a region rich in relict species cut off from their major populations to the north, south, east, and west. It is also a region of endemics, those species peculiar to a region and restricted to it by dispersal barriers. The Meramec River, for example, is nationally noted for a large number of fish taxa. The exceptional diversity of microenvironments in the St. Louis region for both aquatic and terrestrial species promotes a rich biological diversity. Diversity is further enhanced by the region's central location in the continent, which makes it susceptible to species migration from all directions; and by the converging fluvial system, which promotes the dispersal of some species, as the Mississippi Flyway does for waterfowl.[36]

The St. Louis region, so biologically diverse, may thus be interpreted as a longstanding zone of tension between true grassland and forest biomes (figure 4). St. Louis City itself was a mixture of grassland (approximately sixty percent of the area) and forest or woodland.[37] Although climate is the greater determinant of broad-scale patterns of grassland and forest, fire, whether naturally or human set, is a major determinant of details in the distribution of grasses and trees. Both climate and fire produced and maintained the "prairie peninsula," the eastward extension of grassland into the middle Mississippi valley and beyond.[38] The so-called "forests" of the Ozarks were naturally more open, or savanna-like, from fire, with abundant grasses amid the trees; they would be better referred to as "open forests" or "woodlands." The French in pre-American Missouri referred to the tree-covered hills as *bois*, not *forêt*. Human management of the Ozark woodlands in the twentieth century has traditionally promoted tree growth and density for economic reasons at the expense of restoring natural conditions.

Figure 4. *Map by Walter Schroeder, Cartography by Adrianne Nold, Department of Geography, University of Missouri, Columbia.*

Because of St. Louis's location in this zone of encounter between two great biomes, it has exploited the resources of both. The grasslands were first used as open rangelands—first bison, later cattle—then converted into productive croplands. The woodlands of the Ozarks produced pine lumber and hardwoods for St. Louis and cross ties for railroads radiating from St. Louis. In their natural state they were also hog and cattle grazing lands and home to valuable wild game, such as deer and turkey. In the twentieth century these woodlands, now human-managed forests, are a major recreation area for St. Louisans. River bottoms also served St. Louis well as a source of lumber, but more distinctly for beaver and otter during the pre-American years before their near extinction.[39] Bottomland timber provided a convenient fuel supply for steamboats, and the rampant deforestation of river banks and bottoms destabilized the river banks and accelerated channel shifts of the large rivers.[40]

However, the division between grassland and forest biomes is too simple a dichotomy. Within each is a spectacular variety of smaller-scale phytogeographic and zoogeographic regions. A range of vegetative associations and structures form an intricate mosaic when mapped. Among these are various kinds of glades and fens, riparian woods, and wetlands. Differences are as small as those between north- and south-facing slopes in the same valley; various stages in the succession of plants on abandoned crop and pasture lands; and the curious environmental niches of an urban region such as parks, backyards, levees, and vacant lots of demolished buildings. The biogeographical diversity of the St. Louis region is dynamic and virtually infinite in its spatial complexity.[41]

Diversity in species, structure, and location is due to both human and natural processes working over the past few thousand years. Even early human societies had an effect on the region's biology. Prehistoric Indians used fire to create grasslands and probably helped exterminate large Ice Age animals like the mammoth, mastodon, sloth, pecarry, and musk ox.[42] They may have affected the dominance and distribution of trees and shrub species by selective gathering of acorns and seeds. Maize and other useful crops were brought into the St. Louis region over fifteen hundred years ago.[43] Thirty thousand Indians in the Cahokia village complex needed a large and dependable food supply, which they derived from field crops.

But it has been during the past two hundred years, the latest great chapter in environmental history, that the most spectacular and pervasive biologic changes through human intervention have come. Humans have introduced, intentionally or not, new species into the region and have caused, usually unintentionally, the removal of others. They have increased the relative numbers of some, creating monocultural croplands and providing expanded habitats for cedars and hard maples, for example, but they have reduced others to the status of endangered and rare. Deer and turkey, beaver and otter, whose numbers had earlier been decimated by humans, have now returned in significant numbers to the region, illustrating how intelligent environmental management can clearly influence the presence and number of a species. More recently, professional manipulation of the biologic environment is tending to focus less on individual species and more on ecosystems that occupy ecoregions. A viable ecosystem is, of course, essential to the success of any one of its constituent species. The "natural" environment of an urban area like St. Louis is thus viewed as a functioning ecosystem itself. A new field of study, urban biology, has emerged to work toward the understanding and improvement of this ecosystem, so woefully out of any semblance of equilibrium in part because it changes so radically and so fast.

## *Conclusion*

St. Louis has an everchanging environment that can be traced back for thousands of years. When it is thought of at all, the prehuman past is usually considered as a benign or neutral state of equilibrium, one in which, for example, plants and animals existed in steady-state, functioning ecosystems.

A little thought, however, quickly dispels this notion. The prehuman past was tumultuous. Floods larger than those now called "500-year events" swept down the Mississippi and Missouri Rivers. Cold eras, centuries of heat and drought, and repeated firings of the land with the associated coming and going of plants and animals and even entire ecosystems are all part of St. Louis's dynamic past. Each wave of change, whether long or short in duration, ended with both subtractions and additions to the long list of components of the St. Louis environment. The result today is an exceptionally diverse environmental region.

Humans have added further dynamism to natural environmental change. The pace of change has accelerated and its intensity heightened in a great urban area of two and a half million persons. St. Louisans, both as individuals and collectively, have taken great advantage of their environmental resources to create a new, "human-made environment." St. Louisans have used metals from the Ozarks; fuels from Illinois; local limestones, shales, clays, and loess; water from the nation's greatest hydrologic system and from subsurface waters; and an array of biotic resources, including timber, grass, and native animals. These environmental resources converged on St. Louis to lay the foundations and continued growth of a great city.

# Culture and Environment in the American Bottom
## The Rise and Fall of Cahokia Mounds

*William R. Iseminger*

The earliest inhabitants in the present-day St. Louis area arrived at the end of the Ice Age, and successive generations experienced and adapted to a number of climatic and environmental changes. This essay examines the evolution of late prehistoric cultural traditions in the vast floodplain east of St. Louis known as the American Bottom, and the impact that humans and environment had upon each other prior to the arrival of the French in the late 1600s, the beginning of the "historic" period. I will focus on the development and demise of the largest prehistoric settlement north of Mexico, Cahokia Mounds.

Cahokia had an impact on its environment—an ecosystem upon which it was dependent—and ultimately overstepped the bounds that kept it in balance with nature, as well as other human groups, affecting regional political and social relations and the general quality of life. But natural forces may also have had a role in Cahokia's demise. Examining Cahokia's rise and fall, we can see parallels with modern society, although on a different scale. Resource overexploitation, crowded living conditions, political and economic disruptions, and climatic change all contributed to Cahokia's decline, all threads of the same tattered fabric that cloaks today's world.

## The Setting

To better understand the interaction between the prehistoric Indians and the environment of the American Bottom of Illinois, we must first examine the setting in which these exchanges took place.

The "American Bottom" (referring to the eighteenth- and nineteenth-century settlement of this region by Americans, who generally displaced the French, English, Spanish, and Indians who had preceded them) is usually considered to be the broad expanse of floodplain on the Illinois side of the

Mississippi River, bounded on the east by the bluffs stretching from Alton on the north to just south of the mouth of the Kaskaskia River near Chester, approximately 160 km. in length (figure 1). The northern portion of the American Bottom, from Alton to Dupo, Illinois, is the broadest, reaching a maximum east-west width of about 18 km. between St. Louis and Collinsville, Illinois (figure 2). This "Northern Bottoms Expanse"[1] is primarily the result of the confluence of the Missouri and Mississippi Rivers, just south of Alton, especially the scouring action of the postglacial meltwaters that flooded these river basins. Between Alton and Dupo, the limestone and sandstone deposits that form the prominent vertical bluffs to the north and south of these communities dip below the level of the floodplain in a geological syncline, and the floodwaters cut into the softer bluffs formed of more easily eroded beds of coals, sandstones, shales, and limestones capped with a thick layer of loess.[2] Later, as the river valley filled with deposits of silt, sand, and clay, the river took a meandering course, changing its route many times and swinging from east to west across the valley. As former meanders were cut off from the main channel, they became lakes, sloughs, and marshes; streams draining the uplands captured other old meanders. These various fluvial features formed an interconnected "inland waterway" beyond the eastern banks of the Mississippi. They also provided a superb resource base of fish, waterfowl and aquatic plants. Periodic flooding of the region also deposited fertile soils across the ridge and swale terrain of the American Bottom.

There were scattered woodlands concentrated around the aquatic sources consisting primarily of cottonwood, willow, sycamore, maple, and hackberry, surrounded by large areas of prairie. Bluffcrests often were topped with hillside prairies and cedar; denser hardwood forests, primarily oaks and hickories, were concentrated along the bluffslopes and adjacent dissected uplands, and tallgrass prairies dominated the interior uplands.

These various environmental zones would have provided a stable set of floral and faunal resources within less than a day's walk from any settlement in the American Bottom,[3] and ethnobotanical evidence from archaeological sites shows that all zones were being exploited, although in varying degrees in different time periods. However, the stability of these resources would be affected by exploitation, especially as population densities and distributions increased through time.

## Cultural Traditions

Archaeologists recognize several prehistoric (pre-European contact) cultural traditions in this region: PaleoIndian, Archaic, Woodland, Emergent Mississippian, Mississippian, and Oneota. In turn, most of these traditions had

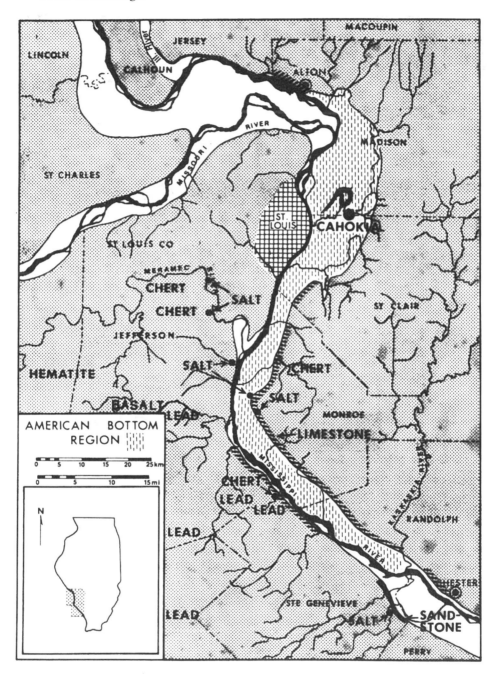

Figure 1. *The American Bottom region (hatched) showing the location of Cahokia, rivers and streams, and some of the local sources for raw materials. Adapted from Kelly 1991b.*

several subphases of cultural development and change. PaleoIndian is generally believed to have ranged from 9500 to 8000 B.C.; Archaic from 8000 to 600 B.C.; Woodland from 600 B.C. to A.D. 800; Emergent Mississippian from A.D. 800 to 1000; Mississippian from A.D. 1000 to 1450; and Oneota from A.D. 1450 to 1550. Actually, the beginning and ending "dates" for these traditions are imprecise and would vary from region to region, but they represent the generally accepted time frames recognized in the American Bottom area. Each tradition would be characterized by an assemblage of diagnostic artifact types and forms, settlement patterns, domicile types, and environmental utilization. The subphase designations and durations are constantly undergoing revision and refinement as new data accumulates from ongoing research.

In the American Bottom region, the first significant occupations were during the Late Archaic, initially as small base camps, and later as extensive occupations of hunting and gathering groups. The fairly permanent settlements were on the higher, more stable clay meander banks and talus slopes.[4] The Early and Middle Woodland settlements were mostly small and seasonal, along cut banks and interchannel ridges, marshes and old lake edges, and low swales in the floodplain. There are some Early Woodland settlements in the uplands, but almost no Middle Woodland ones. The residents focused on exploiting the seasonally available aquatic floodplain and adjacent upland resources. In Late Woodland the emphasis shifted again to mostly upland settlements close to the American Bottom, and a wide variety of flora and fauna from both regions were exploited.[5] Most sites were on forest soils suitable for cultivation, presumably garden plots cleared by slash and burn methods. In early Late Woodland, the lack of significant floodplain occupation may indicate extensive Mississippi River flooding,[6] but by late Late Woodland, although the emphasis was still in the uplands, the first sizeable settlements had begun to appear in the American Bottom. More attention will be paid to Emergent Mississippian and Mississippian settlements elsewhere, but they tended to concentrate in the bottomland areas and major and minor stream drainages, mostly in proximity to tillable soils.

In the central Mississippi valley, the Mississippian tradition began to decline in the thirteenth century, and was essentially gone by the fifteenth century; the mechanisms of that decline are still being unraveled and will be discussed later. Another cultural tradition known as Oneota, which may have its roots in Mississippian, had begun to emerge around A.D. 1100 in the upper Mississippi River valley and spread into the American Bottom by the 1400s.[7] Though only a few scattered sites have been found locally, the Oneota culture seems to have intruded into this area. The Oneota has distinctive tool types, structures, and ceramic decorations that differ from those of the Mississippians.

To the west and north it is believed that the Iowa, Missouri, Osage, Oto, Winnebago, and a few other later tribal groups were descendants of Oneota peoples. It is not known who the direct descendants of the Cahokia Mississippians are, as oral traditions of later groups do not show direct ties to this unique community. As Robert Hall states, "No sites have been located . . . that can provide the positive links necessary to demonstrate whether the Illinois Mississippians just ceased to be, moved southward . . . or remained within the Midwest" as a part of what were later known as Sioux or Algonquin nations."[8]

## Climate and Culture

Although climate change does not determine how a culture will develop, it is one of many factors that influence cultural change and evolution. The cultural traditions summarized above do correlate closely with climatic episodes, which mostly affected the flora and fauna and the hydrology of the area, and thus its occupants.

At the end of the Ice Age, during the PaleoIndian period, the Midwest environment was changing from tundra and boreal forest to one of deciduous hardwood forests and prairies. By 8000 B.C., more than thirty types of large mammals had become extinct, including the mammoth, mastodon, long horned bison, giant sloth, horse, giant beaver, and camel. This was mostly due to changing environment, but the new predator—humans—also had an impact. The Archaic tradition developed as the people adapted to these changes; regional diversity and territoriality became more pronounced. The "Altithermal," a period from 5000-2500 B.C. was up to five degrees warmer than today and was a time of expansion and the development of hunting and gathering Middle Archaic societies. The climate of the "Medithermal," after 2500 B.C., was similar to today's, but with fluctuations or "episodes" that appear to have affected the Indians and their culture.[9]

The "Sub-Atlantic" episode, from 300 B.C. to A.D. 300, was cooler and wetter and closely corresponds to the development of Middle Woodland cultures with their elaborate ceremonialism and cultivation of seed crops. The "Scandic" episode, from A.D. 300 to 800-900, corresponds to the development of the less elaborate Late Woodland tradition; some believe it was a warmer, drier period, while others believe it was cooler, but with a shift in the rainy season. The "Neo-Atlantic" episode, from A.D. 900 to 1200-1300, was basically the time of the Mississippian tradition. The climate started out wetter and cooler and was the most favorable for the development of agriculture, especially the intensive maize agriculture that developed during this time. There was a gradual warming trend that peaked between A.D. 1150-1250, two to three degrees warmer than today, which relates to a time of turmoil at Cahokia. This was followed by a rapid cooling episode called the "Pacific," correlating to the decline of Cahokia and the disappearance of Mississippian culture from the upper Mississippi Valley. There was a short recovery period, the "Neo-Atlantic II," from A.D. 1450-1550, which closely corresponds to the development of the Oneota tradition, but the climate cooled off again from A.D. 1550-1880, the "Little Ice Age." Indian groups in the Midwest still practiced some agriculture, but they had become more dependent on hunting and gathering again, taking advantage of the bison that were expanding into this area as the prairies spread.[10]

## Subsistence

People of all these traditions practiced hunting, fishing, and gathering, with certain resources receiving different emphases through time. In Late Archaic times, Indians in the Southeast and Midwest began experimenting with plant husbandry. By 2000 B.C. squashes and gourds were being cultivated or domesticated, as were certain oily and starchy seed plants, evidenced by the larger seed sizes when compared to those of the wild plants of the same species. In the American Bottom, as elsewhere, the dominant types were the starchy seeds of erect knotweed, and goosefoot or lambsquarters, and the oily seeds of sunflower and marshelder. Additionally, other starchy seeds became important by Woodland times, most notably maygrass and barley; tobacco provided leaves for smoking.[11] This whole complex continued into the Emergent Mississippian and Mississippian periods.

Although corn (maize) first appears in a few Middle Woodland sites after A.D. 200 and a scattering of Late Woodland sites, it does not seem to have become a dominant food source until Emergent Mississippian times, after A.D. 800, when carbonized maize remains occur in 50 to 70 percent of the archaeological features from American Bottom sites.[12] The widespread cultivation of maize helped foster larger population densities or concentrations, the production of larger food surpluses, and the development of more complex political and social organization. Begun initially to create more supplemental foods, the new maize agriculture resulted in an entirely new economic pattern.[13]

A new type of corn (Eastern eight-row or Northern Flint), more adapted to northern climates, may have stimulated Mississippian development. However, this concept has been challenged recently by several paleobotanists who find no substantive evidence in support of that hypothesis, especially when the existing data is put under close scrutiny. They contend that the intensification of maize production and the "emergence of the Mississippian polity at Cahokia site was certainly not fueled by the introduction of Northern Flint,"[14] and is more likely a result of socio-political changes, a "function of such things as individual and corporate group decision-making and information sharing, field allocation policies, and responses to demands for increased surplus and tribute."[15]

Faunal remains recovered from archaeological sites of all periods in the American Bottom, including Cahokia, include at least three dozen types of fish, nearly as many types of birds, a couple dozen mammal species, a half-dozen reptiles, and a few amphibians. During the Late Woodland, Emergent Mississippian, and Mississippian, mammals, particularly deer, were a quite important part of the diet. Along with fish, these species supplied the majority of the meat consumed on a daily basis. Waterfowl represent the most common bird remains, but terrestrial species such as the bobwhite, prairie chicken, turkey, and grouse are also common. Compared to the earlier traditions, the importance of birds increased while fish declined in the Mississippian.[16] The only domesticated animal was the dog, which apparently served as a companion, guard, scavenger, hunting aid, and occasional food source. (Dogs probably accompanied the first PaleoIndians entering the continent from the Old World). Apparently other animal species were not uniformly domesticatable, although individual specimens could be tamed; however, the abundance of wildlife in the region deemed animal husbandry generally unnecessary.

Cahokia's rise to power correlates with the warmer, wetter Neo-Atlantic climatic episode between A.D. 900-1200.[17] For the most part, the Cahokians must have balanced the advantage of increased summer rainfall against increased danger of flooding, probably adapting divided risk cultivation strategies that utilized locations outside the potentially flood-prone bottoms, mainly the terraces, creek valleys and uplands to the east.[18]

Maize, a very productive grain, could be grown in great quantities, producing storable surpluses for leaner times, as well as serving as a trade commodity. Larger populations could be supported and societal ordering became more complex. More well-defined social classes and hierarchies developed; there was increased specialization and division of labor; political alliances became more important; trade was highly structured; conflicts and even warfare between groups and polities increased, perhaps fueled by competition for resources or territory.

## The Rise of Cahokia

The first relatively permanent settlements in the Cahokia region appear after A.D. 700, when Late Woodland peoples established a number of small settlements in the American Bottom and adjacent uplands. Several occupations, some perhaps seasonal or short-term, have been identified in the area that was to eventually become known as the Cahokia site. By A.D. 800, as

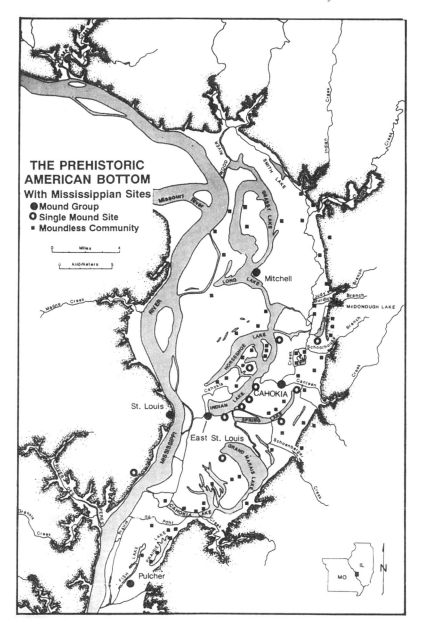

Figure 2. *The "northern expanse" of the American Bottom as it may have appeared around 1800, based on Government Land Office survey records from the early 1800s and early U.S. Geological Survey and other contour maps. Many streams, lakes, sloughs, and marshes provided an "inland waterway," connecting large areas of the bottomlands; most have been drained in modern times. The locations of Cahokia and other Mississippian sites have been superimposed on the landscape. Adapted from map by Mikels Skele, Office of Contract Archaeology, Southern Illinois University at Edwardsville.*

the Emergent Mississippian tradition began to develop, a large portion of the Cahokia site area was occupied. The small, rectangular, single-family dwellings were set in deep basins (up to one meter deep), with individual postholes dug for each wall post. There were also distinctive ceramic vessel forms and decorations. The community pattern usually included groupings of houses and other structures arranged around a courtyard, often with a central post that was sometimes surrounded by pits, and larger structures, probably communal or ceremonial, to one side or in the courtyard area.[19] These formal arrangements suggest the emergence of a ranked form of socio-political organization in the American Bottom region, and perhaps the appearance of chiefs.[20] The presence of large communities suggests population growth, not only at the Cahokia site, but also at other regional sites.

Corn had become an important crop, providing the quantities and surpluses needed to feed larger populations, but the starchy seed crops and many wild plant and animal foods still contributed in important ways to the diet. With this stable food base, a foundation was laid which would support the massive community of Cahokia.

During the Mississippian period, starting around A.D. 1000, several dramatic changes occurred. New architectural forms appeared; the wall posts of houses were placed in narrow trenches. Initially, the house basins were deep, as in Emergent Mississippian structures, but through time the depth decreased almost to surface level by late Mississippian phases. T-shaped structures during the early Mississippian period may have been communal or ceremonial in nature, as were large rectangular structures during later phases. Structure size tended to increase and vary more through time, as did the occurrence of internal storage pits. Initially, structures were clustered in linear patterns at much of Cahokia, generally aligned with the cardinal directions; this gradually evolved into a clustering of structures in apparent household groupings around small courtyards or "patios," with less observance of cardinal alignments;[21] in turn, the courtyard groups tended to cluster around larger plaza arrangements that were often bordered by mounds.

Archaeological evidence indicates that for much of the time Cahokia was occupied, oak, especially white oak, and hickory were preferred as fuel and construction materials; these trees are more commonly found in the adjacent uplands.[22] Indeed, there is a decline in the frequency of nuts and an increase in oak and hickory charcoal in Mississippian features compared to the earlier Woodland site features from the area.[23] This does represent a shift from earlier time periods, when nuts were more important dietary components and these species of trees were less often used for fuel or construction,[24] but with the Mississippian emphasis on cultigens (corn and starchy seeds), nut trees were more expendable for fuel and construction.

New ceramic forms appeared with a greater variety of form and style than previously. Gradually, the majority of wares were tempered with burned and crushed mussel shell, mixed with a paste made from local clay outcrops in the bottomland stream banks and other clay and weathered shale exposures in the uplands. There was an increase in exotic wares from distant regions, primarily from the south, most likely used as containers for commodities being traded rather than as a trade material itself. One variety of local ware, known as Ramey Incised, seems to have originated at Cahokia and was exported to, or copied in, many locations throughout the Midwest, principally to the north. Such extraregional contacts seem more frequent than in prior periods and show that exchange networks were well-developed and expanding, probably under the control of high-ranking personages.[25]

Settlement patterns also changed, and there was greater variety in community size. During most of the Mississippian phases, communities outside of Cahokia were small and moundless, referred to as "homesteads," "farmsteads" or "hamlets" by archaeologists, with from just one or two structures to a few household clusters along the ridges in the bottoms. However, a number of villages of small to moderate size were scattered throughout the area, some with one or two mounds that were probably local centers (figure 2).[26] There seems to have been a nucleation of settlement associated with the Cahokia site and some smaller administrative centers, mostly identifiable as multiple-mound towns such as those near the present-day communities of St. Louis, Missouri, and East St. Louis, Dupo, and Mitchell, Illinois. They were not all necessarily contemporary, nor were their peak periods of equal duration.[27] At their inception, some of these communities may have been equal in power or size to Cahokia, but Cahokia soon outpaced them and dominated the area for a couple of centuries. Pauketat[28] believes that residential density at Cahokia may have been at its greatest during the Lohmann phase (A.D. 1000-1050), but the subsequent Stirling phase (A.D. 1050-1150) was also a time of dense population and elaborate cultural complexity,[29] and Cahokia rose to dominance as the largest Mississippian site in eastern North America.[30]

The dominant features of Cahokia, then and now, are the mounds, as many as 120 of them in Cahokia proper (figure 3). Constructed entirely of earth carried in baskets from Mississippian borrow pits, even where the sites are near sources of stone, they perhaps symbolized ritual links to the earth, the origin of life. The mounds come in three forms: platform, conical, and ridgetop. Platform mounds were the most common, serving as elevated bases for temples, community storage facilities, council lodges, and other important buildings—they were the domains of the elite and shrines to their authority and nodal points of articulation between the community and the cosmos. The

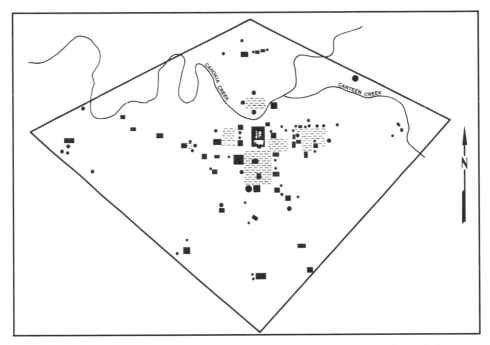

Figure 3. *Distribution, form, and location of the known mounds at the Cahokia site, many of which have been destroyed. East-west dimensions approximately three miles; north-south, two and one-half miles. Monks Mound at center. Hatching indicates known and suggested plaza areas during various phases of occupation. Adapted from Mink, 1991.*

conical mounds have been interpreted as burial mounds but few have been excavated to support this claim; some may have been circular platforms for rotundas,[31] although more work is needed to determine this. The ridgetop mounds seem to mark important locations along Cahokia's axes, and those that have been tested indicate that they did have mortuary functions as well. However, most people were not buried in mounds but in cemeteries; only elite or ritual burials seem to have mound associations. All mounds examined so far show evidence of several construction stages, perhaps commemorating calendric cycles, the deaths of leaders or ascent of new ones, or ritual reburial of the mound in a rite of purification.

Chiefly authority seems to have been consolidated at Cahokia as the site grew to monumental proportions. In time the area generally recognized as Cahokia covered over five square miles.[32] It is also possible that some of the mound clusters represent subcommunities, or suburbs, of the concentration of mounds in "downtown" Cahokia.[33] They may have even functioned as separate communities, perhaps formed by high-ranking lineages that coalesced at Cahokia during the beginning of the Mississippian period.[34]

A majority of the downtown mounds are clustered around several suggested plazas, the largest being the forty-acre Grand Plaza south of Monks Mound (figure 3). Many of the suburban mound groups also exhibit arrangements around possible plazas, while others are more random or isolated.

The huge expanse of the Cahokia site, the large number of mounds constructed, and the massive amounts of soil dug and transported by human labor are just a few of the factors that point to a large sedentary population. Population estimates for Cahokia have varied greatly, from as few as five thousand to as many as fifty thousand. Many of the higher estimates were calculated from the area covered by the site and an assumed consistent occupation density over that area, based on the number of houses exposed in some large-scale excavations in the 1960s. However, many modern researchers tend toward conservatism in conjunction with more recent research and reevaluation of the earlier data.[35] For one thing, not all structures were residences; some were used for storage, processing, communal or ceremonial purposes. Second, not all areas of the site were occupied at the same time or at the same density. Third, not all structures seen in an excavation are contemporary; some were built in the same locale years, decades, or even centuries apart, or individual structures were rebuilt. Fourth, "urban renewal" changed the function of many areas from residential to civic or ceremonial; many of the latter often reconverted to residential usage during later phases of occupation. Finally, some areas considered to be part of the site were unsuitable for habitation, being too low and/or wet.

Thus, considering all the above, modern estimates for Cahokia's peak population between A.D. 1000 and 1200 fall within the ten- to twenty thousand range.[36] Cahokia had the largest known concentration of prehistoric peoples north of Mexico. In conjunction with this fact, there are many archaeologists, myself included, who are comfortable with the use of the term *city* to describe Cahokia, while more conservative colleagues shy away from the term because of the difficulty in substantiating archaeologically many of the technical features that are often considered to define a city or *urban complex*, or who feel that Cahokia never quite crossed that threshold into urbanism.[37] However, Cahokia was substantially larger than any other Mississippian community, the largest of which are usually referred to as *temple towns*, and by virtue of its scale, I believe city is an appropriate term for Cahokia, as it was obviously much more than a larger town.

Economically, Cahokia has been characterized as a *gateway center*[38] on the northern frontier of the Mississippian core area, with Cahokia involved in an ever-changing network of exchange, primarily to the north. Its proximity to the confluence of the Missouri, Mississippi, and Illinois Rivers was probably instrumental in its development as a gateway center. This fortuitous, but probably intentional, location near the confluence of these "highways" for canoe travel and trade gave Cahokia access to the resources provided by the drainages of these great waterways and their many tributaries as they cut through the Ozark Uplift to the southwest, the Mississippi Alluvial Plain and the Coastal Plain to the south, the Interior Low Plateau to the southeast, and the Glaciated Central Lowlands and the Great Lakes to the north.[39] Each had different resources and environments associated with it, and Cahokia had contact with each. Some view such an exchange network as in part a response "to the need for stabilizing intertribal relations, minimizing the threat of warfare, formalizing the etiquette and protocol of intertribal relations, assuring the friendship of allies in times of need, and validating or legitimating these relationships with ritual, religious sanctions, and gifts."[40]

The rise of Cahokia to dominance is in part related to its role in a number of exchange webs that operated both locally and externally. Many exotic materials were brought into the city. Most abundant were marine shells originating from the Gulf of Mexico and the Atlantic; at least nineteen types of marine shells have been identified in archaeological features, primarily the large whelk and tiny marginella.[41] Shells were used mostly for ornamentation, such as beads, pendants, gorgets, and decoration for clothing. Vast quantities have been recovered from Cahokia and surrounding sites, and possible workshop areas have been identified where the raw material was processed into finished goods.[42] Quantities were small at the beginning of Emergent Mississippian, gradually increasing until shells flowed in during the Mississippian era. The acquisition of marine shell was probably under the control of certain elites at Cahokia and other administrative centers, who may have served as patrons to craftsmen who fashioned the shells into ornaments. These elites then controlled the redistribution locally and extraregionally, especially to the north.[43]

Cahokians also imported copper, mostly from the area around Lake Superior, and occasionally recovered from regional glacial till deposits. Almost pure copper nuggets were cold-hammered into ceremonial ornaments and specialized tools. Sheets of mica from the southern Appalachians were often cut and fashioned into ornaments. Other minerals, such as lead, hematite, and ocher were imported, mostly from southeastern Missouri, and primarily processed to make paint pigments or an occasional ornament. The majority (around 80 percent) of the chert (flint) for making tools and weapons came from quarries and outcrops in the Crescent Hills area south of St. Louis, and the rest came from several sources in present-day Monroe and Union Counties in Illinois, as well as smaller amounts from other sources and glacial tills. Salt brines were extracted from springs in numerous locations in southern Illinois and eastern Missouri, and evaporated in large pans to produce salt used primarily in cooking (figure 1).

Thus, Cahokia's trade network was widespread and seems to have increased in time from the Emergent Mississippian through most of the Mississippian phases, falling off as Cahokia declined. At public gatherings such as agricultural ceremonies and other festive occasions, people exchanged items at communal markets in something akin to an annual or periodic *rendezvous*.

## The Decline Of Cahokia: Environmental and Cultural Effects

Any large population center creates consequences for its environment, for other populations, and for its own future, and this is evident at Cahokia. But what caused Cahokia's demise? What were Cahokia's environmental consequences, and how was the city affected by its own course of action and its interaction with others and the environment? There is no single cause or answer, but a combination of factors were involved.

The construction of the many mounds of Cahokia would have affected the local environment, especially when one considers the number and size of the mounds. Monks Mound alone contains 22 million cubic feet of earth. Although no formal tally has been made, it has been estimated that for the 120 mounds (including Monks Mound), Cahokians used as much as 55 million cubic feet of earth. Thus, the surrounding terrain was dotted with mounds and the borrow pits from which earth had been excavated. Many of the latter became ponds or small lakes; the largest covered nearly seventeen acres. These were probably stocked with fish, intentionally or naturally, and attracted other aquatic life and plants. Others were used as community dumps or filled in during urban renewal projects.

In addition, there is evidence that large portions of the Grand Plaza were leveled and filled to produce a flat surface in a normally undulating terrain.[44] There is evidence of filling at other site areas and it is suspected in other plaza locations. In sum, Cahokians moved massive amounts of earth throughout their reign, altering or modifying the natural terrain and creating artificial earthworks.

A population of any size has to be fed and, considering the estimated size of Cahokia, this would have been a major undertaking. As has been noted previously, Cahokia was an agricultural society that relied heavily on the production of maize as well as other crops, with hunting, fishing and collecting rounding out the dietary sources. In order to feed their people, Cahokians allocated massive amounts of land for agricultural fields, clearing many acres of grasses, trees, and brush for areas of preferred soils. Thus, the vegetational patterns of the American Bottom were changed in many locations, and it is possible that there was some siltation from run-off into the various waterways. Land clearing also affects wildlife as habitats are altered or destroyed, redirecting hunting strategies and affecting the availability of certain faunal resources. The deer remains found at Cahokia indicate that Cahokia's deer were harvested, dressed, and butchered at some distance from the city, and the prime meat-bearing cuts transported to the site. Few lower limb bones or skull and neck portions have been recovered.[45] This hunting may have been conducted by Cahokians or by other communities which served as hunting stations, or others that provided meat as a form of tribute.

Much of the land surrounding Cahokia may have been essentially deforested to satisfy the need for firewood and construction timber. However, the source for much of the construction timber would have been the slopes, valleys, and uplands of the bluffs to the east.

The construction of the stockade wall around the central part of Cahokia also involved a tremendous expenditure of forest resources. In my work on the east stockade excavations, I arrived at an average estimate of 20,000 logs needed for each of the four stockade wall constructions, which are estimated

Figure 4. *An interpretation of Cahokia Mounds circa A.D. 1100, when at its peak, although all the mounds and other site features may not have been contemporary. Monks Mound is at the center with the Grand Plaza extending south to the Twin Mounds. The sacred precinct is enclosed by the stockade wall and the Woodhenge calendar stands to the west. Ponds and lakes have formed in borrow pits, while others are being dug. Agricultural fields surround the community. Cahokia Mounds State Historic Site; painting by William R. Iseminger.*

to have been 1.75 miles (2.8 km) long (figure 4).[46] Most of this wood must have come from the eastern bluff oak-hickory forests, some three to five miles away. To fell, trim, debark, transport, and erect the logs would probably have required a minimum of 130,000 job hours per stockade. The reduction in the size of the third and fourth stockades' bastions, which projected from the wall at regular intervals (about 26 meters or 85 feet), suggests an attempt to conserve on the number of logs required, perhaps because suitable timber was becoming more scarce.

The impact of timber acquisition for the Stockade alone must have been great. Large areas of forest were stripped of suitable trees, not only affecting forest cover but also the associated forest flora and fauna important to Cahokians. The construction of thousands of houses (each house requiring nearly one hundred trees) and countless fires burning for hundreds of years also had major consequences. Increased cutting of bluff forests would elevate the amount of erosional runoff and resulting siltation of bottomland streams (this is well documented for many third-world countries).[47] In turn, this would lead to increases in local flooding, endangering croplands. Also, a reduction in local resources meant the Cahokians had to travel greater distances to obtain what they needed. There would be subsequent increased competition, perhaps even conflict, between the regional polities for the remaining resources.

The presence of the stockade indicates socio-political changes and escalating regional stresses. Built between A.D. 1100-1250, the four successive stockades were primarily defensive features—their ultimate purpose was to protect or defend the central, sacred precinct of the community. From the bastions, warriors could launch arrows at attackers, but the identity of the enemy, and whether they ever attacked, is uncertain. Perhaps the increased competition for the existing and less-abundant resources led to interregional conflicts, or maybe the conflicts were intraregional, as local polities became more autonomous and less dependent on Cahokia, occasionally massing to threaten or raid the once-powerful center.[48]

Within the walled area were Monks Mound and seventeen other mounds, the Grand Plaza, and most likely the residences of the ruling class (although excavations have yet to be conducted to verify the last theory). Admittance was probably limited to those who lived there or those who had business with them, or for the general population on ceremonial occasions and for public gatherings. Thus, the wall had a secondary purpose, as a social barrier. We are not sure who lived within, but they were probably affiliated by kinship with the paramount chief. Besides the general population residential areas, there were also definite elite areas outside the wall, but it is not clear what distinguished them from those inside.[49]

Environmental changes may have contributed to the decline of Cahokia. The Pacific climate episode mentioned earlier included increased traumatic weather such as late-spring and early-fall frosts, which would affect cultivated plants and result in a shorter growing season. This was apparently accompanied by a shifting or less-reliable rainy season, leading to a greater frequency of both drought and flood.[50] In addition, similar droughty summer conditions may have increased erosion in the Missouri drainage, leading to increased sediment in the Mississippi and producing a shallower, wider channel more subject to flooding and possibly to heightened water tables in the local area.[51] Coupled with the aforementioned siltation of local streams associated with deforestation and cultivation, flooding from heavy summer thunderstorms would have had disastrous effects on bottomland maize fields.[52] It is interesting to note that during the Moorehead Phase (A.D. 1150-1250) at Cahokia and much of the American Bottom, there is evidence of a decline in population and most settlement is concentrated on the slightly higher elevations. This suggests wetter conditions and higher water tables. There is also a population dispersal and concomitant increase in Moorehead Phase settlements into the uplands.

Prehistoric flooding would not have been as common as in modern times, as there would have been proportionally less runoff due to the absence of massive agricultural fields and paved urban locations. Today, torrential rains cannot be quickly absorbed and are channeled directly into storm sewers and streams, whereas prehistorically, the natural floodplains absorbed all but the most severe floods in the old abandoned channels, sloughs, marshes and lakes (figure 2). Little archaeological evidence indicates flooding problems in the communities, which were usually on slightly higher ground. The Moorehead Phase dispersal is probably due to wetter conditions in low-lying areas rather than the result of major flooding, making the American Bottom a less desirable place to live compared to earlier times.

Agricultural crops were most affected by environmental traumas, and thus the amount of food produced gradually declined. Other flora and fauna were affected and their distributional ranges shrank. Bald cypress, for example, common in the early Mississippian phase at Cahokia, was essentially absent in the later phases.[53] The natural range of cypress is no longer this far north, but its frequency in earlier phase features suggests its range once included the American Bottom or nearby areas.[54]

Hall attributes the decline of Cahokia to "improved techno-environmental adaptations" that favored the adaptability and scale of smaller groups organized as tribes in varied locations. Changes in food and food gathering, particularly in the cultivation of eight-row Northern Flint corn and bison hunting, may have attracted regional populations to the west, "reducing the population circumscription of the greater Cahokia area."[55]

While Northern Flint corn does not appear to have been the stimulant for the beginnings of Cahokia, it may have been involved indirectly in its decline. It is better adapted to shorter growing seasons and fewer daylight hours and resists both rot and drought.[56] Cahokia's neighbors more readily adopted the new corn, as well as protein rich beans, becoming more self-sufficient. Meanwhile, Cahokia remained more conservative, never growing beans and being slow to adopt the new corn. Perhaps Cahokia's fields also were depleted of nutrients, especially nitrogen, which bean plants would have fixed or replaced in the soils.

It is possible that the spread of bison into the region may have also affected Cahokia. With waning local resources, the appeal of bison hunting west of the Mississippi may have encouraged some to leave and pursue this resource, if not from Cahokia itself, at least from some of the surrounding settlements. Bison do not appear to have lived in Illinois until just before European contact (possibly the 1500s) and no remains have been found at Cahokia.[57]

Thus, the combination of increased availability of beans, bison, and better adapted corn could easily have spelled disaster for Cahokia, with there now being fewer advantages to participating in the Cahokia sphere of activities and interchange. Whether Cahokians participated in the shift toward a more balanced hunting and horticultural adaptation, or succumbed to others who did, cannot be said with certainty.[58]

Other factors which may have contributed to, but not caused, Cahokia's decline, include nutritional and health problems. There is some evidence that Mississippians elsewhere, and presumably at Cahokia, suffered more health difficulties than their predecessors. For example, because corn tends to limit the body's absorption of iron, especially among the very young, there was an increase in iron deficiency.[59] In some areas, the trace elements in the bones indicate that higher status individuals often displayed better overall health, having greater amounts of animal protein in the diet. Although this was not always a consistent pattern in the Mississippian world, it would fit with Lucretia Kelly's studies which show that greater amounts of deer bone from preferred meat cuts (high- to mid-utility) are found in features in elite areas of the Cahokia site.[60]

There was also an increase in dental cavities and gum diseases compared to earlier periods, due to the high carbohydrate corn diet, and the stone grit in the ground corn wore the teeth down dramatically. Arthritis was widespread, as was periostitis, which probably resulted from local infections. Less frequent was systemic osteomylitis, a bloodborne infection. Infant mortality was high during the Mississippian period, especially during the first year of life.[61] Some have attributed this to the early weaning onto a corn mush diet, which was nutritionally poor and tended to induce infant diarrhea, leading to dehydration. Few people lived beyond the age of fifty, with the average adult life span being near forty years.

Forms of tuberculosis, blastomycosis, and similar diseases were also apparently more common than earlier. The spread of these diseases may have been due in part to the release of soilborne organisms stirred up by the intensive digging for agricultural fields and mound construction, but the greater concentration of populations living in close proximity to each other played a part as well.

How Cahokians handled human waste disposal is unknown. We do know that individual households had many refuse pits around them, and some of these may have been used for that purpose; or, it is possible that community latrines were used, but nothing we can clearly identify as such has been found in the excavations at Cahokia or other sites. Human waste could well be a source for many pathogens if not properly disposed of. Other types of waste, food refuse, and other debris were often dumped into old house basins, abandoned storage pits, pits dug specifically for refuse disposal, or the borrow pits where dirt had been extracted for mound construction, not unlike a "city dump." In most cases this debris was capped with more soil and occasionally burned, probably to reduce odor and insect problems.

There may even have been "smog," created by the numerous cooking and heating fires that burned daily, producing a smoky haze at Cahokia and throughout much of the American Bottom. One could probably smell Cahokia before seeing it, with all the smoke and trash (this phenomena was even noted by Lewis and Clark when approaching large Indian settlements up the Missouri River in the early 1800s).

It was probably a combination of some or all of the above, coupled with economic and political degradation, that sealed Cahokia's fate. It could never be what it once was. Ultimately Cahokia may have collapsed under its own weight. Recent research indicates that the decline may have begun as early as A.D. 1150, almost a century earlier than once thought, and change was obvious after A.D. 1200. Some researchers see one factor of the decline as a period of political unrest as elites vied for control, with the losing factions becoming "refugees," resulting in the Mississippian expansion to the north.[62] There is no direct evidence of any disaster or traumatic event; it was a gradual process that accelerated during the thirteenth century and by A.D. 1400 or shortly thereafter Cahokia was essentially abandoned. The population gradually dispersed in small groups, probably into the local area at first, especially the uplands, then gradually outward. They may have established new cultural identities or been assimilated into existing groups, perhaps where they had kin ties.

We have seen how Cahokia grew from modest beginnings to become America's largest prehistoric community, how political and economic changes evolved, and how the environment was altered by and affected Cahokia. We often have a romantic image of the Indian living in harmony with the environment, and in most cases this was true, but Cahokia had moved beyond that balance, even though Cahokians were more attuned to their environment than we are today. Cahokia was unique due to its large population and complex settlement system which concentrated large numbers of people; it became a city with city problems. While it could handle these problems for a time, eventually the system began to erode, creating instability. Political, social, and economic controls weakened for reasons we are just beginning to understand.

We are fortunate that Cahokia was located in a primarily rural area, so that much of it survives today, although greatly altered by the plow and the bulldozer; most of the site was once farmed and subdivisions, discount stores, highways, and other construction projects have changed the face of this once great community. The State of Illinois now protects 2,200 acres of it as Cahokia Mounds State Historic Site, but at least one-third of the mounds have been destroyed and the rest of the mounds and the surrounding habitation and ceremonial areas have been heavily altered by modern man. Its sister centers in St. Louis, where twenty-six mounds once stood (thus the nickname "Mound City"), and East St. Louis, where possibly forty-five mounds were located, were destroyed in the 1800s, and many of the outlying communities have also been lost to expanding urbanism, roadways, and farming activities.

Still, much remains. It is estimated that less than 1 percent of the Cahokia site has been excavated, so future researchers have much to examine. Perhaps then we can answer more of the many questions and solve some of the intriguing mysteries of Cahokia.

# Contested Terrain
## Environmental Agendas and Settlement Choices
## in Colonial St. Louis

~

## *Patricia Cleary*

Within months of its founding in 1764, St. Louis witnessed a conflict between French colonists and Missouri Indians over who would occupy the site. While both groups sought to plant a village at the same location on the basis of its perceived advantages, their perspectives on the physical world and the standards they employed in evaluating it differed dramatically. In their confrontation over St. Louis lies the basis for an examination of views toward nature that helped to shape the growth of the eighteenth-century town. Indeed, appreciating how Europeans and Native Americans understood the environment, their place in it, and their relationship to nonhuman nature is crucial to reconstructing settlement choices, race relations, economic developments, and the manipulation of environmental change in the colonial period.

Chance and circumstance dictated the 1764 arrival of French colonists at St. Louis. The previous fall, Pierre Laclede Ligueste had explored the western bank of the Mississippi south of the Missouri River's mouth and had determined the spot to be ideal for a trading post. In selecting the site, Laclede acted according to a set of closely-linked environmental and economic criteria. His decisions, like scores of others by both colonists and Native Americans, provide a prism that illuminates the early history of St. Louis and its environs. By examining how explorers characterized their surroundings and where and when different groups established towns, the centrality of the environment becomes clear. What emerges is a sense of the perceived environmental advantages St. Louis possessed, both intrinsically and in comparison to other nearby settlements.

An exploration of the colonial environment raises a number of historical questions related to the intersecting spheres and influences of the different actors who inhabited the region. How, for example, did people from various cultural backgrounds understand nature and their relationship with it? What were their perceptions of people and place, the role of climate, agriculture, and animals? What did they want from their environment—for example, farmland or access to game—and why? How did they attempt to manipulate the environment to achieve their aims? The presence of game, for instance, was equally desired by those whose diets depended upon hunting and by those who sought gain through the fur trade. How did their wants, related to economic production and subsistence, dictate the contours of their interactions with each other and with the physical landscape as they jockeyed for position and access to resources? Mapping the differing views of Native Americans and Europeans and how their attitudes changed over time offers insight into these questions. Establishing their vision and experience restores both their lifestyle and their influences upon each other and the world around them; taking this approach adds an essential dimension to the history of St. Louis and its earliest inhabitants, grounding it in the evolving context of the physical world.

Although the sources for studying the environment in this period present the typical bias in favor of literate European visitors and colonial settlers, such as that offered by Auguste Chouteau in his narrative of St. Louis's founding,[1] glimpses of the Native American perspective can be gleaned, albeit from more difficult sources: French missionary records and colonial representations—both of which offer a filtered and secondhand view—and archaeological remains. The geographical range of sources for this study is broader than St. Louis itself. Although nineteenth-century St. Louisans confined themselves physically and psychologically to a city of limited size by separating permanently from surrounding St. Louis County, St. Louis in the colonial period must be considered as a city without borders within the context of the territory that it embraced as a center of fur trading. Its inhabitants resided in Upper Louisiana, upon the banks of the mighty Mississippi, in a town populated by different races and nationalities, situated at the shifting crossroads of empire.

When Laclede left New Orleans in the fall of 1763 to search for a good location for a trading post, he did so with particular goals and restrictions in mind. A partner in a firm that had just received a monopoly from French authorities in the Louisiana territory over trade with tribes west of the Mississippi, Laclede wanted a site that would guarantee him maximum access to the greatest number of potential consumers willing to exchange furs for his imported manufactured goods. Thus, he sought proximity to the Missouri River and the nations that lived in its basin. The west bank of the Mississippi was not a matter of choice; with the end of the French and Indian War, territory east of the river became Great Britain's. (Although the western bank was legally the possession of Spain after a secret 1762 treaty and remained so for decades, French settlers preferred it.[2] Some who came to St. Louis did not know initially of the transfer to Spain; others, due to anti-English sentiment, simply wanted to leave Illinois.) After arriving in Ste. Genevieve, the only town on the

Mississippi's western side, Laclede found it unacceptable for his purposes. Finding no building there large enough to contain his goods, Laclede moved on, storing his wares temporarily at Fort de Chartres, in Illinois, while looking for a Missouri site. More importantly, according to Chouteau's narrative, Laclede did not seriously consider settling in Ste. Genevieve "because of its distance from the Missouri, and its insalubrious situation. These reasons decided him to seek a more advantageous site."[3]

Given his trading ambitions, Laclede was willing to move his business and family to an uninhabited spot that met his requirements. He wanted to form "an establishment suitable for his commerce." In other words, location mattered more than the comforts and cultural supports available in a place like New Orleans. Consequently, he promptly began to examine "all the ground from the Fort de Chartres to the Missouri." In Chouteau's version of this journey, Laclede "was delighted to see the situation" where St. Louis now stands, ten miles south of the confluence of the Missouri and Mississippi Rivers, and "did not hesitate a moment" in proposing to build there, persuaded both by "the beauty of the site" and "all the advantages" conducive to settlement that it possessed.[4]

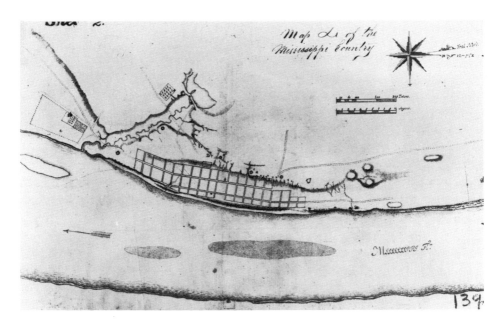

*Map of the Mississippi Country, 1767. St. Louis was established as a trading post, and it lured inhabitants with the notion of riches rather than settlement. This map reveals the concentration of inhabitants, mainly traders, in the village rather than in the surrounding fertile farmlands. The small sectioned-off plots to the south and west of the town mark cultivated fields. Photograph of map by Guy Dupassat.*

From the European perspective, the "advantages" were numerous. Located well above the river's flow, St. Louis, according to one visitor, occupied one of the most beautiful and healthy positions along the banks of the Mississippi.[5] As one early St. Louis historian glowingly noted, the site coupled the advantages of elevation and a limestone shore. "Such situations are very rare," wrote John Paxton, "as the Mississippi is almost universally bounded either by high perpendicular rocks or loose alluvial soil, the later of which is in continual danger of being washed away by the annual floods."[6] As the flood of 1785 demonstrated, Laclede's choice was fortuitous. The flood of that year wreaked havoc throughout the fertile lands along the Mississippi's shifting banks, destroying property and livestock and possibly laying the base for an outbreak of infectious disease. Low upon the river's banks, Ste. Genevieve was devastated, as were numerous other towns.[7] In contrast, St. Louis's site spared it the worst depredations of the flood.

In the eyes of many European visitors, the most notable features of the Mississippi Valley environment were the fertility of the land, its mineral deposits, and the abundance of game, all of which promised wealth to those colonists who would work to secure it. For Europeans, nature was understood, in part, as a source of commodities that could be produced or extracted. Contemplating a settlement on the Meramec River, south of St. Louis, a French promoter argued that the "river where riches abound would offer an infinity of resources and innumerable provisions." Some in the "lands of an ever-renewing fertility" would grow wealthy through farming, "while others with their sharp pickaxes would tear without expense from the entrails of the earth the vast lead mines that it encloses."[8]

For colonists, human domination of the physical world translated into an ordered, enriching landscape. Employing these criteria, British Captain Philip Pittman offered an especially laudatory assessment of the Illinois territory (which included much of contemporary Illinois). Visiting the region in the 1760s, Pittman described the area as possessing pure air and a host of other attributes rendering it desirable for habitation and cultivation. "The soil of this country in general is very rich and luxuriant," noted Pittman; "it produces all sorts of European grains, hops, hemp, flax, cotton, and tobacco, and European fruits come to great perfection." In addition, the land yielded wild foodstuffs: a "very inebriating" wine made from wild grapes, "plenty of fish," and a profusion of other animals, including "buffalo, deer, and wild-fowl."[9] In 1772, an inhabitant of Kaskaskia published an account of the landscape and environment designed to induce settlement in the region. The anonymous author asserted that there was no bad land on either side of the Mississippi, and that the cultivable lands were of such good quality and so extensive that the area could soon boast the most flourishing colony in the world. Interestingly, he noted that tobacco would prove an especially marketable commodity, because the soil of Virginia was nearly exhausted.[10]

St. Louis received similar accolades for its fertile environs. François Marie Perrin du Lac, who visited at the end of the colonial period, averred that the immense prairies surrounding the town naturally produced a wide variety of the grains that Europeans managed to cultivate only with care.[11] In his view, St. Charles possessed meadows "superior to those of St. Louis" with lands that were "better cultivated," and produced "corn, barley, maize, potatoes, in a word, every necessary for man and beast."[12] Perhaps part of his comparison stemmed from the bad reputation of St. Louis's farmers; Perrin du Lac declared that the natural advantages of its fertile lands could have transformed it into the granary of Lower Louisiana if not for the lack of application on the part of colonists who hardly produced grain enough for their own consumption.[13] Indeed, during the colonial period, St. Louis was known as "Pain-court," for its perennial bread shortages.

A map from the late 1760s, which shows the town bearing that designation, underscores colonists' financial perspective toward the environment.[14] The area surrounding St. Louis is described as an "immense prairie where one will locate (or settle) a multitude of inhabitants."[15] Yet the initial St. Louisans failed to farm. St. Louis's profit-oriented first residents had much in common with those of Jamestown, Virginia, the earliest permanent British settlement in North America. There, colonists who preferred to search for gold and other precious metals neglected to plant crops sufficient to feed themselves and suffered through what was known as the "Starving Time" in 1609-1610.[16] Similarly, in "Pain-court," too many of the town's inhabitants engaged in commerce rather than cultivation, leaving the settlers dependent on grain imports from nearby Ste. Genevieve.[17]

Long before Perrin du Lac lamented the lack of agricultural endeavor on the part of St. Louisans, Laclede and his men had undertaken the first step in preparing the area for settlement and cultivation: clearing the land. That was the initial order of business when the trading village was founded in February 1764. Laclede placed Chouteau in charge of overseeing the work of his men, who also constructed cabins and a large structure that would serve as Laclede's house and store. They were soon joined by colonists from Illinois. Apparently pleased with his selection of the location and confident of his fifteen-year-old stepson's supervisory abilities, Laclede returned to Illinois to recover the goods he had stored at Fort de Chartres.

In his absence, the infant settlement of St. Louis witnessed a conflict over the desirability of its site that nearly derailed the town's progress from Laclede's plan. As Chouteau recalled, "[T]here arrived among us. . . all the tribe of the Missouris—men, women and children."[18] At least 150 warriors moved into the village, accompanied by a large number of their families. Imagine the scene from the European perspective: fewer than three dozen men under Chouteau's command and a small number of colonists found themselves tremendously outnumbered by a people of another race, wearing very different apparel and speaking an incomprehensible tongue, who declared their intention to settle permanently on the site. The colonizers found themselves colonized. The immediate result of the Missouris' arrival was the prompt departure of the Illinois colonists. Those who had moved into Missouri to join the new settlement had done so because they preferred not to live under British rule; however, they wished even less to live outnumbered by Indians. They quickly decamped, recrossing the Mississippi to return to their former residences. Faced with the desertion of nearly all of the village's French inhabitants and an unmanageable situation, Chouteau sent for Laclede.

Meeting with the Missouri chief upon his return, Laclede discovered that the tribe wished to settle permanently at his new village; apparently, they found

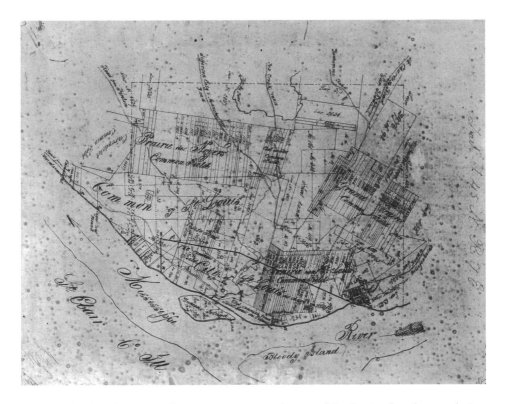

*Fractional Township 45 N, Range 7E, 1847-48. A map of St. Louis after the population expanded west. The land is sectioned in order to display separate land ownership and cultivation. Ink on paper by Julius Hutawa.*

the site as appealing as he had. The Missouris, as Chouteau remembered the scene, described themselves as "like the ducks and the geese, who traveled until they found a fine country, where there was beautiful, open water, that they might rest there, and obtain an easy living."[19] In repeating this characterization, Laclede stated that the Missouris declared themselves "worthy of pity" and similar to these animals in that they "traveled like them to find a place to settle." After such wanderings, the Missouris chose their new home: St. Louis. Laclede paraphrased their decisions regarding the locale thusly: "[Y]ou did not find any one more suitable than that where you are at present; that you wished to form a village around my house." There, the Indians declared, the two races would "live together in the greatest friendship."[20]

The differences between the aspirations of Laclede and the Missouris, their reasons for selecting the same site, and their use of language are all striking. Where Laclede chose the location primarily for its access to trading partners, as well as its apparently healthy situation in contrast to that of Ste. Genevieve, the Missouris, as reported by Chouteau, articulated contrasting goals in a distinctive manner. The Missouris' explanation highlights a world view firmly grounded in the natural order and in the connections between human beings and other living creatures. As Carolyn Merchant asserts for New England's indigenous inhabitants, nature and culture were not separated; human beings and their animal neighbors were closely linked equals participating symbiotically in life's many processes.[21] In similar fashion, employing analogy and metaphor, the Missouri Indians likened themselves to other semisedentary denizens of the river valley, the water fowl, who returned to nesting grounds and moved their homes as resources dictated.

Relying upon the abundant game to supplement their diets, the Indian inhabitants of the area around St. Louis had long incorporated mobility into their lifestyle. They practiced a mixed strategy in securing a food supply, alternating seasons of hunting with planting. Pittman noted that several Illinois tribes—"Cascasquias, Kaoquias, Mitchigamias, and Peoryas"—followed this precise plan. "Except in the hunting seasons," he observed, "they reside near the English settlements in this country, where they have built their huts."[22] In Missouri, the Missouri and Osage Indians followed a similar pattern, spending part of the year in their villages and the winter in hunting buffalo.[23]

A century later, Auguste Chouteau generalized about this practice, averring that the Indians of North America had "always lived in a state of nature deriving their subsistence from the wild animals of the forest."[24] His Eurocentric portrayal smacks of the condescension colonists typically applied to those whom they perceived as living close to nature, and therefore, as "uncivilized."[25] While Chouteau characterized most groups as somewhat settled, he described "the most numerous & powerful" nation on the upper

Mississippi and Missouri Rivers, the Sioux, as leading "a wandering life."[26] They had, he said, "no fixed villages," traveling often, "changing their position with the different Seasons of the year, and as either their wants, or inclination induce them to persue the different Kinds of game with which their Country abounds."[27]

Chouteau's nineteenth-century remarks about Native Americans' aspirations and relationships with nature and wildlife echo the sentiments expressed in his founding narrative. Then, the goal of the Missouris, as reported by Chouteau, was ease of living upon nature's bounty, not the accumulation of wealth. It is not possible to determine, in this case, if the Missouris thought that goal could be more easily accomplished alongside fur traders; during this period, many tribes were becoming increasingly involved in and dependent upon the exchange of furs for consumer goods. In the following decade, when the Missouris engaged in a profitable trade with St. Louis fur merchants, they sowed corn, but apparently not a sufficient quantity to sustain themselves.[28] It is also plausible that for the Missouri Indians, as for those whom Merchant studied, participation in the fur trade led to dramatic changes in indigenous environmental attitudes and practices, transforming beaver, deer, and buffalo from formerly equal beings worthy of respect into resources to be hunted and exchanged for other commodities.[29]

Early descriptions of St. Louis suggest that the region's indigenous population had used burning techniques to manipulate the environment in ways that might have contributed to the proliferation of large animals and the ease of their hunting. Evidence of the extent to which the landscape had been manipulated by human intervention before European settlement is difficult to pinpoint in St. Louis; the impact of agriculture and population growth is clearer in more densely settled pre-contact sites, such as Cahokia.[30] Writing an early history of the city, Joseph Nicollet characterized the site at the time of founding as a plateau that "presented the aspect of a beautiful prairie, but already giving the promise of a renewed luxuriant vegetation, in consequence of the dispersion of the larger animals of chase, and the annual fires being kept out of the country, since the arrival of the whites on the Illinois side."[31] In other words, before the settlement of Europeans, Native Americans used burning techniques, possibly similar to those described by William Cronon in New England, to create a landscape conducive to the flourishing of particular plant and animal species that rendered the setting park-like and full of the game the tribes relied upon for sustenance.[32] Nicollet's more precise description lends support to this comparison: the land "was covered by a growth of heavy timber ... free from undergrowth."[33] In short, the European presence led to the elimination of an environmental practice designed to sustain the local human population. How directly the French influenced the change in policy is impossible to ascertain. When Nicollet wrote his account in the 1840s, he noted that although the "new growth [was] again doomed to destruction," the process was being "carried on with more discernment, and for a more praiseworthy object; it is for the extension of the city, for the erection of manufactories; for clearing arable lands—in short, for all the purposes of a progressive state of civilization."[34]

Burning practices and mobility patterns suggest that the influence of one group upon the other was certainly not unilateral. Whether by constraint or choice, Europeans occasionally followed the example of indigenous mobility, which they characterized as less civilized. Early missionaries followed the semisedentary living arrangements of local tribes in order to proselytize. Gabriel Marest characterized his time in a mission village as spent in constant religious instruction, a flurry of activity in one spot that was followed by dispersal of the inhabitants. "During the winter," he reported, "we separate, going to various places where the savages pass that season."[35] In other words, the missionaries chose to adapt their plans to the native ways.

Later colonists adapted differently upon occasion, rejecting European culture, work patterns, and clothing in favor of Native American folkways and relationships with the natural world. When this happened, European observers remarked upon the phenomenon with interest, criticism, and occasionally disgust. In Cahokia, just across the river from St. Louis, Pittman observed that the inhabitants, many of them French Canadians by birth, "some of whom married women of the Kaoquias nation," did not practice much agriculture, scarcely raising "corn enough for their own consumption." Instead, they depended "more on hunting, and their Indian trade."[36] Of Ste. Genevieve, where the residents did produce enough foodstuffs, the ever critical Perrin du Lac declared that "the children [were] brought up among the savages, contract[ed] their manners, and especially their indolence."[37] Exposure to native lifestyles could have dramatic and highly visible results. At the end of the eighteenth century, Kaskaskia's French inhabitants were described as "accustomed to the Fur trade with the savages"; as a result of their interactions with Indians, the French lived "and the majority of them are clothed in the manner of the Savages. They wear no breeches but pass between their thighs a piece of cloth. . . ."[38] Perhaps the possibility of such a blended culture contributed to Laclede's unwillingness to welcome the Missouris.

When Laclede finally responded to the environmental perspective and agenda presented by the Missouris' declaration and request, he offered a telling statement which demonstrated both his grasp of indigenous politics and imagery and his sense of the deadly competition and conflict taking place upon the frontier of European–Native American contact. His reply began with a succinct summing up: "[I]f you followed the examples of the ducks and the geese in settling yourselves, you followed bad guides." Clearly, Laclede did not want the Missouris to people his infant settlement. Outnumbering the colonists, they would have played a much larger role in determining the shape and course of the settlement's development, possibly precluding the tidy gridwork of streets that Laclede envisioned or changing the function of the fenced common fields that villagers quickly constructed. Until the colonists established control over the contours of St. Louis, they were unwilling to countenance large numbers of indigenous neighbors.

Laclede accused the Missouris of having no foresight, arguing that careful ducks "would not put themselves into open water, so that the eagles and birds of prey could discover them easily." Such an outcome would not befall those who hid themselves in the woods. However, the Missouris would be devoured if they remained in St. Louis. As Laclede exhorted them, "'You Missouris, you will not be eaten by eagles . . . but if [your enemies] learn you are here, beyond the least doubt, they will come to destroy you.'"[39] In other words, a warring tribe, the Osage, with six to seven hundred warriors then at Fort de Chartres, would descend upon the Missouris and slaughter them if they stayed put. Laclede's grisly prediction was designed to undermine the confidence and will of the Missouris and to persuade them to vacate his trading post: "Behold what will happen to you, for wishing to follow, as you say, the course of the ducks and geese, rather than the advice of men of experience."[40]

Whether compelled by Laclede's advice "as a man of experience" or by his warning of a potential attack coupled with no promises of protection or assistance, the Missouris decided to follow his suggestions and leave St. Louis. The same year, the Missouris sought the aid of the French commandant of Fort de Chartres, before the fort was taken over by its new English inhabitants. Louis St. Ange de Bellerive recorded the Missouri tribe's visit to the Illinois post in July 1764, "with their wives, children, arms, and baggage." According to his report, "their fear of the Great Osage . . . caused them to decide to take refuge" at his fort and to urge his intercession in obtaining peace with their enemies. Their wishes did not find a receptive audience. Instead of aiding them, St. Ange, after they had been at Fort de Chartres a month, "persuaded them to return to their villages in order to avoid a greater expense and to give peace to [the] inhabitants."[41] Clearly, the French did not want Indian neighbors.

While the reactions of Laclede and Bellerive to prospective coresidence would suggest otherwise, Missouri Indians had lived in harmony in the vicinity of another French settlement earlier.[42] In the 1720s, the French had constructed a fort close to the Missouri village near the confluence of the Grand and Missouri Rivers in northwestern Missouri. Charged by his superiors in Paris to select an appropriate spot for an outpost that would help the French compete with the Spanish for the Indian trade, Etienne de Bourgmont, commander on the Missouri, traveled up the river. His orders specified that he choose a site very carefully, for its location would determine the success of the venture.[43] Perhaps the memory of their peaceful, albeit brief, proximity to French neighbors contributed to the Missouris' interest in settling in St. Louis.

When the tribe finally prepared to leave St. Louis after encountering a welcome distinctly lacking in hospitality, Laclede attempted to ease their departure. He acceded to the Missouris' petitions to "give them provisions, and a little powder and some balls for the men, that they might hunt while going up the Missouri, and defend themselves, if they were attacked."[44] With "a large quantity" of corn, powder, balls, knives, and cloth, they left after fifteen days in the nascent community. In the end, Chouteau recalled, "all the Missouris went away, to go up the Missouri and return to their ancient village."[45]

This successful conclusion to the conflict over settlement soon worked its magic from the founders' perspective. Within a short time, "those persons who had fled to Caos [Cahokia] on the coming of the savages, returned as soon as they knew that they had gone away, and commenced building."[46] In doing so, they followed Laclede's vision. A network of carefully laid out streets soon emerged, only three blocks deep, parallel to the river, and stretching nearly two miles along its banks. According to Charles Peterson's exhaustively researched history of colonial St. Louis, Laclede's plan "continued the land use traditions" of French villages "and introduced the logic and regularity" of Spanish policies: fields, assigned to particular individuals, were outside of the central residential area, which was organized on a grid that included a public plaza.[47]

The repopulating of the village with French inhabitants signaled that St. Louis would survive not as an Indian settlement built up around a lone trading post but as a town designed to serve European and colonial economic aspirations, cultural designs, and urban plans. Collective needs and financial concerns met in the rapid construction in 1764 of a fence around the common, where the new residents cut wood and pastured cattle.[48] As Chouteau put it, the return of these settlers, along with the arrival of other French colonists from Fort de Chartres, "commenced to give some permanence to St. Louis."[49] Soon thereafter, one missionary described the new village of St. Louis as "formed out of the ruins of St. Philippe and Fort de Chartres."[50]

Given the turmoil that had erupted when the Missouri tribe attempted to join Laclede's nascent settlement, it seems somewhat ironic that a clearly tri-racial society, with distinctive and for the most part welcome contingents of Native Americans, emerged within the first few decades of St. Louis's development. By 1766, a substantial settlement of Peoria Indians appeared at St. Louis's southern borders. According to a British officer, Captain H. Gordon, who reported on the condition of Cahokia in that year, there were "20 Cabbins of Peioria Indians left. . . . The Rest and best Part are moved to the French Side 2

Miles" below St. Louis.[51] Chouteau described the settlement with a slightly different chronology. A few years after a 1766 distribution of land in a common field just to the south of St. Louis, a group of Peoria Indians relocated to the site. The band "obtained Permission to build a village, and they did build one immediately . . . and in after times, this Prairia or Common field was called Prairia du Village Sauvage."[52] Fleeing their enemies in Illinois, the Peoria had sought refuge first at Kaskaskia, and then on the western side of the Mississippi River.[53] Although the village, located according to Nicollet, at the site of the arsenal, did not survive (by 1825, a judge's house stood in its place), its early date of settlement suggests that the initial hostility of Chouteau and Laclede toward Indian cohabitation was a matter of expediency.

Gordon's journal supports this interpretation of the founders' relationships with Native Americans. In characterizing Laclede as "the principal Indian Trader" in St. Louis, Gordon concluded "that the whole Trade of the Missouri, That of the Mississipi Northwards . . . is entirely brought to Him. He appears to be sensible, clever, & has been very well educated; is very active, and will give us some Trouble before we get the Parts of this Trade that belong to us out of His Hands." Given Laclede's control over commercial exchange and contacts with indigenous peoples, Gordon did not anticipate any immediate rewards from journeying upriver. Laclede, he declared, "is readily served by the Indians he has planted within 2 Miles of Him."[54] The French, and Laclede in particular, dominated the trade. As Gordon admitted, "Even the small Quantity of Skins or Furs that the Kaskaskias and Peiorias (who are on our side) get by hunting is carried under our Nose to Misère [Ste Genevieve] and Pain Court."[55]

Indeed, the centrality of the fur trade to the early development of the city required the regular presence of Native Americans. In the late 1770s, the Missouris engaged regularly in the exchange of pelts with St. Louis agents, producing eighty to ninety packets a year.[56] In conjunction with these ventures, the Missouris spent summers living near their trading partners. According to Nicollet's history of the colonial city, the Missouri came downriver in their canoes, carrying with them their wigwams, "and located themselves near St. Louis; their women aiding the colonists in their rural occupations, and in building their houses."[57] Clearly, they were not alone in participating in this business. Among the regular visitors to St. Louis, Nicollet also counted Indians of the Osage and Fox nations.

The numbers of Indians in St. Louis could present challenges for the city's colonial inhabitants. In planning the Revolutionary War attack upon the town, a British military commander argued that it would be relatively easy to take St. Louis "by surprise, from the Easy admission of Indians at that place, and by Assault from those without."[58] Writing in the 1780s, the Spanish lieutenant governor of Upper Louisiana, Manuel Perez, reported an increasing number of

Indian parties coming to St. Louis. Their presence posed problems in maintaining peaceful relations; various groups expected to receive the presents to which they had become accustomed, but authorities lacked even "the wherewithal to make them small presents."[59] By the end of the 1760s, over two dozen tribes were coming to "San Luis" for presents.[60] In 1794, Zenon Trudeau reported that the Loups and the Shawnees had abandoned Cape Girardeau "in order to come to the environs of St. Louis . . . they [had] been won over by the traders or by other counsel."[61] Their presence was invited, perhaps orchestrated, by European traders now confidently in control of the fur economy. The scale of the trade is staggering. A single account of Auguste Chouteau's from 1793 includes in the list of furs 843 bear skins, 38 bear cubs, 98 deer skins, 1,827 shaved deer skins, 25 wolves, 26 cats, 847 raccoons, 201 grey foxes, 2,130 beavers, and 448 buffalo robes.[62] Even at this time, when the fur trade's profits were declining, Chouteau enjoyed a healthy income. His continued riches offer eloquent testimony to the auspicious choice that Laclede made decades before in determining upon the settlement site of St. Louis.

While by the 1790s, who controlled the town, its populace, culture, and economy seemed relatively clear, such matters had been patently uncertain in 1764. Considering Laclede's efforts that year—dissuading the Missouris from remaining in the village and encouraging the permanent residence of French colonists—brings us full circle, redirecting our attention to the consequences of his choices and actions and to the meaning of differing environmental agendas for the people who inhabited the area. European colonists like Laclede had an environmental goal, a vision of a productive natural world subdued by human manipulation. Accordingly, they had a plan for the operation of the human elements within this order as well, with Native Americans cast as subordinate partners producing pelts for exchange, and European colonists dominating the fur trade and agriculture, as well as other enterprises. To control this extractive economic landscape, colonists had to control social interaction, especially because their environmental attitudes were so different from those of Native Americans. Thus, the impact of these two groups upon each other can be understood as resulting from their distinctive understandings of the natural world and from the power dynamics of their interactions.

The repercussions of environmental agendas and community decisions suggest a number of insights about contact experiences and cultural competition. We can begin to survey these by asking how successfully Indians and Europeans chose settlement sites according to various environmental criteria. Colonial developments in St. Louis and other settlements enable us to evaluate how the Mound City's inhabitants fared, in terms of both how they experienced the environment and how they attempted to improve upon and profit from its physical characteristics.

The history of the earliest joint European-Indian settlement in the vicinity of St. Louis, a Jesuit mission village, suggests that the unhealthiness of a site tempered Native American and European enthusiasm for its settlement. Between 1700 and 1703, Father Garbriel Marest headed a mission at the mouth of the River Des Peres.[63] This short-lived settlement, occupied primarily by Kaskaskia Indians, French Jesuits, and some French colonists, may have been abandoned for environmental reasons. The inhabitants, according to one account, found the site unhealthy and removed back to Illinois.[64] Low-lying, swampy lands, such as those at the conjunction of rivers, which tended to flood more often and retain stagnant, standing water, posed the risks of malaria-carrying mosquitoes and higher chances for fecal contamination of the water supply, resulting in what contemporaries called the "bloody flux," most likely amoebic dysentary. The new site of the Kaskaskia back in Illinois did not, in the long run, provide an environment of superior salubrity. Decades later, in the 1760s, traveler George Morgan described the town as unhealthy, with the "Ague & Fever" and a host of other disorders afflicting nearly everyone and leading to high mortality rates.[65] According to a report from the 1780s, the Kaskaskia village, although "handsome," sat on a spot that was "low and unhealthy, and subject to inundation."[66] An unhealthy setting colored the European view of the landscape as commodity; health was a component of their settlement equation.

For Native Americans, sickness in the eighteenth century was more notable as a direct consequence of their interaction with European colonists, who introduced new diseases, than as a result of inhabiting unhealthy sites.[67] Throughout the Mississippi River valley and the Americas, infectious diseases were preeminent in wreaking havoc upon peoples and cultures, devastating entire populations;[68] contemporary Europeans and colonists, however, attributed the destruction of the indigenous population primarily to alcohol abuse and warfare. [69] Perrin du Lac described a group of Peoria Indians in Ste. Genevieve as "the remains of a numerous race, almost extinct by war, small-pox, and especially by the use of spirits."[70] After residing along the Missouri River for nearly a century, the Missouri tribe was destroyed, "conquered and dispersed by the Saukees and Outagamies (Foxes) and other tribes."[71]

In stark contrast to the decimation of Native Americans by disease, clearly the most important factor despite European assertions about alcohol, European colonists thrived in their new setting. St. Louis's environment and situation received numerous commendations in comparison to other colonial settlements. Contrasting the town's characteristics with those of New Orleans and its environs, one late eighteenth-century traveler observed that "those great vast plains and those low swampy lands, such as are seen at New Orleans, are not there, but instead magnificent hills and pleasant valleys," full of trees and grape vines. He further described the healthy environment as the fortuitous result of behavior, city maintenance, and natural attributes. The air, the writer noted, was "very good and healthy. [The people] are sober and not subject to those diseases of contact so afflicting to the human species." Given that the writer was comparing St. Louis to New Orleans, which he described as a city of "debauchery," he most likely alluded to a comparative absence of venereal diseases. "Never," according to the glowing report, "does an epidemic visit them; and those fine people live without pain or torment in their old age and enjoy perfect health."[72] Moreover, he noted, the residents enjoyed streets free of standing water. In 1778, St. Louisans had gathered at the government house one day after mass to effect an agreement "to set the inhabitants to work to drain the streets of stagnant waters."[73] The town retained its healthy reputation for decades.[74]

In conclusion, it is clear that the city's site possessed clear advantages over several others located nearby. Access to trade, indicators of healthiness, safety from a torrential river of known destructiveness, and proximity to possible protectors were just a few of the factors that provided the impetus for the settlement of French colonists and Native Americans in St. Louis's environs. The site appealed to European settlers with an economic understanding of the natural world. For Indians, once some of these groups began to adopt coresidence with European-Americans and to integrate their folkways into the fur market economy, their visits and permanent movement to St. Louis became a matter of course. Yet they lived as temporary inhabitants of a village that would flourish under environmental and urban terms set by newcomers preoccupied with commerce. By the end of the colonial period, St. Louisans of European descent had firmly established a town with recognizable French and Spanish forms and a still perceptible gridwork of streets oriented to and stretched along the river that beckoned them.

# Where Did the Villages Go?

## Steamboats, Deforestation, and Archaeological Loss in the Mississippi Valley

~

## F. Terry Norris

The arrival of the first steam-driven rivercraft, the *Zebulon Pike*, at the village of St. Louis in 1817 heralded an era of unprecedented growth and prosperity throughout the surrounding central Mississippi River valley. The steamboat represented the principle conveyor of Euro-American immigrants into the valley prior to the Civil War.[1] During the first decades of the nineteenth century the port of St. Louis rapidly became the primary point of embarkation to the frontier.[2] Steamboat landings at western ports from Pittsburgh to St. Louis increased exponentially between 1826 and 1847.[3] While such growth was the harbinger of economic prosperity for many, the successful application of steamboat technology in the Mississippi River valley also inadvertently resulted in significant losses for the physical and cultural environments of the region. While the steamboat's role in disseminating Anglo-American cultural traditions throughout the Mississippi and Missouri River valleys has been well documented,[4] analysis of the effects of steamboat technology on the physical and cultural environments of the nation's river valleys has received only limited attention.[5] This essay examines the effect that the application of steamboat technology had upon the ability of modern scholars to comprehend the lifeways of the pre-steamboat era residents of the central Mississippi River valley.

The steamboat industry, and ancillary economic enterprises such as "wooding" (the gathering of massive quantities of combustible fuel to sate the appetites of steamboat boilers), had a profound effect upon both natural landforms and French colonial settlements situated on the floodplain adjacent to the Mississippi. Throughout the early and mid-nineteenth century, the increasing demand for steamboat fuel resulted in widespread deforestation of river banks within the central Mississippi River valley. Deforestation, in turn, caused the banklines of the Mississippi River to become unstable, resulting in significant lateral channel movement. That movement, and associated loss of portions of the floodplain, resulted in the destruction and/or significant damage to all but one of the colonial settlements within the central Mississippi River valley established prior to 1763. During the first half of the nineteenth century, the Mississippi River channel and floodplain situated above the confluence of the Mississippi and Ohio Rivers was the area most affected by the introduction of this technology. The environmental and cultural impact of river transportation in the central Mississippi River valley is the subject of this essay.

## Native American River Travel within the Central Mississippi Valley

Native Americans used the Mississippi River and its tributaries as transportation corridors for millennia prior to the arrival of Europeans. The discovery of prehistoric rivercraft such as the Ringler dugout, a wooden canoe recovered from a prehistoric archaeological context in northern Ohio in 1976, are evidence that Native Americans used the river systems as highways of transportation and trade at least three thousand years prior to the arrival of Europeans in North America.[6]

Figure 1. "Evening Bivouac on the Missouri," *Karl Bodmer, Joslyn Art Museum, Omaha, Nebraska; gift of Enron Art Foundation.*

Analysis of the Ringler dugout revealed that it had been fashioned from a single log of white oak. The presence of several charred areas on the vessel's interior suggest that the passenger cavity had been shaped by repeated episodes of burning and scraping.[7] Other ethnographic and archaeological evidence revealed that such canoe styles remained basically unchanged over several millennia.[8] Comparison of the Native American construction techniques to seventeenth-century accounts in Virginia reveal remarkable similarities.

> The manner of makinge their boates in Virginia is verye wonderfull . . . they raise it [log] uppon po[s]tes laid over cross wise uppon forked posts . . . on the underside they make a fyre accordinge to the lengthe of the bodye of the tree, saving at both endes . . . That which they thinke is sufficientlye burned they quenche and scrape away with shells . . . until the boate have sufficient bothowmes. . . . [9]

In 1989, an extremely well-made Native American dugout canoe, preserved in near perfect condition, was recovered from a side channel of the Mississippi River near Hollandale, Mississippi, during a wildlife habitat improvement project.[10] Dendrochronology dating of that vessel indicates that it was in use at approximately the same time that the above sixteenth-century Virginia journal entry was recorded.[11]

A preponderance of ethnographic and archaeological data suggest that the wooden dugout was the craft of choice for river travel among Native American groups on major river systems within the interior of North America below the Great Lakes. The operation and maintenance of such craft on these river systems would have had little effect on the physical integrity of the river valleys in which they were used.

## The Highway of Empires—Exploration and Settlement of the Central Mississippi River Valley During the Colonial Period

When Europeans entered the Mississippi River valley during the sixteenth and seventeenth centuries, they quickly discovered that the highly maneuverable birch-bark canoes of the Great Lakes region[12] were ill-suited for use in large interior river systems. Ice, flotsam, and even large fish occasionally posed significant obstacles to such fragile craft.[13] Father Marquette, S.J., recorded the following observation following a collision with a large fish near the confluence of the Mississippi and Missouri Rivers in June 1673: "We saw extraordinary Fishes, and one of them was so big, that your Canoe was like to be broke into Pieces, because it run against it."[14] As a result of similar experiences, the French-Canadian *voyageurs* who entered the central Mississippi River valley during the seventeenth and early eighteenth centuries abandoned birch-bark canoes in favor of wooden dugouts, called *piroques,* for prolonged travel on large rivers.[15] Two such *piroques* were encountered by the French explorer Benard de la Harpe on the Lower Mississippi River in 1722.[16] These craft had traveled downstream from the Illinois Country carrying an estimated five thousand pounds of salted buffalo tongues[17] for consumption by the residents of the Gulf Coast communities.

Despite their reliability, piroques were not well suited to transporting grain or passengers.[18] To meet that need, flat-bottomed boats known as *bateaux* appeared in the central Mississippi River valley during the early eighteenth century. William Clark provided an excellent description of a *bateau* in an 1806 journal entry. Clark described a *bateau* as a flat-bottomed craft approximately thirty feet long and eight feet wide, pointed at the bow and stern, and equipped with six oars.[19]

Throughout the eighteenth century, convoys of *bateaux* regularly transported large quantities of various commodities from the Illinois Country villages to the port of New Orleans. Typically, one Illinois convoy carried approximately 50,000 to 100,000 pounds of flour, or other items important to other communities in the Lower Colonies, such as bear oil, hides, salted hams and buffalo tongues, onions, peas, and furs.[20]

Following the Seven Years War (post 1763), the Anglo-American population of the central Mississippi River valley steadily increased.[21] As entire households packed up and moved from various eastern settlements into the Ohio and Mississippi valleys, larger and more substantial craft were required to transport them. Many of these immigrants arrived in the Illinois Country by way of flatboats. The flatboat was one of the most popular and frequently encountered vessels on the Ohio and Mississippi during the late eighteenth and early nineteenth centuries.[22] Frequently, an individual flatboat carried virtually every possession of a farm family. Floating down the Ohio, the flatboats resembled a "mixture of log cabin, fort, floating barnyard and country grocery."[23] Their rugged construction provided adequate defense against any hostility encountered on the frontier.

Despite the popularity of flatboats, they were not the first choice of merchants and traders. While flatboats were well-suited to transport relatively inexpensive cargo like immigrants, their households, and agricultural produce, a more reliable and expeditious means was preferred to transport more valuable cargo such as whiskey, pelts, or affluent passengers downstream to New Orleans. To meet that need, the keelboat was developed.[24] Constructed unlike any other rivercraft that had previously plied the western waters, keelboats were pointed at the bow and stern, and while light of draft and maneuverable, they could carry between twenty and forty tons of freight (figure 1). The name "keelboat" derived from the four-inch square timber that extended along the bottom of the vessel, from the bow to the stern. The hulls of keelboats were constructed of heavy planks and planked ribs and were normally between forty-five to seventy-five feet long and seven to nine feet wide. Keelboats were also fitted with masts and sails.[25] During the colonial period, boatyards in the vicinity of present-day Pittsburgh built the majority of these vessels. No surviving examples are known to exist.

The largest keelboats were built for use on the Mississippi River and were often referred to as Mississippi barges.[26] Despite the fact that keelboat travel was the fastest, safest, and most reliable form of river transportation during the eighteenth century, it was by no means glamorous. The following passage reflects upon the nature of first-class pre-steamboat river travel on the upper Mississippi River system.

> . . . a machine [the keelboat] fifty feet long and ten feet broad, shut up on every side; with two doors, two and a half feet high. It forms a wooden prison, containing commonly four rooms; the first for the steward, the second a dining room, the third a cabin for gentlemen, and the fourth a ladies's cabin. . . . On board were ten women and eleven men passengers, a captain, a mate, a steward, twelve oarsmen, and forty slaves [76 people].[27]

When river travelers ultimately reached port, they were apparently not much better off. At Baton Rouge, ". . . which was filled with tipsy men looking like cutthroat . . . the noise of the drunken, fighting crowd prevented their sleeping . . . when the travelers wrapped up in buffalo robes and lay down . . . they fancied every moment that something terrible was going to happen."[28]

The preceding paragraphs reflect the conditions and nature of river travel and commerce within the Illinois Country throughout the colonial period. For most, river travel was at best a slow, uncomfortable, and often dangerous experience.

While the collective effects of the construction, operation, and maintenance of vessel-types described in the preceeding paragraphs were not particularly disruptive to the physical environment of the floodplain, the next generation of rivercraft that plied the western rivers during the early nineteenth century dramatically, and permanently, altered both the physical and cultural character of the central Mississippi River valley.

## The Voyage of the New Orleans and the Golden Age of Steamboats

The Age of the Steamboat began with the departure of the New Orleans from the Ohio River village of Pittsburg (now Pittsburgh) on October 20, 1811.[29] Given the destruction that this departure portended for the physical integrity of numerous colonial-period settlements within its wake, it was fitting that this event occurred within the shadow of the site of Fort Duquesne. Just as the English General John Forbes had physically swept the living French from that stronghold in 1758,[30] the operation of Anglo-American steamboats would forever sweep a significant portion of the physical evidence of the former French villages from the Mississippi River floodplain.

The maiden voyage of the *New Orleans* successfully demonstrated the feasibility and commercial potential of steamboat navigation between the Illinois Country and the port of New Orleans.[31]

Much has been written regarding that voyage. The vessel left Pittsburg on October 20, 1811, and arrived at the port of New Orleans eighty-two days later, after numerous stops along the way. The boat's downstream speed was between eight and ten miles per hour, resulting in an actual running time between Pittsburg and New Orleans of ten days and nineteen hours.[32] Despite courting disaster on numerous occasions, the voyage of the *New Orleans* was

Figure 2. *Daguerreotype of the St. Louis levee by Thomas Easterly, 1848.*

hailed as an unbridled success.[33] After the boat's triumphant journey, the race to dominate trade on the nation's interior waterways began in earnest. The pivotal role of the steamboat in the Euro-American exploration, settlement, and exploitation of the West was recognized almost immediately. The following statement, made in 1841, mirrored that initial perception.

Steam navigation colonized the West! It furnished a motive for settlement and production by the hands of eastern men, because it brought the western territory nearer to the east by nine-tenths distance. . . . Steam is crowding our eastern cities with flour and western merchants, and lading the western steamboats with eastern emigrants and eastern merchandise. It has advanced the career of national colonization and national production, at least a century![34]

In 1854, less than four decades after the arrival of the first steamboat, Thurlow Weed in the *Albany Journal* reported that steamboats could be seen lined up side-to-side extending for more than a mile along the St. Louis riverfront (figure 2).[35] By 1860, steamboats were ubiquitous on the frontier landscape. Smoke from these vessels were a constant reminder, to all within sight of the river, of both the presence and importance of the steamboat within the Mississippi River valley during the nineteenth century.

The smoke expelled by the powerful steam engines on board these craft resulted from the combustion of organic compounds. The combustible fuel of choice on the upper Mississippi River was wood until the late nineteenth century.[36] The following seemingly innocuous comment taken from the log of Nicholas Roosevelt, written during the initial voyage of the *New Orleans* in 1811, portended the adverse environmental consequences for the central Mississippi valley that were to accompany the steamboat age: "Each afternoon Roosevelt allowed the crew to go ashore and cut enough wood for the next day."[37]

A recent botanical investigation by John Nelson of the impact of nineteenth century settlement on floodplain vegetation concludes that prior to 1850, steamboat demand for fuel wood was enormous. Notes recorded by General Land Office (GLO) surveyors during their efforts to establish section, township, and range coordinates on the floodplain near St. Louis in 1826 contain numerous references to widespread floodplain defoliation. "Timber mostly all cut down near the river bank by settlers living here, but find a black oak stump said to be former lone bearing tree by the present settlers . . . reestablished [corner] in its former position from the remains of former witness trees . . . and the black oak [has been] cut down."[38] In 1842, GLO surveyors noted "cut off timber" in 50 percent of the line descriptions that ended at the river bank. While there is no question that the products of bottomland forests located near nineteenth-century urban centers such as St. Louis were used to build homes and fuel industrial production, the most current literature on the subject demonstrates that the preponderance of riparian deforestation was directly related to the procurement of steamboat fuel wood. Michael Williams[39] used the U.S. Census of 1840 and arrived at the same conclusion. Records showed that sales of cordwood were concentrated along major waterways "due to demands from settlers and hundreds of steamboats plying the rivers. . . . Woodyards became a booming business and many river bank farmers supplemented their incomes by harvesting and selling cordwood from bottomland forests."[40]

Cordwood has been historically defined as wood used exclusively for consumption as combustible fuel,[41] thus differentiating it from construction-grade lumber used in domestic or industrial construction. Based upon the above referenced observations and the traditional definition of cordwood, it is reasonable to assume that most of the wood cut from the Mississippi floodplain during the first half of the nineteenth century fired the boilers of steamboats.

The number of steamboats operating in the Mississippi system increased significantly during the first half of the nineteenth century. In October 1811, the *New Orleans* was the only steamboat in operation on the Mississippi River. Forty-nine years later, in 1860, the situation had changed dramatically. In that year, 735 steamboats regularly plied those same waters.[42] The port of St. Louis recorded 22,045 steamboat arrivals between 1845 and 1852.[43]

The quantity of wood required to support the steamboat industry is staggering. In 1848, a German traveler named Henry Lewis wrote that "The boats [steamboats] on the river all burn wood, and such are the immense quantities destroyed in this manner that, had not nature provided an inexhaustible supply, some other fuel would have long since taken its place".[44] Lewis's observation was quantified by Morgan Neville in *Statistics of the West* (1836). "Steamboats of the smaller class burned from twelve to twenty-four cords every twenty-four hours," Neville reported, "and the larger boats running at mid-century consumed anywhere from fifty to seventy-five cords each day."[45]

To give the reader some rudimentary comprehension of the amounts of wood required by the steamboat industry, the following example is offered. One cord of wood (4 x 4 x 8 ft.) translated into board feet equates to approximately 1,536 board feet of lumber. A framed house 32 feet on each side contains approximately 7,500 board feet of lumber. Large steamboats consumed up to 75 cords of wood per day. Seventy-five cords per day multiplied by 1,536 (board feet in one cord) equals 115,200 board feet of lumber, or 15.36 houses (115,200 divided by 7,500). In other words, one large steamboat consumed enough wood in one day to construct approximately 15 small framed houses. On the eve of the Civil War there were 735 steamboats operating daily on the Mississippi

River in the vicinity of St. Louis. Even if each of those 735 steamboats consumed only one third of that amount of cordwood and only operated half the year, the average daily consumption of cordwood would still have been enough to construct 670,687 buildings in that year alone. The total population of St. Louis in 1860 was approximately 158,000.[46]

By the last quarter of the nineteenth century, the intensive and extensive clearing and gathering of wood, primarily (but not exclusively) for steamboat fuel, had denuded both banklines of the Mississippi River between St. Louis and the Ohio River of most stands of mature trees. Such widespread deforestation resulted in significant changes for both the Mississippi River channel and for many of the colonial-period settlements situated in close proximity to that channel. The following discussion details those changes.

## The Effects of Deforestation Upon Physical and Cultural Environments

The extensive clearing of the Mississippi River banklines during the first half of the nineteenth century resulted in significant changes in both channel depth and channel configuration.[47] This change was most pronounced between St. Louis and the Mississippi and Ohio confluence, a distance of approximately 180 river miles. In a report written to the Chief of Engineers in 1880, Captain O. H. Ernst described the river deterioration. Ernst, a recognized expert on river engineering, concluded that the primary cause of Mississippi River bankline destabilization, erosion, and pronounced decreases in channel depth were the direct result of floodplain forest destruction. After a thorough analysis, Ernst surmised that the ". . . stability of the banks has decreased with the settlement of the country and the clearing away of the forests. Weakened banks permit more rapid erosions, give the river greater width and, therefore, less depth, and navigation is injured. The fact that the river has materially widened within the last 60 years [coincidental with the genesis of the steamboat era] is generally acknowledged by those best informed."[48] Analysis of detailed nineteenth- and early twentieth-century survey maps of the Mississippi River channel on file at the U.S. Army Corps of Engineer District Office in St. Louis quantified the changes perceived by Ernst (figure 3).[49]

Between 1821 and 1888 the river became increasingly wider and more shallow. By 1880, the surface area of the river had increased approximately 50 percent from the area recorded during the 1821 survey. The resulting decrease in channel depth seriously disrupted navigation and created numerous navigation hazards for river vessels of all sizes. Mark Twain, in *Life On the Mississippi*, characterized the late nineteenth century channel as a steamboat graveyard. Twain stated that "a farmer, who lived on the Illinois shore there [approximately eighty-seven miles above the Ohio], said that twenty-nine steamboats had left their bones strung along within sight from his house. Between St. Louis and Cairo the steamboat wrecks average one to the mile—two hundred wrecks altogether."[50]

Paradoxically, federal efforts to maintain an adequate navigation channel between 1824 and 1845 also contributed to accelerated bankline erosion, channel instability, and steamboat accidents.[51] During these years, Congress authorized the construction and operation of snagboats to ply the Mississippi. The mission of those vessels was to search for, and remove, root-wads and tree trunks from the navigation channel. Such obstructions posed serious threats to river craft, particularly to steamboats.[52]

Not all of the activities of the snagboat crews were confined to the Mississippi River channel. In an effort to prevent trees situated near the banklines from becoming future navigation hazards, in many areas, snagboat crews routinely removed large trees to a distance ranging between 100 and 200 feet from the shoreline.[53] Information contained in the Annual Reports to the Chief of Engineers, written by the army officers who oversaw the snag removal program, revealed that during just one three-year period between 1842 and 1845, snagboat crews removed approximately 75,000 trees from the shoreline.[54]

A recent archival study funded by the U.S. Army Corps of Engineers, St. Louis District, gathered data on steamboat wrecks that occurred on the Mississippi between St. Louis and the Ohio. Information obtained from nineteenth-century newspapers, insurance records, salvage company accounts, and other miscellaneous sources were examined to identify the locations of specific shipwrecks within the district boundaries. The results of that investigation revealed that 156 steamboats were lost to snags or rocks between St. Louis and the Ohio River between 1811 and 1899.[55] Another 411 vessels were either damaged or destroyed by explosions, fire, or ice during that same period.[56] Aerial inspection, conducted by helicopter in 1988 during a period of low river stages revealed the remains of only nine steamboats[57] within the study area.

The seemingly contradictory results of the archival and aerial investigation may be explained by the lateral migration of the Mississippi channel. Comparison with the surveyed locations of the nineteenth-century channel below St. Louis, as the channel appeared on a series of U.S. Army Corps of Engineers topographic maps, reveals that the channel was extremely unstable and experienced significant movement throughout much of the century.[58] Many of the steamboat wrecks identified in archives but not observed during the 1988 survey (147 vessels), may be deeply buried beneath the Mississippi River floodplain within former channel locations. The archaeological remains of the *Arabia*, a steamboat that sunk during a storm on September 5, 1856,

**Recorded Changes in Mississippi River Channel Configuration Between St. Louis and the Ohio River During the Mid-nineteenth Century**

| Year of Survey | Surface Area of River | Island Area Only | River Bed Only |
|---|---|---|---|
| 1821 | 109 | 14 | 95 |
| 1888 | 163 | 35 | 128 |
| Change 1821-1888 | 54 (+50%) | 21 (+150%) | 33 (+35%) |

Note: Numerical values denote square miles (2.59 km).
Informatiuon obtained from Stevens (Stevens 1975:120).

Figure 3. *Graph by Terry Norris.*

near present-day Kansas City, was located and removed from a similar bottomland setting in 1988.[59] The examples presented above illustrate the effect that widespread fuel gathering had upon the stability and depth of the Mississippi channel and the adverse consequences for steamboat navigation.

Closely related was the effect that such clearing had upon the physical integrity of the colonial-period settlements located upon the floodplain. Between 1699 and ca. 1752, the French established seven settlements along a sixty-mile reach of the Mississippi River floodplain between present-day St. Louis, and Chester, Illinois (figure 4). Throughout the seventeenth, eighteenth, and early nineteenth centuries, this portion of the central Mississippi valley was commonly referred to as the "Illinois Country" of upper Louisiana. Prior to the end of the Seven Years War (1763), the Illinois Country was an important component of the French Colonial Empire in North America. French settlements along the Mississippi River within the Illinois Country included the villages of Cahokia (1699), Kaskaskia (1703), Fort de Chartres/Village of Chartres (1720), Ste. Philippe (ca. 1722), Prairie du Rocher (ca. 1723), and Ste. Genevieve (ca. 1752), and a small hamlet located at la Saline salt works (ca. 1700).[60] Throughout the colonial period, these settlements provided a wide variety of food and commodities to their Gulf Coast neighbors in Biloxi (1699), Mobile (1702), Natchez (1716), and New Orleans.[61] During the Revolutionary War (1778-1780), the Illinois Country settlements also served as the nucleus for Colonel George Rogers Clark's western campaign against the British military interests in the Ohio and Mississippi valleys.[62]

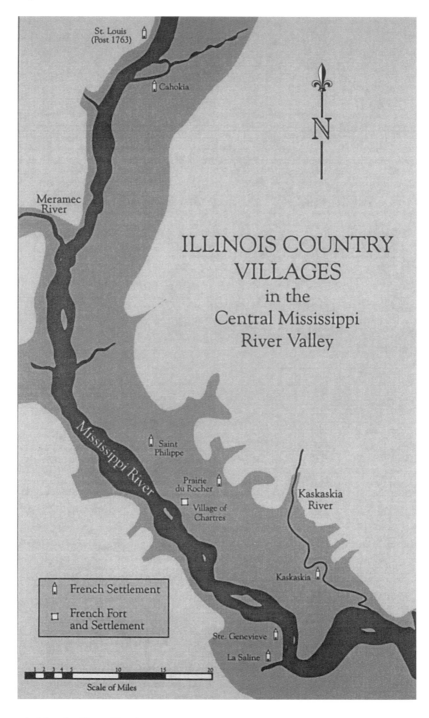

Figure 4. *Map by Terry Norris.*

Despite the important role that the residents of these communities played in the Mississippi River valley during the colonial period, comparatively little is known about their lives. Unlike colonial New England, where seventeenth- and eighteenth-century archives contain numerous first-hand accounts,[63] written observations were rarely recorded by the residents of the Illinois Country. The records that have survived dealt primarily with secular legal and ecclesiastic matters.[64] One study recently concluded that in one such Illinois Country community, Prairie du Rocher, virtually every resident was illiterate.[65] If the majority of Illinois Country residents were, in fact, illiterate, then it follows that most of the surviving first-person accounts and descriptions of village life were written by non-residents. Such individuals would probably have possessed only limited familiarity with the geography of the area and the customs of the people. Logic dictates that such accounts would likely contain significant biases and inaccuracies. An example of this is Charles Dickens's account of the verdant Illinois Country floodplain:

A dismal swamp, on which half-built houses rot away: cleared here and there for space of a few yards; teeming then, with rank unwholesome vegetation, in whose baleful shade the wretched wanderers who are tempted hither, droop, and die and lay their bones; the hateful Mississippi circling and eddying before it . . . a hotbed of disease, an ugly sepulchre, a grave by any gleam of promise: a place [Cairo, Illinois] without one single quality, in earth, air, or water, to commend it.[66]

Residents of the Illinois Country village who undoubtedly observed the steamboat that carried Dickens effortlessly upstream past their villages would probably have found Dickens's description of the nearby community of Cairo curious in the extreme. As historians have long cautioned, the modern researcher should likewise view any and all historical accounts judiciously.[67]

The existing Illinois Country French colonial archives are numerically and thematically limited in their scope. However, one additional perspective on life within the Illinois Country villages is available to the modern scholar: cultural information contained in the archaeological record of each of the villages. Both the historian and the archaeologist share concern with understanding the past. In most instances, the historian's primary sources of information are first person accounts or documents that are contemporary with the event or subject under investigation. For the archaeologist, the primary sources on past events are the unwritten, physical remains (artifacts and artifact relationships) of those activities. For the historian, the primary data source was not the historical event, but rather, someone's recorded interpretation of an event.

Thus, both archival and artifact analyses of historical subjects are minimally one level of abstraction removed from the actual event being investigated[68] and should both be considered as possessing equal (information potential) value during the analysis of historical events. The archaeological remains associated with the Illinois Country villages represent an exclusive primary source of information on these settlements. If unearthed intact, the information contained within the archaeological deposits associated with the Illinois Country villages have the potential to enhance modern interpretations of colonial life within the central Mississippi valley.

Cartographic and field research conducted by the author reveals that lateral movement of the Mississippi River channel severely damaged archaeological remains of four of the original seven colonial Illinois Country settlements. Fortunately, residents of just two of those communities (Cahokia and Kaskaskia) were actually physically displaced by those channel shifts. The original colonial villages of Ste. Philippe and Ste. Genevieve were already abandoned prior to the mid-nineteenth century channel shifts. Residents of Ste. Philippe had left their small farming community in favor of other villages around 1800. Ste. Genevieve relocated to higher ground (the present-day location) shortly after a major flood inundated the community in 1785.

Human displacement notwithstanding, the archaeological remains of the eighteenth-century villages of Cahokia, Kaskaskia, Ste. Philippe, and Ste. Genevieve each represented an important primary source of information regarding the colonial history of the central Mississippi River valley. Archaeological data sets located at each of those locations sustained significant damage or total destruction as a result of steamboat-induced channel migrations. An assessment of the physical extent of that damage is presented on pages 87-89.

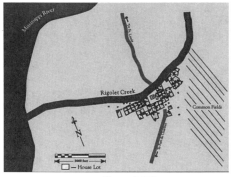 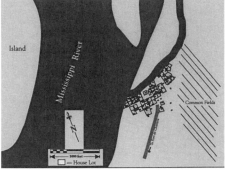

| Circa 1770 | Circa 1870 |

## Cahokia (1699)

*Map by Terry Norris. Depicts Cahokia as it appeared during the mid-eighteenth century, superimposed over a section of a Mississippi River channel map.[69] Analysis of that composite revealed that the Mississippi River channel migration had destroyed the western portion of the village including the sites of at least 10 structures, as well as the "Indian Village and burying ground" as identified on the 1771 Hutchins map.[70] Archaeological investigations later confirmed the accuracy of this hypothesis.[71]*

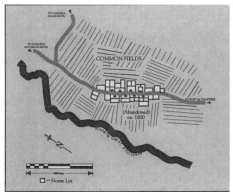 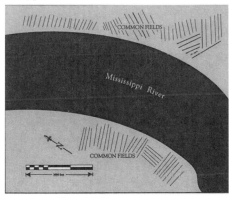

| Circa 1797 | Circa 1870 |

## Ste. Philippe (ca. 1722)

*Map by Terry Norris. Depicts the plan-view image of Ste. Philippe as it appeared to Nicholas de Finiels in 1797, superimposed over a section of an 1866 Corps of Engineers Mississippi River channel map. The control point used to suggest the spacial relationship between the eighteenth-century village site and the 1866 channel location was the General Land Office (GLO) recorded location of the village race (assumed by the author to have been in close proximity to the village). Analysis of that composite image revealed that the original site of Ste. Philippe was totally destroyed by lateral Mississippi River channel migration during the mid-nineteenth century. The author observed no colonial-period archaeological remains during several field surveys of the area and has concluded that the archaeological remains of the small, colonial village of Ste. Philippe have been totally destroyed.*

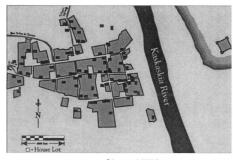
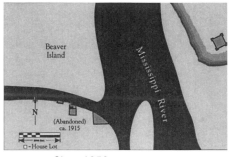

Circa 1770                    Circa 1950

## Kaskaskia (1703)

*Map by Terry Norris. Depicts the plan-view image of Kaskaskia as it appeared to a British military cartographer during the summer of 1766, superimposed over a section of an 1881 Corps of Engineers Mississippi River channel map. Subsequent analysis of the composite image revealed that approximately 95 percent of the original eighteenth-century village had been destroyed by lateral channel migration. Archaeological investigations conducted by the author confirm the reliability of the cartographic plan-view image.*

*Kaskaskia was the largest of the Illinois Country communities situated on the Mississippi River. In 1778, Kaskaskia was the headquarters of Colonel George Rogers Clark's Illinois Country campaign. In 1818, Kaskaskia was designated as the first capitol of Illinois. During the late nineteenth century, the unstable, defoliated bankline of the Mississippi migrated toward the eastern side of the floodplain and destroyed almost all of the physical record associated with those important events.*

## Summary and Conclusions

Information contained in the archaeological record of the original French colonial settlements within the central Mississippi River valley represent an important primary source of data on village life within these communities. Frequently, the settlement pattern, subsistence, and behavioral data recovered from archaeological contexts is not available from other sources. The integration of such information into the image of village life contained in archival documents provide insights into the community that may not be discernable from the archival perspective alone.

From their earliest days, the existence of the Illinois Country villages was closely associated with the river. It was that relationship which dictated the locations of their villages in close proximity to the both the river and the fertile alluvial soils of the Mississippi River floodplain.

Unfortunately, that relationship ultimately resulted in the destruction of portions of more than half of the villages during the latter decades of the nineteenth century. The destruction that occurred at the original sites of the Illinois Country villages (and the corresponding loss of the archaeological data

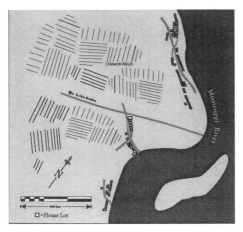
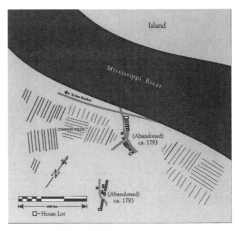

Circa 1777                                 Circa 1890

## Ste. Genevieve (ca. 1752)

*Map by Terry Norris. Depicts the plan-view image of the village of Ste. Genevieve as it appeared to Nicolas de Finiels in 1797, superimposed over a section of an 1881 Corps of Engineers Mississippi River channel map. The control point on this composite is a field road that appears on eighteenth, nineteenth, and twentieth century cartographic images of the area. Analysis of this composite-image interpretation of colonial period archaeological remains recovered from the site (23SG-124) and archival analysis conducted by the University of Missouri, suggest that approximately 66 percent of archaeological remains of the original Ste. Genevieve were destroyed by lateral channel movement during the late nineteenth century.[72]*

base associated with each of these locations) was the indirect product of the "Golden Age of Steamboats." While romantic notions of that era abound, the fact is that the demand for steamboat fuel wood defoliated entire regions of the Mississippi River floodplain and resulted in massive river-channel degradation and lateral movement.

It is impossible to estimate the historical value of the information contained in the archaeological deposits that were eroded into the Mississippi River channel. However, the discovery of a button worn to commemorate the 1789 inauguration of General George Washington from the surface of one of the surviving Illinois Country settlements suggests that much more than the crumbled remains of dwellings may have been lost.

# Paving St. Louis's Streets

## *The Environmental Origins of Social Fragmentation*

~

## *Eric Sandweiss*

From St. Louis's earliest days, the task of making streets forced residents to confront the limits imposed by their natural environment. This essay, which looks at street-making in nineteenth-century St. Louis, explores the compromises and conflicts that citizens faced as they struggled to accommodate civic goals with environmental realities. In the simple process of planning and improving their streets and roads, St. Louisans discovered that the urban landscape can never wholly erase the contours of the natural landscape beneath it. More important, they learned that the "social contours" of the land—that is, the unevenly distributed consequences of environmental conditions—were, if anything, only amplified by citizens' efforts to control them.

In St. Louis, as in other cities, the task of laying streets upon the landscape was among the earliest and most important functions of city government. Auguste Chouteau's primary charge under the city's founder, Pierre Laclede, was to survey and name a series of streets running along the hillside that sloped up from the Mississippi River. Chouteau's plan followed the dictates that had guided European colonial town planning for several hundred years and that could be traced, in some form, as far back as the Roman Empire: his streets paralleled the water, were set at right angles a uniform distance from one another, and gave on to an open plaza near the center of the village (figure 1). Along with the surrounding common fields—the long, narrow strips of land reserved for cultivation—the design itself was but one part of a broader set of dictates by which a familiar social order would be recreated in this wilderness outpost. With it came rules about how to allocate property, where to place various public buildings, and how to maintain land and buildings into the future. In this way, the original street plan of St. Louis rested on two presumptions: first, that predetermined, geometric forms could be imposed upon a natural landscape, regardless of its original contours; and second, that those forms would be integrally related to the maintenance of an equally predetermined social order.[1]

It wasn't long before both of those presumptions were tested to the breaking point. The city's French and Spanish overseers were unable to enforce the kinds of property laws meant to maintain a close, stable community. Just as their idealized society of well-settled farmers had failed to withstand the temptations of mercantile wealth and the transience of the frontier, so had their carefully conceived urban landscape fallen prey to weather, geographic irregularities, and fiscal scarcity. Chouteau's street grid was all but unrecognizable by the time St. Louis was incorporated as an American city in 1823.[2]

Not surprisingly, then, ordinances governing street construction and maintenance were among the first to appear in the new city's books. American lawmakers differed from their French and Spanish predecessors, however, in several related respects. First, they conferred responsibility for initiating and financing street construction upon private citizens as well as on the municipal government, and second, they dropped any pretense of establishing a general plan for the city's streets. Instead, the process would develop according to the wishes of those citizens who owned and subdivided property. Yet even as the Americans abandoned the ambitious social and political agenda of colonial planners, their experience laying streets in the coming decades would lead to the formation of an altogether new agenda—first inadvertent, later intentional—for ordering urban society by ordering the urban environment.

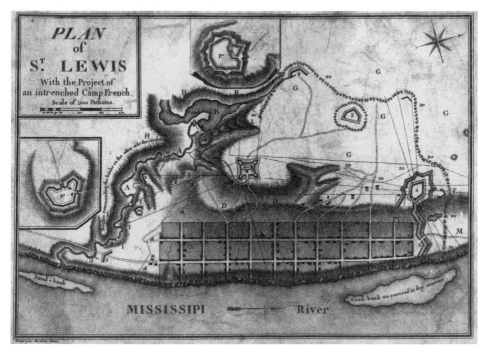

Figure 1. *Plan of St. Louis by George de Bois St. Lys, 1796.*

## *"No Crammed Square Mile": Street-making from 1850 to 1876*

As the city repeatedly expanded its boundaries—in 1841, 1855, 1870, and 1875—to include ever-greater amounts of land for its growing population, street-making remained the most ubiquitous and essential task facing government officials and private developers alike. Yet the men who ran the city government operated with little shared notion of a city-wide street plan. Instead, they shared the more general assumption that the continued development of the land was a necessary ingredient in the city's growth. New streets in any form, as they surmised, would both reflect and contribute to the city's continuing prosperity.

Armed with this faith, the city council blithely imposed a $200,000 annual minimum public expenditure for grading—regardless of whether there were people actually ready to move to the new streets created in the process. The effect of that commitment was dramatic. Once the economic interruption of the Civil War years had passed, the grading appropriation helped to contribute to a period of physical expansion that seemed to some as though it might last indefinitely. "[N]ature has placed no obstacle in the way of its growth in any direction," James Parton wrote of St. Louis in the pages of the *Atlantic Monthly* in 1867, "and therefore there is no crowded thoroughfare, no intense business centre, no crammed square mile." Surveying the new, empty blocks that stretched west toward Grand Avenue, Parton reckoned "that the town could double its population without taking in much more of the prairie."[3]

The story of the rapid transformation of the St. Louis landscape during the period of the city's rise to the ranks of America's great metropolitan centers has in its outlines all the elements of high drama, but the actual details of that story—the ill-considered appropriation bills, the malfunctioning rock crushers, the mud-making street sprinkling wagons—are the stuff of low comedy. For an opening scene, one can do no better than to turn to the clumsy rhetorical flourish of Samuel Curtis, newly appointed to the post of city engineer in 1851. "The day is beautiful," Curtis wrote on 7 January, "but the streets are very bad. What can be done for them?"[4]

That question would go begging for a satisfactory answer as long as public improvement policy was based on the combination of a *prima facie* belief in the virtues of street development on the one hand and an essential unwillingness (after a few years of experimentation with the minimum grading allocation) to require the general citizenry to cover its expense, on the other. Given that combination, at least three primary impediments to a well-maintained, comprehensive street system were inevitable: a reliance on cheap, substandard materials and paving techniques, an unequal geographic distribution of improvements based on existing conditions in the landscape, and the opening of many more streets than could be improved in a timely way. Each of these shortcomings would make tangible, and then amplify, the uneven social impact of St. Louisans' efforts to manipulate their environment.

To understand better how this environmentally rooted imbalance developed, we will take a closer look at the effect of such impediments on South St. Louis: the land that lay on the other side of downtown from the Mill Creek valley. That valley, first the site of the small east-flowing Mill Creek, was dammed in the eighteenth century to create the lake known as Chouteau's Pond. When the pond was drained in the 1850s, the valley soon filled with the rails of the new Pacific Railroad. Like the pond and the creek before them, the railyards set into the ground a basic division that would be highlighted, not lessened, by further efforts to improve the city-wide landscape.

## Problems with Paving Materials

The self-dramatized frustration with which Samuel Curtis embarked on his duties stemmed in part from the city's longstanding reliance on macadamized pavement—a simple, gravel-like surface of crushed limestone laid over a foundation of levelled dirt, which constituted the most frequently used paving material in American cities through most of the nineteenth century (figure 2).[5] Curtis, like others before him, recognized that the limestone used for the city's streets, most of it taken directly either from the bluffs beside the river or from the subsurface of exhausted clay quarries, was of "miserable" quality; that it cracked and turned to dust under the constant stress of city traffic, and that a good rain reduced it to a muddy quagmire.

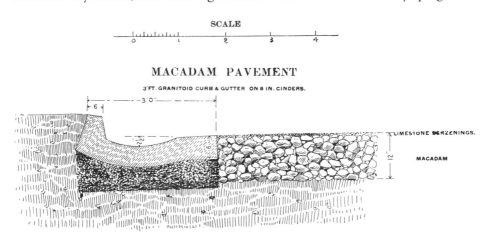

Figure 2. *Cross Section of Macadam Pavement, 1897. Report of Street Commissioner in* Mayor's Message.

Lacking any kind of reliable data on the performance of alternative materials (except for the clearly superior granite block, which was beyond the city's means to afford), Curtis could only recommend that his department begin to experiment in search of materials that presented a more suitable balance of affordability and durability, a potential solution that nevertheless seemed to him "a miserable poor resort in public affairs."[6]

In the face of continuing pressure to pave the greatest number of streets for the lowest possible cost, however, even the miserable poor resort of trial-and-error paving practice failed to gain a foothold in the years that followed. Instead, city paving policy was characterized by a begrudging but unquestioning public commitment to the cheap but short-lived (and high-maintenance) macadam. Under the administration of Curtis's boss, Mayor Luther M. Kennett, the municipal government threw itself wholeheartedly into the task of paving the city's streets by whatever means necessary.[7] Kennett's commitment to quickness and cheapness left a legacy that remained undiminished through three decades of succeeding administrations. From the already remarkable figure of 185 miles of macadamized streets recorded by the Street Commissioner in 1872 (a distance that represented 95 percent of the total mileage of St. Louis's paved streets), the city reached a peak figure of over 300 miles of macadamized thoroughfares by 1881, the year that Mayor Henry Overstoltz desperately pleaded with the House of Delegates that "all extensions of our street system in the shape of new streets be avoided."[8]

But year after year, block after block of macadamized roadway was added, even as professional and layman alike futilely reiterated what Samuel Curtis had pointed out in 1851. Even the introduction, in 1874, of steamrollers to firm up the foundations of macadamized streets made little effective difference in the long run; paving techniques remained, in Overstoltz's words, "utterly inadequate and defective."[9] The daily remarks of ordinary citizens often spoke more eloquently still of the problems that macadam streets engendered for city dwellers: their "soft limestone," wrote one, "quickly grinds to powder; ensuring at all times a disagreeable dust or an equally disagreeable mud." Another wondered, as late as 1897, "when it will cease and become a thing of the past to see a river of mud in the streets." The question was of more than academic interest to anyone who had shared this anonymous diarist's experience of coming home at the end of the day "with enough Real-Estate on my feet to lay off a town-plat."[10]

## Geographic Fragmentation

As poor a surface as macadam was, it represented at least a first step toward easing the difficulties of travel around the city. But streets could only take a person as far as they led. The historical geography of the city placed severe limits on the choices available to St. Louisans as they planned the layout of their city. The boundaries of the old common fields surrounding the original village, for instance, dictated the paths of many of the streets later laid out on the north and south sides of town, despite the problems created by their skewed and clashing grids. More striking in the long run was the effect of the Mill Creek valley, a low-lying swath of land that ran west from the Mississippi at the southern edge of the colonial village. This wide valley, first flooded for the mill dam operated by Auguste Chouteau, later drained and covered with the tracks of the Pacific Railroad, created a major impediment between south St. Louis and the streets of the central corridor, including downtown. Indeed, the most striking aspect of the scattered street improvements made in south St. Louis prior to 1870 is the near-total lack of paved connections between the south side and downtown. With the exception of the parallel streetcar routes of Seventh Street and Carondelet Road (today's South Broadway), not far west of the Mississippi River, no improved street beginning north of Lafayette Avenue continued more than a few blocks south of that thoroughfare. Second Carondelet Avenue (today's Eighteenth Street), which, as its name indicates, should have offered an alternate route from the city center to the village of Carondelet, was not only unpaved at this time but its right-of-way was discontinuous and incomplete. The south side of the city was acquiring a distinct identity—as much through its increasing isolation and its unpaved streets as through the character of its growing German and Bohemian immigrant population.

The social dimension of the street-making process—the interaction occasioned by the actual contracting and carrying-out of improvement work—was as effective as the physical dimension in accentuating regional differences within the city. Contracting may have been authorized at a city-wide level, but its details unfolded in a highly localized way. Grading and paving work was taken on by dozens of individuals and small firms in this period; their chief common characteristic seems to have been either an unwillingness to travel far to work, or a productive relationship with their local alderman. Statistics from the 1870s bear out this impression. All of the contractors who worked on the streets of south St. Louis in the fiscal year extending from 1870 to 1871 lived south of Park Avenue. Only four of them had any road contracts north of the railroad tracks; and of these, only two worked north of Market Street, on what might justifiably be called "the other side of town." Subsequent years showed an even more dramatic degree of isolation.[11] In other words, street improvement remained a highly decentralized and, at the same time, a highly localized profession.

The consequences of this fragmentation of labor were augmented by a series of related circumstances. First, the men who improved streets did so without having to file any plans for the city's advance inspection. The techniques on which they relied were determined by tradition, not by law. Second, the very stone used on streets varied greatly from one end of the city to the other. Macadam made from stone quarried in the south side was not as durable as the rock used elsewhere in the city.[12] Finally, once paved, no street was safely protected by what the city engineer dryly termed "restrictions upon the liberty of disturbance of our pavement by private parties."[13] Even when properly carried out, the typical street repair on a busy, macadamized thoroughfare lasted for only two or three months; hence, the price of each such "disturbance" (for instance, the excavation of a private sewer, or the laying of streetcar tracks) continued to be paid indefinitely into the future, so long as macadam remained the pavement of choice, or necessity, in St. Louis.[14]

## Excessive Street Openings

The combination of a localized outlook and an overriding concern for short-term economizing was responsible, then, for considerable fragmentation and reduplication of effort in the street-making process. That fragmentation was further compounded by the continued legacy of a widely shared faith in the virtues of constant growth. Again the south side offers a case in point. On paper, the area appeared to be growing quickly and efficiently. But in fact the number of streets "opened" there (officially dedicated for public use) far outpaced the rate at which they could possibly be improved. Many of the streets that existed on late-nineteenth-century maps were likely to have consisted of little more than parallel rows of wooden stakes or rock cairns.

How did this come about? The minimal laws drawn up to govern street opening were geared to promoting growth, not controlling it; their methods for apportioning costs ensured that neighborhoods like south St. Louis would never lack for unimproved thoroughfares. Simply to open a street, whether or not it was ready for improvement, cost the public treasury little or nothing. Government-ordered street openings reflected a continuing faith in the power of landscape improvements to catalyze urban development; they also reflected the city's hope of finding cheaper ways to encourage that development than by earmarking great sums of public money for outlying improvements, as they had done in the 1850s. Yet city officials either did not see, or chose to ignore, the environmental underpinnings of their legislative decisions. Because the landscape itself was anything but even turf, the fiscal and political decisions that concerned its improvement could only amplify existing inequities in the quality of people's lives.

The benefits assessment system that applied to street openings provides an illustration of this trend in action. By law, streets dedicated to the city as part of a subdivision were surrendered to the public domain without financial compensation to the original owner. In cases where the city exercised its right of eminent domain in appropriating land for streets, a procedure was established for assessing the benefits and damages incurred by both sides in the transaction. Each time the city proposed to take property for street-opening, the land commissioner convened a jury of citizens to determine, first, the value of the land appropriated (and therefore owed to the property owner), and second, the offsetting *benefit*, or increased value, that would accrue to adjacent land after the opening of the proposed street. If the owner's losses exceeded his benefit, he was entitled to compensation. This system operated through the 1860s with reasonable efficiency. The accounts recorded for the 1856 opening of a stretch of Geyer Avenue, in south St. Louis, offer an example of the assessment practice at work: of thirty-three affected property owners, all received some compensation, and only two (the men with the largest amounts of appropriated land) appealed the jury's decision.[15]

But this relatively neutral system did not last long. In 1867, two new ordinances pushed improvement expenses further from general public responsibility and more squarely into the laps of individual property owners. One limited the city's responsibility for payment to one-tenth of the actual value of the appropriated land. The other extended the definition of who might be assessed for benefits and damages beyond the directly affected, abutting residents, to include any landholder within one-half block or 150 feet of the opening.[16] These rules essentially ensured that the city would never be forced to slow the street-opening process for want of sufficient funds.

In more remote parts of town, like the south side, land values were low to begin with. The taking of property for street construction, then, was nearly always deemed to be a benefit, rather than a damage, to the owner. In fact, only rarely did the city pay *any* street-opening costs in South St. Louis after 1867. In one hearing after another, land juries ruled that south side property owners owed money to the city for the "benefit" of having had their land confiscated.[17]

There might have been some justice to such calculations, had street opening been a reliable harbinger of the impending physical improvement of a neighborhood. But in the relative absence of planning or order that characterized infrastructural improvements in St. Louis at the time, an "open street" was more often a legal convenience than it was a clear right-of-way awaiting the arrival of the steamroller.[18] Camille N. Dry's 1875 bird's-eye views offer graphic testimony of such uneven development on the south side urban landscape. To cite just one example, Crittenden Street, open from Second Carondelet west to a point beyond Gravois Avenue since 1869, is barely visible

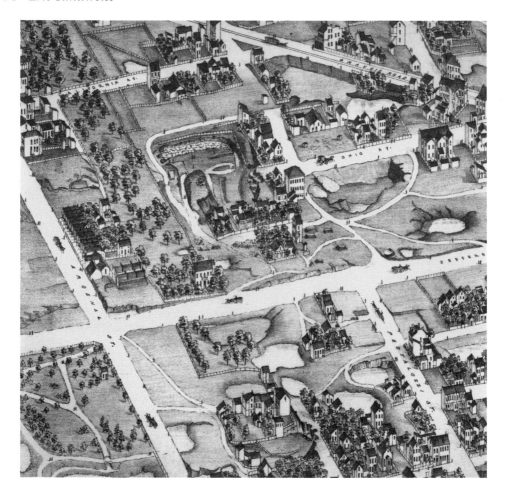

Figure 3. *Pictorial of St. Louis, 1875. Lithograph by Richard Compton and Camille N. Dry.*

in Dry's image as a gap between yards; its route is interrupted by ponds and animal pens (figure 3).[19] A close look at opening and improvement ordinances in one limited, but probably not atypical, portion of the south side—what is today known as the Benton Park neighborhood—offers some measure of the unpredictable rate at which streets, once opened, were improved. The interval between opening and improvement in this area ranged anywhere from a minimum of one year to the remarkable gap of sixteen years that separated the opening and paving of Second Carondelet Avenue.[20]

We can see, then, that the circumstances under which the public streetscape was developed insured little relation between growth and the improvements that made it meaningful. Instead, the city's continuing reliance on cheap materials, highly localized improvements, and cost-free street openings ensured that early street-making would serve as much to separate the socially and geographically disadvantaged neighborhoods of the south side from the rest of the city as to pull them together. Without planning to do so, city officials had hardened the uneven effects of environmental conditions around the city, turning natural happenstance into political fact and creating neighborhoods that looked different from one another, literally from the ground up.

## The Effects of the 1875 Charter on the South Side Streetscape

There were still, by the 1870s, influential voices calling for change in this makeshift state of landscape improvement. Yet their goal was not precisely to rectify the unequal conditions endured by residents of different sections of the city. Instead, they wished to improve the political (and with it, the fiscal) efficiency of the improvement process itself. They realized that goal in 1875 with the drafting of the country's first home-rule charter, a milestone of municipal legislation that has profoundly affected the city, for good and for ill, to this day.[21] The charter was accompanied by a "Scheme for the Separation of the Governments of St. Louis city and County," which removed county authority from within the city limits, and in exchange for assuming the county's entire debt load, ambitiously extended the city's area threefold, moving its western boundary nearly four miles to a line just beyond the edge of the newly planned Forest Park.

The charter, passed with the scheme late in 1875, was packed with a number of features that reflected its framers' disenchantment with past practices of city-building, as well as their desire to prepare a document that would attract the support of the city's working-class electorate. Indeed, the new law contained much to appeal to the citizen of moderate means: it limited property taxes to one percent in the pre-1875 limits and one-quarter of one percent within the new bounds; it lifted the 10-percent limit on the city's share of land appropriation costs, while at the same time relieving landowners of any assessment for street improvement that exceeded 25 percent of the value of their property.[22]

With these fiscal reforms came a more concerted attack on the problem of inefficient, wasteful street improvements. Article 6, section 1 of the charter expressed a broader and more explicit official desire for an ordered landscape than anything seen in St. Louis since colonial days. This clause gave to the municipal assembly the task of "establish[ing] a general plan for the location and graduation of streets within the city"; once done, the newly formed Board of Public Improvements would insure that "in all subdivisions of property hereafter made by the respective owners, they shall conform their streets to said general plan."[23]

But the promise of order, even had it been kept, was only coincidentally related to the achievement of either an efficient system of inter-neighborhood connections or an equitable distribution of improvements. The scheme and charter were organized primarily around a political vision—one that balanced traditional fiscal conservatism with improved coordination of public functions—rather than a spatial vision.[24] The voters of the south side might have been less enthusiastic in their support of the new law had they foreseen the ways in which its rationalizing, simplifying intentions would serve further to confirm and to harden existing inequities in the urban landscape. Newly strengthened municipal regulation often did little more than apply a public-spirited gloss to decisions that, whether based on self-interest, political favoritism, or environmental necessity, had the cumulative effect of neglecting or delaying the much-needed improvement of their half of the city.

The "general plan" called for in the charter provides a case in point. Its long, east-west-running blocks encouraged the smooth flow of traffic west from the river and, indeed, matched the shape of most of the blocks being laid out in the fast-growing central corridor (roughly, from the Pacific Railroad tracks on the south to Morgan Street—today's Delmar Boulevard—on the north). The plan made perfect sense in the context of improving connections from the retail, professional, governmental, and manufacturing facilities that were clustered around the courthouse and the central waterfront, to the residential or secondary commercial area that spread directly west, unimpeded by major geographical irregularities. It did little, however, to redress the isolation of the south side, or to match the existing north-south orientation of most of the blocks already laid out in that part of the city. Instead, it offered a recipe for confusion, ensuring the continuation of difficult street connections between the central city and the neighborhoods to the south.

In any case, the plan quickly became irrelevant. By the end of the year, the Board of Public Improvements, charged with introducing and maintaining order on the chaotic, *ad hoc* city landscape, had given up on the very idea of a "general plan." To properly prepare such a document, they realized, would require years of work. In the meantime, they had been asked to review dozens of new subdivision plans. To postpone approval of these developments in the name of a non-existent plan appeared increasingly ludicrous. By far the most reasonable solution, the board decided, was simply to declare each subdivision, after its approval, "a part of the general plan of the city." They asked for, and received, permission from the city counselor to let this paradigm of cart-before-the-horse planning, essentially a codification of existing practice, substitute for any more positive (and more controversial) action.[25] The idea of the plan was simply too comprehensive, and too far from the prevailing deference to individual initiative, to be successfully implemented.

One area on which the charter did have a marked effect was the rate at which proposed street improvements could be realized. In 1878, the board reported that it had approved just over a third of the street and alley petitions brought before it; by the early 1880s the ratio had declined to 25 percent.[26] A review within the board's *Journal* of street and alley petitions in south St. Louis reveals that this area was, proportionally, even harder-hit by the board's strictness than was the rest of the city. In that period for which records remain (October 1877–February 1880) twenty-six petitions were submitted from this area. Only four were approved.[27]

Why were south St. Louisans so unsuccessful in acquiring street improvements after the charter? The answer lies, once again, in the intersection of environmental conditions and political responses. The Board of Public Improvements proved especially sensitive to the costs of improving uneven, irregular land, something that south St. Louis—crisscrossed with limestone sinkholes and caverns—offered in generous helpings. Time and again, the board turned down petitions for street improvement from those residents who most dearly needed it: people whose property was virtually inaccessible, by virtue either of geological accident or of the scars left by earlier quarrying for the stone used to smooth the landscape of the rest of the city. One block near the corner of Jefferson Avenue and Cherokee Street—a block that had been surveyed and subdivided for nearly twenty-five years—was reported by the board to contain a quarry that extended as far as forty feet below ground level. Residents' petition for an alley through the center of this misshapen land (the construction of which would have necessitated improvement of the entire block) was summarily denied.[28] Certainly, cutting and filling to correct this kind of irregularity, if approved, often served to create more problems. When a group of landowners in the vicinity of Chippewa Street, for instance, saw that thoroughfare being graded in the autumn of 1879, they asked that their own adjacent blocks of Missouri and Indiana Avenues be improved in order to connect with the newly levelled route. This action, the board discovered, would place the petitioners' house lots eight to ten feet below the new street grade; thus the net effect of the action would have been to worsen, rather than better, their predicament.[29]

But it was a measure originally designed to win for the charter the support of voters in neighborhoods like the south side that acted, perversely, to exert the most marked negative impact on the landscape of the area. The owners of cheap lands around the unimproved fringes of the city had been especially hard-hit by the pre-charter street assessment system. For such people, a single paving assessment could actually approach the entire value of their property. It was this perceived injustice that the charter's framers tried to redress by limiting each abutting landowner's share of the cost of street paving to 25 percent of the assessed value of his property.[30] This clause should have given outlying St. Louis residents an affordable, subsidized means of enjoying the improvements (and the attendant appreciation in property values) that others in the city took for granted. But its motivation, to judge from the board's subsequent interpretation, lay less in a desire to see street improvement spread to poorer neighborhoods (that is, in a positive, visual image of the proper course of urban growth) than in a political conviction that the city had a responsibility to keep its citizens safe from excessive taxation. When combined with the equally strong mandate of public fiscal constraint, this conviction served, once again, to ensure that inefficiencies and inequities in the public landscape were amplified rather than diminished.

To judge from their own records, the board opted repeatedly to promote fiscal responsibility over infrastructural investment. Their loss of faith in the once-common assumption that the constant expansion of landscape improvements was a necessary catalyst to urban prosperity was summed up bluntly in their annual report of 1880. The board's glum assessment of the state of the city's public improvements that year betrayed a reticence that contrasted sharply with the optimistic expansionism of the 1850s and 1860s: "Until the many, and wide, open spaces that now separate the built up parts of the city are measurably filled up," it concluded, "the construction of new streets is the least important class of public works [to be undertaken]."[31]

The 25-percent clause proved to be the primary means by which the board rationalized its hesitation to promote the improvement of underdeveloped neighborhoods like the south side. Paving costs were more or less constant throughout the city; land values were not. The improvement of a block downtown on Olive or Pine might have resulted in an assessment of each landowner of perhaps 10 percent of the value of his lot; the same work carried out on Rappahannock or Miami Street might require a tax of 50 percent or more of neighboring property values. Under the charter, the city was now compelled to cover that part of such costs in excess of one-quarter of neighboring land values, yet the board proved repeatedly unwilling to make this commitment. Instead, in case after case, "free" paving in the heart of the city was approved summarily, while "expensive" paving on the outskirts was denied.

At the heart of the board's explanations for its decisions in such cases was a specific interpretation of public and private interest. Growth that came at little or no public cost served (or was at least not injurious to) the public interest. It was allowed to occur unquestioned. Improvements that required substantial public investment, on the other hand, had to be justified in substantially stronger terms: a street had to have a proven value either in carrying traffic from one developed neighborhood to another or in improving drainage over a wide surrounding area. If petitioners were unable to prove such utility, then the board considered their benefit to be "private," and expected them to pay their own expenses. Since the use of one south side street, as the board insisted, "would be confined almost entirely to the wants of the few people living on the street," the petitioners clearly had but one alternative: "[i]f the property owners along the street would club together and build a plank sidewalk along the front of their residences, it would relieve them of the greater part of the inconvenience they now suffer."[32]

Obviously, the city's assessment of a street's "public necessity" had a prophetic as well as a descriptive aspect. Street paving in unimproved or remote sections of town, where the landscape was rough and property values low, was almost certain to require substantial public expense. This locational circumstance was itself, however, an almost certain guarantor that that expenditure would not be approved by the Board of Public Improvements. By remaining unimproved, in turn, such streets acted as impediments to the future improvement of other streets around them; the board had no reason to pave a street that only led from one unpaved block to another.[33] Thus the mandate given the board, particularly the 25-percent rule, served to slow the rate at which the city's streets were improved and to preserve those inequities in the city's landscape already evident prior to 1875. The south side, in particular, bore the brunt of this cycle of caution and neglect.

## Up From the Bottom Line: Establishing an "Imperial System" of Streets

It would seem, then, that no outlying or poorly improved area of St. Louis could have fared well in the late 1870s and 1880s. But the Board of Public Improvements's bottom-line conservatism was belied, here and there, by hints that their definition of the public interest included some surprisingly specific notions about the proper shape of the growing city. Acknowledging the continued isolation of south St. Louis, but denying their own agency in perpetuating it, they reported in 1878 that the railroad tracks in the Mill Creek valley presented "an almost insurmountable barrier to free communication between the two parts of the city, and have seriously retarded improvement of the southern portion."[34] The board members' treatment of a petition for the improvement of the newly opened Lindell Boulevard two years later suggests that this inequity simply bolstered their own inclinations to concentrate public expenditures in the central corridor. The new road, which led west from the intersection of Grand Avenue and Olive Street to the still-undeveloped expanse of Forest Park at the edge of the city limits, was charted through land as unimproved and as inexpensive as any on the south side. To pave this sparsely settled thoroughfare would require the same kind of municipal financial commitment that the board had so often abdicated in the case of south side petitions. But the Lindell application was approved on the first day of its presentation. The board excused its uncharacteristic generosity by explaining that, had they made the more fiscally conservative choice, "we would be justly chargeable with the offense of neglecting an improvement which would greatly tend to the material interest of our city."[35]

The Lindell petition signaled the emergence of a more subjective sense among those responsible for public improvement as to the specific geographic parameters of the public's "material interest." That interest, in this case, apparently lay in promoting the orderly and rapid development of a region whose low density and ample open space already appeared to be less a matter of neglect than of choice. It was the blocks of this burgeoning "West End" of the city that one visiting New Yorker, Walt Whitman, had proclaimed in 1879 "the roomiest by far of any city I have ever seen"; and it was this area that the poet had admired for its "thousands and thousands of fine comfortable 5 or $6000 well built brick or stone houses, with gardens around them."[36] That the favoritism shown toward the affluent West End reflected an apparent class or ethnic bias on the part of the government was, perhaps, not surprising. Beyond that, however, the board's decision on the Lindell petition suggested a shift away from policies based solely on a desire to curb public expense toward those that consciously and actively promoted existing differences within the city. While a new and more specific notion of the proper shape of the city was coming into sharper focus, the rhetoric of street improvement still reflected a fuzzy idea of a city-wide, general good.

The Boulevard Law of 1891, which grew out of the Lindell improvement ordinance, established public powers similar to, but ultimately greater than, the powers that private developers exercised in their own subdivisions. The law gave to the city the right to restrict development along selected streets to residential use only, to establish traffic limitations and uniform building setbacks, and to assess the owners of property along such streets for the entire expense of their construction. This sweeping law was necessarily limited in its application. While Street Commissioner M. J. Murphy promised "a system that will equitably include all [of the city's] interests," the thoroughfares chosen as boulevards continued to reflect the geographical biases of earlier street-reconstruction efforts. Initial speculation about the application of the pending law had centered on Grand Avenue—the original north-south ring road that had traversed the city along its 1855 boundary—and Kingshighway, which served the same function as Grand but ran a mile to the west, through land included within the 1876 limits.[37] While Kingshighway (which connected the exclusive West End to points north and south) was among those streets advocated by the board for boulevard status after passage of the law, Grand

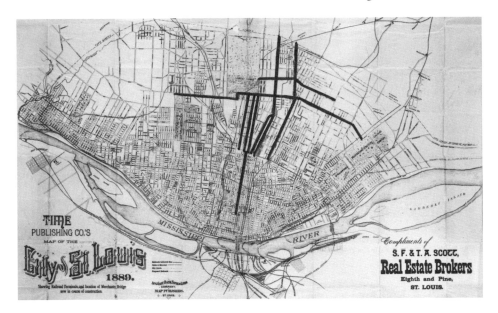

Figure 4. *Map of the City of St. Louis, 1889, showing railroad terminals and location of Merchants Bridge course of construction. Map by A. Gast and Co.*

was not. In fact, the other proposed boulevards constituted an "imperial system" within only the narrowest of empires: they all ran within the central corridor (figure 4).[38] Collectively, they offered further evidence that the decision-makers in city hall had continued to have a blind-sided view of the city. This view focused their attention on infrastructural improvement within a mile-wide strip that included most of the residences and workplaces of St. Louis's wealthiest citizens.

The overall neglect of the south side's streetscape—an undeniable fact in 1900—could be interpreted in several ways, and could suggest several courses of action. For government officials, steeped in the tradition of fiscal conservatism, it simply provided further evidence of the continued good sense of tending to the better-heeled, more easily serviced central corridor. This conviction was central to the agenda of the Civic League, the organization that spearheaded the municipal improvement campaigns of the early 1900s. Opposition to the Civic League and its allies would come in part from the same neighborhoods that had been neglected by previous landscape improvement policies. In articulating their opposition to civic reformers, south side residents would, in a sense, lean on the undelivered promise of the 1875 charter: a promise that the municipal government would take an active role in evening out the urban landscape. Like the reformers, they claimed to speak for the citizens as a whole.[39]

But because the potential of the charter to organize a city-wide response to environmental challenge had never been more powerful than its role in enforcing frugality and expediency, such ambitions had been largely dismissed by shapers of urban policy. Instead, their conception of the "whole" city, of the landscape as it was meant to be, would be molded by the image of the landscape as it *happened* to be; as it had grown under the influence of private developers operating with minimal public guidance and constrained by environmental conditions that differed from one part of the city to the next. As city officials sought to surpass their early trial-and-error responses to the crisis of street-making, they sank ever more firmly into the ruts worn for them over 150 years of continued urban growth. Their efforts only proved, again and again, the enduring power of environmental circumstances to shape the city's political and social order.

# Draining the Metropolis

*The Politics of Sewers in Nineteenth Century St. Louis*

~

## *Katharine T. Corbett*

"The progressive rise of our city is morally certain," declared St. Louis Mayor William Carr Lane in 1823. Its success, destined by geography, would be assured by thoughtful planning for future growth. Health and prosperity alike call for public improvements, especially a city-wide drainage system, "that the rearing of the infant city may correspond with expectations of such a mighty maturity."[1]

Mayor Lane's confidence in anticipating the future of St. Louis built on the then-common liberal faith that private enterprise, technological advance, and social progress all worked harmoniously to produce the greatest good for the greatest number. Over the next several decades the city's location in the path of westward expansion became the impetus for private development. At the same time the geography of that location threatened to impede urban growth: a landscape pocked with stagnant ponds created drainage problems that only a system of sewers could solve. Thanks to the demands of private enterprise, an optimistic theory of urban growth, and a fast-moving river at its doorstep, by 1860 St. Louis was among the first and best-sewered cities in the nation.

By the end of the century, however, the once-progressive St. Louis sewer system was antiquated and over-taxed, mired like the rest of the city in the debris of progress. The same liberal political economy that had driven urban expansion had made it impossible for infrastructure development and maintenance to keep pace. The story of nineteenth-century St. Louis sewers is a cautionary tale of how easily the best of intentions can be undone by a lack of cash, and how the public consequences of private decisions can compromise the general welfare.[2]

Initially, cities built sewers to carry away storm water, but only a few, such as New York and Boston, had sewers for storm water drainage before the mid-nineteenth century; most did not have any underground drains until late in the century. With the exception of human waste, which everywhere went into

*Construction of Mill Creek Sewer, 1868. The illustration reveals the arched construction of brick and the wooden support of the sewer, which was twenty feet across at its base. The primary purpose of the sewer was to drain the watershed and rid the Mill Creek valley of the stagnant polluted water. Daguerreotype by Thomas M. Easterly.*

privies and cesspools, most waste water mixed with storm water in open street gutters and eventually flowed into nearby rivers or other watercourses. Because sewers did not carry waste water, integrated systems that drained large surface areas were only necessary for cities with severe drainage problems. Private sewers or a few large, publicly funded storm sewers were considered sufficient, particularly when there was no obvious final destination. Although stagnant water was considered to be unhealthy, its removal did not usually warrant expensive sewerage. St. Louis, however, was a city with such inhibited natural drainage that stagnant water coupled with frequent heavy storms made sewer construction a community issue in advance of most other municipalities.[3]

The lay of the land largely determined what nineteenth-century St. Louis civil engineers had to do, and explains why it ultimately took so long and cost so much to do it. St. Louis sat on gently rolling prairie that rose from the west bank of the Mississippi River. The city was nearly surrounded by sizeable

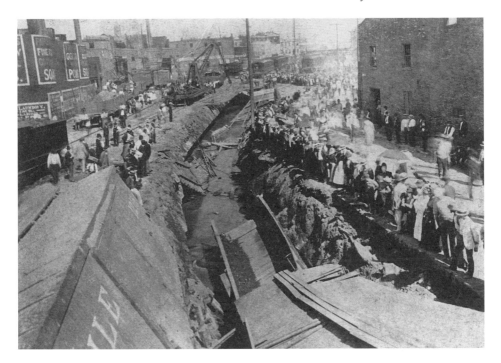

*Mill Creek Sewer Explosion, 1892. On July 26, 1892, more than one thousand feet of the Mill Creek Sewer exploded, killing six people and injuring four. The cause of the explosion was the ignition of oil fumes that entered the sewer during a refinery fire. Because the Mississippi was at flood level, the mouth of the sewer was underwater, trapping the fumes. Photo by Julius Gross.*

streams; its watersheds ran north toward the Missouri River, south toward the Meramec, and east toward the Mississippi. Everyone agreed that the Mississippi was the city's natural sump. Its vast volume and swift currents were more than sufficient to flush St. Louis wastes out of sight and out of mind. No one worried about effluent impact downstream.

On the surface it seemed a simple matter to route trunk sewers along the valleys of the major eastbound watersheds. As the city fanned out toward the west, branching lateral lines would follow development, funneling the community's rain runoff into the mains, and hence to the Mississippi.

Surface topography was deceiving. The watercourses ran downhill through the soil, but the underlying limestone strata rose and fell in ridges running roughly parallel to the Mississippi. Trenching or tunneling sewer lines through successive rocky ridges would prove time-consuming and ruinously expensive.

As rocks went, limestone was relatively easy to pick and shovel and blast. But it had another characteristic that made a drainage system especially urgent in St. Louis. Limestone was vulnerable to chemical weathering from rainwater laced with weak acids from carbon dioxide in the air and organic acids from the soil. Through geologic time, acidic rainwater had percolated down through the limestone underlying St. Louis, widened cracks into fissures and fissures into caves. Often, cave roofs had widened fissures or had fallen in, creating the depressions ("sinkholes") that covered the local landscape.[4]

St. Louisans living in the eighteenth-century colonial fur-trading post found the sinkholes that surrounded their village peculiar, but useful for fishing and occasional waste disposal. Early residents also dammed a creek that entered the Mississippi south of the village for a flour mill, forming a pond that extended west for about a mile. The dam and sluice gates of Chouteau's Pond regulated runoff that cascaded down the Mill Creek valley after every storm. Although the frontier village grew slowly until the 1830s, by 1840 more than 16,000 people were living on less than one square mile. The following year the

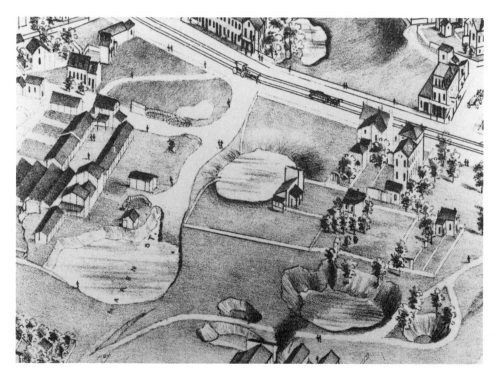

*Pictorial St. Louis, 1875. The effects of chemical weathering from acid rain to the limestone base beneath St. Louis posed a difficult drainage and flooding problem. Especially visible along the local landscape of south St. Louis are the sinkholes, which formed from collapsed caves. Urban development prompted the necessity of a sewer system to drain the sinkholes. Lithograph by Richard Compton and Camille N. Dry.*

city annexed four more square miles, extending the western boundary to 18th Street. Landowners platted dozens of new subdivisions for development.[5]

Anxious to solve the mounting problems of rain-flooded streets and basements in the growing city, the city council passed the first local drainage ordinance in 1841, which encouraged and regulated the construction of private culverts and box drains near the waterfront. The ordinance set grade standards for streets and alleys to insure that water, and whatever else might be in the gutters, flowed directly and quickly into the river.[6] Although development created runoff problems, sinkholes were even more of an issue: they threatened to impede urban growth itself. Because most of the sinkhole outlets within the city limits had long been clogged with debris and garbage, St. Louis was acquiring a reputation as a 'sickly city' surrounded by stagnant ponds from whose "fetid waters was wafted the breath of the dreadful malaria."[7]

In 1841, Street Commissioner Henry Kayser also persuaded the council to appropriate $300 to test his theory that large sinkholes drained through underground fissures to the river and were, therefore, the catch-basins of natural sewers.[8] Kayser believed that if the fissure channels could be kept open, the city would solve its two most pressing drainage problems, surface water drainage and sinkhole pollution, all at once. Kayser tested his theory of natural sewers on a large sinkhole at Ninth and Biddle streets. He excavated twenty feet to expose what appeared to be a drainage channel and observed the flow with dyed water, watching to see whether it drained to the Mississippi. His results were inconclusive. Nearby property owners, impatient with costly experiments, started suing the city whenever rampaging storm water flooded basements and undermined foundations. They demanded that the city council take more direct action.[9]

In 1843, a new city charter gave municipal government the power to regulate water courses and construct sewers for the first time.[10] The city council immediately authorized a sewer to drain the intersection of Wash (now Cole Street) and Seventh streets, but the Missouri courts ruled that the council had no right either to sell sewer construction bonds or to levy sewer taxes. Therefore, throughout the 1840s, all drainage projects competed with the already inadequate street budget for funds. Most efforts centered on draining the busy riverfront commercial area, lest the local economy mire down in the mud.[11]

The St. Louis population tripled in the 1840s to nearly 80,000 by mid-century. As the city grew in size and population, drainage conditions worsened.[12] Kayser, now city engineer, continued his natural sewer experiments, but the outlets of sinkholes on Biddle Street stopped up completely, leaving "a very ugly body of water, which in summer changed to a yellow-green, and [which] emitted vapors freighted with chills, fever, and death." Annoyed residents called it Kayser's Lake, and they wanted it drained.[13]

The sinkhole problem had made St. Louisans unusually conscious of the need for sewers that would drain both surface water and waste water. Earlier, and more clearly than residents of most other American cities, they saw drainage as a matter of public health. By mid-century the rise of the "miasma" theory gave their earlier environmental concerns the sanction of medical science. Miasma was the odorless and supposedly pestilential vapor that rose from decaying organic matter. Physicians and health officials increasingly warned that miasmas rising from swamps and stagnant ponds transmitted epidemic diseases.[14] Draining the St. Louis sinkholes became an urgent matter of public health, not merely public convenience.[15]

In the spring of 1849, after nearly eight years of public debate, the Missouri Legislature finally gave the city the authority under its charter to levy taxes for sewer construction. Coincidently, the following summer a plague of Asiatic cholera wiped out almost ten percent of the local population and further sensitized St. Louisans to the linkage between stagnant water and sudden death. The lesson seemed clear; cholera had struck hardest in the northwest near Biddle and Ninth streets. On July 30, the city council authorized the community's first major sewer, a 12-foot main to drain Kayser's Lake. [16]

A reluctant Henry Kayser was put in charge. Still complaining that his natural sewer idea never had a fair trial, Kayser proceeded to plan the Biddle Street Sewer and its connecting laterals. To lessen the cost of tunneling he proposed making the main sewer smaller than the twelve-foot channel originally specified and reducing its rate of fall. Before construction began, however, a new administration came to power and Kayser lost his job, which had been a patronage appointment.[17]

Kayser's successor, West Point-trained Samuel R. Curtis, completed the Biddle Street Sewer on the original plan, on time, and $25,000 under Kayser's estimated cost of $125,000, in spite of having to drive the tunnel through a forty-foot rocky ridge at Broadway. Competition between contractors had driven down the cost of the connecting lateral sewers, which were paid for by the property owners served. Because they were built with sufficient grade and could withstand heavy flows, the new sewers were self-cleaning. They drained streets and basements and, as promised, enhanced property values.[18]

Curtis next devised an elaborate plan for draining the whole city. He envisioned a single, integrated storm and sanitary sewage system that would carry off "the waste water from the Water Works, the drainage from the houses, the rain that falls on the surface, and the natural fountains that fill the basements and cellars." The deep channel and rapid current of the Mississippi River, lying 150 feet below the highest portions of the city, would be the system's "great trunk." Large public sewers, like the Biddle Street Sewer, would empty into it and serve as stems from which lateral sewers would branch out. These main public sewers, financed by tax revenue, would lie in valleys formerly occupied by streams, or, when necessary, tunnel through ridges to tap sinkhole basins with no other means of drainage. District sewers, financed by the property owners, were grids of branch, or lateral, sewers, which would drain subdivisions as they developed and as the main sewers reached existing neighborhoods.[19] This integrated system, Curtis argued, would increase the health of the people and the value of property. "If to drain the city and promote the health," he wrote,"we shall tax posterity, our descendants will have no cause to reproach us, for they may be indebted to these works for their own lives and fortunes."[20] On July 27, 1850, the city council accepted Curtis's plan in "An Ordinance to Provide a General System of Sewage."[21]

Curtis began with the Mill Creek valley, the 6,400-acre watershed dividing north and south St. Louis. The slow draining of polluted Chouteau's Pond was already underway, but storm water coursing through the Mill Creek valley

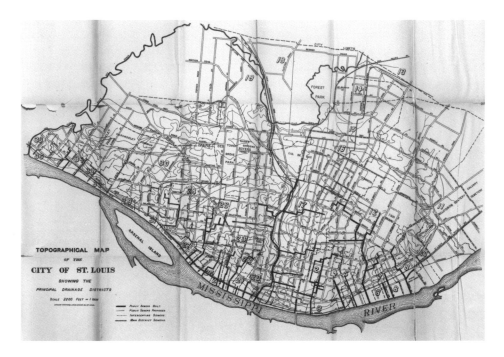

*Topographical Map of the City of St. Louis Showing the Principal Drainage Districts, 1888. Mill Creek Sewer is the primary sewer through the heart of the city, and like all the sewer lines of St. Louis, it drains into the Mississippi. Before the construction of the Pine Street Sewer, which connected to the Mill Creek line east of Forest Park, all drainage north of Forest Park entered the River des Peres. Map by Stephens Lithographs and Engineering.*

frequently overran the dam and spilled down Convent Street to the southeast, flooding the adjacent neighborhood. Curtis proposed to build a sewer twenty-one feet high and thirteen feet wide running due east on Poplar Street to carry the valley runoff into the Mississippi.[22]

When workers began tunneling they discovered a deep strata of quicksand under Poplar Street at Third and Fourth streets. A test bore of fifty-five feet hit no rock. Because there was nothing solid to rest the sewer on for the whole 1,165 feet from Sixth to Second streets, Curtis knew he had to reroute the sewer. Before he could do so, however, a change of administration brought Henry Kayser back to the job as city engineer. Kayser couldn't resist taking another shot at building down Poplar Street. He made the diameter of the channel smaller and devised a plan to reduce pressure on the pipe from ground water in the quicksand by letting some water bleed through the sewer wall. Kayser awarded the construction contract to the lowest bidder, but since no one really knew how to build a sewer through quicksand, he permitted other contractors to experiment at their own expense. One tried to protect his bricklayers by moving a six-foot iron tube through the quicksand. Nothing worked.

Kayser struggled with the Poplar Street project until he left office in 1857. His successor, Francis Hassendeubel, shut it down. Hassendeubel concluded that Kayser's undersized and gently sloped sewer would never discharge fast enough to prevent a stagnant pond from building up behind it. He turned instead to building the Mill Creek Sewer down its natural channel, as Samuel Curtis had originally intended. The largest, most expensive sewer in the city, the Mill Creek Sewer eventually extended more than five miles west of the river to Vandeventer Avenue. It cost St. Louis taxpayers nearly three million dollars before it was completed in 1889.[23]

In 1855, thirty-one main sewers drained more than four hundred acres in the center of the city. That year, voters extended the St. Louis city limits to just past Grand Avenue. In response, Hassendeubel drew up a plan for enlarging the system to drain the land encompassed within the new limits, an area of seventeen square miles. It called for more public sewers along natural watersheds to drain all surface water between the dividing ridges. District sewers would extend from the public sewers toward the ridges. In 1859, a city ordinance established routes of all public sewers started or projected in accordance with Hassendeubel's plan.[24]

Though concerned with health and sanitation, the sewer department's first priority had always been to spur development and enhance property values by draining stagnant sinkholes, containing storm water, and facilitating street openings. St. Louis, the nation's eighth largest city, was home to more than 160,000 people on the eve of the Civil War. For a decade, an average of one thousand new dwellings had been built annually as extended rail and streetcar lines drew residential development westward, particularly along the city's central corridor.[25] Since 1850, workers had completed 10.63 miles of main public sewers and 20.89 miles of district lateral sewers within the old pre-1855 limits. However, very few St. Louis homes had plumbing with sewer connections. Some had piped city water, but most people drew their water from wells and cisterns and used privy vaults in the yard.[26]

By 1861, city engineers had devised a sewer system that its builders and the public believed would be efficient—due in large part to the benefits of geography—and affordable. Taxpayers financed only the main trunk sewers through general revenue; sewer districts insured that property owners bore all other construction costs. Not a pioneering community in any other area of municipal governance, St. Louis had been one of the first to envision a city-wide sewer system for removing both waste water and storm water, and one that was capable of expanding to meet anticipated needs.

During the Civil War, labor shortages, reduced tax revenue, and military priorities slowed St. Louis sewer expansion. The section of the Mill Creek Sewer between Sixth and Tenth streets languished. "Until sewering the Mill Creek valley is completed," declared City Engineer Truman Homer in 1863, "St. Louis may have sewers, but no sewer system." Household and industrial wastes draining into the valley were making "it perhaps the most prolific source of miasma and malaria within the whole city. . . . The fumes and stench rising from them are carried back into the heart of the city by westerly winds."[27] In 1866, a return of cholera—"the stern hand of death"—pointed once again to miasmas from unsewered waste water and plugged sinkholes and to sewer gas escaping from poorly constructed private drains. (Unlike miasma, which later generations familiar with germ theory came to realize was not a disease carrier, methane sewer gas really was a threat to health.) Cholera deaths in 1866 did not reach 1849 levels, which was evidence that sewers were making the city healthier and a compelling argument for building them more quickly.[28]

Extending the system, however, waited on the main public sewers, which were becoming so costly that officials realized "extraordinary means must be provided to pay for them." Sewer systems, among the largest public works undertakings in the mid-nineteenth century, put enormous pressure on municipal budgets, particularly since many cities, including St. Louis, recognized the need for extensive water systems at the same time. Water and sewage infrastructure required huge amounts of capital not available from property taxes and use fees, the usual methods of financing city government.[29] In 1867, a special property tax authorization enabled the city to issue sewer bonds for Mill Creek Sewer construction. The sale raised $300,000 to extend the stone-arched channel east to the river and west along the valley. By 1870, total bonded debt for sewer construction had grown to just over one million dollars, and the Mill Creek Sewer was finished from the river to Fifteenth Street.[30]

St. Louis public sewers were expensive because they were labor intensive and increasingly difficult to build. The east-west mains had to pierce successive rocky ridges so that the district laterals could drain the basins in between. In the early 1870s, crews worked night and day on the Arsenal Street Sewer, blasting an eight-foot tunnel through 1,300 feet of rock. Contractors charged $41,000 in 1872 to build 1,800 feet of the Rocky Branch Sewer in north St. Louis, but charged $160,000 to tunnel the Mill Creek Sewer an equal distance through solid rock.[31]

Urban growth strained old sewers as it demanded miles of expensive new ones. Because St. Louis's sewers were generally straight, well-built, and self-cleaning (sufficient grade and enough storm water made pumping or regular flushing with city water unnecessary), the sewer department did not anticipate spending much of its limited funds on maintenance and repairs. But factories located away from the river poured solid wastes into the sewers and piped excess boiler water and steam down the drain, scalding sewer cleaners. Residents—more than 250,000 in 1870—threw in garbage and ashes, forgetting that solids not flushed with water stayed in the pipes. Slaughterhouses and dairies within the city limits shoveled manure and stuffed animal by-products into sewer pipes, forming cement-like clogs that were nearly impossible to dislodge. Debris coursing down the Biddle Street Sewer regularly damaged the channel, stopped up the outlet, and backed up the waste water. Laws against improper disposal were generally unenforceable, which led the city engineer to press for an ordinance reducing drains to a six-inch diameter in order to limit the size and quantity of refuse violators would be able to cram into the pipes.[32]

Rising costs for maintenance and construction could not easily be met by increasing revenue. Several depressions hit the city and the nation in the early 1870s, just when St. Louis was building a new three-million-dollar waterworks and was under pressure to improve its deteriorating macadam streets. A further complication was an outdated, cumbersome governmental structure that gave too many politicians a voice in administrative and fiscal decisions. For their part, St. Louis taxpayers clamored for lower property taxes and municipal debt limits, while simultaneously demanding more and better infrastructure.[33] In 1873, Mayor James Thomas, resisting pressure to suspend work on new sewers, argued in vain that in the long run it would be good business to incur debt for sewer construction because a well-sewered city promoted growth and increased assessed valuation.[34]

### No 13
### LENGTH OF PUBLIC AND DISTRICT SEWERS. AT THE END OF EACH FISCAL YEAR From 1861 to 1889

| Date | | Length of Public Sewers | Length of District Sewers | Total Length |
|---|---|---|---|---|
| April 1861 | | 10.63 Miles | 20.89 Miles | 31.52 Miles |
| " 1862 | | 11.37 " | 20.89 " | 32.26 " |
| " 1863 | | 12.00 " | 21.43 " | 33.43 " |
| " 1864 | | 12.26 " | 23.13 " | 35.39 " |
| " 1865 | | 12.86 " | 25.78 " | 38.64 " |
| " 1866 | | 14.22 " | 33.88 " | 48.10 " |
| " 1867 | | 15.78 " | 51.12 " | 66.90 " |
| " 1868 | | 18.30 " | 67.00 " | 85.30 " |
| " 1869 | | 20.50 " | 81.60 " | 102.10 " |
| " 1870 | | 22.60 " | 88.53 " | 111.13 " |
| " 1871 | | 24.74 " | 92.42 " | 117.16 " |
| " 1872 | | 26.02 " | 103.23 " | 129.25 " |
| " 1873 | | 28.23 " | 112.77 " | 141.00 " |
| " 1874 | | 29.44 " | 120.56 " | 150.00 " |
| " 1875 | | 32.08 " | 131.31 " | 163.39 " |
| " 1876 | | 33.66 " | 138.34 " | 172.00 " |
| " 1877 | | 34.89 " | 142.64 " | 177.53 " |
| " 1878 | | 36.18 " | 143.09 " | 179.27 " |
| " 1879 | | 39.85 " | 148.41 " | 188.26 " |
| " 1880 | | 43.71 " | 152.64 " | 196.35 " |
| " 1881 | | 45.19 " | 157.47 " | 202.66 " |
| " 1882 | | 46.50 " | 164.80 " | 211.30 " |
| " 1883 | | 47.73 " | 170.53 " | 218.26 " |
| " 1884 | | 48.46 " | 174.92 " | 223.38 " |
| " 1885 | | 49.72 " | 182.38 " | 232.10 " |
| " 1886 | | 50.96 " | 196.14 " | 247.10 " |
| " 1887 | | 54.88 " | 207.90 " | 262.78 " |
| 1888 | | 56.18 " | 214.50 " | 270.68 " |
| 1889 | | 57.78 " | 240.64 " | 298.42 " |

*Graph depicting the length of public and district sewers at the end of each fiscal year from 1861-1889. Population dispersal and indoor plumbing created the need for branch sewers, which put pressure on the city to extend expensive trunk lines.* Mayor's Message and Accompanying Documents, 1889.

From the beginning, the impetus for sewer construction had always come as much from residential developers and civic boosters as it had from officials and citizens concerned about public health. Rapid industrialization in post-war St. Louis made a few people very wealthy and created a small but expanding middle class who could afford new homes equipped with inside plumbing located far from urban grime, congestion, and the increasing numbers of poor. Sinkholes, however, blocked many projected street routes. Until they are drained and filled, lamented Mayor Thomas, "vacant spaces remain which otherwise would be covered with houses."[35] Although developers and home owners paid to construct the district laterals when the main public sewers reached a neighborhood, continued residential expansion depended on the ability of the city to keep extending the sewer system. In the same way, the prosperity of individual private developers depended on the continued public subsidy of city-wide infrastructure.

In 1876, voters tripled the area of St. Louis, bringing an additional forty square miles within the city limits, which now extended about eight miles west of the riverfront to just beyond Forest Park. At the same time, the city withdrew from St. Louis County and assumed all responsibility for infrastructure in the largely undeveloped annexed area.[36] In 1878, 143 miles of district sewers drained

3,722 acres, or nearly a third of the area within the old 1855 city limits—but less than one-tenth the area of the newly enlarged city. Thirty-three miles of public sewers, which had cost taxpayers over 2.5 million dollars since 1851, carried storm and waste water from district sewers to the river.[37] After a decade of effort, the 1.6 mile Arsenal Street Sewer was finally finished. The Rocky Branch and Mill Creek sewers, the city's two principal channels, were still under construction and approaching the old limits at Grand Avenue, some thirty blocks west of the Mississippi. But bond money for both was exhausted, and because the new city charter imposed strict debt limits that made it impossible to borrow more, future extensions would have to come from general revenue.[38]

Statutory limits on the amount of public debt a city could incur was a major influence in decisions about when and where to build sewers in nineteenth-century cities.[39] For St. Louis, however, the problem was particularly acute, because when the city and county separated the city assumed the county's bonded debt. The combined debt of twenty-four million dollars, not out of line with that of other cities, distressed St. Louis taxpayers determined to have cheaper, more efficient city government.[40]

One way to increase efficiency was to reduce the influence of politicians in the day-to-day operation of municipal government. Under the old charter, the city engineer had reported directly to the city council. The new charter empowered the president of a newly created Board of Public Improvements to appoint commissioners to run the infrastructure departments under his direction. The first president of the board was Henry Flad, chief assistant on James Eads's Mississippi River bridge project and one of the city's most respected engineers. The new arrangement encouraged professional standards in the sewer department and led to technological improvements that not only won the St. Louis system a national reputation among municipal engineers, but also made it possible to improve and extend the system despite severe financial constraints.[41]

The city's first sewer commissioner, Robert Moore, was the son-in-law of a former St. Louis mayor. Although he came to the job with no formal engineering training, Moore immediately reorganized the department along more rational and technologically progressive lines. He insisted on detailed specifications for contracted work, conducted cement tests, and introduced clay pipe in district sewers. With an abundance both of clay and bricklayers, St. Louis had a greater percentage of brick sewers than any other large system, but to save money, Moore specified pipe whenever practicable.[42] To rationalize planning he initiated sewer gaging to determine how much ordinary, or dry weather, flow entered the sewers. (Gaging involves measuring the amount of waste water from a number of houses over a specific time.) Although only 15 percent of dwellings had sewer connections in 1880, Moore calculated the size of pipe needed for various numbers of houses in anticipation of the necessity "even in St. Louis of someday building sewers to receive house drainage only."[43]

Moore tackled the on-going problem of drainage violations. He revised permits and codes for private drains and hired inspectors to enforce them by raising connection fees.[44] In 1881, St. Louis passed some of the first ordinances in the nation that limited the size of house drains and required them to be ventilated to keep out sewer gas. After he left office in 1881, Moore became a successful consulting engineer for railroads, but he stayed involved with municipal engineering issues through the St. Louis Engineers Club.[45]

Although improved regulations, stricter enforcement, and new cost-effective technology resulted in better, cleaner sewers, reform alone could not solve the department's bedrock problems: the high cost of extending the main lines through limestone ridges and the expense of repairing or replacing overused old sewer channels, all compounded by steady, low-density development to the west. As the area being drained at the western end of the system grew wider—much like the mouth of a funnel—more and more water was being forced into the main public channels at the narrow end. Between 1880 and 1890 the city spent $620,000 to add thirteen miles of main sewers and $449,000 for maintenance and repairs. At the same time, property owners connected more than 100 miles of new district sewers to the system. [46]

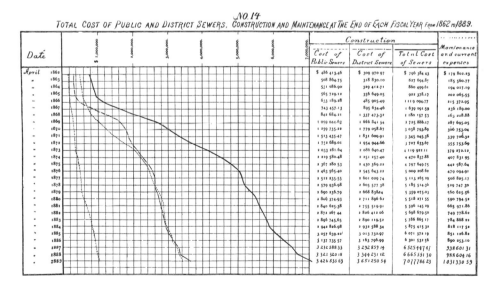

*Graph depicting the total cost of public and district sewers from 1862 to 1889. Annual spending did not keep pace with the need for new sewer construction and maintenance. Mayor's Message and Accompanying Documents, 1889.*

The high cost of building and maintaining public sewers was due primarily to the cost of labor, although securing right-of-way through developed private property became a significant expense as well. Resistance came especially from owners of factories and slaughterhouses and other businesses that would, ironically, gain the most by having sewers.[47] Once a sewer was authorized and land acquired, the department awarded contracts to low bidders. Some contractors used steam equipment, but pick and shovel labor dug most of the trenches and tunnels. Throughout the 1880s, workers slowly excavated west through deep rock to build the Rocky Branch, Utah Street, and Ohio Street sewers. To accommodate the increasingly heavy use of the Arsenal Street Sewer, workers made the channel larger and deeper, reduced the grade, and added tumbling bays that slowed down the flow and kept the brick work from eroding.[48]

While work continued on the west end of the system, on the east end, rising and falling water levels in the Mississippi caused costly damage. In the spring when the water level rose, the mouths of the main sewers were submerged. Storm water rushing through the channel had no place to go but through the top. When the river was low in September 1886, a rush of water created violent eddies that tore away the exposed riverbank, completely wrecking the mouth of the Rocky Branch Sewer. Rotting timbers from the floor of older sewers, like Mill Creek, could break loose any time and block the outlet. In addition to problems caused by rotting, the weight of a sewer and the earth above it compressed material under the side walls. This strained and broke the cross timbers. Eventually, most timber was replaced by inverted arches of stone and cement.[49]

As use of the system increased, routine maintenance problems escalated. Despite prohibitions, people still put manure, garbage, slaughterhouse offal, and ashes into sewers. When stoppages occurred in smaller pipes or near the end of the line, the department's six sewer cleaners had to flush them with city water. Sewer commissioners continually pressed for smaller connecting pipes to discourage dumping of solid waste and petitioned unsuccessfully to have slaughterhouses and dairies restricted to locations on large sewers. More industry meant that more industrial waste entered the sewers, sometimes creating problems with costly solutions. In 1882, a downtown warehouse fire reduced rosin stored inside the building to liquid. It flowed into the sewer, solidified, and stopped up the channel.[50] Oil released from a nearby refinery during a fire in 1892 backed up in the Mill Creek Sewer, which was already obstructed by high water at the outlet. A saloon keeper who had appropriated the top of the sewer for the floor of his basement lit a match in his storeroom. The oil trapped in the sewer below exploded. More than one thousand feet of the sewer blew up through the street, killing six people.[51]

Every year, more human waste was drained directly into the St. Louis system, which had been designed from the beginning to be a "combined system," one that drained waste water and storm water in the same pipes. In 1886, the city gave the sewer commissioner jurisdiction over the construction of vaults, privies, and water closets, in part because waste water seepage was polluting most of the wells in the developed areas of the city. Unlike privies, water closets could flush waste directly into the sewers. By the mid-1880s, nearly twenty thousand dwellings were flushing raw sewage into the pipes and the number of permits for house connections was increasing by 20 percent each year.[52]

In 1880, George E. Waring, Jr., a leading advocate of the sewer gas theory of disease, designed the first system in the nation that separated storm water from sanitary waste water in Memphis. Controversy over the relative merits of the combined and separate systems was the focus of heated debate between civil engineers throughout the decade. Despite the merits of separate systems, the cost of sewering a city with both storm and sanitary sewers was prohibitively expensive for most municipalities. Cities such as Memphis that adopted the separate system in the nineteenth century simply did not build extensive storm water systems.[53]

St. Louisans had realized from the start that they would eventually need to drain the entire city, given the region's geological base, topography, and few water courses. The system had been designed to be expanded, and St. Louis civil engineers defended it as entirely satisfactory for sanitary disposal.[54] Robert Moore insisted in 1885 that a community with a storm sewer system in place would be foolish to build another one for waste water. And, while other cities might eventually need to treat waste water, the ability of the Mississippi "to carry off and harmlessly absorb all that can be brought to it . . . forever settles the question of sewage disposal" in St. Louis. [55]

As early as 1883, however, developers started to lay sanitary sewers without connections to the combined system. House sewage from exclusive Vandeventer Place, a private street west of Grand Avenue in the city's central corridor, drained through fifteen-inch pipes into a branch of the Mill Creek at Grand Avenue, well in advance of the Mill Creek Sewer extension. Unable to keep pace with development, the sewer department was powerless to prevent private individuals from laying pipes that dumped human waste into the city's water courses.[56]

By the late 1880s, development had so far outrun sewer capacity that Sewer Commissioner Robert McMath had to admit that "as the city grows older and larger, defects in the sewer system become apparent."[57] One major defect was aging infrastructure at the narrow end of the funnel where the system entered the Mississippi. Another was the inability of the sewer department either to keep up with private development or to prevent property owners from building private sewers and dumping raw waste wherever it was convenient in advance of main public sewers. From Vandeventer Place westward and north of Forest Park, developers opened new streets with sewers financed, owned, and maintained by private individuals and associations.[58]

In 1887, Robert McMath realized that until he extended the main public sewers into the fashionable West End, developers would continue to pipe sewage into the natural water courses, particularly the River des Peres.[59] Although fifty-five miles of public sewers efficiently drained 263 miles of district sewers into the Mississippi, there were as yet no public sewers west of Grand Avenue. McMath developed a plan to drain 13,200 acres—half belonging naturally to the Mill Creek watershed and the other half to the River des Peres.[60] His proposal involved building intercepting sewers with a method for separating storm water and sewage that would help relieve pressure on Mill Creek Sewer without seriously polluting the River des Peres. The huge Mill Creek Sewer, under construction for twenty years, had nearly reached Grand Avenue, but the completed channel would never be able to carry all the flow directed to it.[61]

In order not to overflow the Mill Creek Sewer, any new sewer emptying into it would need a dam that was higher than the normal flow in dry weather constructed between the main sewer and a connecting storm sewer. Most of the time foul water would flow into the Mill Creek Sewer. During heavy rains, however, more storm water would flow into the sewer, rise over the dam into the new storm sewer, and then flow into the River des Peres, reducing the load on the Mill Creek Sewer. When this happened some foul water, diluted by storm water, would enter the River des Peres. While this scheme would not keep the river free of pollutants, it was the first attempt by the city to control pollution in a watercourse. Until this time, construction either by-passed existing watercourses or enclosed them in the sewer.[62]

McMath's proposal also included plans for some new foul water sewers that would completely separate sewage from storm water. He understood that the germ theory of disease might eventually dictate separate systems, even though he believed the "suspicion now attached to sewage is exaggerated." By the late 1880s, however, the water-borne nature of communicable disease was more widely accepted. These concerns spurred St. Louis city government to finally pass an ordinance prohibiting the discharge of sewage into the River des Peres.[63]

McMath's new drainage plan affected a large area of prime residential development property, extending south from Easton Avenue to Arsenal Street and west from Grand Avenue to the city limits. The centerpiece of the plan was the Pine Street Sewer, an intercepting sewer running southeast from the city limits along the north side of Forest Park and emptying into the north branch of the Mill Creek Sewer. When finished, the Pine Street Sewer would receive sewage from some of St. Louis's wealthiest and most influential citizens. Until then, their waste water would seep steadily into the River des Peres in defiance of the unenforceable ordinance prohibiting it.[64]

The problems created by development in the west drew attention and funds away from the sewer department's second major crisis: the persistent need to rebuild old sewers near the riverfront. Some of the old channels were still adequate for ordinary drainage, but they were too close to the surface for a new generation of office buildings with deeper basements. The Custom House and Post Office, constructed in the early 1880s between Eighth and Ninth streets, had required drainage thirty-two feet below the grade of the street. Since the owners of other commercial buildings in the area wanted deeper sewers too, the city, the federal government, and private individuals split the cost of a deep sewer on Ninth Street. After 1890, anyone building downtown had to pay for a private sewer to connect either with the Ninth Street Sewer or the deep sewer built for the Eads Bridge tunnel in 1874. The city, meanwhile, paid for strengthening sewers under streets being rebuilt with heavy granite blocks.[65] Also, the sewer department now realized that to prevent backup, shallow sewers laid in the flat areas along the riverfront needed to be reconfigured to empty into the Mississippi at the highest level practicable. All the city's older main sewers had to either be made larger, or have relief sewers built parallel to them. "The construction of a sewer on Poplar Street, from the river to 20th Street, is even now a necessity for the relief of Mill Creek Sewer," McMath lamented. "How can the cost, probably $300,000, be met? and other pressing calls also?"[66]

McMath's question about a specific situation went to the heart of the larger problems of infrastructure funding. From the beginning, the St. Louis sewer system was headed for breakdown, or at least failure as a comprehensive, well-functioning system, more for reasons of political economy than environmental factors, system design, or the competence of those in charge.[67] The municipal government that approved McMath's 1887 drainage plan would not authorize enough money to make it work. A pressing need to enlarge the city's inadequate water system had a greater claim on limited resources.[68] Additionally, customers would pay an annual use fee to have water delivered to their homes, but not to have the waste water carried away. In 1893, the city actually decreased funding for sewers and made no appropriation for the extension of any public sewers.[69]

By 1894, the River des Peres was "nothing less than a monster open sewer, poisoning the air with the most dangerous corruption and menace to health known, the corruption of sewage." [70] The beleaguered commissioner pleaded for help: "All that the board has ventured to propose for the coming year is as nothing to the urgent demands of our increasing population." Expansion has created problems "far beyond the resources of the city under its present charter," and extending "far beyond the city limits." [71]

Public spending for sewers had remained static, or even decreased, as population growth, territorial expansion, industrial development, and the popularity of inside plumbing had put ever-increasing demands on the system. Caught between a charter-mandated municipal debt limit and tax-resistant voters, and faced with the high cost of running sewers through rocky ridges, the city could not possibly generate infrastructure revenues fast enough to keep up. Political corruption undercut the cost-effectiveness of awarding construction and repair contracts to the low bidders. Because users paid only a modest one-time connection fee (plus a small portion of property tax), multiplying sewer districts always generated more new sewage than new revenue.[72] And, as development spread beyond the intractable city limits, county-generated sewage began spilling into city drainage basins from areas over which the city had no jurisdiction.[73]

By the turn of the century, nearly six hundred thousand people lived in St. Louis. Waste water and storm water flowed together through seventy-three miles of public sewers to the Mississippi. Four hundred twenty-three miles of district sewers covered much of the northern industrial and residential areas and the Central West End. But in south St. Louis there were no sewers west of Grand or south of Chippewa, except in Carondelet. The decision to host a world's fair in 1903 forced St. Louisans to admit that they could not invite twenty million people to Forest Park without first improving the city's infrastructure. In 1901, voters approved city charter revisions that raised the debt limit to finance the Fair and tackle the central city's most critical needs, which included completing the Pine Street Sewer.[74]

Both driven by and at the mercy of development, the St. Louis sewer system entered the twentieth century in crisis. During the twelve years it had taken to build the Pine Street Sewer, more and more raw sewage drained into the polluted River des Peres. Once completed, the new sewer frequently overloaded the Mill Creek Sewer, again sending sewage into the River des Peres.[75]

In 1910, the city made plans to enclose the polluted watercourse, but could afford only to construct an adjacent sanitary sewer on the lower end. Massive flooding in the River des Peres watershed in 1915 forced implementation. Funded in 1923 with $11 million from a bond issue enhanced with WPA money and labor, the project enclosed the river from the northwest city limits through Forest Park. South of the park a sanitary sewer ran below an open channel to the Mississippi.[76]

The creation of the Metropolitan St. Louis Sewer District in 1954 finally brought city and county drainage under the same jurisdiction, but the sewage generated in the City of St. Louis and near county continued to flow untreated into the Mississippi until 1970, when MSD opened the first of two major waste water treatment plants to serve areas draining to the Mississippi. The

St. Louis region still faced massive environmental problems resulting from decisions made by private individuals, problems of sanitary and toxic waste disposal and storm water runoff that it had a legal and moral obligation to rectify, but little power to prevent. Even mandatory environmental reforms and technological improvements could not, however, resolve the fundamental problem of infrastructure political economy: how to generate sufficient funds from the private sector to build and maintain the public sector infrastructure, that which a community owns in common for its continued health and welfare.

## Acknowledgments

The author would like to thank Howard S. Miller and Andrew Hurlcy for interpretive and editorial advice, Frank E. Janson for sharing his resources and expertise, and Edward A. Reichert and Dennis R. Henson for research assistance.

# Re-Imagining the Urban Landscape

## *Fire Risk and Insurance in Nineteenth-Century St. Louis*

~

## *Mark Tebeau*

On a tranquil St. Louis evening in the spring of 1849, the rhythms of urban life were suddenly interrupted by the kind of noise, confusion, and fear that only a rare emergency could produce. When St. Louisans heard the bells of the docked steamboats ringing just after 10 p.m., they found their curiosity aroused; when fire company bells joined in seconds later, a sense of dread took its place. A city poised on the edge of sleep "became the noisy scene of horrifying confusion." The steamer *White Cloud* had caught fire, broken loose from its mooring, and crashed into other boats, setting them aflame. Prevailing winds from the northeast sent the flames toward the wharf and the city itself. Sparks from the blaze "shot through the sky alighting on the merchandise lying on the wharf and the housetops," and the gathering crowd began to fear for their city in earnest. The heat increased, forcing the large crowd of onlookers southward. Peering over shoulders and around corners, citizens realized that the cause was lost; the fire "spread to the next square from Olive to Pine, and continued in its ungovernable fury. . . ." The Great St. Louis Fire of May 17, 1849 would "rule supreme incapable of being checked by man."[1]

During the nineteenth century, rapid economic growth and congested built environments exposed urban residents and property owners to new and heightened environmental dangers. This essay explores how one such threat—fire—affected the development of the built environment. I consider one way in which fire was conceived as an environmental risk in nineteenth-century St. Louis by studying the business records of a major fire insurance surveying company. I demonstrate how the economic assumptions which framed understandings of fire risk were at the heart of the surveyor's program to reconceptualize and map urban space in the late nineteenth century. By the twentieth century, building patterns in cities like St. Louis began to conform to these revised understandings of what constituted a safe city. In the process, the effects of one environmental hazard were made rational and predictable.

Even as it served as the engine for industrialization, fire threatened the durability and stability of nineteenth-century towns and cities. The scale and intensity of fire use within industrial manufacture grew and its use in the home became pervasive. At the same time, the expanding built environment was constructed of highly flammable materials and structures were clustered more densely. Incidence of fire increased, and the resulting financial losses mounted as capital investment in a shaky infrastructure intensified. Ironically, in mercantile centers like St. Louis, the engines of the city's economic development endangered that growth; most St. Louis merchants warehoused huge quantities of goods along the waterfront, and discovered that steamboats—the lifeblood of the city's widening economic network—often caught fire and burned materials stored along the narrow wharf.

Individual fires threatened to grow and engulf whole blocks. Firemen noted this danger in their ledgers when they wrote that "if it had not been for the activity of our firemen the whole block would have burned."[2] This was not an idle boast. Well into the twentieth century, a large proportion of fires resulted from a blaze that had spread from an adjacent structure. In 1850, some 40 percent of all fires in St. Louis resulted from blazes in adjacent buildings, and as late as 1920 approximately 30 percent of all fires nationwide had been caused by "exposure"—or spread from an adjacent structure.[3] Fires that consumed several structures or entire blocks were not uncommon.

*View of the City of St. Louis: The Great Fire of the City on the 17th and 18th of May, 1849. Lithograph by Nathanael Currier.*

Fires affecting most, if not all, industrializing cities attest to how often and how severely this fear became reality.[4] Between 1818 and 1856, over 400 such blazes caused nearly $2 million in damage in thirty American cities. Urban conflagration, then, was a familiar threat to urban residents. The possibility of a citywide fire imperiled a city's economic fortunes and the solvency of municipal government.[5] In St. Louis, for instance, between 1818 and 1847, approximately two-thirds of all city revenues were collected from property taxes. In 1849, St. Louis burned for nearly two days and more than $3 million in property and goods were destroyed—over 75 percent of the city's accumulated capital.[6]

Urban residents addressed this profound environmental danger in several different fashions: through community voluntary associations, government legislation, and market mechanisms such as fire insurance policies. Undergirding most early nineteenth-century solutions to the danger of fire were volunteer fire companies established, staffed, and supported by various communities within urbanizing cities. Based on reciprocity between communities and their male citizens, urban municipalities sanctioned and encouraged this community solution to the danger of fire. For instance, modeled after laws in Philadelphia and other established cities, in 1826, the St. Louis Common Council authorized residents "to form themselves in fire companies, one company for each ward, to consist of residents of that ward."[7] Municipalities joined private citizens, merchants, and insurance companies in supporting volunteer firemen with generous financial donations. Public funds accounted for half of St. Louis fire companies' operating revenues—over $110,000—in the years before 1850; the remainder was generated by the companies, their communities, and local mercantile interests.[8] Companies used the funds to finance much-needed projects such as purchasing new engines or hose, building an addition to the engine house, or purchasing a company alarm bell. Of course, donations also were used by the volunteer firemen to adorn themselves, decorate their engines, and to parade.

Many cities supported volunteer fire companies by writing common sense preventive practices such as chimney sweeping into statutes, establishing water systems and physical infrastructure to assist in extinguishing fires, and authorizing firemen to destroy buildings in order to thwart the spread of fire.[9] However, most early efforts by local councils throughout the United States appear to have been piecemeal at best—especially when considered in relation to the extensive and systematic standards proposed by the National Fire Protection Association in the early twentieth century.[10] Examining early (and even late) nineteenth-century legislative efforts reveals that attempts to prevent or at least curtail the danger of fire were usually generated by a calamitous fire. Curiously, though, in the nineteenth century, these efforts usually met with little success for a variety of political, social, and economic reasons. In her book *The Limits of*

*Power*, Christine Rosen documents some of these reasons. She argues, for instance, that real estate and other political interests fiercely resisted stricter fire codes even immediately after disastrous fires in Chicago and Boston.[11]

Many urban residents (especially "middling" property owners living in substantially constructed dwellings and merchants) turned to the fire insurance companies to underwrite policies that would indemnify them against financial losses suffered from fires. Though hardly a measure of last resort, fire insurance policies were often expensive and unreliable—especially in the decades prior to the Civil War. Underwriters insured property for up to three-fourths of its total value, and paid claims slowly if at all. Company failure was common, particularly after urban conflagrations. The financial stability of an insurance company depended on its ability to write policies on property which would not burn or to charge premiums equal to or less than the companies' losses. Accomplishing either task demanded that underwriters know when and where fires would occur or, more reasonably, that they could predict how much to charge for insurance in order to cover losses. Successfully predicting losses required that underwriters be aware of how exposed their insured property was to the risk of fire and how frequently fires affected different types of property.

Gaining this knowledge proved exceedingly difficult in practice. As early as the 1810s, underwriters developed commonsense categories of analysis to assess a property's risk of burning, and, over time, refined them. These categories were based on the qualitative "experience" gradually being developed by company officials. In fact, many companies explicitly sought to develop wide-ranging knowledge about underwriting risks. The Aetna Fire Insurance Company's manual, issued in 1825, reflects this agenda. Updated and reissued periodically, this volume instructed agents on which types of structures were the best "risks." It also offered guidelines for setting premiums at levels sufficient to cover company losses. In addition, Aetna corresponded with agents about *every* policy they wrote. Should a policy be written on that particular type of property? Was the premium appropriate? This correspondence—along with requests to survey property—was intended to increase the company's expertise at underwriting insurance.

Despite their awareness of how important understanding fire behavior was, underwriters often failed to attain such knowledge. For instance, despite elaborate procedures, Aetna could not predict how much it would lose from year to year with any certainty. On more than one occasion the company nearly went bankrupt. It also frequently and indiscriminately raised rates to cover unforeseen losses. By 1847, the company had suspended using its *Guide to Agents*, frustrated by its ineffectiveness.[12]

In the 1850s the industry embraced a radically different approach to fire risk—an approach which, curiously enough, relied on many of its previous assumptions. Underwriters reconceptualized the built environment and fire risk in terms of the incipient capitalist economy and objective science. In an 1852 speech celebrating the 100th anniversary of the Philadelphia Contributionship for Loss from Fire, Horace Binney, a prominent Philadelphia lawyer, demanded that fire insurers be "scientific men." He further recommended that they observe "the course of events extensively and accurately." He reasoned that the industry could understand fire's behavior with great certainty.

> Such knowledge may be acquired, and with it a rule of insurance, at least approximately, sufficient for practical use . . . it is possible to obtain what may be called the law of any species of disaster in the place of observation, and in regard to fire something like a mortality table a table of injury as well as of mortality by that element, in the case of houses

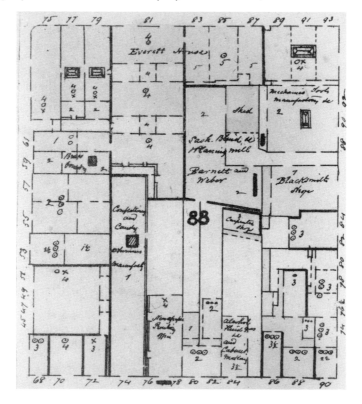

*Bascome Fire Insurance Map, 1857. Block 88 of downtown St. Louis is bordered by Olive, Locust, Third, and Fourth streets, with Locust Street to the north. Fire insurance maps began with the identification of construction, structure, and types of business found on commercial blocks, which enabled the insurance companies to judge the risk involved with each business desiring coverage. Reproduced from the Collections of the Library of Congress.*

and merchandise, and its variations in the case of particular trades, and in the different conditions of the agents and apparatus for arresting and extinguishing fires. Even a year's accurate observations may do something, though perhaps little. Ten years' observations may give a sensible approximation to a rule. And a century may give even the larger variations, the plague and cholera losses, I have called them.[13]

Binney's remarks signaled a significant shift in thinking among underwriters. This "scientific" approach, which was embraced explicitly in industry literature and in business practices, sought to achieve the translation, codification, and objectification of fire risk within the discourse of modern science.

To accomplish these goals, the insurance industry developed and used new information technologies to refine and re-create its previous analytical categories.

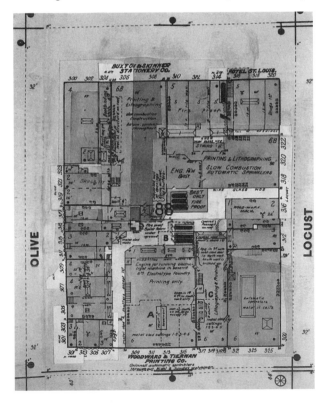

*Whipple Fire Insurance Map, 1897. The details of the maps drastically improved from those of the 1850s as they enabled the insurance companies to better judge the risks involved in coverage. Whipple conducted routine inspections of city property in order to keep their maps up-to-date, but the surveys went beyond the upkeep of the maps to offer a standard for the well-being of the business districts of cities.*

In 1852, for instance, Aetna began collecting, tabulating, and statistically averaging financial loss within different segments of its portfolio according to the physical characteristics of the property. When rating property, the company separated its portfolio into categories of "use" or "occupation"—such as dwellings, breweries, and rope walks.[14] Aetna subdivided these uses into "classes of buildings" distinguished by construction material and technique: first-class buildings were "externally fireproof in all particulars;" second-class buildings were "nearly externally fire proof;" third-class buildings were "ordinary" brick buildings; and fourth-class buildings were "frame."[15] In other words, a premium was assessed by determining a building's use and was adjusted according to construction materials (frame, stone, etc.) and the presence of other hazards.

Beginning in October 1852, Aetna compiled financial information for thirty-five property uses (or occupations.) For each type, it tabulated the total value of the insured property, the amount of premiums collected on it, and financial losses on that type (or use) of property. Next, it calculated the average premium it charged over a six month period. Between October 1852 and April 1853, for instance, Aetna insured "coffeehouses and saloons" valued at $134,599. It collected nearly $2,000 in premiums ($1,947.45), but paid more than $4,550 in losses. In the margins of the ledger, the company noted its loss of $2,602.55 during this six-month period.[16]

Expecting the results of past experience to predict future losses provided Aetna with renewed strategic direction in its daily business practices. In 1857, the company compiled a detailed financial perspective on its losses during the preceding five years. Objectifying fire risk within this classification system provided Aetna the confidence to reissue a new manual for agents in 1857. In its new manual, the company explained the usefulness of its comprehensive categories for statistically analyzing fire risk:

> This classification extends over such a period of time, and covers property to the amount of about one hundred millions annually, thus affording such a basis upon which we can depend with almost entire certainty in adapting rates of premium which will prove adequate to guard the office and its customers from any essential disappointments, provided our views are carried into effect.[17]

The quantitative record of Aetna's financial portfolio became the literal embodiment of fire risk and a guide to business practice. Indeed, the company's statistics reported what Aetna management already knew: insurance on substantially constructed dwellings were its greatest sources of profit. The company's aggregate statistics showed that its premium on dwellings averaged eighty-three cents (per $100 of insurance) between 1852 and 1857. Over the same period, though, the company paid out an average of twenty-three cents (per $100 of insurance) in losses. These statistics remained constant over the next two decades, but Aetna never reduced its rates on dwellings; instead, it preserved this type of insurance as a continual source of profit. By contrast, statistics also revealed seventeen types of property (by use) on which the company had suffered large financial losses, and the manual advised agents not to write policies on these risks.[18]

Statistical representation of risk took on new and magnified importance within the built environment when the insurance industry developed extensive maps of urban space coded according to the industry's organization of good and bad risks. Underwriters' statistical programs were graphically represented on expansive lithographs of most North American cities.[19] This process began when the Jefferson Insurance Company commissioned a map of fire risk in New York City in 1852. Surveyed in collaboration with fire underwriters, fire insurance maps represented the city as an aggregation of many individual, *and interrelated,* fire risks as they color-coded urban areas into districts of greater and lesser risk.

The format and categories used by surveyors were derived from the insurance industry and reflected the criteria underwriters used to set rates—i.e., how buildings were used and constructed. This should not surprise us because, after all, they were commissioned by, or drawn in collaboration with, underwriters. Almost immediately after William Perris published his map of New York City, the Insurance Company of North America bought a copy.[20] The meticulous examination of fire risk in the urban landscape, engendered in fire insurance maps, set new standards within the insurance industry. Between 1855 and 1857, Aetna's General Agent, A. A. Williams, traveled to Montreal and throughout Quebec. He surveyed Montreal block by block and informed agents which neighborhoods and streets in each city were appropriate places to solicit new business and in which areas they should divest themselves of bad risks.[21] By 1857, Aetna incorporated mapmaking instructions into its manuals and included templates that resembled commercial insurance maps as guides to making proper drawings.[22]

The link between fire underwriters and surveyors was drawn even more sharply on the maps themselves. In the 1850s, Perris and other surveyors represented urban fire risk using the language and categories of fire underwriters. Through a system of color coding, dots, and written description, fire insurance maps identified the use of a structure, depicted construction details, and arrayed property in space. They portrayed each of these categories in a different color, giving maps the visual effect of an elaborate quilt. In 1857, Ernest Hexamer, who had worked for Perris in New York City, represented Philadelphia; other major cities were mapped soon thereafter. In 1859, Western and Bascome surveyed St. Louis.[23]

Hexamer's maps represented Philadelphia explicitly in the terms and categories of the Philadelphia Board of Fire Underwriters's standard schedule for rating property. Using a complex matrix of broken, dashed, and whole lines alongside four brilliant colors (now faded hues of green, two shades of pink, and yellow), Hexamer's maps provided insight into building construction and use. They divided "regular" risks such as stores and dwellings into four categories color-coded by both use and construction: "Brick or Stone Stores," "Brick or Stone Dwellings," "Brick or Stone Dwellings with Stores under," "Frame Dwellings," and "Frame Dwellings with Stores under." In addition, Hexamer included a category of "specially hazardous" risks, which he classified according to the danger assessed to them by the Philadelphia Board of Fire Underwriters. For instance, "Bookbinders" and "Brass Founders" were both in the second class of specially dangerous risks, while "Bakers" and "Tobacco Manufacturers" were among the first class.[24] Later versions published by Hexamer (and other surveyors such as St. Louis's Augustus Whipple) dropped the insurance industry's nomenclature ("first class hazards") in favor of simple descriptive language ("brick, stone, . . .").[25]

Surveyors' categories for notating fire risk expanded during the last five decades of the nineteenth century. Map keys grew from one page to two pages as underwriters became more involved in an increasingly minute surveillance of the urban landscape. Such representations became more detailed according to the special conditions that underwriters believed shaped the incidence of fire. Maps listed the width, depth, and height of buildings as well as skylights, boilers, and roof construction. Later maps (those published after 1870) included information on street length and width, wall construction, fireproof construction, breaks between buildings, shutters, thickness of walls, and other architectural details. Finally, most maps diagrammed the relevant fire extinction infrastructure of the city, such as fire plugs, water mains (and their size), and alarm boxes.[26]

Outside the context of nineteenth-century concerns with fire and underwriters' business practices, fire insurance maps appear value free; they seem to be casual, but remarkably detailed, enumerations of the structural features of the built environment. But a closer observation of most insurance maps reveals that they were intensely used by underwriters and surveyors. Most obviously, as suggested above, these maps provided the basic information underwriters required to set rates. As noted above, they identified how a structure was used, how it was constructed, and how the structure was related in space to nearby buildings. Another noticeable quality of many insurance maps are the "pasteovers" covering them.[27] Frequently issued to their customers to be added on top of the existing maps, "pasteovers" kept maps current. Surveyors continuously inspected and regularly reexamined the built landscape as a service to their clients. Keeping the city under constant surveillance not only made insurance maps embody the changing urban environment, but it helped enforce the insurance industry's programmatic fire discipline.

Fire insurance surveys, which had adopted the terms, language, and categories of the industry, were incorporated into underwriting practice gradually over twenty years. Agents marked policy numbers on the maps. Extant maps frequently display penciled-in numbers consistent with underwriters' policy-numbering schemes. In addition to listing policy numbers, underwriters wrote the dollar value of the policies as well as their effective dates onto the maps. If a policy was not renewed, underwriters typically erased the information. Using the maps in this fashion kept agents appraised of where they had policies in force, and out-of-state insurance companies could keep track of all policies written by different agents in a given city. As a result, companies could avoid concentrating too much exposure to the risk of fire within one or two districts of a city.[28]

Beyond setting rates, these maps reveal how underwriters both initiated and were affected by the rationalization of the industry's practices. Objectification of fire risk remade underwriters' conceptions of space. Examining the diaries of A. A. Williams suggests how underwriters "read" the city in terms of this graphic re-imagining of urban space. Between 1855 and 1857, Williams visited the company's agencies throughout New England and Quebec. His diaries meticulously document the risks taken and the rates charged by each agency. In addition, they analyze city streets block by block. Williams's written description takes readers through the alleys, principal streets, and residential neighborhoods of Quebec City, alerting them to the arrangement of space, construction, and use of structures in each block and district.[29]

> Fabrique *[sic]* Street. 17 risks . . . $94,600 . . . Building stone, part wood & part tin covered from 2, 3, & 4 stories high; occupied principally for first class stores; one or two old buildings in this street; avoid them. The risks have been generally fine. Open south upper part of the street; market and open ground in front—French Cathedral stands at the east on upper end of the street.

Williams's diary reads like the insurance maps available in New York or Philadelphia. His description provides the same information as the colors, lines, and symbols of the Perris or Hexamer surveys; each document could provide all the information needed to establish a rate.[30]

When Williams recorded the specific hazards that threatened manufacturing facilities, he often included detailed spatial drawings. He outlined structures, noted building sizes (both the number of stories and the physical dimension), and diagrammed the distance between structures. He depicted the arrangement of the buildings associated with, or unassociated but nearby, a factory, and identified building use and construction details. Though Williams's drawings did not use the key or colored ink recommended by Aetna's manuals for agents, his maps' physical characteristics derive from the "Sample Diagram" provided in the 1857 manual.[31]

To this point, we have seen that fire insurance maps initiated the reordering of urban landscape around the insurance industry's nascent program of "scientific" underwriting. The disparate, seemingly disorganized, and constantly changing urban spatial arrangement was made coherent, and the values of the built landscape took on fixed meaning according to the dictates of fire risk. As read by fire underwriters, cartographic representations objectified fire risk and provided a visual, spatial context for their labor. In addition to conforming to insurance industry business practices, fire insurance maps redrew the relationships between the insured, agents, and fire underwriting companies. Just as Williams's diaries provide insights into how underwriters began to read the city, daily business records of a fire insurance surveying company in St. Louis—the Whipple Fire Insurance Protective Agency—reveal the process through which fire insurance maps shaped the consciousness of those who commissioned, used, and viewed its maps.

The Whipple Company extended the conceptual framework of "scientific underwriting" to the built environment of St. Louis. Active in St. Louis as early as 1870, Whipple maps of St. Louis and other midwestern cities resemble other nineteenth-century insurance atlases. Using the categories favored by insurers, these detailed drawings objectified fire risk in scale drawings of individual lots, blocks, and districts. Like other maps, Whipple's atlases can only tell us how the insurance industry imagined the city. Beyond their superficial function for underwriters, the maps do not provide deep insights into underwriting practice. For that, we need to examine the daily practices of nineteenth-century surveyors, such as those working for the Whipple Fire Insurance Protective Agency.

In 1875, Whipple began to publish *Whipple's Daily Fire Reporter*. This newsletter, published six days a week, offers an astounding comment on the pervasiveness, intensity, and scope of the insurance industry's surveillance of fire risk in the urban landscape. Indeed, the *Daily Fire Reporter* connects the development of "scientific underwriting" and its statistical categorization of fire risk with the spatial representation of those risks in atlas form.

Whipple sold subscriptions of its *Daily Fire Reporter* and other services to customers, including local and national insurance companies, their agents, and owners of commercial and industrial property within the city, as well as the local municipal government. Through the *Daily Fire Reporter*, Whipple performed many services for its subscribers. First, the company inspected and reinspected property (typically in the business district or along the city's wharves). When property owners failed to adhere to practices commonly associated with fire safety, their name, location, and variance were published. Second, Whipple also collected, and daily disseminated, information about the origins, causes, and responses to all fires and false alarms in the city. At the end of each year, the *Daily Fire Reporter* listed the aggregate statistics and often compared them to events in previous years. Finally, subscribers also purchased the opportunity to receive free of charge and/or purchase Whipple's other services. Whipple, for instance, could also be commissioned to survey individual commercial or industrial properties and produce an extensive report of fire risk at that location.

The single most important aspect of Whipple's business was its frequent inspections of property in the city. Whipple's program of inspection served the practical purpose of keeping maps updated and had more far-reaching implications. Inspections constituted a surveillance of property owners which coerced them into behaving according to the insurance industry's standard of conduct regarding the risk of fire. In 1882, for instance, Whipple performed 20,632 "inspections and re-inspections" of 3,267 buildings almost exclusively located in the business district of the city.[32] Indeed, at every location on the block, inspectors carefully examined "every story, cellar and attic of every building." Inspectors surveyed the buildings for any and all dangers of fire, ". . . be it rubbish, dangerous gas burners, defective flues, defective furnaces, careless disposition of ashes, careless use of open lights, etc., etc. . . ."[33] Every day company representatives examined various "blocks" in the city which corresponded to the "block" organization of Whipple Fire Insurance Maps. When Whipple announced it had inspected "Block 123" on September 1, 1882, it directed readers' attention to an area bounded by Franklin Avenue,

> On the second floor of No. 610 Franklin Avenue (R. B. Tunstall & Co.), a stovepipe is not safely adjusted in flue.
> On the attic floor of No. 612 Franklin Avenue (A. Mohl), there is an open stovepipe hole, the flue is used on first floor in cold weather. In the rear of first floor willow baskets are suspended over a gas jet. . . .

Naturally, Whipple's reports employed the language used by insurance companies and which appeared on Whipple's map keys. Agents, underwriters, or anyone familiar with the insurance industry could move from Whipple's reports to its maps to insurance policies with great ease.[34]

As much as they helped to reconceptualize the city's susceptibility to fire risk, inspections provided Whipple the means to physically intervene in the construction of the physical landscape. Each time surveyors discovered a material danger of fire, they brought them to the attention of the occupants and owners of the building. In addition, the next morning the *Daily Fire Reporter* publicized which properties had passed inspection and which had not. Although on some occasions there were no hazards found in a block, usually Whipple's surveyors found fire risks. The *Reporter* would comment on those dangers. An entry from December 1882, noted the hazards that gasoline and rubbish posed:

INSPECTION OF BUILDINGS.
Block 36. At Nos. 514 and 518 South Second Street Gasoline is used.
Ashes and rubbish are deposited against fence and outhouses at Nos.
508, 510, 514, & 518 South Second Street.[35]

A strict program of reinspection buttressed the effectiveness of Whipple's program of inspection—especially when it came to pressuring property owners to accede to Whipple's recommendations. Every Monday, Whipple employees reinspected the risks they had reported the previous week. If dangers had not been removed, the building and its occupants were once again reported:

INSPECTION OF BUILDINGS.
re-inspection.—All dangers of fire reported for the week ending
Thursday, January 19, 1882, have been removed, with the following
exception:
At No. 623 Locust Street (Read's Restaurant), a cooking range is in use,
the floor beneath which is not protected.[36]

Reporting unsafe conditions for the first time almost always appears to have caused the removal of the fire hazard. Announcing the presence of fire dangers for a second time brought even more pressure on the occupants (and/or owners) to remove the dangers of fire. Whipple did more than simply examine the city for fire risk; the company used its program of surveillance to force compliance with the insurance industry's evolving understanding of safety.[37]

Municipal officials confirmed and legitimized Whipple's authority. In the first half of 1882, the Daily Fire Reporter frequently reprinted a small notice from the Chief of the St. Louis Fire Department offering assistance to Whipple. The note from fire chief H. C. Sexton, dated February 1876, commended and approved of Whipple's plan for inspections and further advised that "should parties refuse to comply with your request to have dangers of fire remedied, I (Sexton) will render you such assistance as may be needed."[38] In August 1882, the company announced that it had received a letter from John Beattie, Commissioner of Public Buildings, regarding its system of inspection:

> I have investigated your system of inspecting buildings (for the purpose of abating fire dangers), and in approving the same, I will say, that wherever dangers of fire exist and the parties responsible refuse or neglect to comply with your requests in the premises, I will render you all necessary assistance.[39]

At regular intervals and in their year-end assessment of risk in the city, the company reiterated its relationship with the building commissioner and the municipal government. Whipple explained how its relationship with the building commissioner's office operated. If a property owner refused to remove fire hazards after a second visit by the company's inspectors, then in addition to publishing a notice of the hazard in the *Daily Fire Reporter*, Whipple sent the "party a notice signed by Mr. John Beattie, the City Building Inspector, who is legally authorized to enforce the removal of dangers by fire. We have a volume of blank notices in our office made in duplicate—when we send a notice to the party we also send a duplicate to the above named official so that he is informed of what use we are making his name." In cases of particularly acute danger, Whipple skipped the process of reinspection and immediately informed Beattie's office. The *Daily Fire Reporter* noted that the notices sent to the building commissioner "usually" had their desired effect; further, when no attention was paid by a property owner to a notice of hazard, Beattie "never failed to enforce our recommendations."[40]

Judging from the *Daily Fire Reporter*, however, long before the summer of 1882 the risks of fire discovered by the Whipple Company were removed. This indicates that Whipple's authority in matters of inspection did not solely derive from its relationship to civic authorities. Rather, Whipple's ability to coerce property owners into complying with its suggestions developed out of the company's complex relationship to the fire insurance industry.

Through its program of inspection, Whipple established itself as an intermediary between underwriters, agents, and the insured. Having a third party survey and analyze property eased conflicts between the parties to the fire insurance contract. Whipple performed the inspections that agents were encouraged to do on a regular basis thus lightening the load of agents and giving underwriting companies more control over how the agents conducted business. If Whipple's maps or inspections consistently indicated that a particular "risk" was especially dangerous, insurers could advise agents not to renew that property. Rather than relying on agents to assess the fire risk of a particular property—a decision which some in the industry thought could be affected by agents' desire to get business—underwriters used maps and inspections to assess risk independently of an agent. In addition, companies also could be more bold in entering markets distant from their "home office" because they could be assured quality representations of fire risk in those places.

In addition, Whipple's inspections provided crucial information to property owners. At a time when insurance contracts paid only two-thirds or three-fourths of the value of goods lost, property owners bore a substantial portion of the risk. Consequently, inspections gave them the ability to diminish their financial liability. Inspections also provided evidence that owners were abiding by the strict terms of the fire insurance contract—information that may have been useful when entering into disputes with underwriters about claims or the terms of their contract.

Evidence that the Whipple Company was aware of these relationships appears in its 1883 explanation of its inspection process. The company advised that it is not necessary for "insurance agents with a line on the risk (which did not pass inspection)" to visit the property owner. Through inspection, re-inspection, and publishing the results of its surveillance, Whipple assured its readers that fire hazards would be corrected. Moreover, if that failed, city officials would step in to remedy the problem. The threat of government intervention served as an important supplement to, rather than a substitute for, the authority that the insurance market conferred upon the Whipple Insurance Protective Agency.

By inspecting the built landscape, mapping agencies (such as Whipple) deepened their understanding of fire risk. Yet, property inspections operated less to produce new conceptual information than to codify and apply existing knowledge. But how did the company know what dangers to look for? Certainly, the categories for analyzing this environmental danger derived from common sense. As much as that is true, though, the underwriting community's categories for evaluating danger also developed out of the other cornerstone of Whipple's business (and insurance industry practice)—active enumeration, accumulation, and quantification of the incidence and causes of fire.

The Whipple Agency sought to demystify and comprehend fire in rational terms by dissecting previous incidents of fire. Indeed, while drawing attention to the dangers of fire by underscoring its often dire economic costs in the *Daily Fire Reporter*, the Whipple Agency strove to identify the causes of fire. Enumerating the causes of fire served several purposes. It legitimized Whipple's authority on the subject within the St. Louis community—especially in regard to St. Louis's built landscape. Second, Whipple's expertise at identifying the causes of fires authorized (and was simultaneously authorized by) the company's parallel services of mapping and inspections (more on these in a moment). Finally, Whipple's efforts can be understood as a crucial component of the fire insurance industry's increasingly sophisticated and detailed production of knowledge regarding the risks of fire.

As often as possible the *Daily Fire Reporter* quantified or evaluated everything about a blaze from the total financial loss to insurance loss to the origins of a fire. For instance, on January 24, 1882, the *Daily Fire Reporter* announced that on the previous day a fire was caused when a child lit a match to determine how much gasoline had spilled in the barbershop. At other times, entries were more speculative about the origins of a particular blaze. The Cass Avenue conflagration of July 21, 1882, "originated in the cellar (of the Cass Avenue Planing Mill Co.), which contained main line of shafting, and was probably caused by a hot box." Even so, over 20 percent of the time in 1882, the Whipple Fire Insurance Protective Agency could not determine the origins of a fire.[41]

Whipple expanded and quantified its understanding of fire causes into monthly and yearly reports of the causes, origins, and dangers of fire in the city. In its "Monthly Fire Report" for July 1882, Whipple noted that over $120,000 in fire loss had happened in the city; of that, approximately $115,000 had been covered by insurance. There were 42 fire alarms, 3 false alarms, a second alarm, and 19 "still" fires. Of the 57 "causes" of the month's fires, 19 were unknown, and 10 fires had been caused by fireworks—not a surprising fact given the July 4th holiday.[42] Moreover, just as insurance companies tabulated statistical records of losses yearly, Whipple created a year-end statistical portrait of fire loss and fire risk in St. Louis—a record often placed within the context of statistics gathered in previous years. In 1882, for instance, the company analyzed fire risk and loss in 1881 according to the following categories: "Causes of Fires in the Past Year," "Occupancy of Buildings in which Fires Originated," types of buildings where fires originated, a month-by-month accounting of "Loss," "Insurance," and "Loss to Insurance Companies," "Recapitulation for the Past Thirteen Years," and the "Building Inspections."[43]

At the same time, The *Daily Fire Reporter* gave each fire a cash value, thus identifying the threat of fire (to the well-being of both the community and property owners) as being primarily economic. An early morning blaze in January 1882 caused $100 of damage to a barber shop and another "small loss" to a perfumerer. Not all blazes caused such small losses. On July 19, 1882, a fire destroyed an entire block of Cass Avenue (813 to 825) and the Cass Avenue Planing Mill Company. The *Daily Fire Reporter* listed all twenty-seven insurance companies which had insured the Planing Mill Co. for $4,500 on damage to the building and $23,500 on the "contents"—both stock and machinery. The same blaze also destroyed a furniture factory:

> Nos. 809 and 811 Cass Avenue, a two story brick building owned by
> Wm. Medley, and occupied by Wolf, Kraemer, and Co. as a furniture
> factory. Stock and machinery destroyed. Building well burned out.
>
> Wolf, Kraemer & Co.'s Insurance

| | Stock | Mach'y. |
|---|---|---|
| Firemen's, of Ohio | $250 | $500 |
| Metropole, of Paris | 375 | 125 |
| American Central | 1,000 | |
| Pennsylvania Fire | 500 | |
| State of Iowa | | 500 |
| Amazon, of Cin | 375 | 125 |
| Phoenix, of London | 750 | 500 |
| Total | $3,250 | $1,750 |

In addition to the loss on Cass Avenue, other unrelated fires in the city in the early morning hours of July 21 caused over $100,000 in damage and substantial loss to insurance companies.[44]

The *Daily Fire Reporter* valorized fire insurance as the best method to combat fire. Emphasizing that fire danger could be combated, the *Daily Fire Reporter* distinguished between property and business owners who purchased fire insurance and those who had not. In January 1882, it contrasted an uninsured barbershop owner who lost $100 with the perfumerer who suffered a small loss but had "$600 in the Watertown." The Daily Fire Underwriter did not just encourage the purchase of insurance (or more of it). It also provided object lessons for underwriters which variated from prudent business practices. For example, the *Daily Fire Reporter* listed conflagrations and large fires in other cities as well as detailing heavy losses which resulted from sweeping fires in St. Louis, such as the blaze along Cass Avenue in July 1882. This warned insurance companies against taking risks that were too large or too closely concentrated.[45]

As the *Reporter* enumerated the horrors of fire, it recognized the benevolence of the underwriting community. In particular, it documented the role fire underwriters played in reducing fire losses by highlighting the work of the Underwriters Salvage Corps in minimizing fire loss. On occasion, the Daily Fire Reporter would praise the corps in short notices:

> The Salvage Corps of St. Louis have made a splendid record for 1881,
> and have saved to the insurance companies and property owners many
> times the cost of their maintenance. We could mention a number of

times the cost of their maintenance. We could mention a number of instances where the value of their services could hardly be overestimated. While the cost of supporting them is large, it is trivial when compared with the services they render. "They come high, but we must have 'em."[46]

Subscribed to by business, insurance agents, and underwriting companies, the salvage corps, or "insurance patrol" as it was sometimes called, used tarpaulins to cover items on the lower floors of a building to prevent collateral damage to property caused by water. Though not formally part of the fire department, the salvage corps quite often helped extinguish fires, as happened on the morning of September 4, 1882, when they put out a fire in a three-story brick building.[47]

Beginning in the 1850s, fire underwriters reconceptualized and objectified fire risk in the language of statistical science; by the 1860s fire insurance mapping companies, such as the Whipple Fire Insurance Mapping Agency discussed in this essay, began to represent "scientific underwriting" of urban fire risks on large-scale maps. By the 1890s, through codifying and inspecting fire risk within the built environment, surveyors helped the work of making urban American safe from fire.

Despite the growing depth and breadth of knowledge about the danger of fire, changes in the built environment occurred gradually, and in piecemeal fashion, through the nineteenth century—and accelerated dramatically during the twentieth century. For example, charting change in St. Louis's congested district demonstrates one way in which the built environment was transformed. A special inset in Whipple's 1896 insurance map depicts all the major buildings in that area which adhered to principles of "fireproof construction." Widespread use of "fireproof" techniques indicates that underwriters' rationalization and reconceptualization of fire risk began to take material form in the built environment during the last decades of the nineteenth century.

Even so, the nineteenth-century insurance industry had not yet developed a unified program of intervention to accompany its commitment to understanding and objectifying fire risk. Immense differences within the industries hindered the development of such a systematic approach; indeed, insurance company practice was determined by their position within the industry vis-à-vis what sorts of risks they took. Although nearly all companies compiled statistics and represented fire risk on insurance maps, how they used that information varied widely. For instance, companies which had a varied business (i.e. wrote policies in many different cities and towns and/or on many different types of properties) sought to make profit by predicting losses and dispersing their financial exposure (to fire risk) across space. These companies were especially interested in diminishing economic losses associated with "sweeping" fires.

By contrast, factory mutual insurance companies, such as the one established by New England textile manufacturers, could not disperse their risks (because they generally underwrote a single type of manufacturing facility). In order to earn a profit they had to find ways to prevent the incidence of fire altogether. Such companies pioneered or were at the forefront of innovations in factory design, fireproofing, and preventive devices such as sprinklers. Such differences hindered the industry, as a whole, from developing a comprehensive and systematic approach to fire risk. In addition, underwriters appear to have had relatively little political power to affect legal reform in building codes. After the devastating 1871 Chicago fire, for instance, underwriters' efforts to curb wooden reconstruction met with surprisingly little success.[48]

Moreover, property owners and builders frequently circumvented underwriters' attempts to shape building practices. Many (though, over time, fewer) property owners did *not* insure their property, and as a consequence, they lay outside the insurance industry's sphere of influence. More often, property owners took advantage of fierce competition among fire insurance agents and companies. Competing on price, which was commonplace within the industry at times during the nineteenth century, undermined the ability of fire underwriters to use economic incentive to reduce fire dangers.[49]

For these reasons, and others, wholesale and systematic changes in the built landscape did not occur until well into the twentieth century. In 1905, the National Board of Fire Underwriters and the National Fire Protection Association first recommended uniform fire codes as voluntary standards. Shortly thereafter municipalities began to adopt such rules and all new construction became subject to building standards championed by the insurance industry. However, at the heart of twentieth-century fire codes lay the work of nineteenth-century fire underwriters, surveyors, and statisticians. By objectifying the risk of fire in the language of statistical science and implementing an expansive program of surveillance, insurers re-imagined fire risk and inititated a program to make cities less subject to that particular environmental danger.[50]

# Busby's Stink Boat and the Regulation of Nuisance Trades, 1865-1918

## *Andrew Hurley*

On the evening of July 18, 1873, several hundred angry residents from south St. Louis, mostly German mechanics in their shirt sleeves, gathered at Union Park to attend a public meeting. As a series of political officials implored them to remain calm and to lodge their grievances with the appropriate authorities, cries of "Cut her loose," "Set her on fire," and "Blow her up," rippled through the restless audience. When the meeting broke up, many of those in attendance returned peacefully to their homes. But about two hundred who were not satisfied with the conservative course urged by the speakers decided to take matters into their own hands and began marching east toward the levee, continuing to chant "Cut her loose! Cut her loose!" along the way. Upon reaching the levee, the protesters were confronted by a squad of armed police officers who forcibly blocked them from reaching the object of their wrath, Busby's stink boat.[1]

Busby's stink boat was a rendering establishment, an enterprise engaged in the business of boiling dead animal carcasses to extract the fat, grease, and bone material for use in other manufacturing processes. Several years earlier, John Busby, the owner of the vessel, had operated his rendering business in the outlying suburban community of Cheltenham. It was a profitable business, because under a special agreement worked out with the city of St. Louis, Busby had secured the monopoly rights to render all animals found dead on the city streets and in the sewers. But Cheltenham residents complained vociferously about the odious smells that poured from the open steam tanks. Determined to drive Busby from their midst, Cheltenham citizens brought several lawsuits against him. Busby, pestered incessantly by his disgruntled neighbors and subjected to a series of fines in county court, asked the city of St. Louis to assist him in moving to another location. As a prominent official in the Democratic party, and a close friend of Joseph Brown, mayor of St. Louis, he was certain that the city would come through for him, and it did. In 1871, the city council voted to buy Busby a steamboat with the provision that he dock it at the foot of Barton Street and take it out on the river before performing any rendering operations in order to spare the nostrils of St. Louis residents.[2]

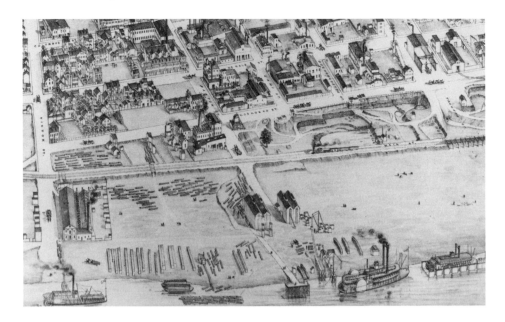

*Pictorial of St. Louis near Barton Street, 1875. The riverfront at the foot of Barton Street was the designated location the city of St. Louis offered to Busby and his stink boat. Lithograph by Richard Compton and Camille N. Dry.*

Busby accepted the city's offer but did not abide by its provisions. Figuring he was immune to the law due to his wealth, power, and prestige—he had recently been elected a county judge—Busby decided to carry on the rendering right there on the foot of Barton street. While the new arrangement suited Busby, the working-class, predominantly German population that lived in the vicinity did not take kindly to this new nuisance in their neighborhood. They already had to contend with the rancid smells from the Schaeffers Soap factory and the equally pungent aromas from a nearby candle works. Yet these smells paled in comparison to those flowing from Busby's rendering boat, which residents described as a "festering sore, breeding sickness and death in our neighborhood."[3] According to one newspaper article, "the villainous smell issuing from that floating stink pot on ordinary occasions is almost unbearable. During the hot nights of summer the people living within ten or fifteen blocks of it are compelled to tightly close their doors and windows to bar out the stench."[4]

Much like their counterparts in Cheltenham, citizens of south St. Louis demanded that Busby clean up his operations or leave. During the spring and summer of 1873, they lodged a series of formal protests with the mayor, the city council, the Board of Health, and the police. City officials, however, were slow to respond. Busby assured his political friends that he had the situation under control, having recently acquired a special "Chicago patent" for consuming offensive stenches. His neighbors remained unconvinced.[5] It was not until the situation became volatile in mid-July, when it appeared as if mob violence might erupt, that the mayor decided to take action. In the aftermath of the incident on the waterfront, Mayor Brown concluded it would be best if yet another location was found for the rendering boat. He determined that Arsenal Island, opposite Cahokia, Illinois, in the Mississippi River, would be the most suitable place and offered his friend Busby a plot of land at that location. Predictably, Busby's move to Arsenal Island ended one chapter of the saga only to open another. Almost immediately, Illinois residents downwind of the new location began to protest, demanding relief from Busby's noxious fumes.[6]

The story of Busby's boat highlights a fundamental dilemma faced by St. Louis as it grappled with new forms of pollution during the Gilded Age: how to balance the needs of manufacturing with heightened popular concern about pollution in a rapidly growing metropolis. As municipal government assumed broader powers to protect the general health and welfare of its inhabitants, this dilemma was thrust upon the stage of local politics. Indeed, the tension between economic growth and environmental quality demanded mediation by governmental authorities and the development of a viable public policy. In many respects, the ad hoc response to Busby's boat foretold the approach that would be underwritten by the official policy of the St. Louis Board of Health, and later codified into law with the adoption of a comprehensive zoning plan in the early twentieth century. To a certain extent, city officials would rely on technological solutions—pollution control mechanisms such as the one that Busby claimed would consume his stenches. The dominant response, however, followed in the tradition of quarantining offensive trades, usually in areas where political opposition was weakest, property values were lowest, and residents were poorest. Thus, the late nineteenth-century approach to industrial pollution had less to do with abating emissions than with allocating social costs. In this way, an evolving policy for addressing nuisances constituted a crucial step in the growing fragmentation of urban space where environmental quality was linked with the social characteristics of particular neighborhoods.

Environmental nuisances were endemic to urban America in the decades following the Civil War. Increased population density in the nation's major commercial centers generated unprecedented levels of garbage and filth. At the same time, the growth of large-scale manufacturing introduced city dwellers to types of waste material they had never before encountered. Oil refineries spilled petroleum and sulfuric acid into waterways and surrounding marshlands. Iron and steel furnaces spewed fine metallic oxides into the atmosphere, obscuring urban skylines in a red haze. Pulp and paper mills were notorious for clogging rivers with lime sludge, bleach, pulp fibers, and assorted dyes and chemicals. While the precise matrix of industrial wastes varied considerably from one city to another, virtually all major metropolises had to put up with the stenches of slaughterhouses, the acidic emissions from gas houses, and the smoke that issued forth from the steam engines that had come to replace raw animal power in large factories and many medium sized craft shops as well.[7]

As one of the nation's largest manufacturing cities, St. Louis generated more than its share of industrial pollution. According to data from the 1880 federal census, flour milling, slaughtering, machine-shop products, chewing tobacco, and malt liquor led the list of manufacturing industries. The city was also a center for paint manufacturing, brickmaking, bag production, and ironmaking. All of these processes generated copious amounts of waste. Brick kilns spewed dust into the surrounding atmosphere; bagging factories discharged fine mists of flax and jute particles; beer brewing left residues of grain laden swill, and paint manufacturing released massive quantities of lead dust.

By the late nineteenth century, St. Louis had already developed a reputation for its smoky skies. The widespread adoption of the steam engine for industrial processing transformed St. Louis into a city of belching smokestacks. The consumption of coal in steam boilers was enormous. Flour mills, for example, consumed up to 50,000 bushels annually. Foundries, steel mills, brick kilns and other industrial operations that required heavy applications of heat used equally large amounts. Making matters worse, St. Louisans relied on a particularly dirty form of bituminous coal that was in great abundance in underground seams across the river in Illinois. Factory discharges were compounded by other sources of coal smoke. Railroads passing through the city left thick trails of black carbon particles in their wake. In and around freight and passenger depots the accumulation of railroad smoke could become especially dense.[8]

Citizens did not accept the proliferation of urban wastes as a matter of course. When pollution aggravated their nerves or caused discomfort, residents voiced their discontent. A sample of complaints delivered to the St. Louis Board of Health during the fiscal year 1878-79 illustrates both the wide range of objectionable practices and the broad geographic scope of the problem. A Cass Avenue brickyard located on the city's near north side drew criticism from local residents when it substituted coal for wood in its brickburning operation. According to city officials, neighbors found the resulting smoke to be "dense, black, and stifling." Breweries were frequently the source of popular grievances. Homeowners and renters who lived in the vicinity of Eighth and Crittenden Streets objected to the incessant clatter and clanging produced by keg cleaning operations at the Anheuser Busch brewery. The proprietor of another establishment on Cowan Street angered people in the area by dumping his waste beer into the street. A south side brewer provoked a similar response when he began discharging swill into a nearby cave. In the same part of the city, an axle grease factory was cited as a nuisance on several counts. Neighbors complained about the unbearable odors arising from the rosin oil and other ingredients of axle grease used during the course of preparation, smoke from the chimney, and the threat of fire due to the handling of highly combustible materials. Even in suburban areas, manufacturing collided with the sensibilities of residents. The inhabitants of Cheltenham, having successfully rid themselves of Busby's boat, still contended with a local silver smelter whose noxious fumes and gases killed shrubbery and trees.[9]

In virtually all parts of the city, stagnant ponds served as receptacles for both domestic and industrial wastes. Some of these ponds were natural phenomena, sinkholes produced by fissures in the underground limestone. Others were created by human action. To procure rocks and soil for the building of roads, workers dug pits in the ground. Over time, dirty water from streets and gutters drained into these gaping holes and accumulated. Manufacturers showed little compunction about adding their own wastes to the already contaminated brew, thereby compounding the problem. During the 1870s and 1880s, city officials received between 50 and 175 complaints annually regarding the sorry condition of these pestilential ponds.[10]

Pollution complaints varied. Sometimes they were simply a matter of aesthetics or of inconvenience. On other occassions, pecuniary concerns were cited. For instance, proprietors of the Schulenburg & Baeckeler Lumber Company maintained that the odors produced by the St. Louis Sanitary Company's rendering plant on Hall Street were destroying their business. Apparently, the stench was so offensive that customers were driven away.[11] Property holders were equally quick to condemn offensive manufacturing operations when their property values were at stake. Such was the case when fifty property owners attended a local Board of Health meeting in the summer of 1893 to voice their objections to the Goodwin Manufacturing Company, a maker of candles. A widow named Meyer informed the board that on account of the smells emananting from the candle works, all of her tenants had moved out, leaving her without any means of support. Another protester claimed that he would be forced to sell his property for half of its original value if Goodwin persisted in its pollution.[12]

Of all the causes for complaint, however, none was greater than the threat that nuisance industries posed to human health. According to the prevailing medical theories of the day, infectious disease evolved from putrefying organic matter and was transmitted by poisonous fogs, or miasmas. As an editorial on the subject in the *St. Louis Globe-Democrat* explained, "the highest medical authorities of great cities have declared that the poison with which the air becomes charged by the decomposition of animal matter is the cause of typhus and scarlet fevers and other malignant disorders."[13] Hence, while fumes from steel smelters, noise from keg cleaners, and smoke from brick yards might generate complaint based on the aggravation they caused, manufacturing establishments that handled decaying animal matter were singled out for especially harsh condemnation.

St. Louisans found plenty to condemn because animal parts formed the basis of an elaborate manufacturing network during the late nineteenth century. The chain began at the slaughterhouses, where live animals were butchered for human consumption. Once all the edible material was carved and packed, however, there was plenty of animal left for other commercial uses. Hides went to hide houses and tanneries for curing. Rendering establishments accepted fatty material from the slaughterhouses along with dead animals from other sources. Together, they were steamed in large tanks to distill tallow and

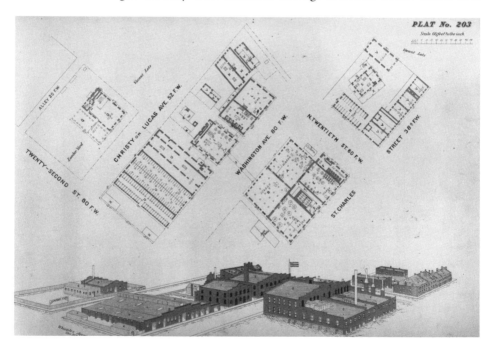

*N. Schaeffer's Soap and Candle Works, 1878. Odors emanating from soap and candle factories were blamed for a drop in property value in the surrounding neighborhoods. Schaeffer, however, kept his factories open due to his involvement with the city council. Whipple's Insurance Maps, 2nd series, special risk revised edition, lithograph by A. Gast and Co.*

lard, products which were then used in the manufacture of soap and candles. Bone-boiling and bone-burning works cooked and ground animal bones for the production of fertilizer and bone-black, the latter being employed to clarify syrups at sugar refineries. Fertilizer plants also received discarded materials from the rendering establishments. Food discarded by kitchens in hotels, steamboats, and boardinghouses was also recycled. Much of this waste, commonly known as slops, went to grease works, where it was cooked in iron-bottomed vats to extract the raw materials needed for soap-making.[14]

Because decaying animal matter generated noxious odors, citizens relied on their sense of smell to detect the presence of disease-producing gases. Indeed, the offensiveness of a stench was taken as a measure of its potency. It was widely assumed that the worse something smelled, the more injurious it was to human health. Hence, complaints about particular nuisances were usually laced with vivid descriptions of the odors produced and the effects on people's olfactory sensibilities. Offal and spoiled meat carted from slaughterhouses to soap factories was described as "so putrid that a wagon loaded with it can be smelled for miles. . . and while rendering the fetid smell sickens inhabitants for miles around."[15] In one part of the city, the stenches from a group of bone factories were said to be so powerful that they "slowed the incoming trains."[16]

The frequent epidemics that swept through nineteenth-century cities, claiming thousands of victims at a time, gave particular urgency to these health concerns. Cholera was particularly destructive and dreaded by urban dwellers in St Louis and elsewhere. The disease had ravaged St. Louis in the past, claiming more than 4,000 victims in 1849, and another 1,500 only six years later. Attempts to disinfect contaminated air through the open burning of tar and sulphur and efforts to prevent further noxious exhalations by covering the ground with chloride of lime had little effect, thereby testifying to the potency of the cholera poison in the public mind.[17] Fear of cholera and other contagious diseases kept citizens constantly on the alert for conditions that might generate deadly miasmas.

If post–Civil War St. Louisans were fairly certain about the root causes of their public health problems, they were frustrated with the legal mechanisms available for addressing them. Nuisance provisions in common-law doctrine enabled private citizens to seek legal redress on the grounds that polluters interfered with their property rights. This strategy had severe limitations, however, because it relied on the initiative of individual citizens, many of whom lacked the resources necessary to engage in long and costly legal battles. Furthermore, most courts, eager to promote economic growth, were predisposed in favor of the polluters. Judges interpreted nuisances very narrowly and demanded conclusive evidence linking a particular manufacturing process to a particular social effect. Also, favorable decisions on behalf of plaintiffs did not necessarily result in abatement of the offense; judges could simply reward the complainant with damage payments.[18]

The limited recourse available through common-law provisions prompted many cities, including St. Louis, to broaden their authority to regulate nuisances through the power of the state. On the eve of the Civil War, the city's municipal code already proscribed certain waste disposal and manufacturing practices with the aim of protecting public health. The law explicitly forbade distillers, soap boilers, tallow chandlers, and dyers from discharging "foul or nauseous liquor" upon any surrounding grounds or into any adjacent streets. Slaughterhouse regulations mandated that floors in all such establishments be constructed to prevent the seepage of waste matter into the soil and that drainage gutters be constructed to carry blood and offal to garbage receptacles. The city also employed a team of street inspectors to roam the city in search of any public nuisances and to order their abatement.[19]

It was not until the spring of 1867, shortly after another vicious cholera epidemic claimed over 3,500 lives, that the city established a Board of Health with broad powers to designate and abate nuisances. Previous municipal health agencies, staffed by part-time political apointees, had neither the resources nor the legal authority to compel private property holders to amend their offensive practices.[20] The new board, composed of three physicians and two private citizens, was empowered to "give all such directions and adopt all such measures for cleansing and purifying all such buildings, lots, and other places." In other words, the agency could promulgate new sanitary regulations as it saw fit. In addition, the enabling legislation authorized the agency to monitor the activities of slaughterhouses, dairies, distilleries, tanneries, and "every subject that can possibly affect the sanitary condition of the city." Noncompliance with Board of Health edicts could result in fines of up to five hundred dollars and even the termination of business.[21] Over the course of the next several decades, the city's nuisance codes were expanded to strengthen the agency's hand. By the early 1890s, legislatively designated nuisances included not only slaughterhouses, dairies, distilleries, soap works, and tallow renderers, but also candle shops, varnish works, glue makers, oil refineries, hemp manufacturers, and white-lead factories.[22]

By virtue of its broad powers, the St. Louis Board of Health enjoyed an opportunity to devise and execute a systematic nuisance policy that would not have been possible under the provisions of common law or the weak municipal codes of the pre–Civil War period. A review of its actions during its first few years of operation reveal a fairly ambitious agenda. Initially, a preoccupation with cholera kept the board and its staff busy disinfecting river boats arriving from southern destinations and quarantining sick passengers. Yet, the fledgling agency also devoted a considerable amount of energy to potential sources of disease already existing within the city. A sanitary police force consisting of twelve inspectors—the number was reduced to six during the winter months— was charged to investigate citizen complaints and find remedies. In addition to inspecting the conditions of tenement houses, supervising the collection of garbage, and regulating the quality of ice and milk, the agency monitored the condition of slaughterhouses, stock yards, and tanneries.[23] To further strengthen the regulation of nuisances, the municipal police department was authorized to issue summonses for violation of city pollution ordinances.[24]

Although the Police Department and Board of Health took their mandates seriously, they refrained from heavy-handed actions that might inflict financial harm on manufacturing enterprises. As the president of the Board of Health made clear upon taking office in 1868, "Our Board disclaims any idea or intention of making regulation, or issuing orders, calculated to oppress any business interest of the city."[25] The implications of this approach were that few industries were closed down, even though the agency had the power to do so. As the Board's chief sanitary officer explained some twelve years later, the complaints of citizens had to be weighed carefully against the large amount of capital invested in buildings and machinery by the owners of manufacturing plants. It would not be fair, he maintained, to summarily close down or expel an establishment given the financial hardship that would be placed on the proprietor.[26]

Politics also worked to protect polluters from harsh disciplinary action. In many instances, the perpetrators of public health menaces were among the most powerful people in the city. As the case of Busby's boat illustrated, the owners of manufacturing establishments often held office or were well-connected in political circles. When they found it necessary, they wielded their influence to deflect enforcement of sanitary regulations. Schaeffer's hide house on Easton Avenue was, acording to one aggrieved citizen, "the most abominable stink-house in the city."[27] Appearing before the Board of Health, the owner of the establishment contended that his operation was neither unhealthful nor a nuisance. The board concurred and decided to suspend disciplinary action. The reason, as reported by the press, was simply that Schaeffer was a member of the city council.[28]

Manufacturers also applied political pressure through the creation of formal and informal lobbying organizations. In this manner, the city's brewers were successful in thwarting the Board of Health's efforts to control the sale of adulterated milk. Of the opinion that high levels of infant mortality were attributable to milk from cows fed on distillery wastes, the Board of Health prohibited the sale of brewery swill to dairies in the spring of 1867. The distillers were incensed, claiming that this regulation cut into their profits.

Dairymen also objected and formed an association, the Milkmen's Society, to fight the order. Hiring some of the ablest and most expensive lawyers in the city, the society threatened legal action. At the same time, it swamped the agency with lengthy petitions and arguments. In a matter of months, the board backed down and rescinded the order on a temporary basis. Ten years later, distilleries were still selling the swill to milk dairies.[29]

Given this reluctance to impose financial hardships, city officials were quick to accept the polluter's word that simple technological fixes would alleviate nuisances and solve and douse public rancor. Just as Judge Busby claimed that a recently invented device would eliminate the smells from his boat, other manufacturers made grand claims on behalf of mysterious gizmos and contraptions that promised to purify their emissions and miraculously turn dirty operations into clean ones. When the owner of Hanson's bone factory was hauled before a hearing conducted by the Board of Health, he pleaded for a suspended sentence on the grounds that he had just purchased a "patent stink-killing apparatus" that would render the air emissions "wholesome." The request was granted.[30]

Sometimes, relatively rudimentary devices could make a world of difference. Many of the city's soap-grease establishments cooked kitchen slops in open tanks, thereby allowing fumes to float freely into the atmosphere. By covering the tanks with steam-tight lids and by drawing the gases into the furnace below by means of a pipe, foul emissions could be greatly reduced.[31] More often than not, however, the miracle solutions trumped up by manufacturers failed to meet expectations, forcing the board to pursue a more systematic means of regulating polluters. While health officials continued to lean on sloppy manufacturers to keep their premises clean, to repair leaky machinery, and to apply appropriate pollution control devices where applicable, they recognized that to a large extent, industrial pollution was unavoidable, a price to be paid for the presence of certain types of economic activity.[32] Thus, regulation ultimately boiled down to a question of allocating these costs. Increasingly, the board looked to geography as a means of sparing certain people from the environmental burdens of manufacturing while placing the burden on others.

From its inception in 1868, the Board of Health considered the spatial implications of the nuisance problem. In the opinion of the board, the key issue was the location of slaughterhouses. When the new board took office, 180 slaughterhouses lay scattered about the city. In virtually all of these neighborhoods, the butcheries posed a nuisance to surrounding residents on account of the discarded offal and blood, and the smells generated by decaying animal flesh. But it was not simply the offensiveness of the slaughterhouses that concerned the city's new health officials. Other firms that used parts of dead animals in their manufacturing process tended to locate next to or near the slaughterhouses to procure their raw materials. Hence, there arose numerous clusters of soap factories, tanneries, glue works, and other such establishments. Health officials recognized that these activities were essential to the viable functioning of a thriving metropolis, yet it struck them as unnecessary to subject such a high proportion of the urban population to the undesirable side effects. Better to centralize these offensive operations in just a few locations, they reasoned, so as to minimize the social cost. Since slaughterhouses were thought to be instrumental in determining the location of ancillary animal-product manufacturing, the Board of Health recommended the establishment of highly centralized and highly regulated abattoirs at one or at most, two locations within the city. Not only would the business of slaughtering and packing take place at such abattoirs, but the related practices of rendering, bone burning, and glue making would take place on the premises as well. Thus, rather than suffer from a multitude of nuisance districts, the city would host one or two concentrated nuisance settings.[33]

The board was unable to convince the city council to pass the legislation it wanted, despite the fact that year after year it continued to press the case for centralized abattoirs. As it became clear over the course of the 1870s that a legislative solution was not forthcoming, the board revised its strategy. Using its regulatory authority, the board attempted to counter the geographic dispersal of nuisances through selective enforcement. That is, it sought to enforce nuisance laws strictly in some areas, thereby encouraging the concentration of such activities elsewhere.

By 1880, the Board of Health was explicit about its new policy. In that year, George Homan, the city's Chief Sanitary Officer, observed that the object of policy with regard to nuisances should be "to secure their removal from near the populous residence parts of the city . . . to a locality set apart for them, where, when fully established in conformity with the direction of proper authority, they should be kept under rigid sanitary surveillance, their rights recognized and interests protected."[34] The approach was further justified on the grounds that the concentration of nuisance manufacturing in large establishments would increase the likelihood that they would have sufficent capital to invest in the most technologically advanced pollution control appliances.[35]

In explaining the board's criteria for selecting a location for the agglomeration of nuisance trades, Homan disclosed the influence of factors that had little to do with safeguarding public health. If the board's reluctance to put polluters out of business betrayed a sympathy for capital investment, its policy of selective enforcement revealed its bias in favor of the owners of high-priced residential property. Certainly, the desire to protect as many people as possible from adverse health effects entered into Homan's calculations. But when it came down to a question of whose health would be sacrificed for the good of the larger majority, the overriding determinant was property values.

Ruling out the southern and eastern portions of the metropolis, Homan cited metereological and political factors. Given that summer winds came mainly from the south, any stenches produced in the southern part of the city would spread to the rest of the metropolis, thus defeating the entire purpose of isolating them in the first place. One might drive them out of the city altogether by banishing them to the eastern shore of the Mississippi River. The idea of relegating offensive trades to areas beyond the city limits had been tossed about before. Seven years earlier, one member of the city council suggested that the city purchase land outside of its limits for the sole purpose of housing nuisance industries. But the health officer rejected this idea on the grounds that outside the city's jurisdiction, health officers would have no control whatsoever and manufacturers would likely resort to the most careless practices. On occasions when winds blew fumes back toward the city, the consequences might be unbearable.[36]

It was in defense of property investments and elite comforts, however, that Homan adamantly opposed locating the nuisance district in city's western reaches. As Homan wrote, many of the city's wealthiest residents were moving

*View of St. Louis, 1876. An engraving depicting the extent of riverfront pollution. Engraving by Schell and Hagen, after Vanderhoof.*

into the western part of the city, a development that had prompted the city to extend its boundaries five years earlier from Grand Avenue to Skinker Road, a distance of roughly four miles. Not only would these wealthy suburban residents be put upon by a western nuisance district, but it would have a deleterious effect on property values that were among the highest in the city.[37]

In particular, public officials such as Homan expressed concern about the proliferation of fertilizer and rendering plants in the upscale suburban district of Rock Spring. Named for the the the large spring that was the principle source of the Mill Creek, this area along Manchester Road between Grand and Vandeventer Avenues emerged as a retreat for well-heeled urban dwellers in the early nineteenth century. The Rock Spring Hotel at the intersection of Manchester Road and Vandeventer Avenue served as the focal point of plush country residences and small businesses. The Pacific Railway's decision to run its tracks through the area in the 1850s undermined the bucolic setting, however. Over the next two decades, manufacturing enterprises, including a bone-black factory, a tannery, and a varnish works, arrived at Rock Spring to take advantage of proximity to the city and the recently constructed railroad line.[38] At the same time, suburbanization continued to bring affluent homeowners to the area. Industrial expansion and residential suburbanization proceeded uneasily. As Homan explained, "This is a desirable residence part of the city and has been rapidly built up the past few years, and the occupants of new houses have been unpleasantly greeted in warm weather, when their windows and doors were open, by the smells. . . ."[39]

The major culprit was Ernest Neuer's bone works. For twenty years, the establishment had accepted the skeletal remains of animals butchered at the city's slaughterhouses and had them steamed and ground for the manufacture of fertilizer, glue, tallow, and bone-black. The fumes from these processes drifted west to the the stately homes along Vandeventer Avenue and north to the equally prestigious Stoddard Addition neighborhood. Due to the social composition of these communities, health officials deemed it wholly inappropriate that Neuer's conduct its business at that location, even though it had been there before many of the homes had been built. Homan and his colleagues insisted that the fertilizer manufacturer, along with other offensive factories, find a more suitable location.[40]

That location would be Lowell. According to Homan, this riverfront section of the city, located several miles north of downtown, was the most suitable for the location of offensive trades. Homan admitted that such a concentration would of necessity produce obnoxious odors, but at least, he reasoned, the city could monitor the situation and prevent the most eggregious abuses.[41] Lowell was well on its way to becoming the city's major nuisance district anyway. Along with the adjacent community of Baden, it had become a magnet for nuisance industries over the previous two decades. A report from the early 1870s observed that the "sickening and disgusting odors" produced by fat melters in Lowell "contaminate the atmosphere for at least a quarter of a mile in every direction and make residence in the vicinity intolerable."[42] By 1879 it was referred to as "the favorite site of a large number of bone-boiling, tallow rendering, fat-melting and kindred establishments."[43]

What differentiated Lowell from Rock Spring was the social composition of the surrounding population. Rock Spring in the 1870s was becoming surrounded by affluent suburbanites. Lowell, on the other hand, was described as an area that was "settled almost entirely by the poorer classes."[44] As in Rock Spring, the residents who lived in the vicinity of manufacturing plants complained about their predicament. In 1873, for instance, the Board of Health received a "well written complaint" from a Lowell citizen regarding the offensive smells produced by a bone-crushing plant. The Board voted to defer punitive action in order to give the owner an opportunity to rectify the situation on his own.[45] In the minds of indignant Lowell residents, this response was typical; health officials appeared far more lackadaisical in their approach to enforcing nuisance laws in Lowell than in other sections of the city.[46] Hence, by the time the chief sanitary officer of the Board of Health officially sanctioned Lowell as the city's nuisance district, he merely verbalized a policy that seemed to have been in force through deliberate neglect.

As long as the Lowell factories remained a local problem, city officials were content to turn a blind eye to pollution. But when Lowell pollution threatened to contaminate the city's supply of drinking water as a result of drainage into the Mississippi River, health officers were inclined to take prompt action. While passing through Lowell on their way to the Mississippi, two streams, Maline Creek and Harlem Creek, collected wastes from the rendering plants and dairies that lined their banks. The point at which the streams entered the river lay just above the waterworks. As Lowell residents were quick to point out to their fellow citizens, this situation threatened the purity of the St. Louis water supply, thereby transforming a local problem into one with citywide implications. Petitions to the Board of Health and letters to local newspapers prompted the public outcry they hoped for. In August 1878, a group of prominent St. Louisans, including several physicians, school directors, and members of the Merchants' Exchange, brought their own peitition before the board demanding an abatement of the health-threatening nuisances.[47]

North St. Louis residents had hoped that this popular uproar would result in the abatement of the offensive Lowell manufacturing activities. Instead they got a sewer. City officials reasoned that the simplest way to prevent contamination of the city's water supply was to divert the waste stream to a point on the river below the intake valve. Hence, construction began on an underground sewer which drained the contents of the creeks and emptied them into the river below the foot of Ferry Street. Construction was completed in 1885. Although the city's water supply was spared, the Lowell factories remained.[48]

Summing up the official policy of the Board of Health in 1880, Homan asserted the urgency of isolating polluting industries from residential populations. As he put the matter in his annual report, "establishments giving rise to offensive emanations . . . must accept the inevitable and seek other locations where they will visit no preventable annoyance on the community, nor impair property values in large residence tracts by their presence."[49] Thus, safeguarding the public health required an aggressive campaign to steer offensive trades away from people and residential property. Of course, this was impossible. If slaughterhouses, glue shops, tanneries, and the like were to operate at all within the confines of the city, they would have to intrude upon some residential population. Homan and his colleagues made it quite clear that in practice, nuisance policy would became a matter of protecting property values and maintaining the quality of residential life for those with wealth and political power. The poor, the propertyless, and the politically disconnected would, of necessity, suffer the consequences.

Not that the Board of Health was entirely successful in ridding affluent areas of offensive pollution. Despite its enhanced powers, manufacturers sometimes prevailed over the board in court. The expense of legal battles precluded a systematic attack on all recalcitrant businesses. For example, the city devoted a substantial amount of money and resources trying to remove a slaughterhouse from a "choice residence locality" at the intersection of Gamble Street and Jefferson Avenue. The Board of Health condemned the establishment on account of improper location and the deleterious effect on local property values. The slaughterhouse refused to abandon the site, and eventually the city decided it was not worth the trouble to continue its enforcement efforts.[50] The board was equally unsuccessful in ridding Rock Spring of its nuisance trades. As late as 1896, Manchester Road was crowded with glue factories, brick yards, iron foundries, slaughterhouses, and packing plants.[51] Indeed, the presence of these noxious industrial facilities ultimately spurred the exodus of affluent residents from nearby quarters. Thus, the desired outcome of isolating offensive trades from well-heeled populations was achieved, but through population migration rather than nuisance abatement.

To civic leaders and planning experts, population migration was a wholly unsatisfactory solution to the problem; indeed, it was precisely the situation that they wished to avoid. The destabilization of residential neighborhoods as a consequence of pollution had become so troubling by the early twentieth century that it became one of the major impetuses behind the adoption of a city-wide zone plan. By this time, the preservation of property values had

*Map of the City of St. Louis Showing Industries, 1919. The spread of industries throughout the St. Louis area caused a depreciation of property value in many residential districts. Lithograph by Harland Barthomew.*

superseded public health as the primary justification for rationalizing land use in the city. Medical experts had largely discredited the miasma theory of disease, thereby minimizing the public health imperative of isolating offensive industries. Yet, the persistent expansion of manufacturing into residential districts, largely a result of limited space in older parts of the city, and the concomitant exodus of besieged homeowners wrought havoc on property values and denied the real estate market any vestige of long-term predictability. Fearing a crisis of investment, civic leaders sought a firmer hand in organizing the arrangement of urban space than was possible under the older nuisance laws.[52]

To this end, in 1918 St. Louis became the second major United States city, after New York, to encode land-use restrictions in a comprehensive zoning law. Intent on separating incompatible land uses, planners and engineers carved the city into discrete districts where only certain types of activity could be performed. At the top of the land-use hierarchy stood the single-family residential district, within which apartment buildings, commercial establishments, and factories were forbidden. Additional zones were created for multifamily dwellings, commercial activity, and industry. Special districts, known as unrestricted zones, were set aside for manufacturers that produced the most objectionable noises and emissions. Chemical works, boiler works, reduction plants, slaughterhouses, soap works, and stone yards fell under this designation. Situated far from the first class residential zones, the unrestricted districts posed little threat to property owners in high-priced residential districts. Because planners were concerned more with long-term stability than with rearranging existing land-use practices, unrestricted zones were placed where offensive trades already operated. The northern riverfront, which included Lowell, and the Mill Creek Valley, which included Rock Spring, were among the major corridors designated as unrestricted in the 1918 zone plan.[53]

It is instructive to note that, while zoning kept manufacturers away from residential districts, housing was permitted in all areas of the city. That is, while factories were not allowed to operate in residential zones, homes could stand in manufacturing zones. Not surprisingly, the housing protected by zoning tended to be vested with property values well above the city average. Invariably, these neighborhoods were inhabited by the middle and upper classes, including some of the factory owners responsible for creating industrial pollution. As a means of preserving property values, zoning had nothing to offer the thousands of working-class families who rented their homes. Factory workers who, of necessity, rented dwellings close to their workplace had no claim for protection against local nuisances according to the prevailing tenets of zoning theory. Indeed, zoning reduced their opportunity to escape noxious conditions by effectively barring low-income housing from cleaner, upscale neighborhoods. Clearly, when early twentieth-century planners spoke of isolating manufacturing from the population, what they meant was isolating manufacturing from the better-off population. Zoning was not so much a mechanism for separating residential, commercial, and industrial functions as it was a tool for preserving property values in selected areas of the city and maintaining the high quality of residential life for elites.[54]

As policy, zoning was both comprehensive and unambiguous. Restrictions on land use were spelled out clearly, giving property holders little room to maneuver. Courts routinely upheld the legal authority of zoning commissions, although St. Louis was one of the few localities where a zoning ordinance was overturned on account of the absence of state enabling legislation. A 1926 U.S. Supreme Court ruling sanctioning the right of municipalities to zone land within their jurisdiction, however, settled the matter for good in St. Louis and elsewhere.[55] Certainly, individual property owners might appeal the regulations, and in some cases exemptions were granted. Still, zoning gave city officials unprecedented power to control and order the urban landscape above and beyond what was possible under the older nuisance laws. Whereas nuisance regulation, at best, addressed nuisance problems as they arose in particular areas, zoning precluded them from arising in the first place.

In one fell swoop, then, architects of the zoning plan accomplished what the Board of Health had been attempting for half a century, albeit with a somewhat modified rationale. To be sure, public health had not dropped out of the discourse altogether, as references to the preservation of healthful living conditions in the early twentieth-century zoning literature make clear. But as pollution was seen less as a cause of sickness and disease and more as a threat to urban land values, civic leaders found it easier to justify a land-use policy that encouraged stark inequities of environmental quality among St. Louis neighborhoods. Nonetheless, zoning should be understood, as it was at the time, as an extension of and an improvement on nuisance regulation. From the early years of the Gilded Age, from the days when city officials wrangled over the proper placement of nuisances such as Busby's boat, pollution control had been premised on the notion of a rational urban geography. Technological solutions did and would continue to merit consideration when dealing with industrial emissions. Yet the most enduring legacy of Gilded Age nuisance regulation lay in the attempt to create a hierarchy of place that would coincide with existing hierarchies of social status, political power, and wealth. Begun under the auspices of protecting the general public from disease, pollution control increasingly became a tool for protecting private property and thus, distinguishing the environmental experiences of rich and poor, powerful and powerless.

# Environmental Justice
# on the American Bottom

*The Legal Response to Pollution, 1900-1950*

~

## *Craig E. Colten*

## *Introduction*

By 1910, several industrial towns existed on the expansive floodplain east of St. Louis known as the American Bottom. As emerging rivals to the larger city across the river, East Side boosters sought to establish their own identity: "We are out of the class of small cities to which we belonged in 1890 and 1900. We have stepped into the company of the communities which do big things. The clothes we wore ten years ago don't fit now. We need a new suit and we want things made to order, not hand-me-downs."[1]

By attracting new industry, these Illinois communities were able to drape themselves in a new wardrobe and avoid existing solely on economic "hand-me-downs." Industrial output, however, entailed the production of pollution, and this became a part of the East Side's identity as well. While these towns grew and coalesced, industrial production increased and the American Bottom found itself adorned in a veil of smoke and surrounded by noxious channels of factory effluent.

How did the communities and citizens of the American Bottom respond to the contrasting outcomes of industrial development—economic prosperity and environmental problems—during the early twentieth century? Like communities elsewhere, they voiced opposition to foul air and water by filing nuisance suits against polluters. American jurisprudence has a lengthy history of dealing with such complaints.[2] The prevailing view is that courts employed the balancing doctrine, which aimed to balance the benefits of economic development against the comfort and safety of complaining parties and tended to favor industrial concerns. In a locale where business leaders vigorously encouraged expanded industrial activity, one might expect the courts to rule in favor of the manufacturing interests.[3] Circuit courts in Madison and St. Clair Counties, however, showed a predilection to rule in favor of the plaintiffs, and sometimes their decisions faced reversal at the appellate level. This pattern reveals an emerging public concern with pollution, illustrates how individuals took measures to reduce their own exposure to it, and indicates that in an area which embraced economic development, the courts continued to show sympathy to the victims of that development.

## Environmental Background of the American Bottom

Given the local setting and the nature of nuisance law and its enforcement, several questions arise: How did the state legal and regulatory framework affect industrial waste management practices? How did juries and justices, living amid the same population as the pollution victims, rule? How was the balancing doctrine applied in communities directly dependent on a single major employer? Also, how did local courts rule in an era of massive industrial expansion and during a time characterized as tolerant of pollution?

In an effort to explore these questions, I selected two counties astride the American Bottom (figure 1). Graham Taylor characterized communities in this area as "satellite cities" in his classic treatment of industrial suburbs.[4] In essence, the communities along the Mississippi River from south of Alton to just downstream from East St. Louis were company towns, established to serve single manufacturers. Wood River was host to the Standard Oil Company's refinery and Roxana to Shell's. Granite City Steel created Granite City. National City was the residence of about 100 people and a constantly shifting population of cattle and hogs awaiting the gruesome services of the slaughterhouses and packing plants. Livestock hides were processed in Hartford's tannery. Monsanto (now Sauget) housed Monsanto Chemical Company's Krummrich plant. Alorton and Fairmont also developed as distinct corporate entities around single industrial concerns. Both Alton and East St. Louis had a more diverse manufacturing base, but they too harbored several key industrial concerns.[5]

Early industrial development of this area depended on several factors. The clustering of rail facilities at East St. Louis prompted entrepreneurs to create the National City stockyards and their associated livestock processing and packing facilities. In addition to transportation advantages, the developers bounded the activities usually associated with creating nuisance conditions within their company town and thereby created a territory where such practices were sanctioned. In addition to livestock processing, smelters, coke works, creosote operations, oil refineries, tanneries, and chemical works found sites on the floodplain. Such operations were also commonly identified as nuisance-causing industries by municipal codes. The absence of legal restrictions prohibiting these practices also encouraged certain industries to locate on the American Bottom.[6]

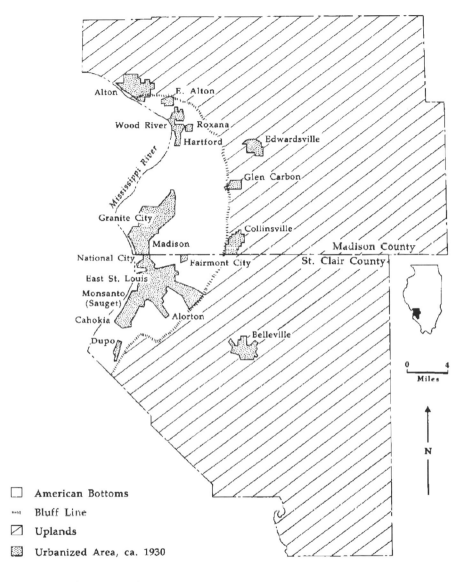

Figure 1. *Map by Craig Colten.*

Another extremely important factor in attracting this particular group of industries to the American Bottom was the availability of inexpensive coal on the Illinois side of the river. Not only were there ample beds of coal in Madison and St. Clair Counties, but local freight charges offered Illinois coal users substantial savings. Consequently, industries using large amounts of coal, such as smelters or coke works, could lower their costs by building in Illinois. In conjunction with direct consumers of coal, companies using coal byproducts typically chose locations near their source of raw materials. Explosives and chemical producers, along with wood preserving operators, joined coal consumers on the American Bottom.[7]

In the early twentieth century, oil refiners also began to purchase sites and add to the landscape of livestock and metal processing and chemical production facilities on the East Side. Citizens held this particular industrial ensemble responsible for producing objectional environmental conditions. The relatively dense, yet politically fragmented, settlement of the American Bottom created an ideal setting for pollution suits. Quite frequently, however, local statutes exempted key industries from the nuisance definition.[8] This arrangement permitted offensive conditions to exist legally within one jurisdiction, but regulations could not confine airborne or water-carried pollutants to the territory where they were allowed. Consequently, neighbors in adjoining municipalities or unincorporated areas took offense to the release of foul air or water that migrated through their communities. Indeed, quite frequently this was the framework for environmental complaint.[9]

By the early twentieth century, the metropolitan St. Louis region had dealt with environmental matters for some time. Struggles with the smoke issue in St. Louis had passed through the first round of reform by 1900 and underwent a second in the 1930s.[10] Flooding and the development of a levee system, particularly on the Illinois side of the river after 1903, were key issues in the early years of the century. In fact, the completion of an integrated flood control and drainage system served to attract industry to the American Bottom during the first quarter of the century.[11] Direct public involvement in these issues alerted the populace to problems of managing the environment in an industrial society. Furthermore, the means for dealing with these issues established a context for future environmental issues, one reflecting the belief that controlling the environment was a local matter. St. Louis citizen organizations and municipal authorities vigorously addressed the smoke issue before 1900. Levee districts, consisting of local entrepreneurs and farmers, organized to raise funds, build levees, and keep flood waters from inundating relatively small areas on the American Bottom during the first quarter of the century. At the time, neither the state nor the federal government were expected to solve these local matters—although by the 1930s the Corps of Engineers reluctantly assumed flood-control responsibilities.

Perhaps even more important was the prominent case heard by the U.S. Supreme Court that pitted St. Louis interests against the Chicago Sanitary District. With the opening of the Sanitary and Ship Canal in 1900, Chicago diverted its sewage into the Illinois River, which emptied into the Mississippi a few miles upstream from St. Louis water intakes. Fearing the delivery of typhoid and cholera bacteria from Chicago, Missouri sought an injunction through the only venue of recourse, the federal supreme court. Extensive St. Louis newspaper coverage of the impending sewage-laden flood portrayed Chicago as the evil upstream villain and clearly linked pollution with an identifiable source.[12] When the courts allowed Chicago to continue using the waterway for sewage removal, St. Louis–area residents were left frustrated, but they were alerted to the possibility of using legal means against unwanted pollution.

Finally, the East St. Louis area developed an early reputation for having a court system sympathetic to occupational health suits. Legal advisors to the DuPont Chemical Company counseled planners to reconsider siting a plant there due to the prevalence of "medico-legal racketeering."[13] Even now, local courts are sought as the jurisdiction for workers's compensation suits. This suggests a long-standing recognition of occupational hazards endemic to heavy industry, coupled with a fundamental mistrust of manufacturers. A strong union presence among the coal miners further shaped popular opinion toward industry. The nuisance suits filed in Madison and St. Clair Counties reflect an extension of this attitude toward environmental issues.

## *Legal Context*

The principal legal means for abating pollution at the turn of the twentieth century was nuisance law. As presented in the leading treatise on the subject, H. G. Wood observed that those creating a public nuisance were liable for damages if they carried on a noxious trade that was "of such an offensive character as to be materially offensive to the senses, and such as impair the physical comfort of those who come within their sphere."[14] Speaking specifically of water pollution, he noted that the discharge of any substance did not provide the basis for legal action, but only those that "impart to the water such impurities as substantially impair its value for the ordinary purposes of life, and render it measurably unfit for domestic purposes."[15] Although establishing a satisfactory definition of "measurably unfit" was problematic, nuisance law offered a means to contest pollution.

In an effort to provide greater clarity to the nebulous common law principle, many states and municipalities passed statutes that defined certain activities, including industrial pollution, as nuisances. By the early twentieth century many state laws specified wastes from slaughter houses, packing plants, sawmills, and gas works as nuisances.[16] Such legislation provided a general means, although not a specific method, to address pollution. In the absence of active pollution abatement agencies that carried out regular inspections and water quality evaluations, enforcement depended largely on citizen suits.

Court decisions on private nuisance suits tended to follow several basic trends during the early years of the century. According to the U.S. Public Health Service, courts generally found that industrial discharges into a stream that resulted in material damage to a downstream user were a nuisance and consequently exposed the releaser to liabilities. In addition, the courts frequently ruled that the economic importance of a manufacturer did not excuse it from penalties if its pollution caused injury.[17]

Illinois's criminal code at the turn of the century declared that the corruption of any spring, river, stream, pond, or lake "to the injury or prejudice of others" was a public nuisance. It also defined the use of a building for any trade that caused "noxious exhalations, offensive smells, or otherwise, is offensive or dangerous to the health of individuals, or the public" likewise a nuisance.[18] This statue provided the context for much of the legal action carried out during the early years of the century, but it did not provide for aggressive enforcement, as did the St. Louis smoke ordinances.

Knowledge of nuisance law was not restricted to jurists and lawyers. Industrial spokesmen indicated that manufacturers understood the existing penalties for polluting behavior. Treatises on industrial plant siting recommended that factory builders consider local attitudes about pollution and encouraged them not to transgress local laws.[19] Writing to an audience of industrial engineers, James Tobey stressed that "the discharge of raw sewage, brine, acid, and untreated industrial wastes into a stream is not a reasonable use of it. . . . The person injured by such practices has suffered a legal wrong, and for every legal wrong there must be a right."[20] The outward position of those writing to and for industry was that pollution had legal consequences, not that the law provided special favors to manufacturers.

In a 1920s survey of public health authorities, a researcher with the Illinois State Water Survey offered several insights into prevailing attitudes. The majority of respondents favored the discharge of crude sewage into streams under certain circumstances. They qualified their answer by pointing out that releases should be permissible only if the waterway was already polluted or was in such a condition that no user was injured. This opinion ran parallel to the state nuisance law. When queried if the pollution of streams by industrial wastes or sewage to the point of creating malodorous or unsightly conditions should be permissible, the majority offered a negative response. One respondent clarified his answer by observing that "industrial sewage can be purified to a point short of actual nuisance and at an expense not prohibitive."

Nevertheless, the surveyor concluded, the consensus was that when government-required treatment would cripple a significant industry, some nuisance should be tolerated.[21] The survey of practitioners reflected a common acceptance of the notion that industrial pollution should be allowed to a certain extent. And indeed, it was, but the law also provided means to contest damaging pollution.

## *Agency Action*

Shortly following the 1911 survey, Illinois formed its first statewide pollution abatement agency—the Rivers and Lakes Commission. The state empowered this commission to hear complaints from citizens who objected to water pollution and authorized it to render judgements, which included the power to order a halt to pollution. Its actions were based on "the best use of the stream for the public." Accordingly, the commission considered the dilution capacity of the stream, the distance from discharge to a downstream user, and the use made of the water.[22] In effect, the commissioners accepted the principle that is was reasonable to expect waste treatment before an effluent was released to a waterway used for drinking water, especially where there was no alternate water source. Their expressed policy embraced the balancing doctrine and called for consideration of the public utility of the water against the costs of pollution abatement to manufacturers. Indeed, when evaluating the need to impose treatment orders on manufacturers, the commission stated that it was "a question of allowing a certain degree of local stream pollution or of abandoning the industry."[23]

During its five-year existence, the Rivers and Lakes Commission heard a number of complaints against both municipal and industrial dischargers. A private complaint against Edwardsville, the seat of Madison County, charged the town with polluting Cahokia Creek, which flowed across the American Bottom and emptied into the Mississippi River. The commission investigated the situation and determined that Edwardsville was "offensively polluting" the stream and recommended that the city modify its sewage disposal practices to prevent objectionable odors.[24]

The following year the commission heard three more complaints in the Madison and St. Clair Counties area. Two complaints against upland municipalities, Belleville and Collinsville, alleged that domestic sewage discharges were fouling streams. The commission conducted local hearings and brought in the scientists from the State Water Survey to evaluate conditions near Belleville. Ultimately, they ruled that Belleville's discharges did not cause "material damage" and concluded that Collinsville's sewage system was adequate to treat the community's sewage load. When complaints about Belleville's sewage releases surfaced again, the commission admonished the city to seek advice from the state board of health. The third case initiated a long-standing conflict between East St. Louis and its neighbor, National City. This complaint objected to effluent released to Cahokia Creek from the packing plants. The same charges were aired again the following year and a hearing was scheduled.[25] Although the commission acted with some caution in this situation, they had issued cease-pollution orders in several other cases throughout the state. Indeed, after investigating a complaint that a fish packing operation in Grafton, a small river town on the Mississippi, was fouling the river with dead fish, it served a written notice to cease the practice.[26] These incidents reflect a greater tolerance for municipal use of rivers to transport sewage—a legally accepted practice at the time. On the other hand, the more vigorous action taken against the fish house, located on the Mississippi River with its abundant dilution capacity, although several miles upstream from Alton's and St. Louis's water intakes, reflected the view that the ultimate use for human consumption influenced the degree of pollution permitted.

The commission reported hearing relatively few cases involving manufacturers in the American Bottom; nonetheless, between 1913 and 1916, it considered a total of forty-five cases involving industries statewide. In twenty-six cases, it issued cease–pollution orders; in another five instances it called for the pollution sources to install or improve their sewage treatment process; and in only six cases did it dismiss the complaint.[27] Despite an expressed policy of permitting some pollution to protect manufacturers, the commission apparently did not find the cost of pollution control onerous. In balancing the social benefits against the economic costs, the state agency frequently imposed costs on industry by acting to protect water quality.

Several government agencies struggled for a number of years to resolve the pollution problem caused by the National City stockyards and packing plants—to the expense of the industry and the benefit of the citizenry. Beginning in 1904, the St. Clair Board of Supervisors declared Cahokia Creek a "great menace to East St. Louis" when it disgorged its contents of offal and packing plant sewage on the stream banks. The board of supervisors recommended a direct channel from the stockyards to the Mississippi River that would detour around East St. Louis and eliminate the offensive conditions.[28] The problem persisted, however, and the local sanitary district reported in 1915 that "firms and corporations have . . . encroached upon the channel of said Cahokia Creek and obstructed the same so that filth and stagnant pools of water accumulate and stand and contribute a menace to the health of the inhabitants."[29] The following year the Rivers and Lakes Commission heard complaints on the subject.[30] Ultimately, the stockyards and meat packers constructed private sewers to the river and relieved the city of its exposure to offensive effluents.[31] As with other situations involving manufacturers, industry ultimately bore the cost of negating the nuisance, after some delay and discomfort to those living nearby.

In 1929, Illinois created a second agency with pollution abatement responsibilities. The Sanitary Water Board, like its counterparts elsewhere, resided in the state public health department and received authority to define and abate pollution. Its responsibilities extended not only to public water supplies, but also to water used for recreational purposes, for watering livestock, or for fishing.[32] The Sanitary Water Board, although possessing the authority to initiate legal action against polluters, sought cooperative solutions to pollution problems. In 1936, the Sanitary Water Board reported that its efforts resulted in the successful installation of "thousands of dollars in equipment" at refineries on the American Bottom.[33] This resulted in minimizing objectionable tastes in water supplies obtained from the Mississippi River. In effect, the Sanitary Water Board secured abatement without legal confrontation while passing the costs to the waste generators.

The general policy of the Sanitary Water Board, like its predecessors, was one of cooperative pollution control, but they took the explicit position that the cost should be borne by industry. In a general statement concerning the board's position shortly after World War II, the Chief Sanitary Engineer enumerated the following points:

a. the industry is responsible for the solution of its problem,
b. as a public agency, the Sanitary Water Board will analyze industrial waste and its impact upon streams, but industry must effect a solution,
c. the solution to any specific industrial waste problem can be found if sufficient time and study is given the problem by the industry,
d. the degree of treatment should be commensurate with downstream usage, safety of public water supplies, and volume of natural stream flow.[34]

Thus, early in the postwar period, the state maintained a policy that clearly placed the burden to minimize public harm due to water pollution on industry and recognized waste treatment as a viable option, while also considering the potential assimilative capacity of waterways and the needs of downstream water users.

## The Courts and Pollution

Local courts in Madison and St. Clair Counties ruled in favor of individuals complaining of personal or property damages due to polluting industries in several cases. In some instances, appeals courts overturned these rulings, suggesting either local judicial sympathy with the complainants, or perhaps a county judiciary out of touch with the broader principles of nuisance law.[35] Whatever the fundamental reason for differences between the local rulings and the appeals court decisions, there was an apparent divergence between the two levels of judiciary.

In one of the local cases later overturned, a neighbor of the Aluminum Ore Company plant near East St. Louis claimed that a substance released to the atmosphere by the manufacturer damaged her eye in 1922. Although nuisance suits generally do not consider personal injury, both the local and the appeals courts found that personal injury was included under the broad provisions of nuisance law, and that in this situation it was not necessary to demonstrate negligence. Based on testimony by the plaintiff and circumstantial evidence of emissions from the plant causing other personal and property damage, the local courts found in favor of the plaintiff and awarded her what was a rather sizable sum for the time: $3,000. Upon subsequent review, the appeals court reversed the local court, arguing that the appellee did not prove the material that burned her eye was released by the appellant's plant. The initial decision, apparently, did not consider a fine to be burdensome to the large manufacturing concern, and the appeals court found fault with the circuit court's use of evidence without considering the balancing principle.[36]

A second case involved a Hartford oil refinery that released industrial wastes into the lake of an adjoining property owner. The refinery, one of three in the immediate vicinity, constructed a series of ditches in 1919 to carry liquid effluent into the nearby Grassy Lake. As years passed, the refiner added traps to intercept the oily wastes and reduce the amount of oil entering the lake. Nonetheless, wastes continued to enter the lake, and by 1925 the buildup of chemical residue had caused vegetation to die and aquatic life to disappear. Between 1925 and 1928, oil fires repeatedly broke out on the lake surface. In response, the land owner sought an injunction in 1929 for the nuisance caused by the refinery. A master of chancery considered seventeen hundred pages of evidence and collected more than five hundred pages of abstract in the case. Ultimately, the master ruled that the refinery was guilty of maintaining a nuisance and ordered the injunction. On appeal, the defendant argued that another refinery, along with the local tannery, had caused the pollution, that its extensive waste collection and treatment systems prevented any harmful substances from entering the lake, and that an injunction would cause it great harm. Although the master agreed that others may have contributed to the pollution, he did not find the other arguments sufficiently compelling to accept the defendant's position. The appeals court confirmed the decree, ordering an injunction on the waste disposal practices of the refinery and thereby placing greater value on the cessation of pollution than on the economic benefits of the refinery.[37]

Several years later (1938), another party living near a major manufacturer complained that chemical releases caused her to become ill and requested a payment of $3,000 under the state nuisance law. The existing law stated that it was a public nuisance to use a building as a place of manufacture which released "noxious exhalations" that were dangerous to individuals or the public. The jury found in favor of the plaintiff and awarded her $2,500. In a series of instructions, the circuit court judge reminded the jury that the plaintiff had to demonstrate that the emissions were released by the defendant's plant and that they constituted a hazard. Furthermore, this decision required a showing of negligence. This factor raised the burden of proof, which in the eyes of the jury was accomplished. The manufacturer filed an appeal, but there is no record of an appellate decision.[38] Once again, the local courts found in favor of the victim of pollution and passed the costs of causing personal harm back to the manufacturer.

In still another case where the county court awarded damages to plaintiffs, the appeals court reversed the lower court's finding. In *Gardner et al. v. International Shoe*, several Hartford homeowners took action against a large tannery that discharged its wastes to a large settling basin on its property. The neighbors complained that gaseous emissions from the disposal basin created a nuisance by virtue of the offensive odor, resulting in damages to property and also depriving them of wholesome enjoyment of their homes. The local jury found the tannery guilty of nine counts and the court entered a $1,200 judgement for all but one of the counts.[39] The case was appealed and the findings reversed, whereupon the state supreme court upheld the appellate verdict.[40]

In this case, the nuisance issue pitted several residents of a town with about sixteen hundred residents against the community's leading employer—in 1941 it engaged about six hundred workers. The confrontation emerged after the state public health agency required the tannery to treat its effluent before releasing it to the Mississippi River. Consequently, the tannery constructed a settling basin to allow solid, biological wastes to precipitate before the clarified liquor flowed into the Mississippi. It was the decomposing solids, produced by the state-approved treatment system, that gave rise to the offensive odors. The new conditions prompted neighboring residents to complain that the odors emanating from the lagoon caused nausea and headaches and that at times they had to leave home to seek fresh air.

This was a classic conflict between individuals and the community's principal employer. The state supreme court observed that the key point of the litigation was

whether a plaintiff can recover for any odor that comes from a manufacturing plant that disturbs him in the enjoyment of his premises, or whether such enjoyment is limited to any extent by his living in the neighborhood of an industrial community where various smells, odors, gases and vapors are absolutely necessary to the carrying on of the business of producing articles of commerce or use for the public generally.[41]

Numerous defense witnesses testified that the odors were not offensive or were only occasional. Indeed, the defense even brought in the state department of health's industrial hygiene investigator to document the level of emissions arising from the pond (he reported measurements of hydrogen sulfide below harmful levels).[42] Furthermore, the defendants argued that numerous other sources of offensive odors existed—both industrial and domestic. The defense asserted that the tannery and waste facility operated in an approved manner and that a tannery could not operate without producing odors. Therefore, they argued, there was no negligence. In considering the evidence presented to the two lower courts, the Illinois Supreme Court concluded that the waste pond was part of an industrial complex and that the odors were reasonably necessary, especially considering the neighborhood. Consequently, the justices upheld the appellate decision and permitted operations to proceed without payments to neighbors.

These four cases suggest that local courts sympathized with their peers who suffered perceived discomforts or damages due to pollution. Despite prevailing public policy that sought to permit a degree of pollution in the interest of maintaining the economic benefits of major employers, some local citizens considered pollution a behavior that warranted compensatory payments or injunctions.

## Conclusions

In an age when urban residents increasingly came into direct contact with byproducts of industrial expansion, courts struggled to balance the benefits of economic development against the costs of pollution. Considering pollution as a nuisance, the courts could impose an injunction, award the plaintiff a fine, order a modification of waste disposal practices, or let existing conditions stand. The general early twentieth-century view was that industry offered employment, produced goods necessary to the public, and provided a social good that offset pollution. Such basic positions were inherent in the policies of the Illinois pollution control agencies. Yet courts in the Illinois counties east of St. Louis, in a group of nuisance cases, found that polluters were liable for damages or that abatement was not beyond the means of the polluter.

This is an important revelation for two reasons. First, it illustrates the concern of individual citizens and groups of citizens with industrial pollution before 1950. Not only did they find emissions and effluent offensive, but they took steps to either obtain compensation or to halt the offending practice. These citizens were able to mount a legal battle with leading local employers and to present a convincing case that industrial pollution was the cause of their discomfort. Second, they won cases and secured the backing of the courts at the local level. Circuit courts awarded damages or imposed injunctions in several instances in the East St. Louis region, indicating that local opinion held manufacturers accountable and did not consider the costs of pollution control excessive.

The appellate decisions, while likely reflecting national patterns of jurisprudence, were not wholly in accord with local jurists. This suggests that we might do well to investigate the popular perceptions of pollution problems and legal remedies. The judges and juries in Madison and St. Clair Counties found sufficient evidence to issue rulings in that particular social and environmental context. How would similar events be ruled upon elsewhere? Furthermore, the popular actions at the circuit court level did not run exactly parallel to expressed state policy, which was more accommodating of industry, even though the actions of pollution abatement agencies could be somewhat less tolerant. Overall, the rulings on pollution matters at the local court level suggest that there was a powerful undercurrent that swept along beneath state policy and the appellate courts. This undercurrent carried the notions that neighbors of polluters were justified in demands for compensation, and that industrial polluters would not be destroyed by the addition of adequate treatment equipment or payment of fines. Fueling this undercurrent was a general mistrust of industry and the belief that local environmental issues could be managed at the local level.

## Acknowledgments

Funding for this project came, in part, from the Hazardous Waste Research and Information Center, a division of the Illinois Department of Natural Resources. The opinions expressed by the author do not necessarily reflect the views of the Center. Ted Samsel crafted the map.

# "The Land of a Million Smiles"

*Urban Tourism and the Commodification of the Missouri Ozarks,*
*1900-1940*

~

## *Jennifer A. Crets*

"The Ozarks have two great needs," the *Kansas City Star* proclaimed in 1912. "Good hotels and a persistent press agent. The most beautiful spots in the range are remote from cities and there is a lack of the conveniences of civilization that spells discomfort for visitors dependent on local accommodations for food and lodging."[1] However, by the outbreak of World War II, the Ozarks had changed drastically. Lake Taneycomo and the entire Ozark region of southwest Missouri marketed itself to the nation as "The Land of a Million Smiles," and the many resort communities and tourist courts which followed the highways and lined Taneycomo's shores had to compete for vacationers. Many offered brand-name conveniences and comforts that would specifically attract the urban consumer: Superfex heated cottages, hot and cold running water, individual radios, Simmons beds, Beauty Rest mattresses, private toilets and baths, and Hot Point electric ranges.[2]

In less than thirty years, tourism had transformed the remote rural and wilderness region of the Midwest known as the Ozarks into an extension of the white, middle-class urban cultural landscape to be found in St. Louis and other adjacent cities. Triggered by urbanization and industrialization, the Ozarks became a valuable vacationland commodity to be purchased by urban travelers and transformed by their culture. During the first four decades of the twentieth century, tourism reorganized the Ozark region's economic hierarchy, redefined its space, and even reshaped the land itself.

In the mid-nineteenth century, the Ozarks were essentially unknown to people living in Missouri's urban areas. A region in the middle of the country overlapping four states—southwest Missouri, northwest Arkansas, northeast Oklahoma, and extreme southeast Kansas—the Ozark landscape, comprised of rugged, hilly terrain interlaced with numerous spring-fed streams and rivers, made travel difficult at best. Thus, the region lay isolated and seemingly frozen in time, its inhabitants living a frontier-like, pre-industrial existence. In stark contrast stood the city of St. Louis, located on the northeastern margin of the region. By the end of the previous century, the city had become an ugly, noisy, polluted metropolis. In addition, its population had grown increasingly diverse—culturally, racially, and economically—much to the dismay of the city's white upper and middle classes. For these latter groups, St. Louis seemed an urban prison from which escape provided the only relief.

Each summer, many of St. Louis's wealthy closed up their urban residences and fled to fashionable eastern resorts or country villas. Others built elaborate suburban residences but remained tied to the city year-round by the growing number of suburban commuter trains. For the less wealthy middle classes, however, escape was not as economically feasible. Some took advantage of the Wabash Belt Railway to enjoy a day at Rosedale, Huntley, Ferguson, Jennings, and other suburban resorts which had begun to encircle St. Louis in the 1880s.[3] Others rode the St. Louis, Iron Mountain & Southern Railway to an increasingly popular St. Louis County attraction, Creve Coeur Park, for company picnics and holiday celebrations.[4] Parks and suburban retreats such as these—settings suggesting the antitheses of work and urban cares—attracted an urban public hungry for arcadian pleasures. These, in turn, became early, convenient, and affordable tourist attractions for the middle class. Thus, as railroad-building expanded the city ever-outward and decreased the distance between city and country, the Ozarks grew in importance to even more potential urban escapees. Sites along the Meramec River took on special significance to St. Louisans, especially places like Valley Park and Meramec Highlands, both reached by the St. Louis & San Francisco Railway (nicknamed the Frisco). During the St. Louis World's Fair, the Frisco offered visitors special excursion rates to Meramec Highlands, allowing tourists to be whisked from the urban perfection of the fairgrounds to the arcadian perfection of the Meramec River resort.[5] The cooling springs and rolling hills of the Ozark landscape offered nature-starved St. Louisans a picturesque wonderland and an antidote to the ills created by the rapid pace of urbanization and industrialization.

Ironically, St. Louis's initial connection with the Ozark region was sparked by these two forces, and not by those seeking a cure for urban malaise. The city was positioned on a nearly direct line between the Ozarks and the industrial sections of the north and east, and after the Civil War the city's capitalists began to take notice.[6] They built railroads to the Ozarks to tap the vast natural resource potentials of the region for industrial purposes, especially to access the rich iron and mineral deposits, and to build transportation connections to the lucrative markets of the country's southwestern states. But tourism followed these paths of industrialization, and once the tracks of the St. Louis, Iron Mountain & Southern Railway and the St. Louis & San Francisco Railway sliced through the rugged Ozark hills in the latter half of the nineteenth century, trains brought many St. Louisans, with their romantic preconceptions

*The expanding service of the St. Louis & San Francisco Railway brought the picturesque wonderland of the Ozarks within reach of St. Louisans seeking escape from urban life. In 1908 the Valley Park Hotel offered guests first-class accommodations overlooking the scenic Meramec River. Postcard Collection, 1908.*

of country life, into the picturesque landscape of southwestern Missouri for the first time. Consequently, the region soon became known for its idyllic scenery, if not for its comforts. The completion of the railroad corridors and the establishment of commercial centers in the rural hinterlands caused rural retreats to spring up in the newly accessible regions.

Indeed, those same industrialists who built and used the St. Louis, Iron Mountain & Southern Railway (later renamed the Missouri–Pacific) to supply their St. Louis-based factories with Ozark mineral resources also enjoyed the access to the pastoral delights of ruggedly picturesque Iron County, center of iron-mining country. There, approximately eighty miles south of St. Louis, the residential village of Arcadia was established and became "a 'suburban' hamlet . . . a center of late-Victorian resort society," where the main pastime was "remaining long enough to renew old friendships and spend a few hours among the club's rustic beauty spots."[7] Along the Frisco Line overlooking the Meramec River, the Valley Park Hotel declared that it was "situated so very conveniently to St. Louis [that] . . . the business man can send his family and have all the comforts of home, and he can get in to St. Louis at all times of day to attend to business, and when the day is over, return to this cool resort to recuperate for the next day's work."[8] Likewise, in 1906, near the Arkansas-

Missouri border, rural Taney County began to welcome its first tourists after the completion of the White River Division of the Missouri–Pacific. From this early urban connection grew the towns of Branson and Hollister, both designed and laid out with the help of railroad company architects and town planners. Slowly, the Ozarks were brought into an urban social network quite distinct from the industrial resource supplier role it initially played and continued to play. Indeed, Hollister recognized early the economic potential of remaining picturesque; the entire town was designed and constructed in the architectural theme of an old English village.[9]

As commercial conduits, Missouri's railroads continued to determine the locations of the earliest Ozark estates, resorts, and attractions and expanded the reach of urban culture by guiding its flow from city to country. But, entrenched in their function to serve industry and urban growth, railroads also remained tied to strict schedules, small town hotels, and single-destination traveling. Without the automobile revolution, Ozark touristic development could not have enlarged its sphere of influence nor profoundly affected the landscape as it soon did.

*Auto-Touring in the Ozarks, ca. 1910. Early automobile enthusiasts knew that promotion was the key to fixing Ozark roads. Well-publicized cross-country auto-tours, like this one around 1910, helped advertise the wealth of Ozark touring possibilities to other automobile owners, who in turn lobbied Missouri's government for a state highway system. Photograph by Bill Trefts.*

In 1910, only 510,000 motor vehicles existed in the entire United States, most of these with urban owners. Indeed, while St. Louis boasted 4,832 registered motor vehicles within the city limits in 1911, many remote Ozark counties had none. Taney and Stone Counties together had only one registered vehicle.[10] By 1921, automobile ownership across the country had reached more than ten million. That same year, automobile travelers outnumbered railroad passengers six to one.[11] But unlike the railroads, which connoted urbanism and industrialization, the automobile symbolized and granted freedom from the constraints of modern city life. Thus, its recreative potential was the essence of its desirability.[12] As the ultimate consumer product, the automobile's ever-expanding use directly aided and expanded Ozark tourism and the commodification of the entire vacation experience. Perhaps sensing this, the Frisco attempted to accommodate the sightseers by proffering auto service to nearby scenic wonders along its many stops in the Ozarks. For example, the Frisco published a guidebook to Sequiota Cave and Park, located five miles from Springfield, Missouri, emphasizing that "first and foremost among [its] attractions . . . is its easy accessibility." Located on the Frisco's Chadwick Branch, a sightseeing trip to Sequiota took "about fifteen minutes in each direction." On weekends, when train service could not hope to accommodate the touring crowds easily, "hourly motor car service [was] maintained to and from the park." During the rest of the week "there [was] a train from Springfield to the park in the morning, and one back to Springfield early in the afternoon." To make the trip as convenient as possible for its weekday visitors, the Frisco train stopped "exactly at the entrance gate," which was less than a hundred yards from the mouth of the cave.[13]

But without rigid time schedules and unwanted stops, the automobile allowed middle-class families to see a lot more of the Ozarks in much less time. Limited road access did, for a time, control auto touring in the Ozarks, but as roads and their markers slowly improved, sightseeing gradually replaced the earlier single-destination vacation goal offered by railroad resorts and attractions. Automobile enthusiasts knew that the wealth of touring possibilities, formerly accessible only by train, needed advertisement. "Thousands of persons have lived in St. Louis all their lives without knowing that within 25 miles of the Court House there is scenery that rivals that of Switzerland, the Rockies, the Blue Ridge and the famous Piedmont Valley," declared the *St. Louis Times* in 1918. "The only correct way to see this scenery is by an Automobile. Do not deny your family this privilege."[14] Only the lack of any total road system in the state blocked their way.

In fact, the existing Ozark roads were fraught with danger, preventing many automobile owners but the most daring and resourceful to attempt a weekend trip. Without any road numbering system or even the certainty that roads would be passible, the *St. Louis Times* aided potential motor tourists by publishing incredibly detailed itineraries through some of the more scenic sections of the region.[15] Even more helpful, though, were organizations like the Automobile Club of St. Louis, which "donated several thousand *[sic]* of dollars and many hours of work" to various counties with scenic attractions.[16] Similarly influential were the regional road improvement groups, especially the Ozark Trails Association, which not only "pioneered . . . a system of marked highways from St. Louis to Las Vegas," but championed "a system of good roads connecting the four states of Arkansas, Kansas, Missouri and Oklahoma" with markers "so the travelers would have no difficulty in following the same, never losing their way and having no uneasiness of mind, as to the route while traveling."[17] In so doing, they and groups like them across the country paved the way for modern state and federal highway systems. The importance of these regional groups in effecting highway modernization, partly to aid economic progress and partly to promote Ozark tourism, helped shape a unique landscape based on consumption rather than production.

Missouri's efforts to build a statewide highway system began in 1907 with the appointment of a state highway engineer to improve certain county roads that would eventually serve as state roads. Various legislation and bond issues were enacted over the next fifteen years until the 1921 centennial road law established a state road system "designating control points through which such roads must pass."[18] Touristic considerations played no small part in the state's planning process. Indeed, one such planned road, known later as part of U.S. Route 66, was recommended by the State Highway Commission in 1922 to "afford a direct connection between St. Louis and the Ozarks and the southwest portion of the State" and to link "the largest population centers of the State with a playground that is unsurpassed in the middle west."[19] The relationship between vacationlands and their connecting highways was made even clearer when in 1924 the National Conference on Outdoor Recreation proclaimed that the "whole world of outdoor recreation is at the command of the motorist. One end of the road is at his doorstep. At the other end is the place of his desires. The outdoors invites him."[20]

To attract the increasing numbers of middle-class consumers, the Ozarks were marketed in a variety of ways by their urban investors during the first decades of the twentieth century, all leading to economic and environmental transformations. Although no urbanites wanted raw nature, different traveling groups sought different destinations and experiential goals. Generally, the Ozarks were marketed over the first four decades of the twentieth century as three distinct landscapes: hunter's paradise, health resort and spa region, and family vacationland. Each of these touristic objectives required certain modifications on the landscape and involved different emphases in marketing the landscape. Each contained a social component—the implied or bluntly stated goal of white, Christian, middle-class exclusivity. And each increased the Ozark region's value in the vacation marketplace.

Initially, when limited urban conveniences posed problems for many travelers, the Ozarks attracted those willing to rough it amid the idyllic scenery. Coinciding with the national back-to-nature movement at the end of the nineteenth century, the wealthy urban sportsmen treasured its rather "primitive" condition and sought to recapture a pioneer lifestyle of sorts through such simple recreative activities as camping, hunting, fishing, and floating the rivers in the Ozark country "where the forest rules supreme."[21] However, even the most ardent sportsmen wanted certain elemental luxuries to ensure a successful trip. Historian Dona Brown has noted that "Romantic travelers [in the last century] could turn to Nature as an escape from the crude commercialism of their society—but not before they had purchased the railroad ticket, the trunks, the hotel room, the elegant bound journal, and the guidebook."[22] Likewise, in the twentieth century, the touristic experience of rugged, outdoor life required consumption.

The wealthier sportsmen often set up their own hunting lodges, complete with sufficiently rustic urban comforts, and sold memberships to their urban friends. For example, the little town of Hollister on the White River became a tourist center "largely because of the actions of a group of St. Louis sportsmen." In 1905, after the Louisiana Purchase Exposition in St. Louis ended, these men bought, dismantled, and moved the huge spruce log building that had served as the State of Maine's exhibition hall to Hollister, Missouri, using the just-completed White River Division of the Missouri–Pacific Railroad. There it was reassembled to become the centerpiece of the Maine Club, a formalized organization for Taney County's sportsmen tourists. Significantly, the building was "the first major freight to arrive" in the White River Country, and the St. Louis sportsmen, bedecked in their city clothing, were the first passengers ever to detrain in Hollister.[23]

For those not of the sporting gentry, rural residents started businesses which catered to a middle-class hunting and fishing crowd. For example, Perry Andres of Arlington, Missouri, made his living renting much-needed camping equipment: boats, tents, cots, complete cooking outfits with stoves for baking, table-ware, lanterns, axes, camp chairs, fishing tackle, and ammunition. Even guides, cooks, and hunting dogs could be hired on the spot.[24]

Recognizing the consumer market to be tapped by promoting the sporting life, the Passenger Department of the Frisco published one of the Ozarks' earliest vacation guidebooks in 1898. Entitled *Feathers and Fins on the Frisco*, the guidebook described in detail the best locations in the Ozarks for sportsmen to enjoy a true wilderness vacation—all conveniently adjacent to the tracks of the Frisco, of course.[25] Through this successful marketing strategy, the vision of the sportsman's paradise dominated St. Louis's conception of the Ozarks at the turn of the century. Indeed, in 1904, one of the concessions at the St. Louis World's Fair even sought to re-create the experience for its visitors. "Hunting in the Ozarks" claimed to be "the largest and most unique shooting gallery in the world," and boasted "A Reproduction of a Scene on the Frisco System. Trees, Mountains, Running Water, Moving Animals, and Birds."[26]

In addition to its vast, unspoiled forests filled with fish and game, the Ozarks also contained some of the nation's largest and most beautiful springs, natural wonders which attracted many late-nineteenth and early-twentieth-century St. Louisans who literally traveled in search of health. Around 1890, wealthy St. Louis businessmen established The Gasconade—a resort hotel at Lebanon, 180 miles southwest of St. Louis by way of the Frisco—because of a magnetic spring thought to contain curative properties. However, in addition to restored health, the resort also granted its visitors social status, thus fulfilling "a 'long felt want' of [St. Louis's] people for a strictly first-class place near at home where health, rest and recuperation could be found amid surroundings as elegant and congenial as any offered by similar resorts in the East, that are reached only after a long, tedious and expensive journey."[27]

Much more successful in this regard was Eureka Springs, a resort town founded in 1879 in northwest Arkansas just south of the Missouri border. After several documented and well-publicized "cures," the town experienced a gold-rush popularity and, after the advent of railroad service, quickly became the definitive Ozarkian spa, drawn into an urban social and economic network.[28] So noteworthy had the spa become in just five years that the Eureka Springs Improvement Company—a corporation which included influential St. Louisans Arthur H. Foote, auditor and passenger agent for the Frisco Railroad; Richard C. Kerens and Charles H. Smith, president and secretary respectively of the Western Anthracite Coal Company; and Isaac Taylor, the city's noted architect—financed, designed, and built the Crescent Hotel in 1886 on the highest point in the town.[29] There, "amid sunshine and greenness and mountain air," praised one Frisco brochure, "Hundreds of people sit the summer through upon [its] porches . . . in calm enjoyment of an undefined something, drinking the waters as almost their only occupation, and looking across the top of a mountain world with that sense of contented pleasure which has its source in something not describable by way of words."[30]

Not all of Missouri's springs experienced the enormous resort popularity that some eventually achieved. As Ozark historian Milton D. Rafferty explains, "No doubt the reason for this was that to command anything more than area trade it was necessary for a resort to be located no more than a few miles from

*Crescent Hotel Guests, 1889. On the front steps of the Crescent Hotel in Eureka Springs, a genteel group of guests gathers for a souvenir photo in 1889. Many late-nineteenth-century St. Louisans of the leisure class literally traveled in search of health and status. Eureka Springs, a health spa founded in 1879 in northwest Arkansas, experienced a gold-rush popularity after the advent of railroad service, and quickly became the definitive Ozarkian spa. Photograph by Barker's Views of Eureka Springs.*

a railroad over rather easily traveled roads. By the time railroads had penetrated the remote sections of the Ozarks, the spa era had passed."[31] Although Eureka Springs had no railroad nearby, its amazing popularity brought the tracks right to the town limits. Several of the Eureka Springs Improvement Company's stockholders were Frisco officials who saw the profits to be made. The railroad subsequently built a nineteen-mile spur line which ran excursion trains to the spa from Seligman, Missouri.[32] Thus, the Frisco provided the "main line of travel connecting the region with the world," conveying thousands from city to spa across the Missouri and other Midwest borders.[33] At the turn of the century, the railroad even supervised the operations of the Crescent Hotel, which it described as a "first class, thoroughly modern resort hotel." During St. Louis's Louisiana Purchase Exposition, the Frisco lost no opportunity to market the Crescent Hotel and Eureka Springs in the *World's Fair Bulletin,* as well as in its own brochures.[34]

"Taking the waters" at these fashionable resorts required leisure time and money found only in the genteel circles. When the medicinal waters lost their power to attract a populace increasingly impressed with medical science, Eureka Springs and other resorts like it in Missouri continued to lure this class of vacationing St. Louisans in search of arcadian healing. Even at the height of the spa's curative fame, the Frisco's promotion of Eureka Springs acknowledged that "those who come are not always sick . . . and the commonest scene is the group of women with flushed faces and wind-blown hair who gather on verandas and tell each other where they have been, and what a delightful how-many-miles it was. And if anywhere needed, there are places to go. . . . To go, to ride, to be out of doors—this is the only thing really."[35]

The health resort craze among the leisure classes of the nineteenth century helped popularize the cyclic summer vacation and define a vacation ideal for the less affluent, more privacy-oriented middle classes. As a ritual and symptomatic antidote to modern living, the Frisco urged potential vacationists to "Find out about the pleasures that it is every one's natural Summer right to enjoy."[36] In 1911, the railroad announced the Ozarks' ability to cater to all tastes and pocketbooks: "there are now many clubs, private lodges, farms and cabins where parties can spend a day, week or month according to their own opportunities and conveniences." The Frisco's Vacation Department even offered to "make all the arrangements free of charge."[37]

Despite the democratic rhetoric, much of the appeal of these early spas and resorts resided in their exclusivity. Indeed, one 1891 guest list from The Gasconade included only St. Louis's most wealthy business gentry, including Jules S. Walsh, president of the Mississippi Valley Trust Company, and three of his company's directors. Even though 1908 found more of St. Louis's comfortably middle-class families sharing in the health-giving delights of the Palace Bath House and European Hotel in Eureka Springs, these spas and other such exclusive resorts continued to function as sanctuaries from both the physical and social discomforts of the urban environment.[38] Indeed, investors marketed the entire Ozark region as safe for discriminating families. The White River Railway even boasted of the social advantages of living in the region, suggesting that the morality, religious spirit, education, temperence, and law-abiding character of its residents surpassed all expectations.[39] In vacationland, a family could reside temporarily, but absolutely, with whomever they perceived to be their own kind. Such discrimination was upheld by simple economics: if a resort's customers dropped too low in class definition, the wealthier patrons soon moved on to more suitable surroundings, leaving the resort to deteriorate, socially and physically. In fact, the main reason for the demise of Meramec Highlands in the early part of the century, located in far west St. Louis County, was "the resort's proximity to the city which attracted an undesirable element who drove away the well-paying clientele. Without the latter, it could not survive."[40]

While unspoiled wilderness, scenery, and healing springs continued to draw St. Louisans and other midwest urbanites to the Ozarks, the White River region became infused with a literary fantasy that still permeates the region today. In 1907, Harold Bell Wright, an itinerant preacher, had retired to the Ozarks because of failing health. While there, he wrote the novel *The Shepherd of the Hills*, using the arcadian setting of the White River valley and local residents as models for his characters. After publication, the fictional story assumed an historical life of its own, attracting tourists who wanted to see the sites of Wright's "Shepherd of the Hills Country," sought to experience first-hand the Ozark atmosphere, and were willing to pay for the privilege. Local residents, including the models for the characters themselves—such as Old Matt, Uncle Ike, and Sammy Lane—obliged. Wright had endowed the Ozarks with a fictional culture attractive to an urban reading, traveling, and consuming public. The region itself soon became a valuable commodity.

Indeed, Mr. and Mrs. Jimmy Elwell of Kansas City, on their honeymoon in the summer of 1915, "took the wonderful 'Shepherd of the Hills' country trip on horseback lasting three days." Striking out from the Taneycomo Club at Hollister, their vacation headquarters, they dined with "Old Matt and Aunt Molly," took their pictures, and were then pointed toward Notch by Mr. Ross (Old Matt in Wright's novel) where they met Uncle Ike. They then rode "over to the W. H. Lynch home, the office of Marvel Cave," where they spent the evening. They "started the next morning by the old mill site up the trail 'nobody knows how old' to Old Matt's cabin" where they "encounter ten other tourists and feast on fried chicken." Next they rode "to Dewey Bald where we stand on 'Sammy's Lookout' and cut our initials on the signal tree." Afterwards, the owner of Pete's cave sent them on "the trail through Mutton Hollow past Jim Lane's cabin where we register and resume our way to Taneycomo Club via Branson and Hollister."[41]

The drawing power of Wright's novel did not wane with the advent of automobile travel. Indeed, many roads in Taney and Stone County were established to provide easier access to the sites, with local residents reaping the rewards of Ozark tourism.[42] Pearl Spurlock, an entrepreneurial Branson resident, for many years provided a taxi service and served as tour guide for the many Wright-inspired vacationers.[43] In 1930, St. Louis teenager Eleanor Klouzek drove with her family to see Marvel Cave, the proprietors of which had tailored their tourist business specifically to visitors with automobiles.

> There were signs all around advertising Marvel Cave. . . . After paying admission "we were given two signs . . . for the bumpers of our cars. The woman [who owned the cave] said that she hoped that we would carry those signs all the way back to St. Louis. . . . The woman also gave

us several pennants in orange and black with the words 'Marvel Cave' across them, and a box of some of the views in the cave. She told us that Marvel Cave was the true 'Shepherd of the Hills Country' that we had come to see. She showed us a map of the surrounding area and explained its history to us."[44]

Automobile tourism allowed an even wider spectrum of St. Louisans to experience the Ozarks and the vacation ritual in general. Indeed, any family who could afford an automobile became potential vacationists, and the ability to vacation at all became a symbol of middle-class status. Many took advantage of the geographical freedom inherent in automobile travel. Some literally camped by the roadside, hauling with them the needed domestic equipment to set up makeshift kitchens in the out-of-doors, a practice that, for rural residents, was fortunately short-lived.[45] To alleviate the problem, many Ozark towns established municipal tourist camps for automotive travelers, and these "towns vied for motorists with attractive campgrounds."[46] In 1926, Joplin's "unusually modern tourists's camp" offered motorists a resort-like atmosphere, "with shelters, kitchens, swimming pool and an excellent 18-hole municipal golf course."[47] However, as more choices in lodging became available to the touring customer, "the Pierce-Arrowing millionaires began to desert the [free municipal campgrounds]," followed closely by the middle-class families. Consequently, the camps, like Meramec Highlands, deteriorated into crowded, unsanitary, even crime-ridden hives of "tin-can tourists."[48] The International Association of Tourist Camps met in Detroit in 1925 and collectively determined to "drive the tin-can travelers to places other than the regular camps" by charging $1.50 a day per vehicle.[49]

Restrictions on socio-economic class, race, and religion continued to be a feature of Ozark resort life well into the twentieth century. For example, Pippin Place, a family resort on the Gasconade River one hundred sixty-five miles southwest of St. Louis by way of the Frisco, required references from potential vacationers, "the endeavor being to restrict the place in such a manner as to make it appeal to families and all discriminating people." Eden, a similar resort on the Gasconade River near Hazelgreen, Missouri, bluntly advertised that they catered "to gentiles only." Vacationers were thus assured to "bring the kiddies—they will be safe here." Likewise, Cassville, the seat of Barry County near the Missouri-Arkansas border, tried to attract tourists by promoting itself proudly as "100% percent white."[50]

In fact, by the 1930s, tourists had so many choices of where to stay that they became as discriminating as the early spa-goers of the last century, seeking status through their choice of accommodations. For example, Anchor Tourist Village in Branson attracted no business until the owner changed the name on his sign to Anchor "Travel" Village. Mr. Madry, the owner, explained the reason: "We had a constant stream of that class of tourist who travels with everything in his car. . . . We learned that the customers we were after resented being classed as 'tourists.' They are travelers."[51]

As Dona Brown observes in her recent history of nineteenth-century tourism, "Vacations did not unite middle-class tourist. . . . Vacation communities were divided by extremely fine distinctions of class, religion, family, and ethnicity; they were far more segregated than most urban neighborhoods."[52] Just as in the previous century, vacations in the twentieth century "enforced profound class divisions. It widened the gulf between the growing minority who could aspire to such leisure and the great majority for whom a week away from work would mean unemployment and a slide into poverty."[53]

St. Louisan Eleanor Klouzek and her family belonged to the latter group. As a teenager in 1930, Eleanor's first trip to the Ozarks proved the fulfillment of her and her family's five-year wait to experience a real vacation. So special was the experience, she recorded each step of the entire trip in a diary. California had been the Klouzeks' first choice, but her father, a St. Louis policeman, could never get a furlough. Nevertheless, they were "still eager to take a trip somewhere," and a four-day vacation in the Ozarks was planned for late July. With fourteen extended family members and three automobiles, they drove the three hundred miles from their flat on Arsenal Street in St. Louis to their Ozark destination.[54]

But even among "equals," the consumer culture of tourism divided Ozark customers by vacation goals, and these divisions usually fell along gender lines. For instance, at Rockaway Beach, fishermen and hunters could feel especially comfortable at Cap'n Bill's Hotel; however, they may not want to stay at Barde's Cottages, which offered domestic surroundings for a "family clientele."[55] Even individual families were subject to the divisions promulgated by touristic culture. Thus, vacationing families sought resorts which indulged each member's interests and desires. Indeed, while the Klouzek kids were swimming, "the women folk had gone to Mueller's store to buy some post-cards to send back home . . . [and] the men folk had gone down to the lake to try their luck at fishing."[56] Although the Klouzeks may not have always played together, they did stay together—at Rockaway Beach, first resort community on Lake Taneycomo.

In 1913, Missourians witnessed the completion of their state's first hydroelectric development, Powersite Dam, located in Taney County in southwest Missouri just above the Arkansas border. Built by the Ozark Power and Water Company, the dam impounded and harnessed the power of the often raging and unpredictable White River, forming the state's first human-made lake. Called Lake Taneycomo, it covered 2,000 acres of land and created 53 miles of scenic shoreline.[57] Not only did the project bring jobs, flood control, and the long-awaited electrical modernization to the southwest region of the Ozarks, local residents and urban visitors saw immediately the lake's scenic and recreation potential. Taney County historian Elmo Ingenthron points out the lake's importance to the Ozarks, stating that "Even though it [Powersite Dam] was a capitalistic venture with a profit motive, the non-profit side effects have been substantial. The creation of Lake Taneycomo ushered in the tourist business, which is now the lake region's largest enterprise and chief source of income."[58]

The creation of the winding but extensive body of water increased the number of picturesque locations for private and commercial resort-building and the potential for region-based tourism not possible with isolated resorts like Valley Park, Meramec Highlands, or Eureka Springs, and consequently allowed for a more numerous and economically diverse clientele. So totally were the Ozarks brought into the urban hierarchy that, by the 1920s, Lake Taneycomo and its surrounding attractions had become known both regionally and promotionally as "The Playground of the Middle West," attracting visitors from all the major urban centers in Missouri and its surrounding states. As Linda Myers-Phinney has noted, the region's appellation actually reflected reality and is evidenced "in the resorts which bore place names. Among these were Camp St. Louis, Camp St. Joe, Kansas City Club, Tulsa Club, and the Big 8 Club of Kansas City."[59]

However, more than just names were transplanted. First established by a railroad economy, rural Ozark towns had subsequently grown into thriving commercial centers in response to motor-touring and road-building. Like the old suburban villages, their transportation and communications connections to St. Louis and Kansas City transformed these tiny hamlets into urban gateways through which vacationers passed going to and from the Ozarks.

One such town, Joplin, was originally established as a railroad center for the mining industry of southwest Missouri. Described by *Saint Louis Magazine* in 1880 as "being hardly more than a mining camp" along the tracks of the Frisco, Joplin had grown by the 1920s into a "modern city of 35,000" which advertised itself as the "Gateway to the Ozark Playgrounds." As such, Joplin promoters played up the contrasting urban and rural images of their gateway town specifically to attract urban consumers. In Joplin, one guidebook boasted, "The hotel accommodations are surprisingly excellent. The eight-story Connor Hotel is favorably compared with hostelries of cities many times the population of Joplin." But unlike bigger cities, Joplin sat close enough to "beautiful parks with clear running streams, lakes and swimming pools . . . to hold pleasure seekers for a few days on their trip into the Ozarks." Indeed, "Just a fifteen-mile automobile ride out of the gateway town," the guidebook stated, "the tourist finds himself in beautiful foliaged hills, with clear-running fishing streams and scenic panoramas to delight the eye." Served by several highways, the guidebook went on, "Joplin also proves an ideal [vacation] headquarters, as many of the beautiful Ozark resorts are within from one to four hours drive over beautiful scenic roads."[60] The Ozarks offered tourists a familiar urban environment without the taint of big-city commercialism. As more and more Ozark towns announced themselves as gateways for tourists in the vacation literature, the "formerly independent towns and villages and also rural territory [became] part of [an] enlarged city complex."[61]

Moreover, the commercial playground associations were centered in these rural towns, organizations of tourist businesses which benefited from their new mini-city status in the urban hierarchy. Significantly, Joplin was home to the Ozark Playgrounds Association. Incorporated at the close of 1919 after an inspirational trip to Eureka Springs,[62] the business men and women in the cities, towns, and resorts of the vacation region in southwest Missouri and northwest Arkansas came together to "cultivate and promote the recreational features and bring about a closer cooperation of their citizenship." The Ozark Playgrounds Association produced highly detailed road maps which not only showed potential vacationists where to stay and what to see but which helped to establish a unique Ozark regional identity.[63] That identity synthesized the contrasting rural and urban images of the Ozarks into one harmonious and desirable whole which the Ozark Playgrounds Association then used to advertise the Ozarks as a vacationland to the nation at large.[64] Indeed, for many years, the association's brochures and guidebooks pictured its headquarters—an appropriately rustic cabin-like building—which contrasted sharply with the distinctly urban background of Joplin's business district. With that single image, the Ozark Playgrounds Association emphasized urban/rural harmony and proclaimed Joplin a portal to vacationland.

Around Lake Taneycomo, many resorts themselves became self-supporting communities, fulfilling the role of the larger gateway towns, but located much closer to the attractions. For example, in 1930, urban conveniences offered at Rockaway Beach caused the resort to grow into a complete community which boasted in one advertisement the following amenities: "Grocery store, filling stations, coffee shops, garage, daily mail service, long-distance telephones and telegraph, gift, tourist supply and curio shops, boats, canoes, outboard motors, big passenger-boat trips, [and] fishing guides."[65] And as commercial tourism in the Ozarks grew in popularity, more variety in facilities and attractions were offered.

But more than just conveniences attracted vacationists. Investors and promoters alike developed marketing strategies which targeted the various levels of urban, middle-class family values. The slogan "The Land of a Million Smiles" publicized the image of the family playground. Clearly, by the 1930s, when the vacation habit had become a rite of middle-class life and middle-class aspirants, traveling families tried to experience an ideal, that somehow the automobile, the scenery, the cottage, and the fun activities of vacationland would help them attain. Indeed, Eleanor Klouzek thought that even the family meals seemed better while on vacation: "We all assembled before dark when everyone decided it was time for supper and such appetites we had! I had never before seen one big family of fourteen get along so splendidly!"[66]

The attraction of families to a playground atmosphere testified to the all-pervasive culture of consumption in American society. More and more, the intangible experiences of vacations were for sale. Even urban home life incorporated the recreative associations found in vacationland, and many new middle-class suburban communities around the country boasted homes amid playground-like settings, emphasizing status and outdoor recreation. Indeed, in 1926, when the new residential suburb of Osage Hills formally opened to home buyers on the former site of Meramec Highlands, developers asserted that its uniqueness and exclusiveness lay in its recreational focus. Such amenities as golf courses, a swimming pool, tennis courts, boating, and bridle paths would grant the Osage Hills homeowner "recreational facilities and social opportunities and contacts possible of achievement at the best country clubs."[67]

Likewise, Rockaway Beach, Lake Taneycomo's first major resort center, promoted a recreative and residential atmosphere. According to a 1926 brochure, "Rockaway Beach is a real pleasure resort—not just a place to go." The brochure then listed every kind of activity a middle-class urban family could want: fishing, swimming, dancing, boating, horseback riding, hiking, and tennis.[68] As art historian David Quick says, "while Rockaway may have started as a place for people to be, it became a place where they went to do."[69]

In addition to espousing a family-oriented, recreative ethos, proprietors of Lake Taneycomo resorts and many other Ozark accommodations developed a nostalgic architecture most appealing to middle-class tourists. The most important element in the building of a vacation landscape lay in the accommodations offered and the arcadian ideals they symbolized. The bungalow even came to symbolize the 1920s suburban housing ideal. But Marguerite Mooers Marshall noted in *Good Housekeeping* that the bungalow was "primarily the resort of white-collar workers . . . all of them with wives, and most of them with children." According to Marshall, the bungalow structure not only symbolized the arcadian ideals of vacationland, but also "other old-fashioned American ideas, including the idea that the members of the family really prefer being together to being apart!"[70]

Perhaps more than any other landscape element, the bungalow cabin or cottage standardized destinations and expectations. It helped to establish a geographical realm connoting rusticity, outdoor recreation, and the simple life—images in stark contrast to city living.

Some families, building on their automotive independence in vacationland, built their own accommodations. The vacation-home appealed to the middle-class love of simple living and financial modesty. Donald Powers, writing in the *Missouri Game and Fish News*, concluded that "A cottage or cabin that is all your own will add to the joy of outdoors for you." According to Powers, a pretentious summer home was unnecessary. "It can be a simple, one-room affair," he suggested to his middle-class readers, "and still return you a big dividend of pleasure on the small outlay of capital necessary."[71] Indeed, the possibility of owning a suitably arcadian cabin in vacation country appealed immensely to families who delighted in personalizing and shaping their own domestic spaces.[72] These do-it-yourself vacation cabins put families in direct contact with arcadian and patriotic values. *Woman's Home Companion* advised its readers that "The Old Fashioned Log Cabin is the new-fashioned summer camp, with all of the comforts of modern life and all of the picturesqueness of pioneer days."[73]

Cheaper and cruder in both construction and decoration than a permanent residence, a family could own and enjoy a visually rustic cabin with all the interior comforts of a miniature, but less complex, suburban home. The Murphy Door Bed Co. of St. Louis and Kansas City told potential vacationists "WHAT TO BUILD IN THE OZARKS." For "Small Cost [and] Lots of Room . . . The two Murphy Beds add two extra Bedrooms without the cost of building or furnishing them; a Murphy Kitchen saves work and a Bennett Fireplace guarantees heating comfort."[74] Indeed, minimizing space and work helped families, especially mothers, enhance the experience of the simple life. Furthermore, the vacation cabin offered families a unique realm of decorating possibilities, a personal space in which to display the family symbols of arcadian life. *Good Housekeeping* advised its female readers that "If a moose head, a brace of wild ducks, or a sailfish are the pride and joy of the sportsman of the family, do not banish them to the attic—take them to your summer camp where they will feel at home."[75]

For those not wanting to bother with or pay for a "second home," there were many other accommodations from which to choose. As roadside camping lost favor with more "respectable" tourists, commercial resorts began attracting a wider economic spectrum of middle-class America by offering a variety of accommodations to meet most middle-class desires and pocketbooks. By the 1930s, tourist courts had replaced tourist camps, emphasizing in the name-change the new permanence and quality of popular roadside lodging. *Harper's Monthly* pondered the success of the tourist court business in 1933 and concluded that "the decade just behind us was one in which millions became accustomed to certain elementary luxuries; hence the rush to those tourist cottages prosperous enough to provide comfortable mattresses, electric refrigerators, and modern plumbing for guests who often did not have these things at home." Significantly, tourist courts across the nation were one of the few businesses which continued to thrive, even grow, during the darkest days of the Depression.[76]

*Harper's* also noted in the tourist court trend the diversity of the bungalow/cottage form, reporting "innumerable treatments of the log cabin . . . prize specimens of car-barn Moorish; amazing marriages of Dutch and Mission, of tea shoppe and Pueblo; the valiant responses to local scenery and history of those who . . . 'try to cash in on their geographical assets.'"[77] Recognizable for its low, horizontal lines, wide eaves, and natural structural materials, tourist court owners found that the bungalow design was adaptable to just about any form or historical style, or even to any climate or local style, without destroying its overall sense of naturalness and simplicity. Anna and Willard Merriam, the Kansas City couple who founded Rockaway Beach, built their bungalow on the shores of Lake Taneycomo and called it "Whylaway," a "rambling Craftsman summer home . . . with light-colored rubble stone walls and flared eaves, which gave the building a strong Oriental flavor."[78] The Merriams must have liked the motif, for they used it repeatedly in developing their resort, as evidenced in their popular Brookside Bungalows. Eleanor Klouzek noted in her diary that both the dance pavilion and the Taneycomo Hotel were "made Japanese style."[79]

However, the most popular bungalow form in the Lake Taneycomo area was the pioneer-inspired log cabin—as could be obtained at the Sammy Lane Resort in Branson or at the Shepherd of the Hills Estates at Forsyth—mainly because of local tradition.[80] An evocation of pioneer days, "cabin" accommodations offered urban families the ultimate visual link with the "simple life" popularly associated with the Ozarks. However, as David Quick has observed, "While log or log-appearing buildings are common in the Taneycomo area and range from cabins of round logs to others with siding cut to appear log-like, almost none of these buildings reflect the characteristic Ozarks hewn log house. This indicates that most tourist and summer residents responded to a preconception . . . that did not include the Ozarks hewn log house despite its picturesque qualities."[81] As with most merchandise of urban consumer culture, the vacation cabin was not designed to offer tourists an authentic pioneer experience. Instead, it provided an urbanized version of a rural residence for which only symbolic concessions to Ozark culture were necessary to impart an Ozark experience.

Eleanor Klouzek recalled the cottage she and her fourteen-member family shared in 1930: "Our cottage was about half-way up the hill. . . . Its name was 'J. Hawk'. . . . It was one long one-story building with a screened-in porch all the way across the front."[82] Indeed, the earliest cottages and cabins in the lake area, as art historian David Quick has noted, "utilized screen windows and porch to keep the tourist close to nature."[83] Natural materials emphasizing ruggedness, earthy colors, and low horizontal lines were used "to imitate the natural complexity of the physical world."[84] Verandas and screened-in porches literally joined the outside to the interior and provided fresh air for its residents in the days before air-conditioning. But the verandas and screened porches also supplied the families with one last barrier against nature, something urban tourists did not want to face defenseless.

The bungalow tourist courts especially appealed to traveling women. The individual cottages and cabins exuded a residential domestication that seemed far removed from the inflexible and impersonal big-city hotels. Historian Warren Belasco observes that "unlike the male atmosphere of commercial hotels, cabin camps displayed a distinctive woman's touch: chintz curtains, doilies on the dresser, rockers, flower boxes. Such home-like extras were said to put traveling women at ease, and this was essential in attracting the family trade."[85] Sensing this fact, Taneycomo resort owners and associations consistently promoted the domestic ideals inherent in their accommodations. In a direct appeal to the domestic and consumptive role of women in middle-class families, the Ozark Playgrounds Association announced the region's elimination of "the fancy frills and tinsel of mansion-like hostelries." Ozark accommodations "boast not of 'cuisine' but of their abundance of fresh eggs, good rich milk and butter, delicious fruits and berries and the safest and purest of cold spring water." For wives and mothers looking for privacy and personal freedom while on vacation, "there are cottages, cozy little dwellings, with full equipment for 'keeping house' and directing one's own hostelry. There's a touch of color and true Ozark atmosphere about these rustic little homes which appeals to the home-loving family."[86]

However, the symbolic facades of domestic simplicity and outdoor values masked the true role of the Ozarks' tourist courts—vacationland commodity. Indeed, Dona Brown recognizes the "ultimate irony of the industry . . . that [tourists] inevitably bought what they did not want. . . . [They] turned away from the allure of the marketplace to travel straight into the arms of the marketplace."[87] With an ever-increasing standardization of urban amenities and comforts, the sense of place required only symbolic concessions.

For example, the Ozark Playgrounds Associations endorsed reputable Ozark resorts in their travel literature in the years before standardized motel chains. Like department store catalogues, Ozark Playgrounds Association guidebooks enticingly displayed the choicest of views, expertly creating desire through effusive and romantic descriptions of landscape and attractions. At the same time, they offered detailed lists of all modern conveniences to be found at Ozark vacation spots. To help advertise and assure tourists of quality accommodations in vacationland, the Ozark Playgrounds Association designed an insignia, an "Ozark trade-mark," as one guidebook called it. Since

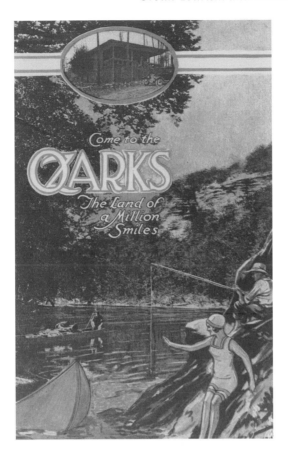

*The Ozark Playgrounds Association created the slogan "The Land of a Million Smiles," publicizing through their guidebooks the image of the happy family playground. When the vacation habit had become a rite of middle-class life and its aspirants, traveling families sought "togetherness"—an elusive ideal which the automobile, the scenery, and the playful atmosphere of vacation land would help attain. Booklet compiled by Ozark Playgrounds Association, ca. 1925.*

the organization restricted its use and distribution, the potential visitor was assured truth in resort advertising. "This Ozark Insignia, then, is your guarantee," the association declared. "It is your safeguard in selecting a resort or location in 'The Land of a Million Smiles.'"[88] Historian Mary Ann Beecher notes that the "emphasis on modern equipment provided manufacturers with opportunities to advertise their products in motels' promotional literature, in the hope that tourists using their products on the road would decide to purchase them for their own homes."[89] The Ozark Playgrounds Assocation marketed an increasingly standardized Ozark experience to urbanites all over the Midwest.

*By World War II, Lake Taneycomo resort and business guidebooks marketed an increasingly standardized Ozark vacation experience to urbanites all over the Midwest. With eye-catching graphics and effusive descriptions of landscape, accommodations, and attraction, they effectively used the art of advertising to create a landscape of consumption. Booklet compiled by William L. Barde, ca. 1939.*

Indeed, Lake Taneycomo resorts supplied visitors not only with an arcadian experience, but also with first-class accommodations brimming with certain elemental luxuries, and updated endlessly to compete for tourist dollars. As early as 1915, just two years after Taneycomo's formation, the owners of Cedar Park resort "spent a large amount of money in the erection of buildings, installing water and electric light systems, building drives, bridle paths and walks throughout the Park, and establishing such improvements as Tennis Courts, splendid Dance Pavilion, Camp Grounds, Swings, Rustic Bridges, Boats and Docks, Bath House, [and] Shower Baths."[90] Significantly, Cedar Park Resort tourists enjoyed electricity four years before the town of Forsyth, the Taney County seat![91]

In 1926, the Lake Taneycomo Chamber of Commerce predicted that "You will enjoy Hotel Taneycomo with its rustic effect, its roominess and the comforts it offers you here. You will be living in the midst of nature and yet the advantages and conveniences of this modern hotel." Hotel Taneycomo boasted running water, electric lights, private shower baths, and toilets in every room. Both lobby and dining room were equipped with "the large electric ceiling fans, which make life comfortable." Nearby, housekeeping bungalows were completely furnished except for "all linens and silverware." Light, airy, and well-screened, the bungalows offered "running water, modern toilet conveniences and shower baths, electric lights and electric hot plates for cooking." And as if that wasn't enough, "You can use your irons and toasters."[92]

But perhaps, Anchor Travel Village put it most succinctly in 1939 when it stated in its advertisement, "Let this be Your Home in the Ozarks. . . . 22 Strictly Modern Cottages overlooking Lake Taneycomo."[93] By that time, experienced tourists knew what "Modern" meant. Urban amenities were

*Ozark Recreation, ca. 1930. One history of resort culture speculates that vacationers crowded Ozark beaches in this manner not simply because they "were people of small means and could afford nothing grander but . . . because they were city-dwellers, accustomed to and enjoying close contact with their neighbors." By 1930, tourists in The Land of a Million Smiles "were content to fish, swim, and sunbathe right next door to each other, because solitude held a hint of menace to them." Photograph by Pete Hangge.*

crucial to the success of resorts, and proprietors knew that they had to convince urbanites that their needs for modern comforts would be met—even in "The Land of a Million Smiles."

By World War II, resort areas, even individual tourist courts, had acquired the look and feel of expertly landscaped subdivisions. Lined up, side by side, facing a road or parking area, appropriately historic or rustic in design, built of native wood and stone, and often with attached carports, Ozark tourist accommodations in "The Land of a Million Smiles" were promoted as "overnight homes" and "travelers homes."[94] David Quick finds this aesthetic noteworthy, representing as it did "the tendency to make the motor cottage appear to be a miniature version of a fashionable house type of the time."[95]

One history of resort culture speculates that "the cozy cottages . . . stood herded together on narrow plots . . . not simply because the purchasers . . . were people of small means and could afford nothing grander but . . . because they were city-dwellers, accustomed to and enjoying close contact with their neighbors."[96] Indeed, at Rockaway Beach and throughout "The Land of a Million Smiles," isolation did not exist. Barde's Cottages boasted they were "just a few steps to every activity." The proprietors of Brookside Bungalows even measured such distance in urban terms to reassure their vacationists that their accommodations stood "within four city blocks of all the resort activities."[97] Such tourists were content to fish, swim, and sunbathe right next to each other, "because solitude held a hint of menace to them." Indeed, they feared the isolation of a true wilderness and "liked looking out at night and seeing through a nearby scrim of trees a lighted window."[98]

The consumer culture of tourism standardized the promotional rhetoric, visual cues, and amenities of the Ozarks vacationland. This in turn connected the cities, suburbs, towns, and resorts of the region into a middle-class consumptive domain, where romantic scenery, urban comforts, and social exclusivity were purchased by travelers seeking escape from city life. Thus, during the first forty years of the twentieth century, St. Louisans and other urban dwellers commodified the Ozarks and reshaped the land according to their ideals.

# The Struggle for Smoke Control in St. Louis

*Achievement and Emulation*

~

## Joel A. Tarr and Carl Zimring

## Introduction

Industrial cities such as St. Louis, Pittsburgh, Chicago, and Cincinnati experienced their major growth from approximately 1850 to 1950. These decades were marked by great tension between the forces of growth and production and the surrounding environment. Air, land, and water resources were debased, and landscapes transformed. In the late nineteenth century, reformers, women's groups, and engineering and public health professionals launched numerous campaigns to improve the environmental conditions under which urban populations lived. Two of their most significant accomplishments were to improve the quality of drinking water supplies and to eliminate dense smoke from the urban atmosphere.

The movements to obtain clean water and clean air began at approximately the same time in the late nineteenth century, but several decades separated their accomplishment. Water came first, and by World War I many American cities provided drinking water to their citizens that had been filtered, chlorinated, and freed of bacterial pollution. Smoke control, however, was more elusive, and while after World War I the majority of urbanites were drinking treated water free from water-borne epidemic diseases, many still breathed smoky air.[1] As a leading chemist noted in the 1920s, "while we have made marvelous advances in cures for human ills, in bacterial control, in hygiene and sanitation, so far as water and waste are concerned, sanitation of the air stands today just where it did one hundred years ago."[2] No city, in fact, effectively controlled its heavy smoke until St. Louis did so in 1940.

This essay will explore the reasons for the lag between water and air clarification by focusing on the St. Louis experience in successfully eliminating dense smoke from its atmosphere after decades of failure.[3] Water, however, provided the precedent. St. Louis suffered from turbid and contaminated water into the twentieth century. In 1901, however, driven by both civic pride and a concern over the public health, St. Louis improved the quality of its water supply, drawn from the Mississippi River at the Chain of Rocks Waterworks (built in 1894), by subjecting it to a clarification process. Between 1908 and 1915, St. Louis made further improvements to its waterworks, constructing a new coagulating plant and the world's largest sand filtration operation.[4] While St. Louis also attempted to control its smoke emissions during this period, it was unsuccessful, and the city suffered from severe smoke pollution for several more decades.

In 1940, however, under the leadership of Commissioner of Smoke Control Raymond R. Tucker, a former Associate Professor of Mechanical Engineering from Washington University in St. Louis, Mayor Bernard F. Dickmann, and James L. Ford, Jr., chair of the Citizens' Committee, the St. Louis municipal government enacted the most far reaching smoke control program of its time. The city's previous success in improving water quality furnished a powerful analogy that shaped its approach. The St. Louis program rested on a series of ordinances approved by the Board of Aldermen between 1937 and 1940. Their implementation not only removed dense smoke from the city's air after years of futile campaigns, but also provided a model for smoke control that cities throughout the nation emulated.

## The Smoke Problem in St. Louis

St. Louis's smoke problem, like that of other smoky cities, was caused by a reliance on bituminous coal for its primary fuel. The city is located between two contrasting natural regions, the Ozark dome, which provides numerous metals, and the Illinois basin, containing large deposits of carbon fuels. Energy consumers in St. Louis took advantage of cheap coal from Illinois mines, using it in ever increasing quantities during the nineteenth century. By 1900, the city's industries, utilities, commercial sector, railroads, riverboats, and residences were burning approximately four million tons of coal a year. Illinois bituminous, especially the cheaper versions from western Illinois mines, was a "dirty" fuel, containing large amounts of sulfur compounds and fly ash that combustion released into the air.[5]

While St. Louis has an excellent urban site, it is also an area with a proclivity to fogs and atmospheric inversions, or high pressure systems. Like all cities, St. Louis is a heat island, absorbing solar radiation in the day and releasing it at night. The range of bluffs on the eastern side of the Mississippi River, however, occasionally inhibited pollutants from dispersing, and they often combined with fog to form masses of stagnant and polluted air that greatly reduced visibility and increased the discomfort of those suffering from pulmonary diseases. Residents of St. Louis called these air pollution episodes

"Londoners," a combination of trapped smoke and fog that became a common fall and winter occurrence, as the smoke "hovered where it was made."[6]

Because of its gaseous and particle contents, smoke had a blighting effect on many areas of urban life. In the 1920s, St. Louis engineers calculated that smoke deposited about nine hundred tons of solids per square mile in the city, while the annual cost of "black smoke" was about $15 million (mostly cleaning costs). The smoke reduced the hours of sunlight, blackened building facades and destroyed stonework, injured vegetation, discolored clothing and fabrics, and deposited grit and dirt throughout homes. Smoke increased the costs and labor required to clean homes—a burden that fell with particular intensity upon women.[7]

The Missouri Botanical Garden was located near a St. Louis industrial and railroad district, surrounded by apartment houses and homes. "Much smoke is constantly pouring out of the stacks," the Garden's *Bulletin* reported, with

*Washington Avenue West to Grand Avenue, 1935. Illinois coal was the primary fuel used in St. Louis; it was deemed "dirty" due to the amount of sulfur and fly ash released from the burning coal. Photograph by Block Brothers Studio.*

devastating effects on roses and other plants. Throughout the city the sulfuric acid from smoke, the lack of sun, and air contamination by coal particles produced wilted gardens and blighted trees.[8] People suffered as well as plants, and sulfur compounds irritated the mucus membranes of the upper respiratory system, increased the distress of people with pulmonary problems, and was suspected as a factor in the prevalence of diseases such as pneumonia and tuberculosis.[9]

While smoke emissions could be reduced and even eliminated through the use of several different methods, including substitution of clean or smokeless fuels for dirty fuels, careful firing methods, and technological fixes such as automatic stokers, all of these methods potentially raised costs. From the perspective of many energy users, the benefits of cheap coal were more important than clean air. Most energy users, therefore, found limited economic incentives for smoke reduction. This was especially true for consumers who used relatively small amounts of coal, such as households and small businesses. Mobile boilers, such as railroad locomotives and river boats, which were among the most notorious smoke producers, faced special problems in reducing emissions because of problems of limited boiler space. Large coal-using industries were often also major polluters, although the incentives for them to burn fuel more efficiently could and eventually did reduce emissions.

St. Louis, as well as other soft coal burning cities such as Cincinnati, Cleveland, Chicago, and Pittsburgh, launched campaigns to stamp out the "smoke evil" in the late nineteenth century. As signified by the use of the term "evil," these initial crusades frequently relied heavily on moral arguments for smoke control. Progressive reformers (or "positive environmentalists" as historian Paul Boyer calls them), also attacked smoke as a threat to the physical and moral order of the city, believing that its prevalence destroyed personal impulses towards proper behavior.[10] Howard W. Evans, a Chicago physician active in smoke control, for instance, commented that a "spotless town is a more moral town than an air-polluted town. It is hard to have clean children in a dirty town, and physical dirt is closely related to moral dirt, and both lead to degeneracy."[11]

Reform groups, such as the Civic League of St. Louis and the St. Louis Citizens' Smoke Abatement League, led anti-smoke movements, with women and engineers playing especially important roles. Women's groups in cities throughout the nation, most with middle or upper middle class memberships, were heavily involved in anti-smoke campaigns. As mothers and homemakers, women had to cope with smoke's negative effects upon family health and the burden of extra cleaning that dirt and soot caused. In addition, working for urban environmental improvements such as smoke control or sanitary reform provided a form of empowerment for women who otherwise had limited political influence.

Urban scholars have traditionally called such women's environmental activities "municipal housekeeping," but these "feminist perspectives," as one historian entitles them, also aided in broadening the attack upon smoke by "establishing a natural, moral, and legal right to clean air."[12] Women environmental reformers in Chicago, argues historian Maureen A. Flanagan, "tended to see the city as a shared home, so they promoted public policies to make the city more livable for all."[13] In St. Louis, women were important activists in the smoke control movement from the 1890s through its successful completion in 1940.

In the 1890s, for instance, the Wednesday Club, an elite women's club, played an active role in publicizing the harm done by smoke and in pushing the initial drive for smoke control legislation. "The present condition of our city," complained club spokeswomen, "endangers the health of our families . . . and adds infinitely to our labors and expenses as housekeepers." In 1907, the Wednesday Club formed a special "Women's Organization for Smoke Abatement" to help enforce existing statutes. The organization divided the city into five districts, each with volunteer observers who reported on smoking chimneys to the Smoke Abatement Department and to the newspapers, and pushed for the prosecution of law violators. In 1915, women's groups played a similar role.[14] In 1923, the Women's Organization for Smoke Abatement helped form the Citizens' Smoke Abatement League, the most influential smoke control group of the 1920s. In 1939 and 1940, women's groups such as the St. Louis League of Women Voters and the Women's Chamber of Commerce provided important support for the successful passage of a strong smoke control ordinance.[15]

But while campaigns by women's groups raised public consciousness about the evils of smoke pollution, engineers played the critical role of clarifying the technical issues and proposing solutions for what they saw as a technical problem. Mechanical engineers specializing in combustion viewed smoke as a sign of inefficient and wasteful fuel consumption that bore high social as well as economic costs. Although there were complaints about smoke pollution in St. Louis as early as the 1820s, the first attempt to mitigate the problem came in 1867, when a new city ordinance required that any smokestack should be at least twenty feet higher than adjoining buildings. In 1891, a meeting composed of "prominent citizens, representing fifteen city clubs and commercial bodies," with the approval of Mayor Edward A. Noonan, secured the appointment of a committee of seven engineers to study the smoke problem. After reviewing technical and fuel conditions, the availability of smoke control devices, and the experience of other cities in regulating smoke, the report recommended St. Louis's first substantive smoke control ordinance.[16]

*Raymond Tucker, Mayor of St. Louis, 1956. As smoke commissioner from 1934-50, Tucker led the movement to clarify the St. Louis air. His leadership resulted in a program for smoke control that was duplicated in other industrial cities.*

Throughout the history of the city's smoke control efforts, engineers such as Victor J. Azbe, Edward Flad, and A. S. Langsdorf sought to define the problem and to develop technological and fuel improvements. Eventually, it was Raymond R. Tucker, a mechanical engineer who became the first smoke commissioner and then mayor of St. Louis, who devised the successful strategy that brought smoke under control. It was probably no coincidence that Tucker's father was also an engineer and had participated actively in a 1904 anti-smoke campaign.[17]

## Smoke Control Policy, 1893-1934: A Record of Frustration

St. Louis passed its first major smoke control legislation in 1893, following the recommendations of the engineering committee. The Board of Aldermen approved bills declaring "the emission of dense black or thick gray smoke to be a nuisance," and authorized the creation of a commission (the St. Louis Smoke Commission) to define permissible smoke emissions and to test smoke prevention devices.[18] The ordinances appear to have been relatively successful in reducing some of the worst smoke nuisances, but in 1897 the Missouri Supreme Court declared them unconstitutional on the grounds that cities did not have the right to declare dense smoke a nuisance.[19] Subsequently, the Missouri State Legislature passed a law declaring the emission of dense smoke into the atmosphere of cities of 100,000 or more to be a nuisance. The St. Louis Board of Aldermen passed ordinances regulating smoke in 1901, 1902, and 1904, but they had limited effects because of weak enforcement features.[20] In 1912, for instance, the Inspector of Boilers,

Elevators and Smoke Abatement attempted to enforce the smoke control ordinance with a staff of four smoke inspectors and one photographer. He complained that because of a lack of inspectors, he often had to resort to court proceedings to get violators to cease.[21] Passage of a new city charter in 1914 and a new state smoke nuisance statute in 1915 also accomplished little. Agitation by women's organizations as well as the Civic League resulted in limited prosecution of law violators, but on the whole, smoke conditions remained oppressive.[22]

In 1923, the Committee on Smoke Abatement of the Chamber of Commerce, led by John H. Gundlach, in league with the Women's Organization for Smoke Abatement, formed the Citizens' Smoke Abatement League to begin a new assault on St. Louis smoke. Eventually, eighteen civic organizations joined the league. The attack focused on the "Black Smoke Tax," emphasizing the cost of smoke to St. Louis citizens.[23] Research revealed that the tax was costing every man, woman, and child in the city of St. Louis anywhere from twenty to forty dollars a year. The league's basic position was that the smoke problem resulted from people's ignorance of "how to properly burn fuel." Therefore, they had to be educated to "understand that a smoky

The Citizens' Smoke Abatement League was a leader in the anti-smoke movement, and it consisted primarily of women, who had to deal closely with the effects smoke had on a family's health and home. Billboard, 1939.

atmosphere is neither a necessity nor an advantage but that it is a selfish infringement on the rights of others," and trained to burn low-volatile fuel in a smokeless manner.[24] The Associated Engineering Societies of St. Louis accepted responsibility for determining the best fuels and furnaces for smokeless combustion and developing an efficient and simple method of firing for citizen use. In addition, the Division of Smoke Regulation attempted to enlist coal distributors in the campaign, providing them with "the proper kind of coal" and instructions as to its "proper burning."[25]

The league raised two hundred thousand dollars from nine hundred individuals and firms to educate the general public on the advantages and methodology of smoke elimination. It distributed literature and organized talks before civic and fraternal organizations. It helped form a "firing school" for janitors and householders, and sent inspectors to different neighborhoods to identify polluters and to teach them proper firing methods.[26] A "surprisingly effective" strategy was for inspectors to photograph buildings with smoking stacks and send copies of the pictures to the owners.[27] As part of their campaign, the league pushed for an enlarged smoke abatement department, a broader definition of a smoke nuisance, and broader inspection powers for inspectors.The Board of Aldermen approved an ordinance with these provisions in 1924.[28]

The Smoke Abatement League claimed that its campaign had produced major smoke reductions from a variety of sources.[29] The average St. Louisan, however, did not perceive the improvements, and popular enthusiasm and participation in the clean air drive waned.[30] Although thousands of people had been taught proper firing methods, there were still many others who would not use such methods due either to ignorance, apathy, or inconvenience. Smoke conditions in St. Louis appeared to be as bad as they had been before the Smoke Abatement League's drive. The apparent failure of this campaign showed the limitation of a solely educational approach to the smoke problem. As Tucker later noted, this experience "taught the City of St. Louis the futility of endeavoring to educate eight hundred thousand people in the art of firing a smoky coal."[31] As if to confirm the end of any serious attempt to control smoke, in 1932 the city combined the Department of Smoke Regulation with the Department of Boilers and Elevators, with the consequent weakening of any control effort.[32]

Up to the early 1930s, St. Louis's efforts to abate its smoke pollution had followed a course common to that in other smoky cities. The cycle was usually begun by a women's organization in coordination with engineers and other reformers. These movements often produced statutes that defined black smoke as a nuisance and that set limits on its emission. Divisions or Departments of Smoke Control with small staffs of inspectors were responsible for enforcing the act, frequently aided by volunteers from the citizens' organizations. Tucker observed that these smoke control movements had an episodic character:

> After each unsuccessful attempt a feeling of apathy descended upon the community. For a period of three to five years nothing would be done, then conditions would become so severe that small groups of citizens would again become aroused and a new attempt would be made. These attempts were not successful because they either failed to realize, or saw fit to ignore, the weaknesses of all previous attempts [which] had depended upon innocuous legislation without attacking the core of the problem.[33]

Penalties for breaking the statutes were usually limited, and smoke control departments viewed their functions as educational, not punitive. Occasionally, departments did make spirited attempts to secure real penalties for ordinance violators, but such efforts usually died out relatively quickly, quashed by court actions or by political pressure.[34]

The reality of the smoke problem, as Tucker and other engineers increasingly realized, was that it resulted from the actions of thousands of separate actors: large and small businesses and industries, railroads and tugboats, public and private institutions, and many, many private households. The smoke situation, therefore, resembled the water supply system *before* supplies were centralized, when households drew their water from multiple local sources such as wells, ponds, and streams, and/or purchased them from water vendors. In order to effectively cleanse water supplies, they first had to be centralized and then treated before distribution. "Would it have been possible for us to practically eradicate typhoid fever in the City of St. Louis," Tucker asked rhetorically, "if we had 140,000 possible sources of contamination?" The answer, of course, was no, and the water analogy suggested that effective smoke control would only come through control of the quality of the fuel supply.[35] Such an approach, however, had not been tried in any city, but engineers active in the smoke control movement believed that such "radical" methods were required.[36] As Victor J. Azbe, Chairman of the Research Committee of the Citizens' Smoke Abatement League noted in 1931, "Nothing will ever clear the air of smoke except smokeless fuels or the completely smokeless firing of coal. . . . One must be merciless and allow no compromise. The evil is too deeply rooted for mild methods."[37]

But could such "radical" measures be accomplished? Changing the fuel type and/or the combustion practices of soft coal consumers was difficult enough with large factories or railroads, but even more problematical with householders who used a variety of types of heating equipment. By the mid-1920s, however, combustion engineers had concluded that domestic heating plants as well as those in smaller business establishments were at the root of the smoke problem's persistence. As engineer Osborn Monnett, former chief of Chicago's Smoke Abatement Division noted, "as far as the great mass of small household heating plants are concerned, there has been no advance in methods of burning coal in the last 100 years."[38] These plants were commonly in bad repair, with inexperienced or poorly trained persons firing them. They often used the cheapest fuel that produced the "very worst smoke." It often contained phenols and other acid compounds, producing "irritating effects" on the mucous membranes of the nose and throat. Furthermore, chimneys on homes and small businesses discharged smoke at low levels, thus causing it to hang close to the ground.[39]

A 1930s federal Works Projects Administration (WPA) survey of 104,000 St. Louis heating units showed that 38.5 percent were individual room coal stoves and 58.4 percent were central heating units. All of the stoves and a majority of the furnaces were hand fired, and often designed to burn coal of higher quality than Illinois coal.[40] Regulation of these heating units and their fuel required powerful laws supported by a consensus of the city's citizens and political and economic elites.[41] "Legislation alone cannot clear the atmosphere," Tucker noted. "It must have the active support as well as the moral support of the community if the community desires to have smoke abated."[42]

A major question involved the availability and price of smokeless fuels. Ranked in terms of their smoky qualities, the dirtiest and also the cheapest coal available was western Illinois bituminous, followed by bituminous or semi-bituminous (Pocahontas, for example) from other more distant coal regions, and anthracite, the most smokeless but also the most expensive. Byproduct coke, made by the carbonization of bituminous coal, was smokeless, but also considerably more expensive than Illinois bituminous. Made in high temperature retorts, coke was used primarily for industrial purposes, especially in steel making, although the byproduct gas produced was frequently sold to cities for purposes of cooking or heating hot water. Byproduct firms also occasionally produced domestic grade low temperature coke such as char or briquettes, but in small quantities since it was less profitable than the industrial product.

In the 1920s, engineers and entrepreneurs conducted a number of experiments with different processes to produce a smokeless fuel from low-quality bituminous coal at a reasonable price. The appeal of the smokeless fuel was that it promised to reduce smoke from domestic stoves without requiring the expense of new combustion equipment.[43] Edward Flad, a well-known St. Louis engineer, advocated a plan in the late 1920s by which coke, made from Illinois coal from a low temperature carbonization process, would be supplied to all residences, apartments, and small stores in the city at a price competitive with Illinois coal. However, probably because of the cost of constructing the byproduct plants, his proposal was not given serious consideration.[44]

By the mid-1920s, other smokeless fuels appeared on the market which eventually threatened the dominance of coal as a domestic fuel. Some homes, for instance, had adopted oil heat, while others used various forms of gas supplied by utilities that had recently entered the home-heating market. These included manufactured gas, natural gas, or a mixture of both. The number of St. Louis households, however, that used gas of any kind for home heating remained minimal. The Laclede Gas Light Company, which had been chartered in the middle of the nineteenth century, had a "perpetual" monopoly of the St. Louis gas market. It appears to have made little attempt to aggressively pursue the home heating customer. In 1934, it had almost 168,000 domestic customers, but most used gas for lighting, cooking, or heating hot water; only about 29,000 used manufactured gas for heating purposes (about 25,000 individual gas heating units and 4,000 for central-heating furnaces).[45] While the Illinois and Missouri Pipeline had brought natural gas from Louisiana fields to St. Louis in 1928, the Laclede Company, which controlled the St. Louis gas distribution system, only sold to industrial users because of price and load problems with the domestic markets and because it wanted to protect its investment in its manufactured gas plant. Through its privileged franchise position, it was able to block natural gas companies from entering the city.[46]

Engineers argued that both "personal" and "social" factors contributed to the choice of fuel. From a personal perspective, a fuel's heat value and combustion qualities had to be considered; from a social perspective, its smokiness and sulfur content were most important. "The lesson in this," Victor J. Azbe observed, "is not to burn the cheapest, but the best fuel not only from a personal but from a community standpoint."[47] But he also realized that for most low income coal users, the appeal for smoke abatement was "in vain, if it means an initial burden of added cost."[48]

Thus, smoke control, as with many environmental issues, posed important equity issues. If smoke control was to garner the necessary political support, some means to either limit fuel costs or to convince users that the higher costs of clean fuel were warranted had to be found. Engineers could design technical solutions to the smoke problem, but their implementation would require not only an understanding of the technical issues, but also the political skills necessary to win popular support for the policy. The man who embodied this balance was Raymond R. Tucker.

## Achieving Smoke Control

In 1933, after years of Republican rule, St. Louis elected Democrat Bernard L. Dickmann mayor. Dickmann proceeded to appoint Raymond R. Tucker as his personal secretary with instructions to "clarify the air as a previous administration had clarified the water."[49] Dickmann's willingness to take on this issue in the middle of the Great Depression was a tribute to his political courage. Dickmann also appointed a blue ribbon citizen's committee to advise him on smoke elimination. The committee reported that only the use of smokeless fuel or of mechanical stokers would bring success, a conclusion that the nation's leading combustion engineers had already reached. At approximately the same time, a St. Louis Medical Society committee reported that smoke, while not directly implicated in the cause of any specific illness, could be a contributory factor in poor health.[50]

Tucker was an astute and shrewd judge of people and of situations. He realized that only a well thought-out strategy that differed sharply from past approaches would bring smoke control to St. Louis. This approach would require both engineering and political skills, and Tucker believed that he possessed both. Speaking to the Engineers's Club of Philadelphia in 1941, he described the type of person who could accomplish smoke control:

> You must have a man in charge who possesses the essential engineering knowledge to formulate these rules and to enforce them, and, above all, he must have a keen sense of public relations. He must be capable of going before organizations of this character . . . telling them his problems, telling them where they can assist, and, if he does that, he will get their support.[51]

Tucker, of course, was describing himself and the strategy he had followed in his battle for smoke control.

Tucker and Mayor Dickmann recognized, however, that powerful forces opposed changes in fuel supply and combustion technology. Coal dealers and Illinois mine owners and miners were the most adamant, fearing the economic consequences of a policy requiring the replacement of Illinois coal with a smokeless fuel, such as gas or coke, or a cleaner coal. The Coal Operators' Association, an organization of the Illinois mine owners, threatened to sponsor a commercial boycott of St. Louis if a strong smoke control ordinance was approved.[52] Since the Illinois coal regions supposedly spent forty million dollars a year in St. Louis, the threat was formidable.

People with older heating units, especially the city's poorer residents, also were skeptical about the benefits of smoke control. They worried that fuel prices would rise if smokeless fuel was required or that they would have to replace their heating units with more expensive ones. In order to overcome the opposition, Tucker believed that public opinion had to be aroused to a state where "the people would be willing to take the necessary steps to correct the evil."[53] A master at public relations, he astutely used the radio and newspapers to campaign for clean air and to argue that any increase in costs for households and industry would be offset by the savings produced by a cleaner city.[54]

Tucker understood that a new strategy was required if the administration was to avoid repeating past failures, and he hoped to get an unbiased source, the Bureau of Mines, to outline it for the city. The mayor requested a $15,000 allocation from the Board of Aldermen for a study of the problem with recommendations, but the board would only supply $7,500. The bureau, however, refused to undertake the study not because of the reduced sum but because it believed that making recommendations was beyond its authority. Tucker proceeded to hire Osborn Monnett, a noted combustion expert recommended by the bureau, to do the work.[55] While the consultant's report deviated only slightly from what had been done in the past, Tucker added a clause to its recommendations. Known as the "washing clause," it established the principle that St. Louis had the right to control the type of fuel consumed in the city.[56]

The "washing clause" required that coal sold in the city had to be treated to remove its impurities, especially sulfur and fly ash, before sale. Tucker hoped that it would also produce a "fuel of uniform quality with higher calorific value which would adapt itself more readily to underfeed stokers."[57] The washing clause was directed primarily at Illinois coal, and that state's coal firms and miners protested vigorously. The Board of Aldermen, however, adopted a smoke control ordinance incorporating the clause as well as other important provisions on February 11, 1937. The ordinance defined acceptable smoke and ash emissions, limited the size of burnable coal to no more than six inches, and required all fuel exceeding those standards to be treated by a washing process (either with water or air) until it conformed to the ordinance's standards. It mandated the use of the Ringleman chart—a simple visual but "practical" device that used different gradients of gray and black as standards—to measure smoke. And, it reduced the amount of time available for railroad locomotives to produce heavy smoke.[58]

The ordinance also contained provisions creating a division of smoke regulation, including the appointment of a commissioner and the hiring of smoke inspectors. On September 15, 1937, the St. Louis Joint Engineering Council, which the mayor had given the power to chose the smoke commissioner, named Tucker to the position. With the help of the council, Tucker proceeded to prepare an examination for smoke inspectors to staff the new division with professionally qualified individuals.[59]

While the washing clause gave the city the right to control fuel quality, it lacked enforcement provisions. Therefore, on October 28, 1937, the Board of Aldermen passed a second ordinance regulating the importation, storage, hauling, and distribution of fuel within the city. It also gave the smoke commissioner the power to require permits of fuel dealers backed by a one thousand dollar surety bond. If a dealer was convicted of violating the solid fuel law, the Board of Public Service could revoke their permit. The division prepared a list of acceptable coal types that it supplied to dealers.[60]

The new ordinance also contained a clause requiring that the smoke commissioner certify and license plans for building new or reconstructing fuel-burning plants. This requirement pertained mainly to industrial users, since it only applied to fuel used in new equipment with a capacity of 1000 square feet steam radiation or equivalent load. Anyone using equipment with a capacity below this—effectively all domestic users—was exempted from the 1937 ordinances. Tucker sought to require domestic installations to use mechanical fuel burning equipment or smokeless fuel, but the city appeal board ruled that the smoke commissioner did not have the authority to make such demands.[61] Thus, two major sources of smoke emissions, domestic stoves and furnaces, were still not effectively controlled.

The Division of Smoke Regulation, in cooperation with the WPA, surveyed smoke conditions throughout the city during the last three months of 1937. They found that the 1937 ordinances produced a substantial reduction in the density of smoke discharged from all sources, but especially from commercial and industrial ones.[62] However, the city's air showed almost no visible smoke reduction. Unregulated fuel sold to domestic users continued to generate approximately half of St. Louis's smoke.[63] The Division of Smoke Regulation reported in December of 1938 that "a solution would not be had until there was an adequate amount of fuel available for domestic use which was smokeless and which could be sold at a price commensurate with its value."[64] The division recommended that the state of Illinois (which produced most of St. Louis's coal) initiate a research program for the development of a smokeless fuel. Further recommendations on the use of fuel and fuel-burning machinery were made through the next year, as the St. Louis smoke pollution persisted. As late as autumn 1939, St. Louis experienced smoke palls worse than any in the city's history. "Visibility was reduced to a matter of a few feet. One could not see across the main thoroughfares."[65]

As public outrage increased and demands for action escalated, Tucker suggested to the mayor that the Joint Engineering Council review his department's work, arguing that decisions should be made on "sound engineering principles rather than the result of hysteria."[66] On Sunday, November 26, the *St. Louis Post-Dispatch* published an editorial titled, "An

*Black Tuesday, 1939 (Civil Courts with cars in front). In autumn 1939, St. Louis was coated with the worst smoke problem in the history of the city. The result was the formation of a citizens committee, which stated that either smokeless fuel or the correct burning equipment must be used.*

Approach to the Smoke Problem," in which it presented a plan for joint community action against smoke. The editorial proposed that the city use a combination of market forces and centralized power to put smokeless fuel into consumers' hands. More specifically, it suggested that the city ask "producers of smokeless fuels to bid for the city's business;" that it purchase fuel from the lowest bidders; and, that it sell the fuel on a "cash-and-carry basis" to consumers and licensed dealers. The plan would be administered by a non-partisan board. "As soon as sufficient supplies of smokeless fuels were available at reasonable prices," noted the paper, the city should approve an ordinance that prohibited the use of other fuels except in smokeless combustion equipment.[67]

A wave of favorable responses greeted the *Post-Dispatch* editorial, and Mayor Dickmann responded by inviting those citizens of St. Louis "expressing a desire for drastic action" to a meeting at city hall to discuss strategy. From this group of forty-eight men and four women, he appointed a blue ribbon citizen's committee to prepare recommendations that would hopefully end the city's smoke crisis.[68] The committee was composed of James L. Ford., Jr., Vice President of the First National Bank, chairman; Kelton E. White, retired broker; Gaston DuBois, Vice President of the Monsanto Chemical Company; Dr. Alphonse McMahon, past president of the St. Louis Medical Society; Chase Ullam, a retired realtor; John B. Sullivan, Secretary to the Mayor; and Tucker. H. A. Buehler, Missouri State Geologist, and M. M. Leighton, chief of the Illinois State Geological Survey, were appointed as technical advisers.[69]

The committee introduced its report with much of the same rhetoric Tucker used in persuading audiences that smoke control was in the city's best interests, talking of its effects upon health, property values, and quality of life: "Our citizens have a right to the pleasant life, a life full of well-being and well living, as well as the right to the protection of their health and economic welfare."[70] It emphasized that education alone could not solve the problem, invoking Tucker's favorite clean water analogy to prove its point: "One might as well argue that the city . . . furnish untreated river water to its citizens provided it gave them full directions and instructions how to eliminate the impurities, and policed them to see that it was done."[71] Some critics of the Tucker approach had raised concerns about the higher cost of smokeless fuel for the poor, but the committee argued that the net savings from heating efficiency, reduced cleaning, and better health would offset any increase in fuel cost. It maintained that while Illinois coals should be considered first for the manufacture of smokeless fuels, several other types of smokeless fuels should also be accepted. It acknowledged, however, that while various types of processed smokeless fuels such as solarite, carbonite, and disco were available, their price was too high for many consumers.[72] However, it explicitly repudiated the idea that the city subsidize purchases of smokeless coal, arguing that while more expensive, the fuel would have higher heating value. In addition, it maintained that such a policy would have to apply to all fuel purchasers, not only to the poor.[73]

The committee examined possible approaches that would have involved major system changes such as district heating, construction of a municipal gas or coke plant, and natural gas distribution.[74] It rejected these as inappropriate, often due to the expense, although it accepted natural gas and district heating as partial solutions.[75] The committee's cardinal recommendations were based upon the two principles that prominent St. Louis engineers had first enunciated in the late 1920s: first, that all those who desired to burn high-volatile fuel must employ mechanical fuel burning equipment; and second, those not using mechanical fuel burning equipment had to use smokeless fuel.[76] These requirements applied to all fuel users in the city, including railroads. The committee recommended that railroads operating within the city limits should be required to submit a definite program outlining which of these methods they intended to employ and setting a date for compliance.[77]

At the same time the Citizens' Committee made its report, a Special Smoke Committee of the Joint Council of the Associated Engineering Societies of St. Louis, formed at the mayor's request, also reported. Its recommendations agreed fully with those of the Citizens' Committee. On April 8, 1940, under great pressure from over one hundred voluntary civic groups, various elites, and the media, the Board of Aldermen approved an ordinance incorporating these principles.[78]

The smoke control law, Tucker recalled years later, changed "the buying habits of approximately 1,000,000 people . . . [and] the merchandising habits of practically all the fuel dealers in the city of St. Louis."[79] Not only were fuel dealers controlled, but all firms selling combustion devices had to report all sales and the names of customers to the commissioner of smoke regulation. Faced by the new regulations, those who did not have or could not afford mechanical equipment had to scramble to find smokeless fuel, defined as any fuel containing less than 25 percent volatile matter. The ordinance provided for the sealing of fuel-burning apparatus if it was not licensed or if there were more than three violations of the smoke law within a twelve month period.[80]

The key to program success in the first year was existence of a supply of reasonably priced low-volatile fuel. Tucker and the staff of the Citizens' Committee scoured the markets for coal that could meet the city's requirements. Processed smokeless fuel such as disco or solarite proved too expensive, but a supply of low-volatile coal was available from mines in Arkansas. The price of the Arkansas coal was higher than the cheapest Illinois bituminous, but it burned cleanly enough to conform with the new ordinance and cost less per ton than the most expensive coke and bituminous coals. The Citizens' Committee obtained railroad agreement to reduce the shipping cost of Arkansas coal to two dollars per ton, but enactment of the rate also required Interstate Commerce Commission (ICC) approval. In a special appeal to the ICC, committee chair James L. Ford, Jr., wrote ICC chair Joseph B. Eastman that the committee was requesting a rate adjustment to "largely benefit the poor of our city":

> I do not feel that our request, while unusual, is out of line . . . railroads in the past have been permitted in times of pestilence, floods and other dire calamities to name unusual rates even to the extent of

giving free transportation. While we have no pestilence or flood, we do have condition of a dire effect upon the health, well-being and economical welfare of our city.

Although a number of eastern railroads protested the lower rate, the ICC granted permission for the rate adjustment, and over a million tons of low-volatile fuel became available for heating purposes for the 1940-41 heating season.[81]

## Smoke Control Success and Transfer of the St. Louis Model

The 1940 Ordinance brought marked improvements to the St. Louis atmosphere as well as experiencing some predicted difficulties. Many of the problems involved the low income population. Due to the regulation of coal quality, the price of coal per ton to individual users increased, causing hardship among many of the city's poorer residents. One "widow," for instance, wrote to Mayor Dickmann that she "would rather put up with the smoke than to see my family freeze. . . . I know you don't realize how we poor people have to scratch to get along." Many of St. Louis's working class citizens purchased their coal by the basket on a weekly basis from street peddlers because they lacked the cash to buy in large quantities and because their tenement apartments lacked storage space. One coal merchant maintained that the smoke ordinance would force the small dealers out of business, leaving only the large companies who had the resources to survive the change.[82] Joseph M. Darst, director of the city's Department of Public Welfare, warned the mayor that the high price of coal and the inability of the poor to purchase baskets of coal on the street would cause suffering: "Any amount of money necessary," he wrote, "should be spent to assure the poor of St. Louis being able to buy . . . their coal supply at not one dime more than it cost them last year."[83]

A number of incidents of price gouging and short weights in regard to bushel sales did occur, forcing the administration to take action in December 1940. Tucker and Ford, chair of the citizens' committee, made arrangements with the St. Louis Coal Exchange and the Authorized Fuel Dealers Association, representing 135 coal yards, to sell basket smokeless coal at their yards on a cash and carry basis. Because the Division of Smoke Regulation had difficulty regulating price and quality among the basket coal peddlers, in the summer of 1941 the smoke ordinance was amended to cover their activities. [84]

While equity problems did develop in regard to the effects of the ordinance, organized labor did not oppose it, expressing public enthusiasm about the benefits of smoke control. The Board of Aldermen made no attempt to repeal the smoke ordinance, evidencing its political popularity.[85]

Generally, the Division of Smoke Regulation followed a cooperative rather than a coercive policy in enforcing the ordinance against violators, whether domestic, industrial, commercial, or transport.[86] Normally, a source would be permitted three violations before definite steps would be taken to eliminate the offense. Improper adjustment of equipment or mechanical failures, rather than use of illegal coal, caused most violations. Where cooperation failed, offenders were charged in Police Court. In the ordinance's first year, small coal dealers and peddlers made many attempts to smuggle Illinois high-volatile coal into the city. The division stationed inspectors on the bridges over the Mississippi River to block them, revoking the licenses of dealers convicted of law violations. Finally, the division issued fuel equipment installation permits and inspected installations. From 1940-44, households replaced almost 30,000 hand-fired heating plants with mechanical ones (23,000 coal stokers, 3,300 gas plants, and 2,200 oil burners). Railroads also altered their technology, replacing 200 steam locomotives with 100 diesel electric locomotives.[87]

The fuel and equipment controls mandated by the ordinances approved from 1937-40 produced dramatic results. The United States Weather Bureau provided one measure of these with its smoke observations, which divided smoke for any given day into the categories of "moderate" and "thick," as determined by the visibility of established landmarks. Between the winters of 1939-40 and 1940-41, the Weather Bureau estimated that the hours of "moderate" smoke decreased by 70.3 percent and those of "thick" smoke decreased by 83.6 percent. The U.S. Weather Bureau Senior Meteorologist commented that the 1940-41 heating season was "the first in many years that St. Louis failed to have a really good smoke." The Missouri Botanical Garden provided another measure—a comparison between the hours of sunshine at the St. Louis Garden and its Arboretum, located thirty-five miles from the city. Prior to the passage of the 1940 ordinance, observed the Garden's *Bulletin,* the Arboretum always had a larger number of sunshine hours compared to the Garden. In 1941, however, there was only a thirty-four-hour difference.[88]

These improvements continued year by year (albeit at a slower pace because of the demands of the war effort), proving the effectiveness of St. Louis's smoke controls and demonstrating a city's ability to achieve environmental improvements with the proper strategy. Building facades were cleaned of black soot, the labor of housekeepers was reduced, and hotels and department stores encountered lower cleaning costs and merchandise spoilage. Physicians reported reductions in infections of the upper respiratory passages, such as colds, sore throats, sinus infections, bronchitis, and pneumonia. Thus, as J. H. Carter, smoke commissioner in 1946 wrote, smoke abatement could only be accomplished with "cost to the taxpayer," but when asked the question, "Does smoke abatement pay?" St. Louis answered an emphatic "Yes!"[89]

Cities across the country noticed St. Louis's achievement. By late February 1941, eighty-four municipalities had sent delegates to the city to examine the basis for its successful smoke control policy. In February 1941 alone, Pittsburgh, Cincinnati, Chicago, and Kansas City sent delegations to St. Louis to learn about the program. By 1944, 230 cities had requested information on the St. Louis smoke ordinance.[90] After the war, a number of cities passed St. Louis-derived smoke control laws, and Tucker served as a consultant to many of them. Pittsburgh was the only major city to approve a smoke control law similar to that of St. Louis before the war, acting after a group of councilmen visited St. Louis to marvel at its clean air; the law, however, was not implemented until 1947.[91]

The effort to keep St. Louis skies clean and to free them from further pollution was simplified by the Mississippi River Fuel Corporation's completion in 1949 of a 664-mile natural gas pipeline to transport the natural gas from wells in the south. In 1949, the Laclede Gas Light Company, serving 310,000 customers, completed the conversion of its system from mixed gas (natural and manufactured gas) to natural gas. In 1950, J. H. Carter, Commissioner of Smoke Regulation, wrote Tucker that "the advent of natural gas into the city has completely changed the aspect of the smoke abatement problem." Whereas at the end of the war only 5 percent of the city's homes used gas and 68 percent were hand fired, by 1950 36 percent of the homes used gas for heating, 21 percent used oil, 12 percent used stokers and only 31 percent hand fired smokeless coal. Carter observed with satisfaction that instead of requiring over a million tons of low-volatile coal a season, only five hundred thousand tons were needed.[92]

## Conclusions

St. Louis shared with other cities a history of unsuccessful smoke control efforts. These included enactment of anti-smoke ordinances of varying severity, episodic enforcement, and various educational programs. The initial anti-smoke ordinances focused on heavy smoke emissions from large point sources such as industrial and commercial establishments and steam locomotives. Although cities often prohibited "dense smoke" regardless of its source (usually for a specific time period), before enactment of the 1940 St. Louis ordinance, no city had seriously attempted to regulate domestic smoke. This was undoubtedly because of the political and administrative difficulties enforcement posed, and because industrial, commercial, and railroad sources seemed the obvious primary polluters.

By the 1920s and 1930s, however, the character of the smoke problem had changed considerably. Many large and medium sized firms had shifted from hand-fired boilers to mechanical stokers, or to fuels other than soft coal, largely because of energy costs. Large centralized utilities rather than small and scattered generators now provided electric power. Industries used manufactured gas more widely, while breakthroughs in pipeline technology made natural gas available in cities hundreds of miles distant from gas fields. Many firms had shifted to oil as a fuel. And, various smokeless fuels derived from coal, such as disco or solarite, as well as domestic-grade coke, appeared on the market. Observing these developments, engineers concerned with air quality concluded that large point sources, such as industries and railroads, had receded as contributors to the smoke pall compared with the contribution of domestic coal users.

Numbered in the many thousands and including a wide range of types of heating equipment scattered over the city, domestic sources posed a major problem. There was no easy method by which they could be controlled, and attempts to do so posed political as well as administrative issues. Working class urbanites who heated with individual room stoves and kitchen ranges were especially problematical. To a large extent, these households depended on cheaper forms of coal that were purchased on a weekly basis from itinerant coal dealers, and they could not afford to replace their equipment or to purchase smokeless fuels.

By the late 1920s, engineers realized that controlling smoke bore many similarities to the clarification of drinking water—that it required treatment at the source, using smokeless fuels and/or combustion equipment that produced no smoke. Attempts at causing behavioral change—e.g., making people better fire-makers through education—were downgraded in importance, although public support was recognized as essential for any new program. The regulation of a city's fuel, however, was more complex than the regulation of its water supply. Fuel supplies were not centralized, making the control problem especially difficult. Multiple interests opposed the fuel regulations, including coal mine operators, miners, and coal dealers. Many citizens worried about potential rises in fuel prices. Fuel regulation was thus a political issue much more controversial than water treatment, and implementation of an effective policy required more time and political skill than did water clarification.

Raymond R. Tucker demonstrated the necessary mastery of political and administrative as well as technical skills. Though Tucker was an engineer, he astutely framed the terms of the debate in a manner that couched political change in the language of scientific expertise.[93] Astutely, he used newspapers, radio, and public speaking engagements to garner support from citizens' groups and to convince the public that smoke control would improve the public health, reduce housewives' burdens, and be economically and physically beneficial to St. Louis. Representatives of women's groups played an important role in regard to publicity about the smoke evil and in support of strong legislation, although not appearing in a decision-making role. Mayor Bernard L. Dickmann provided Tucker with the essential political support and cover to accomplish his program. Once popular backing had been generated for tough legislation, Tucker, Mayor Dickmann, and Citizens' Committee Chair Ford used it to pressure the Board of Aldermen into passing the required ordinances. Low-volatile fuel from locations other than Illinois and new alternative smokeless fuels enabled users with limited resources to adhere to the strict emissions regulations.

In 1940, St. Louis provided an example of a city that had apparently solved its smoke problem. In addition, it had used a model that was transferable to other cities. The visible signs of its success drew many observers and would-be emulators from other cities, but most lacked political leaders with the skill and technical knowledge of Tucker. Tucker himself became a consultant to a number of these cities, and some, like Pittsburgh and Cincinnati, followed the path of St. Louis in requiring smokeless fuels and mechanical stokers. Eventually, coal lost out completely to natural gas and to oil as a domestic fuel, while the diesel-electric locomotive displaced the smoky steam locomotive.[94] The adoption of these cleaner fuels and technologies, however, does not obviate the importance of the 1940 smoke control ordinance. The requirement for smokeless fuel and equipment undoubtedly increased the rate of natural gas adoption after World War II, while the reduction of "visible smoke" permitted a shift of focus to other types of air pollutants. Those who bore the larger share of the ordinance's costs, unfortunately, were members of the working class, as well as the producers and distributors of high-volatile coal. By the 1960s, however, concern over domestic smoke was largely gone from the clean air agenda, to be replaced by concerns about other air contaminants, such as smog from leaded gasoline and various industrial fumes. It is doubtful that most present-day environmentalists even know of the St. Louis achievement, but it stands as an important marker in the struggle of American urbanites for clean air.

# River Dreams

*St. Louis Labor and the Fight for a Missouri Valley Authority*

⌒

## *Rosemary Feurer*

Recent environmental dilemmas seem to pose an inevitable conflict between workers' interests and environmentalists' concerns. The debate over the northern spotted owl and further cutting of Pacific Northwest timber, for example, is almost always posed as one of "jobs vs. the owl." Saving the environment, according to this perspective, means sacrificing workers' livelihood. Similarly, St. Louisans might recall the dispute over the Calloway nuclear power plant in the late 1970s and early 1980s, when the Building and Construction Trades Union Council of St. Louis and Missouri actively defended construction of the plant. Some environmentalists, bitter over their loss on this issue, have derisively joked that "some St. Louis unions would pave the Mississippi if it provides jobs for their members."[1]

By focusing the issue in these terms, however, the larger problem—the fact that workers are left with few choices beyond supporting "development" in the hands of private corporate interests—is obscured. As James Bellamy Foster has argued, the common opposition between workers and environmentalists is not inevitable, but rather the outcome of historical and political contingencies.[2]

This paper explores a brief moment when other possibilities for workers' involvement in environmental choices arose. The campaign for a Missouri Valley Authority, had it been successful, would have established an agency modeled after the Tennessee Valley Authority and empowered to plan for and develop the nine-state area along the Missouri River valley. In 1944, a St. Louis union began organizing the campaign, which expanded into a coalition of unions, farmers, and citizens' groups in St. Louis and elsewhere in the Missouri River states. The campaign developed when an opening for the "planning idea" arose in the context of the debate over the postwar economy. The campaign started out of a concern about the need for postwar jobs. However, as the coalition began to explore seriously the costs of environmental devastation, many developed a more expansive view. Seeking to balance development with the needs of the natural environment, the coalition tried to develop alternatives to counter the consequences of leaving environmental decision making in the hands of private interests and government bureaucrats.

By the end of World War II, the Tennessee Valley Authority (TVA) enjoyed growing public support and was considered a hallmark of New Deal achievement. The TVA was popular, its adherents claimed, not only because it brought electrical power to the Tennessee valley and solved navigation problems, but also, according to David Lilienthal, head of the TVA, because it was an example of "Democracy on the March," the title of his acclaimed 1944 book. Lilienthal promoted the idea of the TVA as a new decentralized regional planning approach that worked in conjunction with the people who lived in the valley rather than as a distant federal bureaucracy. Later TVA, developments and analyses of the authority raised questions about the legitimacy of Lilienthal's claims. Nevertheless, in the 1930s and 1940s, the "TVA idea" continued to be associated with the popular notion of decentralizing power from the growing federal bureaucracy.[3]

Bills for the establishment of other river-based authorities continued to be submitted throughout the 1930s. In a 1937 message to Congress, President Roosevelt endorsed the establishment of seven other authorities. Among the duties of Roosevelt's National Resources Planning Board (NRPB) was that of researching and advocating these proposed authorities. There was little grass roots support for these authorities, however, and as the New Deal's political fortunes began to collapse after 1938, the prospects for the NRPB's proposals eroded. In 1943, as World War II mobilization eclipsed concerns for New Deal planning, Congress easily dismantled the NRPB. Despite TVA's popularity, prospects for other planning authorities seemed dismal indeed.[4]

Then, in the spring and summer of 1943 and 1944, record flood waters came sweeping relentlessly through the lands bordering the lower Missouri River, especially from Sioux City down to the confluence with the Mississippi twelve miles above St. Louis. The floods on the wildly fluctuating Missouri River resulted from the annual runoff of melting snow combined with record rains in the upper valley states of Montana and the Dakotas and caused record damages of more than $110 million dollars in these two years. From Kansas City to St. Louis, levees built by towns and farmers' districts succumbed to the muddy waters that brought sand and dirt from as far away as Montana, and the Missouri inundated thousands of acres of farmland. It forced the evacuation of thousands from St. Charles and left thousands more homeless. In St. Louis, it contributed to the rising Mississippi crest, as the Coast Guard, army engineers, and civilians struggled to protect the city with thousands of sandbags.[5]

The devastation caused by the floods provided an opening for the Army Corps of Engineers (ACE) to expand its role in Missouri River development. The ACE drew much of its support from private interests that supported improved navigation and had been mainly concerned with deepening the Missouri River channel. Since the 1930s, it had been given a Congressional mandate for flood control.[6] Seizing the opportunity provided by the floods to expand its control over the Missouri River, ACE representative Colonel Lewis Pick, "a shrewd, ambitious bureaucrat-soldier," submitted to Congress a brief, hastily drawn proposal comprising twelve pages, which called for $661 million and promised "complete protection for this area against . . . all floods," as well as providing for full development of the irrigation in the dry upper-valley states of Montana and the Dakotas. The plan, writes one historian, "proposed the complete dismantling of the natural river." It proposed to construct a series of dams and reservoirs on the Missouri's main stem and the lower Missouri's tributaries and a series of agricultural and municipal levees from Sioux City to the mouth. Simultaneously, the ACE submitted separate legislation to another committee that proposed extension of the lower Missouri's river channel from six feet to nine feet. Because deepening the channel required the release of additional waters from the upper valley, especially in dry spells, to sustain it, the ACE's twin proposals made its claims to balance flood control, navigation interests, and upper-valley irrigation interests dubious. Nevertheless, the Pick Plan was passed by the House Flood Control Committee in March 1944.

The Pick Plan met immediate opposition from interests in the upper Missouri valley who viewed it as a threat to their claim on water resources for irrigation. The Bureau of Reclamation (BR), an agency created in 1902 and mainly supported by irrigation interests in the upper valley, reacted to the threat that the Pick Plan represented to the BR's role in the upper Missouri valley. Charging that the ACE was using the flood control plan to mask its navigation interests, the BR proposed their own "Sloan" plan (named after its author, W. Glenn Sloan) that protected irrigation on the upper Missouri valley. The plan incorporated some of the flood control features of the Pick Plan, but also sought to construct eighty-nine new reservoirs in the upper valley in order to furnish irrigation to dry land and hydroelectric power to rural residents, at an estimated cost of $1.3 billion. Sloan's plan excluded navigation provisions, thereby defining the major conflict over water use between the two agencies, and between the upper and lower river interests. As one historian puts it, "one agency wanted to spread the river over fields while the other insisted on letting it flow in deep steady currents in order to float commercial traffic."[7]

As the Pick Plan rolled its way toward Congressional approval, the *St. Louis Post-Dispatch*, in a widely disseminated editorial, called for a campaign for the creation of a Missouri Valley Authority, in order to implement a unified plan for flood control and Missouri River development. An MVA, the *Post-Dispatch* argued, would replace the patchwork approach and bureaucratic haggling between the federal agencies (and the private interests that backed these agencies) over river issues. The *St. Louis Star-Times* also quickly backed the idea and called for a "genuine grassroots movement" up and down the valley for an MVA.[8]

The call for a grassroots MVA campaign would likely have remained just a call in the lower Missouri valley if not for the initiative of District Eight of the United Electrical Workers, headquartered in St. Louis. In order to understand the motivations involved in District Eight's campaign, we must look at the District's early development and union leadership, as well as the context of workers' concerns during World War II.

District Eight of the United Electrical Workers grew out of a local drive to organize the St. Louis electrical industry in the 1930s. This was part of the newly formed Congress of Industrial Organizations, which sought to organize all workers in the industry rather than following skill divisions as had many of the American Federation of Labor craft-based unions. Workers at Emerson Electric started the organizing drive in 1936. In March 1937, workers at Emerson joined the wave of sit-down strikes across the country that riveted the nation's attention. The Emerson plant occupation not only succeeded in organizing that company, but proved an effective catalyst for other organizing drives and the formation of the entire St. Louis CIO movement. By mid-1937, the "big three" of the St. Louis electrical industry (Emerson Electric, Wagner Electric, and Century Electric), as well as a series of other smaller companies had signed contracts with the union.

The CIO movement raised hopes among labor activists that united workers would be a force for change not only on the shop floor but in the larger society. This was especially true of the aspirations of District Eight's leaders, who brought a background and perspective that affected the style of the MVA campaign. Much of the District's strategy was influenced by Bill Sentner, District Eight's president. Sentner was a Communist Party member. Despite perceptions of dogmatic Communists adhering to a Party line, Sentner was in fact deeply committed to the extremely democratic structures of his union. He stood for election directly by the membership every year. Sentner, a native St. Louisan, had developed a community-based focus to organizing that derived from his politics, his experiences in the early 1930s as a union organizer, and his experiences with workers in the CIO. The CIO was, to a great extent, a community-based coalition in its formative period. Sentner believed that labor as an institution would be the leading force behind social transformation if it became the key civic institution within the community. Any attempt to build shop floor power, he argued, depended on the development of the union as a key "civic" organization in each of the communities. Power, in other words, was gained by creating a dynamic relationship between the union and the community. That dynamic required that people recognize labor as representing the "public interest" at the same time it fought for more voice for workers in public discourse.[9]

The initial success of the 1937 organizing drives, however, was partly turned back by a counterattack unleashed by employers after recession took hold in fall 1937. Then, as wartime production picked up in 1941, the district also faced further erosion of its base because almost all of the companies that it already bargained with, or hoped to organize, were small, niche manufacturers. Wartime defense contract allocation policy was oriented to major employers such as General Electric and Westinghouse, who were given "cost-plus profit" contracts; by fall 1941, smaller electrical companies were already threatened by the pending curtailment of production.[10] These problems sparked District Eight's call for war and postwar planning.

National CIO leaders had offered an alternative to the corporate-dominated defense mobilization. They proposed an Industry Council Plan (ICP), which called for organizing "industry councils" composed of government, labor, and management representatives that would be given the power to allocate natural resources, to distribute orders for production and to direct manpower in a rational way. Rather than allocating mainly to large businesses, these councils would manage the nation's wartime production needs by taking into account plant facilities, labor supply, and housing availability; they would ensure that small business received a share of contracts. Already becoming mired in an increasingly bureaucratic structure, however, the CIO did little more to promote the plans than make appeals to higher governmental echelons. Its own representative in the government war mobilization apparatus refused to advocate them.[11]

District Eight, in contrast, organized a grassroots drive for such an approach. The campaign resulted in a huge midwest meeting of civic, labor, and small business owners. The labor delegates influenced the conference to formally endorse "equal participation of management and labor in determining a proper and adequate retraining program and allocation of primary and sub-contracts," along the lines of the ICP. Sentner was named to a committee to draw up the program and served as one of two Washington representatives of the group. As a consequence, Evansville, Indiana and Newton, Iowa, two areas where District Eight had members or were organizing, were named as a Priorities Unemployment area and were given contracts on that basis.[12] But even as District Eight entered into this community-based movement for wartime planning, top CIO officials committed to the ICP had lost interest in it, and they dismissed the UE's argument that the CIO should adopt this approach in order to bring planning into the forefront of wartime issues.[13]

During the war, nevertheless, District Eight expanded its base of members considerably, especially in the St. Louis area. St. Louis business and civic leaders had taken for granted the dominance of big industry in wartime allocation, but had conducted plant surveys in order to get subcontracts for the area's medium-sized and smaller companies. Through an aggressive organizing campaign in some of these plants, the UE became the largest union in the St. Louis CIO. An intense and acrimonious campaign resulted in District Eight's organization of the largest St. Louis armaments plant, the Small Arms plant on Union and Goodfellow, whose work-force grew by 1943 to 35,000, a majority of them women and a substantial number of them black workers.[14]

Sentner and other district representatives remained highly critical of the basis of wartime mobilization and what it implied for the postwar era. District Eight's wartime workers, especially those at Small Arms, experienced the continual threat of layoffs and insecurity after 1943. District representative Robert Logsdon complained that wartime planning which excluded labor's concerns—maldistribution of war contracts, failure to consider available manpower, and the failure to make full use of women and African Americans in

*William Sentner, president of District Eight of the United Electric Workers, addresses a rally of small arms workers following a series of layoffs in the 1940s. Washington University Archives.*

the war effort—signified not only a bad approach to the war, but held deep implications for the postwar world. In a letter to Sen. Harry Truman, Sentner wrote, "Apparently it is left to the hit-or miss procedures of a loose labor market to see that laid off men and women are reabsorbed—a fantastically inadequate arrangement for an area like St. Louis."[15] Citing surveys showing that women wanted to continue working after the war and suggesting the need for "advancing democratic opportunities for Negroes to retain their newfound jobs," Sentner chided leading St. Louis businessmen who assumed that blacks and women would be shunted back to their prewar positions in the economy.[16]

Thus, for Sentner and many other workers, war and postwar concerns were intertwined. How would workers fare in an economy no longer lifted by war production? Would the U.S. fall back into Depression Era conditions? After 1943, district representatives continually sought to raise other possibilities for the postwar economy and to place workers' concerns at the center of postwar economic and political discussion. Sentner argued that the postwar economy could only be just if labor had a major role in planning it. District representatives succeeded in getting St. Louis mayor Alois Kaufmann to establish a city-based postwar planning committee that included representatives of the CIO and AFL, suggesting that this kind of committee was the "first step in a nationwide application of the principles of community cooperation" for a new postwar world. They also organized a CIO shop steward council to discuss the postwar economy as a base for future mobilization.[17]

In 1944, the district hosted five conferences on postwar planning. Worker representatives were elected on the basis of two men and two women from each factory department. The St. Louis conference discussed expansive views of a new postwar order. Sentner suggested that a postwar world of "unemployment and chaos, human misery and despair can and will be avoided. . . . Community planning for postwar conversion and employment will guarantee successful national planning for postwar conversion and employment." Sentner advocated planning for an economy that would create more interesting jobs and a reduction of working hours to thirty per week after the war.[18] In a preview of future battle lines, however, George Smith of the St. Louis Chamber of Commerce interrupted to remind workers that the point of the free enterprise system was not to create jobs, but to make profits. On the other hand, Stuart Symington, president of Emerson Electric, seemed supportive. Symington had secured war contracts for Emerson through personal connections with some of the financial interests in government who were in charge of the wartime production allocation. He reminded the audience that the fruits of wartime prosperity had been produced by government planning, and indicated support for a limited role for labor in local and national planning.[19]

Delegates to the St. Louis shop delegate conference enthusiastically endorsed the establishment of an MVA as a means to promote postwar planning on a local and regional level. By the time of the postwar planning conferences, District Eight's executive board had already voted to give full financial support, including one staff research job, to the promotion of an MVA. District Eight's leadership viewed a campaign for the MVA as a way to promote postwar planning for full employment, as well as to place labor at the center of the "public interest" in the postwar era. The MVA "is the type of broad planning that is needed throughout our land to satisfy the needs of demobilized war workers," the executive board urged in explaining its decision. They also argued that an MVA would mean "control, in the public interest, of the flow of waters and the erosion of land."[20]

District Eight's campaign began with a pamphlet titled, *One River, One Plan*, which outlined a comprehensive plan for the river development. In keeping with the district's stress on postwar planning for jobs, the pamphlet predicted that five hundred thousand jobs would be created within five years from projects such as dam building, irrigation, electrification, soil conservation, reforestation, etc. In many respects, the pamphlet agreed with the dominant view expressed by the ACE about control of the natural river for development or economic growth purposes. It stressed that electrification of rural areas (only thirty percent of all farms in the Missouri River basin had been electrified) through cheap public power would create a new market for the region's electrical products. Irrigation would become available to small farms, opening up opportunity that had mainly accrued to agribusiness. Through postwar planning for the Missouri River valley basin, "its abundant resources ought to make for significant peace-time expansion." On the other hand, the pamphlet and press releases accompanying it stressed that only through regional, decentralized planning could the river "be harnessed for the public good" and the various concerns of Missouri Valley citizens be reconciled. The pamphlet stressed that public involvement in utilization of water resources would bring overdue consideration of the "devastating effect of exploitation." Moreover, inclusion of soil and water conservation, as well as reforestation, were aspects left out of both the Pick and Sloan plans.[21]

District Eight distributed *One River, One Plan* widely to launch a community-based grassroots campaign in support of MVA, a campaign they sought to keep out of the hands of the technocrats who had dominated the NRPB. Naomi Ring, the district's staff researcher for the MVA, suggested to a correspondent that while the district had been approached by "every liberal from Washington D.C. to Canada writing us veiled suggestions that they would like to get in on paying organizational publicity jobs for this deal." The district sought instead to "concentrate on actual organizational affiliations of farm and labor groups," into "one broad committee that can pull in as many farm, labor, industry and civic people," in order to increase the effectiveness of the campaign as well as to establish its style. She concluded: "It is important to get good people in on this from the ground up because even after the bill is passed, there will be many issues that will be settled according to the wishes and mass action of the citizens in the valley."[22]

District Eight staff soon found the "right" liberal engineer to help them formulate the bill. Walter Packard had been director of the New Deal's Resettlement Administration in five southwestern states; one historian suggests that Packard represented the prototypical "community" oriented type of New Dealer, committed to planning and a "cooperative commonwealth" in the United States. Packard was one of the most vocal critics of agribusiness interests and private power within the Reclamation Bureau, where he had worked on the Central Valley Project, an irrigation and power project in central California. His critique of the Central Valley Project for helping to entrench large growers had earned him the rage of western corporate and agricultural interests. He wrote to Sentner, "Our experience with the Central Valley Project in California amply demonstrates the need for vigilance in protecting the rights of labor and the consumer, both in the setting of policy and in administration." He concluded: "It is not enough to secure an authority. It is equally important to see that the authority represents sound public policy. This can be accomplished only by a determined drive by labor, farmers, consumers and liberal elements, generally. These groups should be brought together in a concerted campaign in the public interest."[23]

The response to *One River, One Plan* was encouraging, "exceed(ing) UE's wildest dreams," both among their own members and workers in other unions, including the rival AFL unions. Later Sentner reflected that the issue "caught on like no pork chops issue ever did" not only because of workers' concerns for postwar security but "also because there's hardly a union man or woman [in the district] that isn't tied either through family or tradition to the rural areas and the woes they've suffered through Old Man River." Indeed, many electrical workers and especially many defense workers had only recently migrated from the rural areas of Missouri, and maintained ties to their rural past. James Davis, an autoworker and secretary of the Missouri CIO, who outside of Sentner became the most important advocate for the MVA from the CIO, was "raised within three-quarters of a mile of the Missouri River," and later remarked that "I have seen the place I was raised on covered with about a foot of sand that probably came from Montana." These ties suggest that viewing industrial workers in "special interest" terms neglects the multi-dimensional characteristics of working-class formation. Many of these same workers no doubt shared Sentner's avid enthusiasm for recreational activities, such as fishing in Missouri's outstate regions. Workers were concerned not only for jobs but also were drawn to hopes for a broad enhancement of life in the postwar world. Sentner's visionary hopes for the new era thus resonated with many industrial workers.

Thus, it was not only the promise of jobs that attracted workers and unions to the proposal. After all, the army engineers' plan also promised development and jobs. In Iowa, AFL leaders, with whom CIO unions had forged the type of cordial relations that often eluded the rival federations in other states and whose leaders deeply admired and respected Sentner, helped District Eight representatives gain the cooperation of building trades unions for the proposal. The attraction of an MVA here was founded not only on some of the same rural ties, but, as Sentner noted, a high level of enthusiasm from Iowa AFL leaders for establishing a place for labor in postwar planning. Further, the Army Engineers had traditionally bid out contracts for their projects, often resulting in undercutting the union-established prevailing wage for construction work. The MVA, its supporters argued, would follow the TVA's practice of hiring workers directly and paying prevailing wages.[24]

Farmers and farm groups also responded enthusiastically to the district's campaign and would soon take a central role in it. District Eight increased contact with farmers across the nine states, especially with two important farm organizations, the Missouri Farmers Association and the National Farmers Union.[25] These organizations bitterly opposed the Army Corps of Engineers based on past experience. Writing to Sentner in summer 1944, Missouri Farmers Association leader H.E. Klinefelter condemned the Pick Plan as an "army engineers' scheme." He charged that the Corps had "all but ruined the Missouri River with their attempts to develop a 6 foot channel. Now they talk of a 9 foot channel." Klinefelter favored any plan that would "take authority away from the army engineers and give it to some independent agency that hasn't any axes to grind."[26] The *Missouri Farmer*, journal of the eighty-six thousand member organization, endorsed the MVA "in the hope that by superseding the new flood control law with an MVA, at least SOME of these monumental dams might be replaced with extensive soil conservation measures which are quite as effective as dams—if not more so—in holding back floods." In the upper valley, according to a *St. Louis Star-Times* investigation, "many small farmers, dirt farmers, [and] small town merchants" were "skeptical toward grandiose plans for irrigation," such as those proposed by the BR which had usually benefited large farmers only.[27] But the MVA pamphlet pledged that water resources would favor small farmers over agribusiness. In addition, the pledge of public power from water resources won over many farmers. The National Farmers Union, a grassroots organization headquartered in Montana, had proposed in 1942 that the "TVA be made a pilot operation for the nation." By late August, NFU had begun to launch its own campaign among its 250,000 members, using *One River, One Plan* as its tool. Glen Talbott, president of the North Dakota Farmers Union and chair of the NFU's water resources conservation committee, wrote that the organization would "do everything in our power to secure this type of approach."[28]

The coalition with farmers would have a pronounced effect on the perspectives of the labor activists, especially regarding the farmers' stress on soil conservation over dams for flood control, a point, as we shall see, that would eventually challenge notions of "taming the river." Naomi Ring, the district's MVA staff researcher, received a series of letters from farmers and soil conservationists stressing that an MVA should make soil conservation and erosion a central consideration. In August, she wrote somewhat contritely that *One River, One Plan* (for which she had apparently been the primary author) had been her first "encounter with river development . . . I have come to the conclusion that more stress should have been put on irrigation, soil conservation and the general well-being of the farmers."[29] Within a short time, District Eight supporters of the MVA sought to assure their farmer allies that the structure of an MVA would take their concerns into consideration. Sentner wrote to another correspondent who worried about the navigation provisions of the MVA that "MVA would only undertake regional projects that are both feasible and benefit a maximum amount of the people in the valley; therefore, I am sure we will have no worry." Klinefelter wrote Sentner, with regard to concerns about soil and flood control issues, "I do not believe we are very far apart on the subject."[30]

MVA supporters recognized that it would encounter stiff opposition from the BR and ACE, but were gratified to win support from the Rural Electrification Agency (REA), a governmental agency that had promoted public power projects and cheap electricity for rural regions in the New Deal Administration; the REA was defunded during the war and its staff had an obvious interest in promoting the MVA. Ring used Packard's contacts in the REA to secure staff support and advice. She reported to Sentner that after a meeting between herself, Packard, and REA, REA was willing to "go along" with the labor-farmer coalition that was developing out of the UE's efforts because of the respect they had for Packard, adding that "the fact that you and Packard are so 'close' gave them more confidence in the role labor will have to play in an MVA organization."[31]

In August 1944, MVA legislation, written by Packard, REA staff and District Eight representatives, was submitted by Senator James Murray of Montana. Later, Missouri Representative John Cochran submitted the House version of the bill.[32] Both bills allowed the authority two years to develop a plan that would "reconcile and harmonize" the requirements for flood control, navigation, reclamation, power, and other needs "in such a way as to secure the maximum public benefit for the region and the nation." The plan would then require Congressional approval. The MVA would be governed by a board of three directors, who "would utilize to the fullest possible extent the advice and assistance of the people of the region, including local and state governments." Missouri Valley Authority directors were barred from having any financial interest that would benefit from any potential development. The bill gave the MVA "broad powers to sell and distribute electric power and water and to fix rates" for sale to consumers, with a preference for sale to cooperatives. The legislation barred dams not approved by the MVA. Further, evidence that environmental concerns had already gained ground in conceptualizations of the MVA were apparent in a provision that gave the authority the power to "prevent pollution of the waters of the Missouri and its tributaries."[33] On September 22, FDR sent a message to Congress strongly endorsing the bill and calling for more authorities. Vice-presidential candidate Truman also made a wholehearted endorsement.[34]

In the fall, the grassroots campaign for the MVA began to take shape. UE delegates wended support for the bill through the Missouri CIO convention, which endorsed the MVA and voted to call a nine-state meeting of CIO unions to help organize for it. The Missouri CIO and UE representatives pushed the national CIO convention, held in November, to make the MVA part of their "People's Program of 1944."[35] Farmers' groups also increased their efforts. The Cooperative League, a two million member association advocating cheap power, enthusiastically endorsed the MVA. The Consumers Cooperative Association, a similar group based in Kansas City, also endorsed it.[36]

The momentum for an MVA was strong enough to force what James Patton of the National Farmers Union called a "shameless, loveless, shotgun marriage" between the Army Corp of Engineers and the Bureau of Reclamation. In early November, the two agencies quickly collaborated on a new proposal comprising six pages, called Pick-Sloan, which combined the elements of the two plans into what the agencies claimed was a comprehensive Missouri Basin Plan. They divided up jurisdiction, with the BR having authority over the upper valley and the Corps retaining control on all navigation and lower valley projects. As one scholar has pointed out, "the new plan said nothing about how the water would be proportioned to meet conflicting needs," and while it called for hydroelectric power, it did not call for public power projects. Finally, as the *Post-Dispatch* later noted, Pick-Sloan even violated the standing principles of the Bureau of Reclamation, however loosely they had been enforced, that those who benefited from irrigated water would pay for the costs, and even retroactively applied its provisions to money still owed to the BR. Pick-Sloan was nothing more than "a subsidy for the privileged interests," wrote Walter Packard. There were no provisions for soil conservation or other environmental measures.[37]

Pick-Sloan sufficiently united congressional supporters who argued that it was a comprehensive plan that obviated a need for an MVA. Pick-Sloan legislators included provisions in their bill that would prevent the future creation of an MVA. After much wrangling, and fearing that Pick-Sloan might be approved with the anti-MVA provisions, MVA congressional supporters worked out a compromise with Pick-Sloan backers despite protests from grass roots supporters in farm and labor groups. Murray consented to postpone the push for MVA legislation until the next Congress in return for the elimination of provisions from the Pick-Sloan bill that would prevent the ability of MVA to supersede it and the promise of early hearings. Murray reasoned that because only four hundred million dollars had been appropriated for the initial phase of the Pick-Sloan, the fight for an MVA was best postponed until more momentum could support it. The Pick-Sloan bill passed Congress in late December 1944. MVA proponents were buoyed by FDR's statements that Pick-Sloan should not be considered a substitute for the MVA, and that its provisions could indeed be integrated with an MVA. Vice-President-Elect Truman was also considered an "ardent advocate of MVA."[38]

Even as hopes for an MVA were collapsing in Congress, a new determination had taken hold among MVA advocates. In a representative expression of that urgency, the *Missouri Farmer* excoriated the intentions behind the Pick-Sloan plan with extensive detail of what it would mean to Missouri farmers and rural residents. The editorial charged that the twenty-six proposed Missouri dams were intended chiefly for a deeper channel as desired by Kansas City commercial interests, rather than for the ostensible purpose of flood control. The commentary estimated that the dams would "ruin approximately 900,000 acres of Missouri's best farm land, and force some 20,000 families out of their homes." The dams would "ruin" six counties and parts of five others. The proposed Table Rock Dam in Taney county would flood "most of the best land" in three counties. Parts of other counties "will be flooded while lakes of water and mud will destroy, permanently, some of the world's finest springs and beauty spots in Wayne, Reynolds, Shannon, Carter and Ripley counties." Chillicothe "will be located on a peninsula—an enormous lake will almost cover up Livingston County and a corner of Linn county." A dam on the Grand River meant that a fourth of Davies County "will be inundated," and dams on the Meramec River and Big River would "blight Franklin and Jefferson counties." The editorial concluded that most Missourians in the affected areas "appear not to comprehend what has been done to them," and that "the few" who understood Pick-Sloan "seem to believe that their Government 'will not do this thing to us' as one of them recently put it."

Warning that without action on the part of the citizenry "it will be done!" the *Missouri Farmer* predicted "that when the people living in these condemned areas of Missouri learn the full import of the new flood control law they will never return any Missouri Congressman to office who voted for it!" Upper Missouri farmers also argued that navigation would dominate the purposes even under this "compromise" plan.[39]

In mid-December, Sentner outlined a plan for a grassroots campaign to coincide with the next legislative session. Noting the momentum toward an MVA, and the way it was able to unify various labor, farmer, and consumer groups, Sentner outlined plans for a "movement [that] should become the Broadest movement developed since the days of the Populist(s)." Sentner emphasized that the "movement should be local in character but should be linked with the national program." Unions could "be the force that ties in these regional projects with the overall national program, thus prevent[ing] these projects from becoming a political football with regional trades in congress, etc." In order to move on the program, District Eight representatives persuaded their national union office to allocate a staff member to work for the establishment of a St. Louis MVA committee, a nine-state committee, and a national committee to support the MVA.[40] UE's new staffperson assigned to the MVA campaign, William Chambers, emphasized to their farm organization friends that they preferred to get "community people to take the lead rather than one of the Congressmen," as some had suggested, in order to keep the campaign a grassroots drive.[41]

In January 1945, the St. Louis committee was formally established, with Raymond Tucker as chair and with representatives from labor, law, veterans groups, women's groups, and church groups, though Chambers and Sentner worried that the committee was "weak on industry people," whom they thought were necessary to combat criticism of MVA.[42] Under Chambers's and Sentner's guidance, the group established a speakers bureau to expand their outreach. Over the course of the next few months, the St. Louis committee speakers went before groups such as the St. Louis Women's Chamber of Commerce, Liberal Voters League, St. Louis Branch of the NAACP, local posts of the Veterans of Foreign Wars, Missouri Federation of Women's Clubs, and many church groups. By spring 1945, the campaign was yielding "strong official backing from the Catholic Church." This campaign also helped to develop a bit of support among business, especially among small businesses, using the argument that by electrifying farms in the Missouri valley, industrial expansion would accrue to many St. Louis businesses. Then, in April 1945, the St. Louis committee scored a major victory when, in a referendum, the St. Louis Chamber of Commerce members voted to endorse the MVA.[43]

By early 1945, other city-based committees were being organized in the nine-state region, including one in Kansas City and another in St. Charles County. In February 1945, through District Eight's push, a national CIO committee for an MVA was established and declared plans for "reaching every CIO member in the nine-state region on the importance of regionally administered MVA." In addition, other state CIO federations pledged to organize for an MVA and to disseminate educational material and information on MVA through local unions to individual CIO members.[44] Further, the seeds planted in 1944 among the AFL groups were beginning to develop into a real coalition. In Kansas City, the AFL "has taken hold and is circulating all the building trades unions in the nine states for support" and was starting to establish a nine-state building trades MVA committee. Both the AFL and the CIO held valley-wide conferences on the MVA to promote and organize for it. Finally, in spring 1945, a "Friends of the Missouri Valley" national committee was established, chaired by Thurman Hill of Washington, D.C., claiming it would "coordinate efforts of state and local proponents of the MVA." While Sentner was gratified that he was included among the endorsers, he stressed that the impetus for the campaign should remain at the local level.[45]

As the campaign progressed, and even as the issue of jobs and development remained a primary emphasis in the arguments for an MVA, proponents sought to differentiate their proposal from Pick-Sloan by arguing that only through the MVA would concerns for the environment be taken into account. Listen, for instance, to this example speech for the speakers' bureau, (probably written by Sentner):

> We are in the process of closing a three-century long epoch of planless exploitation of the human, natural, and physical resources of North America. During these three centuries, it has been assumed that untrammelled individual initiative would somehow yield the greatest long-run social progress. Now we know the error of that assumption. The practices of the past compel the immediate formulation of regional and national plans. Not to do so now may lead to disaster not many years hence.

Another CIO representative suggested that the "present practice regarding rivers is to work backwards. We spend millions of dollars to buy fertilizer to replace ruined soil. We spend millions of dollars to purify river water polluted by soil. But we refuse to spend money to eliminate the conditions which lead to soil protection and a pure flow of water."[46]

The new Murray Bill, submitted in February 1945, put more emphasis on soil conservation and promised to "restore the declining water table, protect wild game; conserve water, soil, mineral and forest resources" in addition to development through energy dispersion in the upper valley. It also added to the MVA's duties the "disposal of war and defense factories to encourage industrial and business expansion," again emphasizing the decentralization of power from Washington, D.C. Structurally, it added an advisory committee to be composed of representatives of labor, farmer, business, and citizens' groups, reflecting proponents' attempts to enhance the viability of public input into decentralized, regional planning.[47]

By summer 1945, the ranks of supporters of the coalition had expanded, and the campaign began to influence sentiments and opinions in the nine-state area. In May, a "Missouri Conference on MVA," organized by the St. Louis group, was sponsored by over fifty organizations.[48] This meeting spurred the organization of a Regional Committee for an MVA, founded at a July 1945 convention and headquartered in Omaha. There, hundreds of leaders of various groups, including farmers' groups, labor groups, women's groups, the National Association for the Advancement of Colored People, the Veterans of Foreign Wars, and others voiced their commitment to organize a petition drive for one million signatures to spur Congress to support an MVA.[49] The progress of this group and the others in building support for the MVA was indicated in a Gallup Poll during the summer, which revealed that three out of every four people in the Missouri River areas favored an MVA.[50]

But the MVA's political fortunes in 1945 certainly didn't match the expectations raised by such polls. Murray had expected the bill to be sent to the Agriculture Committee as he had requested, and as had been the case with the TVA and similar legislation. But Vice-President Truman, in the first of what many in the campaign would later view as a series of outrageous betrayals despite his vocal support, referred the bill to the Commerce Committee, chaired by a senator hostile to MVA. Others understood that since his early political career Truman had been a close ally of the ACE and Kansas City navigation interests, and in fact "was a friend of Pick's."[51] The MVA bill faced an uphill battle as it steered slowly through two subcommittees, whose chairman, John Overton, was head of an organization formed to oppose the MVA.[52]

Behind these strong congressional opponents was a growing overlapping coalition opposing the MVA, totalling thirty organizations, which began to organize and spend exponentially over the $10,000 that the pro-MVA forces raised for the entire campaign in 1945. Leading the opposition was the National Association of Electric Companies, formed in the summer of 1945 and composed of 170 private power companies who undertook a richly financed campaign to influence public opinion against the MVA. It placed full-page advertisements in newspapers across the nine-state region, financed a weekly radio program, and subsidized the publication of a book attacking the TVA.

(A later investigation suggested that the NAEC had made kickback arrangements with their suppliers to finance anti-MVA propaganda in each state.) Another powerful new organization was the Missouri Valley Development Association (MVDA), which worked with the power interests but also started to organize the many other groups that had a stake in keeping out an MVA. They coordinated an array of groups already opposing the MVA, including, for example, upper-valley cattlemen (who opposed it because they feared loss of rangeland to irrigation), barge-line operators and river construction contractors (two of many groups with a financial stake in navigation), the Associated General Contractors, (who opposed it because the MVA would hire workers directly instead of contracting out to private companies), the National Reclamation Association, an upper-valley group composed of power companies, railroads, chambers of commerce, and corporation ranchers who sought to maintain their entrenched position with the BR. The Mississippi Valley Association, which represented navigation interests and was headed by St. Louisan Laclan Macleay, lined up the key testimony at the congressional hearings. The MVDA especially was successful in organizing governors and state legislatures and business groups to go on record against the MVA.[53] Finally, the MVDA set up an anti-MVA office in St. Louis to specifically target the St. Louis Chamber of Commerce. By October, they were successful in keeping the Chamber of Commerce from moving on its favorable referendum vote to support MVA. As commentators noted, that vote had been "a blow" to anti-MVA forces, and had "hampered their campaign ever since. . . . When they attempt to brand MVA and its supporters as 'socialistic,' opponents lay themselves open to the retort, 'The St. Louis Chamber of Commerce voted to support MVA. Is that organization socialistic?'"[54]

Opponents were unified in their arguments against the MVA: it was unnecessary in light of the Pick-Sloan plan, it would establish a "super-government" and was a step toward "state socialism." As Sentner later put it, "All of these organizations assailed MVA as 'unAmerican' and a 'threat to private enterprise.'" Disputing the constant pleas of MVA supporters that their plan was a move away from distant government bureaucracy and would place more control in the hands of the citizens of the valley, the opposition groups suggested that the power placed in the hands of the MVA advisory board would interfere with state government's ability to control their own destiny and the waters that ran through their states. Anti-MVA pamphlets with titles such as "Totalitarianism on the March" suggested that sinister forces were involved in the MVA campaign. The MVDA called for an investigation of the pro-MVA campaign for "unAmerican activities."[55]

The tack in Congress also added another dimension, suggesting that most of the pro-MVA advocates at the congressional hearings were "unqualified" to testify on river problems. Autoworker James Davis, secretary of the Missouri CIO and head of the CIO nine-state committee, chafed at this charge. He retorted that he had "seen with his own eyes" the "mistakes made by army engineers," which had ruined the farm owned by his family in the Missouri bottomlands.

> I worked for the Army Engineers when they threw the dikes up on the Missouri River. . . . I have seen, in the last four years, land worth $200 an acre covered over with willows and sand because of certain dikes in there, when the floods came. No one up there had any way of knowing which way they were going to channel the river. My experience has been very practical, something I could see.

Davis criticized Pick-Sloan for ignoring "any attempt to integrate soil conservation, erosion control, community development or cheap power," as called for by the citizenry. He also noted that Murray's bill at least provided a role for "the farmer, the business man, and labor, does this and reaches all walks of life."[56]

By the fall, when it was clear that the MVA Bill was being picked apart in committee hearings, Murray asked that further hearings be postponed. Meanwhile, Sentner and other activists outlined the longer-term political fight that would have to be fought, state by state, around the issue. Sentner reflected cogently on the entrenched opposition, but he remained focused on the growth of the coalition that had come together over the issue. The campaign for the MVA, he noted, "has united progressive forces . . . as they have never been united before," had been the catalyst for the organization of citizens' groups in various cities, including St. Louis, and had united farm and labor groups in a way that no other issue had been able to do: "Farmers Union and MFA leaders addressed Labor Day picnics and are speaking at the state conventions of labor organizations this fall," while new groups, such as the Catholic Rural Life Congress, had become energized over the issue. The "movement has grown . . . and no longer can be considered as a simple movement in support of a piece of legislation. It is and must be considered as a major political movement with all of the elements of populism which is so native to our section of the country . . . this movement if given proper support and guidance, can go out in the 1946 election campaign and make a major contribution to the election of progressive members of the U.S. Congress and Senate."[57]

Sentner's vision was never realized, and while from 1946 to 1948 hopes continued to be raised that the MVA would find the political momentum to match its popularity, these hopes were dashed. What happened to the vision that Sentner articulated?

In many respects, we can say that postwar era labor politics dashed it. Postwar strikes, beginning in late 1945 and continuing through the biggest strike year in history, 1946, consumed the attention of most labor unions. Then beginning in 1946, as the cold war began to escalate, there was an intensification of the existing internal polarization over the role of leftists such as Sentner within the CIO. The CIO hierarchy sought to exclude Sentner for instance, from any representation of MVA boards. (Ironically, Sentner, enjoyed more support from the St. Louis MVA committee, a community-based coalition, and especially its executive secretary, who relied constantly on his advice, than he did from the national CIO.) Of course cold war politics elevated the issue of Communists in the labor movements to a new level and became an all-consuming job for Sentner. Meanwhile, beginning in 1945, the national CIO centralized the CIO campaign from Washington, D.C., appointing lackluster bureaucrats to organize it. This was certainly not the locally based campaign Sentner envisioned.[58] Further, the CIO's legislative efforts became concentrated on attempting to prevent anti-labor legislation such as the Taft-Hartley Act as the labor movement found itself fighting a rearguard action. Finally, while still publicly calling for planning in the postwar era, the CIO's commitment to it floundered on the shoals of a booming postwar economy. The immediate postwar years did not prove to be the return to Depression-era conditions that many had predicted. Pent-up consumer demand boosted the economy until late 1948, when a severe recession set in. Then, with the onset of the cold war and the hot war in Korea, defense spending surreptitiously crept in as a jobs program that both the CIO and conservatives could accept. In St. Louis, Emerson Electric was just one of many businesses which benefited from these developments. It was a new kind of planning that replaced the grand visions articulated during the war.

Just as important, however, was the continual floundering of the campaign under the momentum of legislative defeats and the inability to get committee hearings. In 1946, Murray submitted a revised bill which included representation from federal agencies in the MVA structure. But after the 1946 elections, a conservative Congress took office. When, in spring 1947 devastating floods came again, President Truman nodded in the direction of an MVA but asked Congress for four billion dollars for Pick-Sloan, thus boosting it to what the *New York Times* called a "bustling reality." In 1948, the election of a more progressive Congress (including fifteen congressman and two senators who had won on a pro-MVA platform) renewed hopes among MVA proponents, but a revised bill (which agreed to use existing agencies and not to disrupt Pick-Sloan projects underway) was unable to make it out of committees still controlled by opponents of the idea. Throughout these legislative attempts, MVA supporters found that Truman remained an obstacle. A chronicler of the MVA's legislative fortunes has argued that Truman "deserved much of the blame for the continued frustration among MVA's supporters." After becoming president, he continued to publicly pledge support, but helped to torpedo it even when it enjoyed positive prospects, such as in 1948 when the election of a more progressive Congress inspired the last substantive push among supporters.[59]

What was lost with the defeat of the MVA and the demise of the coalition that had generated it? Clearly, the fledgling development of alternative environmental approach to natural resources that had taken root among many farmers, workers, and citizens. This approach appeared to deepen even as the prospects for MVA dimmed. In the years that Pick-Sloan began to become a reality, the critique among those who held the coalition together even under unfortunate circumstances yielded unprecedented perspectives about the value of technological solutions to river management and considerable evidence of a growing understanding of the relationship between floods and human activity. The MVA coalition continued to attack the premises of Pick-Sloan, arguing that it failed to recognize that "the cause of floods originated almost wholly upon the land. It is what is done on the land that conserves water."

By 1948, as W.C. Etheridge, a coalition advisor from the College of Agriculture at the University of Missouri, put it in one speech before the Regional MVA group, there was a complete "loss of faith in dams as a means to control floods." Etheridge recounted the "long story of the attempts to control floods by the building of dams is one of more and bigger dams and *more and bigger floods*. The dams have mounted in height and number and cost but they have nowhere permanently curbed the torrents. To the lay mind the whole situation seems extravagant and foolish." When combined with the destruction of fish and wildlife that Pick-Sloan entailed and other developments such as the "denudation" of land instead of reforestation, the "natural means to flood control" were being further eroded. Etheridge proposed to the group, in a widely disseminated speech, an argument that a kind of "chaos theory" would defeat the Corps's plans—suggesting that the siltation of reservoirs and the loss of volume in dams proved their conviction "that the purpose of high dams as the major means of flood control is ultimately defeated by the imponderables." The Missouri group also issued a resolution criticizing TVA's lack of attention to soil conservation and reforestation, called for "extensive areas" to be "designated as protected from development," and suggested that any kind of "regional planning should prevent urban congestion and work for the decentralization of industries and cities into smaller and more liveable communities—sound, democratic, social planning by public agencies having power would attempt to deal with long commutes by workers."[60] The CIO Committee on Regional Development drafted a pamphlet (ironically in consultation with Sentner, who they had sought to keep out of the coalition) in the late 1940s that also sought to articulate clearly these ideas:

> Too long our American forests, rivers, minerals have been exploited for private profit. Too long our soils have been neglected and abused. . . . Our life becomes constantly more urban and more mechanical. We are losing our contact with nature, with the outdoors and with the leisurely pace of living which characterized America in its rural epoch. The speed-up has spread throughout our entire civilization and is no longer to be found only in our industrial plants. . . . [We must choose] long-range goals with care. It means we must be very much on guard against taking over into our social planning the same standards of value which created our difficulties. In the field of resource development and conservation, it means an emphasis on the so-called renewable or living resources; forests, soil, waters, wildlife, recreation, and scenery. In regional planning, it means the dispersion of industries and cities and the encouragement of our smaller communities. This is not to disparage our engineering works. . . . But it is to say that men do not live by consumers' goods alone.[61]

The expression of such sentiments indicates just how far the interaction with farm constituency and conservationists had moved labor from the developmental perspective. Nevertheless, the structure of the CIO and labor politics in the postwar era had ensured that these lofty ideas lacked a community-based grassroots campaign that could have brought them to the center of public discourse.

By 1951, Pick-Sloan had used 1.25 billion dollars to build dams and levees on the Missouri and its tributaries, yet the floods of that year were the worst in history up to that point. Yet despite its defeat, one scholar of Missouri river development suggests that the "MVA specter haunted the agencies" and "served as a latent threat," forcing them eventually to give up some planned dams and navigation projects. Particularly important in this was the work of Missouri Farmers Association leaders who continued to push Missouri Congressman Clarence Cannon to restrict the Corps's activities. In 1954, Cannon succeeded in "prohibiting the use of funds in the stretch of river from Kansas City to the mouth 'for any purpose other than bank stabilization work,'" thereby preventing plans to deepen the channel, at least until 1963, when Cannon's health failed and Congress "with no mention" in published hearings, renewed the navigation channel appropriations.[62]

# Floods, Rats, and Toxic Waste

*Allocating Environmental Hazards Since World War II*

~

## *Andrew Hurley*

On the face of it, the Great Flood of 1993 served as a reminder that despite advances in engineering and information technology, the human ability to control nature has its limits. The deluge did not come as a complete surprise. Television and newspaper reports followed the approaching swell as it devastated one upstream community after another. People who lived and worked in the floodplains of the Missouri and Mississippi Rivers, along with those who occupied land along its tributaries, the Meramec River and the River des Peres, worked relentlessly to contain the overflow by fortifying flood walls and constructing sandbag barricades. The rivers did not cooperate. From July 16 through August 1, the rushing waters pummelled protective levees, yanked barges from their moorings, and flooded businesses and homes. On the night of July 30, the force of the Mississippi River snapped the metal cables that held fifty-one propane tanks to their waterside mounts. Bobbing freely in the water, the tanks shook the feeder pipes violently, straining them to the point of possible rupture. Had the highly flammable propane gas escaped, a massive conflagration would have been likely. Fortunately for the several thousand nearby residents, the pipes held.

While local and national media portrayed the Great Flood of 1993 as a calamity visited upon an entire city, in fact, most of the metropolis was spared from destruction. For the majority of St. Louisans, the flood was a spectacular drama witnessed vicariously through television, or by firsthand observation for the more adventurous. For many citizens, the flood also provided an opportunity to exercise civic altruism through sandbagging and relief efforts. However, the number of people who lost their homes or suffered property damage was relatively small. Seen from this perspective, the Great Flood of 1993 was less a reminder of the human inability to control nature than an illustration of some people's ability to successfully insulate themselves from the vagaries of sudden environmental change. Indeed, one can read the entire environmental history of St. Louis in terms of the relative success of certain groups in controlling nature, often at the expense of their neighbors. Given the severe disparities that govern the physical condition of the urban landscape, it is certainly an appropriate framework.

If we apply this perspective, not only to the impact of natural disasters, but also to the differential impact of shifts in flora and fauna, waste disposal, and the quality of the city's built infrastructure, we can discern clear patterns that expose the way class and race have conditioned the relationship between the urban population and the environment. Through an examination of the urban response to flooding, the proliferation of rats, and the disposal of toxic wastes, this concluding essay aims to explore the public and private means by which class and race have become imprinted on the allocation of environmental amenities and disamenities in St. Louis, especially in the years since World War II.

## Floods

St. Louis's geological and meteorological features leave its inhabitants exposed to natural disaster in the form of periodic tornadoes, earthquakes, fires, and floods. To some extent these disasters are governed by forces beyond human control--wind patterns, fluctuations in atmospheric pressure, tensions along subterranean faultlines, and so forth. Yet, the hand of human history is very much behind the precise pattern of destruction and the way that different portions of the population are affected. In an earlier essay, Mark Tebeau observed how changes in the insurance industry during the late-nineteenth century altered people's relative vulnerability to urban fires. In similar ways, human activity has conditioned the social impact of tornadoes and floods.

Although tornadoes do not act with intention when they strike, the shoddy structures that stand in their path are more likely to fall than those built of sturdier materials. The wealthy are not always spared, but their financial resources often give them a decided advantage.[1] Consider the repercussions of the tornado that ripped though the metropolis in 1896. It was the most devastating in the city's history, killing more than two hundred people. Crumbling buildings, flying bricks and glass, and electrical fires caused an additional one thousand injuries. Human suffering was concentrated in the working-class districts of the city's south side, although not on account of any predisposition on the part of the tornado. The cyclone tore a path through rich and poor neighborhoods alike. Among the first sections of the city to bear the force of the eighty-mile-per-hour windstorm were the fashionable residential districts of Compton Heights and Lafayette Park. Grain elevators, warehouses, and manufacturing plants along the southern portion of the riverfront also sustained damage. But while the cyclone took sizable bites from the stone and brick mansions in the wealthy districts and dislodged brick and glass from the factory facades, it completely toppled many of the more rickety homes and shops that lay in between. On one corner alone—at the intersection of Seventh and Rutger Streets—seventeen people were smashed to death under the weight of collapsed wooden and brick buildings. Just a short distance away along Broadway, "massive business blocks reeled and crumbled like card houses, and in many places the dead and injured outnumbered the unscathed," according to one observer.[2]

In terms of actual property damage, the elite residents of Lafayette Park and Compton Heights undoubtedly suffered the greater financial loss on account of the higher values of their homes. One must keep in mind, however, that wealthy property holders were also in a better position to rebound from such financial setbacks. By the early part of the twentieth century, they were also able to take out insurance policies to protect against catostrophic loss to their property.

In contrast to the precautions taken to minimize the impact of earthquakes and tornadoes, which were largely inadvertent, St. Louisans have pursued flood control with sustained purpose for more than two centuries. The founding of the city at a point high upon the western bluffs of the Mississippi affirmed the importance of achieving immunity form the seasonal variations in river flow. On occasion, even the bluffs failed to offer sufficient protection. When the river surpassed the forty-one-foot gauge in the spring of 1844, muddy water lapped at downtown storefronts and homes. Refugees took shelter in Colonel Brant's tobacco warehouse. Madame Chouteau salvaged her expensive furniture by hauling it through her attic windows.[3]

The movement of population and industry into the low-lying floodplains north and south of downtown over the next century, along with metropolitan expansion on the American Bottoms in Illinois, placed more people and property at risk.[4] Desirable residential districts tended to spread along high ground, but by the turn of the century, factories and working-class homes had sprung up on many of the most vulnerable points along the riverfront. Urban development of the floodplain was tied directly to the coming of the railroads in the second half of the nineteenth century. Railroad companies chose to lay their tracks in the floodplains leading from downtown because the flat valley floors provided an ideal surface for construction. Industries gravitated to these riverside corridors to take advantage of both rail and water transportaton. To house the workers who toiled in these factories, developers erected modest homes in the vicinity.[5] On some portions of the riverfront, squatters raised ramshackle homes close to potential sources of employment.[6] Thus, the extent of human disturbance on account of flooding increased considerably. When unusually high water rolled by the city in 1903, it drove twenty-five thousand people from their homes.[7] Twelve years later, another deluge wrecked hundreds of small wood framed homes along the River des Peres. Twelve people lost their lives along with an estimated 500,000 chickens.[8] Although the people who purchased or rented homes in the floodplain may have been cognizant of the risks, proximity to work and cheap housing costs probably overrode concerns about flooding.

Repeated damage to property along the bottomlands prompted industrial and commercial concerns to build protective walls and levees. Railroad companies that laid tracks along the floodplains were among the first to construct a series of earthen embankments along the Mississippi River to keep periodic floods from interrupting the flow of commerce. To protect its new steel plant and the homes of laborers in Granite City, Illinois, the Niedringhaus family helped to finance the Madison County levee, the largest protective levee in the metropolitan area, in 1893. For the most part, however, privately funded flood protection worked to the advantage of highly capitalized enterprises rather than residential property. It is instructive to note that while the Madison County levee staved off disaster for the factories and working-class residents of Granite City during the 1903 flood, an African American community located further downstream was afforded no such protection and was overrun by the Mississippi River in many places.[9]

Indeed, for unprotected residential communities, the cumulative effect of levee construction was to exacerbate the destructiveness of periodic flooding. By obstructing the free flow of water across lowland areas, the levees only squeezed greater volumes of water downstream; by confining the river to a narrower channel, the levees pushed water past the city at ever higher levels. Unprotected areas that had once been relatively safe from flooding became increasingly vulnerable. As early as 1851, Charles Ellet, Jr., of the U.S. Army Corps of Engineers, recognized that floods in the Mississippi Valley were increasing in height because levee obstructions forced the river to rise higher and flow faster downstream in order to discharge the same volume of water.[10] Subsequent investigations showed the problem growing worse as more railway inclines, protective levees, piers, and warehouses crowded upon the river. Although the floods of 1881 and 1951 carried nearly the same amount of water, the latter passed the city at a level six and a half feet higher.[11]

Several other factors contributed to the problem. With the construction of a vast network of storm sewers, a development described in detail by Katharine Corbett in her essay, rainwater that once seeped into the soil to replenish groundwater supplies was now siphoned to the Mississippi River, adding to the total flow. Sediment accumulation along the river bed also raised the water level. River confinement, however, remained the primary culprit of worsening floods.[12] There were offsetting factors, to be sure, as Walter Schroeder noted in the first chapter of this book. Yet, continued urban development in the floodplain and the heightened destructiveness of floods caused considerable alarm among civic leaders by the twentieth century.

Curiously, the predominant response to this predicament was to build even more levees. During the 1940s, civic and business leaders saw levee construction as an integral part of a scheme to revitalize industrial development along the St. Louis waterfront. By this time, St. Louis was running out of vacant land for factory construction and city planners had identified the riverfront as the only viable place for future industrial growth. But the risk of river flooding deterred manufacturers from sinking large sums of capital into expansion or new construction projects. Hence, industrial development hinged upon flood protection.

The city's hopes for providing such protection were buoyed by legislation passed by Congress in the 1930s that had made federal funds available for this purpose. In 1947 a group of industrialists who operated facilities along the riverfront spearheaded the campaign for federally funded flood protection by forming the St. Louis Flood Control Association. The following year, Aloys Kaufmann, mayor of St. Louis, submitted to Congress a formal request for a series of protective levees along the Mississippi River stretching from one end of the city to the other. The proposal, as originally drafted, also included provisions to contain the River des Peres, which was subject to backflow from the Mississippi River at high water stages. Ironically, the channelization of the river in the 1920s and 1930s, which reduced the risk of flooding somewhat, spurred new residential and industrial development along its banks in south St. Louis, thereby exposing more people to a danger that still existed.[13]

After subjecting the plan to a cost-benefit analysis, the Army Corps of Engineers determined that some portions of the riverfront simply weren't worth protecting. Only where property values were high or were expected to increase as a result of flood control did the Chief of Engineers recommend the allocation of public funds. The key variable in assessing the value of particular parcels of riverfront property was the extent of industrial activity. Hence, the city had no trouble justifying its request for sections of the riverfront just north and south of downtown where several manufacturers operated plants and where the city planned for further industrial expansion. Here, the Army Corps of Engineers calculated that the economic benefits of flood control would far outweigh the costs of construction.[14]

Corporate interests that stood to benefit from the project lobbied Congress to secure the necessary appropriations. To arouse sympathy among federal lawmakers, industry leaders cited the hardships caused by previous floods and predicted tremendous damages that would result from future ones. Speaking before a Senate subcommittee, the executive vice-president of the St. Louis Car Company described how high water on the Mississippi forced his company to relocate equipment and curtail operations every few years. A Ralston Purina Company vice-president detailed the inconvenience and expense involved in sandbagging, pumping water, and constructing portable embankments every time the rising river threatened Purina's grain elevator on the waterfront. A representative from the Mallinckrodt Chemical Works added that while his firm was able to weather minor overflows, a major flood would cost the company as much as 2.5 million dollars and idle one thousand workers for an indefinite period of time.[15] Apparently, such testimony convinced Congress, and it authorized the appropriation. In 1959, construction began on a network of concrete flood walls and earthen levees stretching from Maline Creek in the city's northern reaches to Chippewa Street, eleven miles to the south.[16]

In the working-class residential districts farther south where property values were comparatively low, anticipated costs exceeded potential benefits and federal funding was denied. Thus, the flood wall stopped where factories and warehouses gave way to homes. Only in one section of Carondelet did cost-benefit ratios work out favorably for flood protection, largely due to the presence of industry. But the Great Lakes Carbon Corporation, the major industrial concern in the area, lobbied *against* inclusion on the grounds that a flood wall would interfere with its operations. In this instance, industry used its political muscle to subvert the operative policy-making formula; no wall was constructed in this reach of the river. Residential property owners enjoyed no such clout.[17] Thus, although federal government largesse enabled the city to protect a larger portion of its riverfront than would have been possible otherwise, funding formulas and the political process continued to favor industry and commerce over the interests of local residents.

The inherent biases contained within the federal funding formula were evident during the Great Flood of 1993. While the factories of the Monsanto Corporation and the John Nooter Boiler Works remained dry behind the massive floodwall, the residential communities located a little further south were awash in muddy water. Damage was especially severe in Carondelet and the south St. Louis neighborhoods alongside the River des Peres. Sandbags piled high along the banks of this normally benign tributary saved some homes but were not nearly as effective as the concrete flood walls. Basements were flooded, streets were converted into streams, and thousands of residents had to be evacuated from their homes. More than one hundred houses in south St. Louis were damaged beyond repair.[18] Such was the legacy of more than one hundred years of flood control in St. Louis.

## Rats

Fossil remains from Cherokee Cave suggest the tremendous change in the composition of natural fauna in the St. Louis region over the centuries. Long before the Lemp Brewery used the subterranean cavity on the south side of St. Louis to store lager beer, the cave provided a habitat for armadillos, black bears, beavers, wolves, porcupines, woodchucks, and pecarries. Few of these species inhabit St. Louis today; some—the pecarry and armadillos, for instance—have become extinct, while others have moved beyond the range of urbanized settlement to more hospitable settings.[19] While urban growth proved to be incompatible with many of the species that inhabited the wetlands and woodlands currently occupied by the city of St. Louis, other species flourished in the new urban environment amid the backyard gardens, warehouses, alleyways, and kitchen cupboards built by human hands. Isolated from wilderness predators and furnished with an almost unlimited supply of food, readily adaptable animals such as the cockroach, the pigeon, the grey squirrel, the housefly, and the rat have found an ideal home in the modern city. To be sure, urbanization has reduced the variety of life forms drastically, but the city remains a thriving habitat for many nonhuman animals nonetheless.[20]

In some cases, human settlers deliberately populated the city with imported species either to perform useful tasks, to provide companionship, or to add to the diversity of natural life. Pigs performed a useful function for the city's earliest settlers by roaming the streets and consuming the food slops discarded by taverns and households. Prior to the invention of electricity and the internal combustion engine, horses served a variety of transportation purposes. By the latter part of the nineteenth-century, St. Louis streets teemed with the equestrian beasts. In 1880, more than two thousand horses were employed in the street railway system alone. Considering that the average horse produced about twenty pounds of excrement each day, one can begin to appreciate the horse's environmental impact.[21]

Following the common post–Civil War practice of introducing wild European birds to American soil, two prominent citizens released several varieties of exotic finches into Lafayette Park in 1870. Most of the birds did not take to the south St. Louis environment and perished, but twenty European tree sparrows thrived and multiplied, living off the bountiful grain supplies stored on the premises of the numerous breweries in the area. Several years later, most of the tree sparrows had been driven to more remote locations by a more aggressive European import, the English sparrow, a species which has since become ubiquitous, not only in St. Louis, but in most north American cities. In the 1930s, the city became host to yet another alien avian species, the European starling. Fifty years earlier, Eugene Schieffelin had brought the bird to America as part of his effort to import all the birds mentioned in William Shakespeare's works. Although Shakespeare only gave the starling a minor role—it appeared in one passage of *Henry IV*—the bird took top billing on the American stage. Gravitating to the warmer temperatures of dense urban areas, the European starling thrived among perforated trees, rotted eaves, and abandoned buildings, displacing many native species.[22]

In other cases, additions to the biotic pool were the result of inadvertent, and often unwelcome, importation. Such was the case with the brown Norway rat, which arrived as a stowaway on transatlantic ocean voyages in the eighteenth century. Few species have thrived so successfully in the urban environment; few have been perceived as more dangerous. Rats tend to follow people wherever they settle in large numbers because they enjoy the same foods—meat, fish, vegetables, fruit, and grain—and because they can make easy use of human-built structures for breeding and sheltering their young. Still, rat populations at any given place and time will vary according to the generosity of their human hosts. Due to their nocturnal habits and their penchant for occupying dark, enclosed, subterranean spaces, humans rarely glimpse the full dimension of rat proliferation in their cities. A rule of thumb for the recent twentieth century has been about one rat per person. In St. Louis during the early 1940s, however, the number of rats was estimated at 1.8 million, or roughly two rats per person. Rats in St. Louis were particularly fond of the numerous ashpits that people kept on their property prior to the establishment of municipal rubbish collection. In addition, sanitation services were notoriously poor in many St. Louis neighborhoods.[23]

Although it has been much maligned, and with good reason, the rat does provide some useful functions. Historian Sam Bass Warner, Jr., has noted that like mice, sparrows, cockroaches, and ants, rats assist humans in cleaning up the city by consuming discarded trash.[24] In this way they perform a scavenger role analogous to early nineteenth-century urban pigs. Apparently, they also served as a source of adventure. During World War II, children in some St. Louis neighborhoods organized rat hunting expeditions. Outfitted with hunting equipment, clubs, and sacks, they stalked rodents in infested innercity alleyways, sometimes bagging as many as twenty in one evening.[25]

In the eyes of most humans, however, the Norway rat has been viewed as a serious pest. Despite the relative rarity of bubonic plague in the United States, rats have posed, and continue to pose, a threat to public health. Their bites cause infections and fevers while intestinal parasites can pass through rat feces and urine into the human digestive system. Certain forms of habitual rat behavior contribute to other hazards and inconveniences. By burrowing below ground, rats frequently undermine building foundations; many urban fires owe their origins to rats gnawing through the insulation on electrical wires. Hungry rats have a reputation for being especially brazen about stealing exposed food from pantry shelves and garbage containers.[26]

Like other environmental disamenities, the hazards associated with rat infestation have not been distributed evenly across the urban population. Rats tend to gravitate to the centers of poverty. Certainly this has been the case in St. Louis since 1940, a period for which numerous studies of rodent activity have been undertaken. At the root of the relationship between rat infestation and poverty lies systematic disinvestment and neglect. By allowing housing units to fall into disrepair, urban slumlords have provided ideal harborage for rodents, especially in the form of dilapidated sheds and garages. Poor sanitation service, in turn, has ensured a veritable smorgasbord for hungry rats. The limited financial resources of impoverished tenants have not afforded them with an opportunity to compensate for the transgressions of property owners and city officials, and have often made the situation worse. In high crime areas, for instance, St. Louisans have been reluctant to invest in secure garbage containers, anticipating theft. In recent years, the rat problem in innercity St. Louis has been compounded by rapid depopulation which has left in its wake abandoned buildings and vacant lots.[27]

For those forced to live in such areas during the post–World War II era—residents in these districts suffered from limited mobility options on account of race and income—rat encounters conditioned daily life. Homes with broken walls and punctured floors allowed rodents to come and go as they pleased. Rat bites were common, forcing parents to keep a vigilant watch on their children. The case of Ricky Curtis Stewart, a three-month-old infant who was taken to the hospital after being bitten on the foot by a rat that crawled under his bed clothes, was not unusual in north St. Louis neighborhoods in the 1940s. Many families receiving public assistance in these years complained to their caseworkers about the rats that scampered across their childrens's beds delivering bites to the scalp, arms, and legs. One mother of five living in a dilapidated tenement on the city's north side was in the habit of burning lights through the night to keep the rodents away from her young children. To prevent them from chewing up their new clothes, she packed them in a box which she hung from a nail on the wall.[28]

By the 1950s, the most thoroughly infested area of the city was the Mill Creek valley. Here, in what was considered to be the city's worst slum area, 90 percent of all households lacked private baths while more than half had no running water. Most of the inhabitants were African American. Disinvestment by property owners, many of whom probably lived in other parts of the city, had left virtually the entire neighborhood in a state of dilapidation by the end of World War II.[29] It was a haven for rats. Yet, only after an incident in which a rodent chewed off the ear and gashed the forehead of a two-month-old boy, causing him to be admitted to Homer G. Phillips hospital in serious condition, did the rat problem in the Mill Creek valley generate any publicity.[30]

The persistent proliferation of rats in poor and predominantly African American neighborhoods is all the more appalling given the city's concerted efforts to eradicate the pest. Its failure to do so over a fifty-year period attests to a policy approach characterized by short-sightedness, limited political will, and at times, blatant discrimination. At best, rat control efforts in St. Louis have been sporadic, ebbing and flowing in tandem with the flickering spotlight of media attention. The predominant weapon in the war against rats has been poison. In 1942, the city inaugurated its rat-burrow dusting program, which relied on the spraying of calcium-cyanide in rat holes. To implement the program, the city trained more than sixteen hundred citizen volunteers in the use of spray guns and set them loose in their neighborhoods. Over time, the city turned to more lethal forms of poison, including anticoagulants.[31]

Poisoning, however, has proven to be of limited effectiveness. Rats are not only intelligent but have a keen sense of taste. Hence, a rat fortunate enough to survive a bout of poisoning is not likely to nibble at the same type of bait again. More importantly, poisoning has failed to address the conditions of poverty that have facilitated rat breeding in the first place. Whenever spraying activities were scaled back, as they have been following the subsidence of media publicity, rat populations have climbed rapidly to previous levels.[32]

Public health officials have recognized this failing and have, on occasion, called for more thorough and permanent solutions. In this vein, the city council in 1946 passed a comprehensive rat control ordinance based on U.S. Public Health Service recommendations, mandating that all property owners seal holes in walls and floors and keep their premises clear of loose trash. The law provided for inspections of "rat-stopped" buildings every forty-five days. Shortly thereafter, the city instituted municipal refuse collection to eliminate the ashpit problem.[33]

Unfortunately, enforcement of the ordinance lagged after a few years, and vanished completely in parts of the city where it was most desperately needed. In 1955, J. Earl Smith, St. Louis's health commissioner, came under fire for admitting that the city had all but abandoned rat control in the Mill Creek valley. He justified this inaction on the grounds that it was neither feasible nor practical to devote resources to rat control in areas that were slated for eventual slum clearance. Attempting to shift blame from his own department to the financially strapped residents who could hardly afford to take care of the problem on their own, Smith remarked, "a rat doesn't go anywhere unless he's invited."[34]

Perhaps the matter would have rested there had it not been for the concerted protests lodged on behalf of Mill Creek residents by Teamsters Local 688. In an earlier chapter, Rosemary Feurer highlighted organized labor's role as an advocate of environmental protection in the context of the fight for a Missouri Valley Authority. Only a few years later, organized labor would again lend its political muscle to the cause of improving environmental conditions, albeit through a different union and in a very different setting. Teamsters Local 688 represented several families who lived in the Mill Creek valley. Shocked by the widely publicized story of the infant who was hospitalized for rat bites and incensed by the health commissioner's indifference and insensitivity, union leaders decided to make rat control the priority of its Community Action program. Union members toured slum areas, photographed unsanitary conditions, and interviewed tenement dwellers. Then, the union took its case to the Board of Aldermen and secured its assistance in calling for stricter enforcement of the city's rat control ordinance. Frustrated with the administration's lethargy, however, the Teamsters decided to file suit against the city for failing to enforce its rat control and housing standard ordinances in the Mill Creek valley. The Teamsters Union won the suit and a circuit court judge ordered that the laws be enforced in all areas of the city, including those considered blighted.[35]

In time, the rat problem in the Mill Creek valley was solved, but only because the entire neighborhood was razed for urban renewal. As displaced residents filtered into neighborhoods on the city's north side, disinvestment in basic infrastructure followed, and so did the rats. A study conducted in 1968 found that roughly 70 percent of all reported rat bites in the city occurred in the corridor that stretched from downtown to the city's western border between Delmar Avenue and Natural Bridge Road. Inspections in low-income neighborhoods found evidence of rat infestation in 53 percent of the dwelling units. The corresponding figure in high-income areas was only two percent. The report criticized the city for emphasizing the provision of rat bait to disgruntled residents over thorough inspections of property.[36] A similar investigation conducted in 1980 reported little change in the situation, finding the heaviest incidence of rat infestation not only in the same northside neighborhoods identified in the 1968 report, but in adjoining tracts as well.[37]

## Toxic and Hazardous Waste

When St. Louisans think about toxic waste disposal, the tragedy of Times Beach comes to mind. Following the discovery of dioxin contamination in 1982, the entire suburban development was evacuated and the United States government eventually bought out the homes. Since then, controversy has raged regarding the most appropriate way to dispose of the contaminated soil. With respect to toxic waste contamination in St. Louis, however, Times Beach represents only the tip of the iceberg. Over the past century, manufacturing firms have used a vast array of dangerous chemicals and substances to produce industrial goods. While much of that waste matter has long since been carried away by waterways and wind, large quantities remain in the soil and groundwater. Today, the metropolitan area is pockmarked with sites where hazardous and toxic materials have been precariously disposed on land.

In recent years, the issue of toxic waste has been linked with the phenomena of environmental equity and environmental racism. Studies in various cities have uncovered evidence indicating that exposure to toxic pollution correlates with class and race: poor and minority residents tend to live closest to hazardous waste sites. A 1987 report issued by the United Church of Christ concluded that communities hosting active hazardous waste facilities consistently contained higher percentages of racial minorities than those without any and that, in addition, three out of every five Black and Hispanic Americans lived near at least one uncontrolled abandoned chemical waste site. Finding it unlikely that these patterns result from random chance, authors of the report inferred that deliberate racial discrimination on the part of polluters was responsible.[38]

In St. Louis, it is difficult to find conclusive evidence of deliberate racism on the part of polluters, but it is clear that class and race have been determining factors in exposure levels. With respect to race, much of the correlation can be attributed to real estate dynamics that brought certain types of people into certain types of neighborhoods in the decades following World War II. Thus, if racism was at work, it was a much more institutionalized, and arguably more insidious, variety.

The dimensions of the toxic waste problem in St. Louis are staggering. Wherever manufacturers handled hazardous materials prior to the advent of strict environmental regulations in the 1970s and 1980s, they left a trail of poison. Some hazardous waste sites in St. Louis date back to the nineteenth century. Many more reflect more recent manufacturing activity in the field of petrochemical production. The total number of sites in the St. Louis area where there is the potential of hazard to human health and the environment exceeds three hundred. Of these sites, at least fifty have been deemed sufficiently serious by federal and state regulatory agencies to warrant investigation or remedial action.

Lead is perhaps the most ubiquitous of the industrial toxins introduced to St. Louis during the nineteenth century. The opening of lead mines in southern Missouri around mid-century made the city an ideal location for the manufacture of various lead products. The Collier White Lead Works grew to become the largest manufacturer of lead-based paints in the west by the 1870s. With a workforce of 150 men, the company churned out four thousand tons of white lead ground in oil and two thousand pounds of red lead each year, along with even larger quantities of castor and linseed oil.[39] In addition to the manufacture of lead paints and oils, St. Louis produced lead pipes, sheet lead, lead shot, and lead batteries.

To this day, many former production sites are infested with contaminated soil and groundwater. Since the late-nineteenth century, the National Lead Company has operated several plants in the St. Louis area. At its Granite City, Illinois, location, fallout from the smelter stack over the decades rained down upon the surrounding soil and seeped into the underground aquifers. The handling of lead-based ores in the production of paints and clays produced similar levels of toxicity on the premises of the company's facility on Manchester Road. State regulatory agencies consider both sites to be among the most hazardous in the St. Louis region today.[40]

Of course, lead-based products manufactured in St. Louis and elsewhere made their way into people's homes, continuing to pose a hazard for as long as they remained there. Most St. Louis homes built prior to World War II were coated with lead paint. Even though the Missouri legislature banned its use in home interiors in 1950, the danger remained as long as it covered the walls. The problem was most acute in poor neighborhoods where malnourished children craved contaminated plaster that was easily picked from peeling tenement walls. When Ivory Perry, a local civil rights activist, toured slum dwellings in north St. Louis in the early 1970s, he was shocked at the number of children who suffered from skin problems, runny noses, and recurring colds related to lead ingestion.[41]

After 1940, the most hazardous wastes were those that derived from the defense and chemical industries. Since 1942, when the Mallinckrodt Chemical Company began processing uranium ores for use in the manufacture of atomic weaponry, the disposal of radioactive materials has posed a problem for St. Louis. Until 1957, when Mallinckrodt terminated its defense contract, the company carted its uranium residues to a twenty-one-acre site immediately north of Lambert airport. There, the radioactive material was stored in uncovered heaps and in drums. In 1966, the Atomic Energy Commission transferred the waste piles to a site about three-quarters of a mile away, at 9200 Latty Avenue, and deposited them directly on the ground. Over the next two decades, the ore residues were moved to several locations, including other properties along Latty Avenue. At each storage site, as well as at the original production site, radiological investigations reveal excessive levels of uranium, thorium, and radium.[42]

St. Louis was well represented in the explosive growth of petrochemicals after World War II. Advancements in the field of organic chemistry made possible a host of useful new materials that quickly won acceptance among farmers, industrialists, and ordinary household consumers. To boost agricultural output, farmers sprayed their fields with miracle herbicides and pesticides. Petroleum derivatives such as benzene and toluene found widespread use in a variety of industrial operations. Meanwhile, American consumers garbed themselves in polyester and nylon, scoured their bodies with newfangled detergents and cleansers, and cluttered their homes with plastic dishware, toys, and furniture. Unfortunately, the same properties that made these materials so valuable, in particular, their resistance to degradation

*Until 1957, the Mallinckrodt Chemical Company disposed of radioactive waste in drums just north of Lambert airport. The company was processing uranium for the production of atomic weapons. Courtesy of the U. S. Department of Energy.*

from natural organic processes, made them especially destructive to humans and the environment. With a tendency to accumulate in the fatty tissues of living organisms, they passed quickly through the food chain, endangering all forms of life. Rachel Carson alerted the nation to dangers of DDT with the publication of *Silent Spring* in 1962, but lesser known synthetic chemicals, including vinyl chloride, polychlorinated biphenyls (PCBs), and dioxin, have been found to be equally destructive.[43]

Wastes generated in the postwar period tended to be disposed of differently than in earlier times. After World War II, heightened popular concern about the environment prompted localities, states, and the federal government to promulgate regulations restricting the disposal of untreated hazardous waste into the air and water. Regulations pertaining to the disposal of hazardous wastes on land were not as comprehensive, and it was only after 1970 that solid wastes began to elicit the same scrutiny as airborne and waterborne wastes.[44] Thus, while cities such as St. Louis were making great strides in cleaning rivers and the air, land was becoming increasingly contaminated with mounting levels of synthetic chemical waste.

Dioxin provides an excellent example of how rapidly such substances were diffused throughout the urban environment. The story of dioxin contamination in St. Louis revolves largely around the activities of one man, Russell Bliss, a purveyor of waste oil. Bliss routinely purchased used oil from garages and service stations in eastern Missouri and then resold it to refineries or used it to spray dirt surfaces as a means of suppressing dust. On occasion, Bliss also offered his services to manufacturers who wished to get rid of their chemical wastes. In 1971, Bliss secured a contract to dispose of dioxin generated by the Northeastern Pharmaceutical and Chemical Company (NEPACCO) in Verona, Missouri.[45] Dioxin was a byproduct in the manufacture of hexachlorophene, a skin cleanser. Upon receiving the dioxin residues from NEPACCO, Bliss proceeded to mix it into his existing stock of crankcase oil. From the storage tanks, the dioxin-contaminated oil found its way to twenty-seven sites in eastern Missouri where the Bliss Oil and Salvage Company sprayed it on dirt roads, parking lots, and horse arenas.

Times Beach was one of these sites. During the early 1970s, the city had it roads sprayed for dust control annually and hired Russell Bliss to perform the work. Dioxin contamination was found to be so extensive, covering more than five hundred acres, that the federal government spent 3.3 million dollars to buy out all homeowners in 1983. Today, the town is abandoned.

A number of trucking terminals within the city of St. Louis also contracted with Bliss to spray their properties, sometimes at the prodding of city officials. In 1972, the Hammill Transfer Company on Chouteau Avenue was pestered by a city air pollution control inspector because dust kicked up in the trailer parking lot drifted into the street and interfered with motor traffic. The inspector recommended Russell Bliss as a remedy. Shortly after a Hammill employee contacted Bliss, a tank truck pulled up to the site and discharged oil over three blocks of company property. Unbeknownst to the Hammill Company, the oil was tainted with dioxin.[46]

The Bliss tank truck made an appearance at other sites around St. Louis in 1971 and 1972, dispersing dioxin widely throughout the metropolitan area. A nursery in Chesterfield purchased the waste hauler's services, as did a lumber yard in Hazelwood. Two churches in Manchester hired Bliss to tamp down their dusty parking lots. The municipalities of Eureka and Castlewood contracted with Bliss to have some of their streets oiled. At all of these locations, dioxin was subsequently discovered.

Not all dioxin contamination in St. Louis resulted from spraying. The poisonous chemical also leaked from storage tanks that Bliss maintained in the western suburb of Frontenac. In 1980, a housing contractor discovered dozens of waste drums wedged in the banks of Caulk's Creek, a small stream that meandered through a wooded area adjacent to Bliss's residential and commercial property in Ellisville. Further investigation revealed another cluster of decaying drums in a nearby trench. Bliss denied any involvement in the matter.[47]

The story of dioxin's dispersal across the metropolitan landscape is somewhat unusual. Toxic materials originating from a particular source rarely find their way to so many sites. More commonly, toxic materials are buried at or near production sites. Over the course of about sixteen years, from 1962 until 1978, the Lanson Chemical Company in East St. Louis dumped its wastes into a low lying marsh adjacent to its property. Lanson was in the business of making ingredients for paint and floor wax, and the hazardous materials handled at the work site included solvents, oils, and resins containing PCBs. Much of the excess chemical waste was disposed of in the marshlands. In addition, the company stored approximately fifty thousand gallons of contaminated resins in drums around the property.[48]

Along the riverfront, just south of downtown St. Louis, workers at the American Car Foundry spilled more than twelve thousand gallons of organic solvents over a thirty-six-year period in the process of cleaning paint from stencils. Upon seeping into the soil, the chemicals migrated through groundwater to cover an area more than ten times the size of the original stencil cleaning site. Among the toxic chemicals that infested the underground aquifers and soil were trichloroethene, tetrachloroethene, methylene chloride, dichloroethene, benzene, toluene, and xylene. Most of these organic compounds affect the central nervous system in humans; trichloroethene, tetrachloroethene, methylene chloride, and benzene are classified as carcinogens.[49]

Other toxic waste sites in St. Louis originated as landfills or dumping grounds that accepted wastes from a wide variety of industrial plants. Among the most notorious of these is a small stream that runs through Sauget, Illinois, known by the apt name of Dead Creek. Prior to the construction of a sewer line, local industries simply let their wastes flow directly into the creek. From the 1930s through the 1970s, manufacturers in Monsanto, Illinois, handling materials too toxic for the sewer system, handed them over to village president Leo Sauget. The roster of companies included American Zinc, Darling Fertilizer, Federal Chemical, Lewin Metals, Lubrite Refining, Monarch Petroleum, US Chemical Warfare Service, and Monsanto Chemical Company. Sauget proceeded to dump the material along Dead Creek. Other waste haulers in the area also found Dead Creek an ideal depository for wastes. The volume of contaminated material there is estimated at more than 7.5 million cubic yards, enough to fill 200,000 large dump trucks. The toxic stew at Dead Creek includes chlorobenzene, PCBs, dioxins, and assorted heavy metals and pesticides.[50]

Historically, human exposure to toxic waste has been conditioned by both class and race. Because toxic substances have appeared in the largest quantities and the most concentrated form inside factories, industrial laborers have occupied the front lines of exposure. Workers at the Collier White Lead plant in the 1870s were subjected to the inhalation of so much lead dust that they were required to wear face masks. Yet even the masks did not provide sufficient protection. Persistent illness among the workers prompted Thomas Richeson, the owner of the company to take further precautions. He employed steam power to pump lead through pipes to the grinding room to minimize handling of the dangerous metal and installed a revolving fan inside the grinding room to suck lead dust from the air.[51]

Well into the twentieth century, exposure to lead remained a major occupational health hazard. Since 1922, for instance, workers at the ACME Battery Manufacturing Company were exposed to dangerous levels of lead in the form of lead dust and lead oxide, a pasty compound that facilitated absorption of lead through skin pores. By the 1980s, the plant generated more than 150,000 pounds of lead waste annually. An examination of employees in 1968 revealed twelve cases of elevated lead levels in blood; one worker was diagnosed with lead poisoning.[52]

Workers were also among the first to suffer from exposure to the many varieties of synthetic waste that became so prevalent in the years after World War II. At the Wagner Electric plant in Wellston, Missouri, many of the workers who built electrical transformers drenched themselves in PCB-laden oil on a daily basis. At least one worker attributed his cancer affliction to contact with the toxic chemical.[53] Workers at several St. Louis trucking terminals also attributed various health ailments to their exposure to toxic chemicals. In 1987, fifty laborers who worked at the loading docks of Jones Truck Lines brought suit against their employer, claiming degraded health as a result of dioxin exposure. At a nearby terminal, one worker blamed dioxin poisoning for a sudden paralysis of his hands and feet. Meanwhile, truckers who worked out of the Hammill Transfer facility reported health afflictions to their union including cancer, skin disorders, and neurological problems.[54]

Off-site migration of toxic wastes from landfills, factories, and storage sites has expanded the number of people affected by toxic pollution to include nearby residents. Those who live downwind or downstream from pollution sources can be even more vulnerable to the effects of toxic exposure than workers, especially if they are very young, very old, or already sick. Moreover, movement of buried wastes through underground aquifers can spread pollution and pose a threat to residential neighbors long after companies have shut down their facilities. Due to the industrial origin of most toxic wastes, those most severely affected have been those residing in or near manufacturing districts.

Several recent studies suggest that in the 1990s, African Americans and the poor are disproportionately represented in St. Louis neighborhoods that contain abandoned toxic waste sites. As Thomas Lambert and Christopher Boerner, the authors of one such report, explain, "the percentages of poor and minority residents living near industrial and waste sites are significantly larger than the percentages of such individuals living in tracts without facilities."[55] Yet, it does not appear that this environmental disparity results primarily from deliberate racism on the part of polluters. Indeed, evidence indicates that the social bias in levels of exposure has had far more to do with inequities in the real estate market over the past forty years.

Most of the chemical companies and heavy industries responsible for generating the wastes at these now-abandoned sites operated facilities in either innercity areas—along the riverfront in St. Louis, or the Alta Sita district in East St. Louis, for example—or in heavily industrialized suburbs such as Wellston, Missouri. Few of these were African American neighborhoods when industries first introduced hazardous substances to the local environment. There were exceptions. Large sections of East St. Louis, for example, have been inhabited by both African American households and offensive industries since the 1940s. But because heavy industry relied on a predominantly white labor force in the immediate post–World War II period, surrounding neighborhoods tended to be populated by white, working-class families. In recent years, however, many of these neighborhoods have witnessed dramatic demographic transformations, attracting poor and minority households at an unusually fast rate.

*Wagner Electric Company, general view of large assembly bay in transformer shop, 1930. Factory workers came into contact with toxic waste at its most concentrated form. At Wagner Electric, workers were afflicted by PCB-laden oil. Photograph by Oscar Kuehn.*

Lambert and Boerner suggest that the presence of pollution contributed to the flight of white residents and a consequent depreciation in property values, especially after 1970 when Americans developed a heightened environmental consciousness. According to their hypothesis, poor and minority families in search of affordable housing then moved into these contaminated communities on a voluntary basis.[56] While Lambert and Boerner may be correct in asserting that pollution was partly responsible for white flight, their contention that African American in-migration was voluntary ignores the racist dynamics of the housing market in postwar St. Louis.

When large numbers of African Americans migrated to St. Louis from the rural South in the decades after 1900, very little housing was available to them outside the eastern half of the central corridor. In the northern, western, and southern reaches of the city, developers and property holders frequently inserted restrictive covenants in their deeds to prevent the sale of homes to racial minorities. Real estate interests were complicit in the solidification of a segregated housing market; the St. Louis Real Estate Exchange formed a standing committee on segregation to enforce a de facto policy of separate housing for black and white citizens. By 1940, these practices effectively barred African Americans not only from elite white neighborhoods, but from white working-class communities where homes were more affordable.[57]

After World War II, slum clearance programs displaced thousands of African Americans from their homes, forcing them to seek housing in new areas of the city. Although the striking down of restrictive covenant enforcement and the passage of fair housing legislation facilitated the movement of African Americans into neighborhoods that had once been off-limits, many areas of the metropolis remained closed to them. For the most part, it was older working-class neighborhoods on the edge of existing African American settlement that experienced an influx of minorities. In part, this was due to the affordability of housing in these areas and in part it was due to deliberate steering on the part of realtors. During the 1960s and 1970s, realtors orchestrated the racial transformation of many innercity industrial neighborhoods using a technique known as blockbusting. Employing the fear of integrated housing to scare white homeowners into selling their property at cheap rates, realtors resold homes to African Americans with limited housing options and turned a tidy profit in the process. In this way, entire neighborhoods changed from white to black in a short period of time. Older industrial districts with a deteriorating housing stock proved to be especially fertile ground for blockbusters. In Wellston, Missouri, a blue-collar community that once employed thousands of people in manufacturing jobs, mostly in the electrical industry, the percentage of white residents fell from 91 to 30 percent between 1960 to 1970. Industrial districts along the riverfront just north of downtown experienced a comparable swing in the following decade. The African American families who were guided, en masse, into neighborhoods such as Wellston and north St. Louis, rarely had any idea of the environmental timebombs that lay ticking in their backyards.[58]

Uneven investment patterns in the physical landscape have accounted for disparities in environmental quality since the earliest years of the city's history. Through the mechanism of private market forces, class and race have mediated the relationship between people and their surroundings by conditioning the type of work they perform, the quality of housing they can afford, and the neighborhoods they are able to inhabit. Several factors, however, distinguish the past half century's allocation of environmental amenities.

First, suburbanization exploded the spatial dimensions of the metropolis, thereby affording privileged groups greater opportunity to remove themselves from zones of poverty, pollution, and decay. Consider the fact that from 1950 to 1990, land use increased by 455 percent while the population grew by only 33 percent.[59] The channeling of investments in the physical landscape to newer developments has produced stark contrasts between the postwar suburbs and older innercity areas in terms of the condition of recreational facilities, the quality of the physical infrastructure, and the salubrity of air.

Second, divisions of class have become increasingly correlated with divisions of race. Because postwar suburbanization has been, for the most part, a white phenomenon, African Americans have been disporportionately relegated to those innercity districts saddled with decaying physical structures and relict wastes.

Third, the relationship between environmental quality and both race and class has become increasingly embedded in public policy, in the cost-benefit formulas that govern the location of environmental improvements, and in the selective enforcement of laws.

Whether two hundred years of environmental change in St. Louis has been for the better or worse is a tough or perhaps impossible question to assess. Insurance policies have minimized fire risks, sewer construction has reduced the incidence of epidemic disease, and smoke control programs have cleared the skies of heavy soot. At the same time, urban growth has destroyed many plant and animal habitats, river constriction has increased flooding, and industries have introduced new and dangerous forms of chemical waste into the air, water, and soil. Beyond debate is the fact that over the two hundred years, the benefits and liabilities of environmental change have not been equally distributed.

# Contributors

*Patricia Cleary* is associate professor of history at California State University, Long Beach. A specialist in early American history, she received her Ph.D. from Northwestern University. Recent publications include "'She Will Be in the Shop': Women's Sphere of Trade in Eighteenth-Century Philadelphia and New York," in the *Pennsylvania Magazine of History and Biography*.

*Craig E. Colten* is associate professor of geography at Southwest Texas State University. He is the author of *The Road to Love Canal: Managing Industrial Waste Before EPA*. He received his Ph.D. from Syracuse University and spent ten years as associate curator at the Illinois State Museum in Springfield.

*Katharine T. Corbett* has published on nineteenth-century St. Louis history and the history of African Americans in St. Louis. She has an M. A. from the University of Missouri–St. Louis and teaches at University College, Washington University. As director of interpretation at the Missouri Historical Society, she was responsible for interpretation for the exhibits "Saint Louis in the Gilded Age" and "Meet Me at the Fair: Memory, History, and the 1904 World's Fair."

*Jennifer A. Crets* is assistant curator of photographs and prints at the Missouri Historical Society. She received her M.A. from the University of Missouri–St. Louis. She is the author of "Water of Diamond Transparency: The Legacy of Chain of Rocks Park," published in *Gateway Heritage*, and a contributor to the exhibition catalog *Plains Indian Ledger Drawings, 1865-1935: Pages from a Visual History*, edited by Janet Catherine Berlo.

*Rosemary Feurer* teaches labor history at Northern Illinois University. Her recent publications include "The Nutpickers Union, 1933-1934: Crossing the Boundaries of Community and Workplace" in *"We Are All Leaders": The Alternative Unionism of the Early 1930s*, edited by Staughton Lynd. She is also editor of *The St. Louis Labor History Tour*. She is completing her Ph.D. at Washington University in St. Louis.

*Andrew Hurley* is associate professor of history at the University of Missouri–St. Louis where he teaches urban and environmental history. He received his Ph.D. from Northwestern University. He is the author of *Environmental Inequalities: Class, Race, and Industrial Pollution in Gary, Indiana, 1945-1980.*

*William R. Iseminger* is curator of archaeology at Cahokia Mounds State Historic Site, where he has worked for twenty-five years. He received his M.A. in anthropology from Southern Illinois University–Carbondale. He has authored or co-authored numerous articles on the Cahokia settlement, most recently "Mighty Cahokia" in *Archaeology Magazine.*

*F. Terry Norris* is the district archaeologist for the U. S. Army Corps of Engineers, St. Louis District, and a research associate of the Colonial Studies Program at the Illinois State Museum. He is a doctoral candidate in American Studies at St. Louis University and has published the results of various Mississippi valley prehistoric and historic archaelogical investigations over the past twenty years.

*Eric Sandweiss* is director of research at the Missouri Historical Society. He received his Ph.D. in architectural history from the University of California, Berkeley, and is the author of several published works on the development of St. Louis and San Francisco, including "Fenced-Off Corners and Wider Settings: The Logic of Civic Improvement in Early Twentieth Century St. Louis," in Mary Corbin Sies and Christopher Silver, eds., *Planning the American City Since 1900.* He is currently writing a book on architecture and social change in St. Louis.

*Walter Schroeder* is assistant professor of geography at the University of Missouri–Columbia. He received his M.A. from the University of Chicago and is a Ph.D. candidate at the University of Missouri. He has published widely on Missouri geography, including *Presettlement of Missouri,* and *The Biodiversity of Missouri: Definition, Status, and Recommendations for Its Conservation* (co-authored). He is currently preparing studies of the landforms of Missouri and the historical geography of the eastern Ozarks.

*Joel A. Tarr* is the Richard S. Caliguiri Professor of Urban and Environmental History at Carnegie Mellon University. He recieved his Ph.D. from Northwestern University and has published widely on the history of the urban infrastructure and the urban environment. He is the co-editor, with Gabriel Dupuy, of *Technology and the Rise of the Networked City in Europe and America.*

*Mark Tebeau* is a doctoral candidate in social history at Carnegie Mellon University. His dissertation is titled "'Eating Smoke': Masculinity, Technology, and the Politics of Urbanization, 1850-1950." He has held research fellowships from the Missouri Historical Society, Harvard University, and the Smithsonian Institution and is curator of an exhibit on nineteenth-century firefighting at the Bucks County Historical Society in Pennsylvania.

*Carl Zimring* is a doctoral candidate in social history at Carnegie Mellon University. He holds an M.A. in the social sciences from the University of Chicago.

# Notes

## *Andrew Hurley,* Introduction

1  See, for example, Gary Ross Mormino, *Immigrants on the Hill* (Urbana: University of Illinois Press, 1986); George Lipsitz, *The Sidewalks of St. Louis: Places, People, and Politics in an American City* (Columbia: University of Missouri Press, 1991); and Lipsitz, *A Life in the Struggle: Ivory Perry and the Culture of Opposition* (Philadelphia: Temple University Press, 1988); David Roediger, "Not Only the Ruling Classes to Overcome, but Also the So-Called Mob: Class, Skill and Community in the St. Louis General Strike of 1877," in *Journal of Social History 19* (winter 1985), 213-39; Rosemary Feurer, "William Sentner, the UE, and Civic Unionism in St. Louis," in *The CIO's Left-Led Unions*, ed. Steven Rosswurm (New Brunswick, N. J.: Rutgers University Press, 1992).

2  William Cronon, *Nature's Metropolis: Chicago and the Great West, 1848-1893* (New York: Norton, 1991).

3  *Report of the Secretary of War*, vol. II, House of Representatives 42d Congress, 2d session, Ex. Doc. 1, pt. 2 (Washington: Government Printing Office, 1871), 321-24.

4  For an introduction to the literature on urban environmental history, the reader should consult the following works: Martin V. Melosi, "The Place of the City in Environmental History," in *Environmental History Review* 17 (spring 1993): 1-23; Christine Meisner Rosen and Joel Arthur Tarr, "The Importance of an Urban Perspective in Environmental History," in *Journal of Urban History* 20 (May 1994): 299-310.

## *Walter Schroeder,* Environmental Setting of St. Louis

1  Tectonic Map of the United States (at 1:2,500,000), U.S. Geological Survey and the American Association of Petroleum Geologists (Washington: U.S. Geological Survey, 1962); A. G. Unklesbay and Jerry D. Vineyard, *Missouri Geology* (Columbia: University of Missouri Press, 1992), 39-40.

2  Walter A. Schroeder, "Landforms of Missouri" (in preparation).

3  Unklesbay and Vineyard, *Missouri Geology*, 162.

4  Ibid., 159-60; N. M. Fenneman, *Physiography of the St. Louis Area*, Illinois State Geological Survey, Bulletin no. 12 (1909), 66-67.

5  David D. Denman, "History of 'La Saline': Salt Manufacturing Site, 1675-1825," in *Missouri Historical Review* 73, no. 3 (1979): 307-20.

6  Paul W. Gates, "The Railroads of Missouri, 1850-1870," in *Missouri Historical Review* 26 (1932): 126-41.

7  Nicolas de Finiels, *An Account of Upper Louisiana*, ed. Carl J. Ekberg and William E. Foley (Columbia: University of Missouri Press, 1989).

8  Fenneman, *Physiography of the St. Louis Area*, 66, 68.

9  Gary Ross Mormino, *Immigrants on the Hill: Italian-Americans in St. Louis, 1882-1982* (Urbana: University of Illinois Press, 1986).

10  W. J. Burton, "History of Missouri Pacific Railroad." Unpublished. Prepared under instructions from P. J. Neff, President. St. Louis, 1956, vol. 1, 100; McCune Gill and Isaac A. Hedges, *The Romance of Chouteau's Pond, St. Louis, Missouri* (St. Louis: n.p., 1941).

11 J. Thomas Scharf, *History of St. Louis City and County* (Philadelphia: Louis H. Everts & Co., 1883), 1:748.

12 Thomas R. Beveridge, *Geologic Wonders and Curiosities of Missouri*, 2d ed., revised by Jerry D. Vineyard, Educational Series, no. 4 (Rolla: Missouri Division of Geology and Land Survey, 1990), 161-62.

13 *Régistre d'Arpentage* [collection of land surveys by Antoine Soulard 1796-1806]. Original in the Missouri Division of Geology and Land Survey, Rolla.

14 Fenneman, *Physiography of the St. Louis Area*, 68; Scharf, *History of St. Louis City and County*, 1:772-78.

15 Beveridge, *Geologic Wonders and Curiosities of Missouri*, 157.

16 J. D. Landraum, "A Foundation Investigation of Cherokee Cave Under Route I-55, City of St. Louis," in *Proceedings of the 15th Annual Highway Geology Symposium, 1964* (Rolla: Missouri Geological Survey and Water Resources, 1964), 81-93.

17 Schroeder, "Landforms of Missouri."

18 Ibid.; A. G. Goodfield, "Pleistocene and Surficial Geology of the City of St. Louis and the Adjacent St. Louis County, Missouri" (Ph.D. diss., University of Illinois, Urbana, 1965), 17-19, 22, 114, 116.

19 J. L. Hough, *Geology of the Great Lakes* (Urbana: University of Illinois Press, 1958), 284-96.

20 Beveridge, *Geologic Wonders and Curiosities of Missouri*, 59.

21 Schroeder, "Landforms of Missouri."

22 Unklesbay and Vineyard, *Missouri Geology*, 135-36; William W. Rubey, *Geology and Mineral Resources of the Hardin and Brussels Quadrangles (in Illinois)*, U.S. Geological Survey Professional Paper 218 (Washington: U.S. Government Printing Press, 1952), 88.

23 Fenneman, *Physiography of the St. Louis Area*, 6-8, 18, 59-61; Rubey, *Geology and Mineral Resources of the Hardin and Brussels Quadrangles (in Illinois)*, 88; Goodfield, "Pleistocene and Surficial Geology of the City of St. Louis and the Adjacent St. Louis County, Missouri," 26; N. M. Fenneman, *Geology and Mineral Resources of the St. Louis Quadrangle, Missouri-Illinois*, U.S. Geological Survey, Bulletin no. 438, Washington, D.C., 46-47; Beveridge, *Geologic Wonders and Curiosities of Missouri*, 38.

24 Fenneman, *Physiography of the St. Louis Area*, 6-7; Scharf, *History of St. Louis City and County*, 1:748.

25 Schroeder, "Landforms of Missouri."

26 Rubey, *Geology and Mineral Resources of the Hardin and Brussels Quadrangles (in Illinois)*, 127-28.

27 Ibid., 128-29.

28 Fenneman, *Physiography of the St. Louis Area*, 13-14; Rubey, *Geology and Mineral Resources of the Hardin and Brussels Quadrangles (in Illinois)*, 127-28.

29 Daniel Drake, *A Systematic Treatise, Historical, Etiological, and Practical, on the Principal Diseases of the Interior Valley of North America* (Cincinnati: Winthrop B. Smith and Co., 1850), 138-41.

30 U.S. Army Corps of Engineers, St. Louis District. "Melvin Price Locks and Dam." 1993.

31 Scharf, *History of St. Louis City and County*, 2:1053-60; James Neal Primm, *Lion of the Valley: St. Louis, Missouri* (Boulder, Col.: Pruett Publishing Co., 1981), 155-57; Frederick J. Dobney, *River Engineers on the Middle Mississippi: A History of the St. Louis District, U.S. Army Corps of Engineers.* (Washington, D.C.: U.S. Government Printing Office, no date), 24-31.

32 Fenneman, *Physiography of the St. Louis Area*, 73-74.

33 Jim Silver, "The Past, Present and Future of Times Beach," in *Missouri Resources* 12, no. 4 (1995-96): 10-15.

34 Alan H. Strahler and Arthur N. Strahler, *Modern Physical Geography*, 4th ed. (New York: John Wiley & Sons, Inc., 1992), 442-43.

35 Ibid., 443-44.

36 Timothy A. Nigh, et al., *The Biodiversity of Missouri* (Jefferson City: Missouri Department of Conservation, 1962), 4-19; Jon L. Hawker, *Missouri Landscapes: A Tour Through Time* (Rolla: Missouri Department of Natural Resources, 1992), 1-4.

37 Walter A. Schroeder, *Presettlement Prairie of Missouri*, Natural History Series, no. 2 (Jefferson City: Missouri Department of Conservation, 1981), 15-18.

38 John R. Borchert, "The Climate of the Central North American Grassland," in *Annals of the Association of American Geographers* 40 (1950): 1-39; Douglas Ladd, "Re-examination of the Role of Fire in Missouri Oak Woodlands," *Proceedings of the Oak Woods Management Workshop* (Eastern Illinois University, Charleston, 1991): 67-80.

39 Carl O. Sauer, *The Geography of the Ozark Highland of Missouri*, The Geographic Society of Chicago Bulletin no. 7 (Chicago: University of Chicago Press, 1920), 56-60, 116-23, 152-53.

40 O. H. Ernst, *Annual Report of the Chief of Engineers, U.S. Army, to the Secretary of War for the Year 1880*, Executive Documents, 46th Cong., 3d sess., 1880-1881 (30 volumes), vol. 4 (Engineers), no. 1, pt. 2, vol. 2, pt. 2, Washington, D.C. (serial set 2012): 1369-70. See also Terry Norris's essay on environmental change in the bottoms, this volume.

41 Missouri Botanical Garden, "An Introduction to the Biological Systems of the St. Louis Area," vol. 1. no date, St. Louis.

42 Maurice G. Mehl, *Missouri's Ice Age Animals*, Educational Series, no. 1 (Rolla: Missouri Geological Survey and Water Resources, 1962), 45-73; Hawker, *Missouri Landscapes*, 181-84.

43 Hawker, *Missouri Landscapes*, 194.

## *William Iseminger,* Rise and Fall of Cahokia Mounds

1 Timothy R. Pauketat, *The Ascent of Chiefs: Cahokia and Mississippian Politics in Native North America* (Tuscaloosa: University of Alabama Press, 1994), 45.

2 Ibid., 46.

3 William B. White, Sissel Johannessen, Paula G. Cross, and Lucretia S. Kelly, "Environmental Setting," in *American Bottom Archaeology*, ed. Charles J. Bareis and James W. Porter (Urbana: University of Illinois Press, 1984).

4 Andrew C. Fortier, Thomas E. Emerson, and Fred A. Finney, "Early Woodland and Middle Woodland Periods," in *American Bottom Archaeology*, ed. Bareis and Porter, 59.

5 John E. Kelly, Fred A. Finney, Dale L. McElrath, and Steven J. Ozuk, "Late Woodland Period," in *American Bottom Archaeology*, ed. Bareis and Porter, 111, 125.

6 Ibid., 126.

7 Robert L. Hall, "Cahokia Identity and Interaction Models of Cahokia Mississippian," in *Cahokia and the Hinterlands: Middle Mississippian Cultures of the Midwest*, ed. Thomas E. Emerson and R. Barry Lewis (Urbana: University of Illinois Press, 1991).

8 Ibid., 19.

9 William R. Iseminger, "Relationships Between Climate Change and Culture Change in Prehistory," in *Illinois Antiquity* 25 (spring 1990): 2-4.

10 Ibid.

11 David Rindos and Sissel Johannessen, "Human-Plant Interactions and Cultural Change in the American Bottom," in *Cahokia and the Hinterlands,* ed. Emerson and Lewis (Urbana: University of Illinois Press, 1991): 41; Neal H. Lopinot, Lucretia S. Kelly, George Milner, and Richard Paine, "Part 1: Archaeobotanical Remains," in *The Archaeology of the Cahokia Mounds ICT-II Biological Remains*, Illinois Cultural Resources Study, no. 13 (Springfield: Illinois Historic Preservation Agency, 1991), 168-72.

12 Pauketat, *The Ascent of Chiefs*, 51.

13 Brian M. Fagan, *Ancient North America: The Archaeology of a Continent*, 2d ed. (London: Thames and Hudson Ltd., 1995), 432-33.

14 Lopinot, et al., "Part 1: Archaeobotanical Remains," 169.

15 Gayle J. Fritz, "'Newer,' 'Better' Maize and the Mississippian Emergence: A Critique of Prime Mover Explanations," in *Late Prehistoric Agriculture: Observations from the Midwest*, ed. William I. Woods, Studies in Archaeology, no. 8 (Springfield: Illinois Historic Preservation Agency, 1992), 29.

16 Lucretia Kelly and Paula G. Cross, "Zooarchaeology," in *American Bottom Archaeology*, ed. Charles J. Bareis and James W. Porter (Urbana: University of Illinois Press, 1984), 215-32.

17 Hall, "Cahokia Identity," 23.

18 William I. Woods and Sidney G. Denny, "Mississippian Horticultural Exploitation of Upland Alluvial Settings: An Example Study from the Cahokia Region," paper presented at the Fifty-fourth Annual Midwest Archaeological Conference, Cleveland, 1982.

19 John E. Kelly, "The Impact of Maize on the Development of Nucleated Settlements: An American Bottom Example," in *Late Prehistoric Agriculture: Observations from the Midwest*, ed. William I. Woods, Studies in Archaeology, no. 8 (Springfield: Illinois Historic Preservation Agency, 1992); George R. Milner, "American Bottom Mississippian Cultures: Internal Development and External Relations," in *New Perspectives on Cahokia Archaeology: Views from the Periphery*, ed. James B. Stoltmann, (Madison, Wis.: Prehistory Press, 1991).

20 John E. Kelly, "Range Site Community Patterns and the Mississippian Emergence," in *The Mississippian Emergence*, ed. Bruce Smith (Washington, D.C.: Smithsonian Institution Press, 1990), 99.

21 James M. Collins, *The Archaeology of the Cahokia Mounds ICT-II: Site Structure*, Illinois Cultural Resources Study, no. 10 (Springfield: Illinois Historic Preservation Agency, 1990), 224-26.

22 Lopinot, et al., "Part I: Archaeobotanical Remains."

23 Rindos and Johannessen, "Human-Plant Interactions," 42; Lopinot, et al., "Part I: Archaeobotanical Remains," 166-67.

24 Rindos and Johannessen, "Human-Plant Interactions."

25 John E. Kelly, "The Evidence for Prehistoric Exchange and Its Implications for Prehistoric Cahokia," in *New Perspectives on Cahokia*, ed. Stoltman, 65-92.

26 Milner, et al., "Part III: Human Skeletal Remains," 33-34.

27 Ibid., 30.

28 Timothy R. Pauketat, *Temples for Cahokia Lords: Preston Holder's 1955-1956 Excavations of the Kunnemann Mound*. Museum of Anthropology, Memoirs, no. 26. (Ann Arbor: University of Michigan Press, 1993), 5.

29 Milner, et al., "Part III: Human Skeletal Remains," 34.

30 John E. Kelly, "Cahokia and Its Role as a Gateway Center in Interregional Exchange," in *Cahokia and the Hinterlands*, ed. Thomas E. Emerson and R. Barry Lewis (Urbana: University of Illinois Press, 1991), 61-80.

31 Pauketat, *Temples for Cahokia Lords*, 145-56.

32 Melvin L. Fowler, *The Cahokia Atlas: A Historical Atlas of Cahokia Archaeology*, Studies in Illinois Archaeology, no. 6 (Springfield: Illinois Historic Preservation Agency, 1989), 201-2.

33 Ibid., 34.

34 John E. Kelly, personal communication, 1995; Pauketat, *The Ascent of Chiefs*, 65.

35 Milner, et al., "Part III: Human Skeletal Remains," 74.

36 Claudia G. Mink, *Cahokia: City of the Sun* (Collinsville, Ill.: Cahokia Mounds Museum Society, 1992).

37 William R. Iseminger and John E. Kelly, "Partitioning the Sacred Precinct," in *Cahokian*, Summer (Collinsville: Cahokia Mounds Museum Society, 1995): 3-4; George R. Milner, "The Late Prehistoric Cahokia Cultural System of the Mississippi River Valley: Foundations, Florescence, and Fragmentation," in *Journal of World Prehistory* 4 (1990): 1-43.

38 Kelly, "Cahokia and Its Role."

39 Pauketat, *The Ascent of Chiefs*, 43-44.

40 Hall, "Cahokia Identity," 27.

41 Kelly, "The Evidence for Prehistoric Exchange," 87.

42 Pauketat, *Temples for Cahokia Lords*.

43 Kelly, "The Evidence for Prehistoric Exchange."

44 George R. Holley, Rinita Dalan, and Philip A. Smith, "Investigations in the Cahokia Site Grand Plaza," in *American Antiquity* 58, no. 2 (Washington, D.C.: Society for American Archaeology, 1993): 306-19.

45 Lucretia Kelly, "Faunal Remains," in *The Archaeology of the Cahokia Palisade*, ed. William R. Iseminger, et al., Illinois Cultural Resources Study, no. 14 (Springfield: Illinois Historic Preservation Agency, 1990), 109-34.

46 William R. Iseminger, "Features," in *The Archaeology of the Cahokia Palisade: East Palisade Investigations*, ed. Iseminger, et al., 1990, 33-37.

17 Lopinot, et al., "Part I: Archaeobotanical Remains"; Neal H. Lopinot and William I. Woods, "Archaeobotanical, Environmental Degradation, and the Collapse of Cahokia," in *Plant Production and Social Relations in the Eastern Woodlands*, ed. C. Margaret Scarry (Gainesville: Ripley P. Bullen Monographs in Anthropology and History, University of Florida Press, 1991).

48 Iseminger, et al., *The Archaeology of the Cahokia Palisade*; Iseminger and Kelly, "Partitioning the Sacred Precinct."

49 Iseminger and Kelly, "Partitioning the Sacred Precinct."

50 Hall, "Cahokia Identity," 23.

51 William I. Woods and George R. Holley, "Upland Mississippian Settlement in the American Bottom Region," in *Cahokia and the Hinterlands: Middle Mississippian Cultures of the Midwest*, ed. Thomas E. Emerson and R. Barry Lewis (Urbana: University of Illinois Press, 1991), 59.

52 Ibid., 60.

53 Lopinot, et al., "Part I: Archaeobotanical Remains."

54 Pauketat, *The Ascent of Chiefs*, 46.

55 Hall, "Cahokia Identity," 33.

56 Ibid., 25.

57 Ibid.

58 Ibid., 26.

59 George R. Milner, "Bioanthropology," in *American Bottom Archaeology*, ed. Bareis and Porter, 238.

60 Lucretia Kelly, "Analysis of Faunal Remains from the 1982-1985 East Stockade Excavations," in *Cahokian*, Spring (Collinsville: Cahokia Mounds Museum Society, 1995): 3-6.

61 Milner, "Bioanthropology," 236.

62 Thomas E. Emerson, "Some Perspectives on Cahokia and the Northern Mississippian Expansion," in *Cahokia and the Hinterlands*, ed. Emerson and Lewis, 221-36.

## *Patricia Cleary,* Settlement Choices in Colonial St. Louis

1 In his firsthand account, penned well after the city's inception, Auguste Chouteau recalled the process that went into the choice of the site, as well as the initial conflict that erupted over who would occupy it. Fourteen when he accompanied his stepfather

Laclede up the Mississippi River in the fall of 1763, Chouteau played an important part in directing and recording the course of St. Louis's earliest history. All of the English translations of Chouteau's account come from Auguste Chouteau, "Narrative of the Settlement of St. Louis," in *The Early Histories of St. Louis*, ed. John Francis McDermott (St. Louis: St. Louis Historical Documents Foundation, 1952) (hereafter *Early Histories*). The French original appears as "Chouteau's Journal of the Founding of St. Louis," Missouri Historical Society Collections 3, no. 4 (1911), 335-49.

2   Under the terms of the secret Treaty of Fontainbleau of November 1762, Spain accepted the Louisiana Territory from France as compensation for losses suffered as France's ally during the Seven Years War. See William E. Foley, *A History of Missouri, Vol. 1: 1673 to 1820* (Columbia: University of Missouri Press, 1971), 16.

3   Chouteau, "Narrative," *Early Histories*, 48.

4   Ibid.

5   Perrin du Lac and François Marie, *Travels through the Two Louisianas, and among the Savage Nations of the Missouri*, translated from the French (London: Printed for Richard Phillipps, 1807), 48.

6   John A. Paxton, "Notes on St. Louis," 26 May 1821, in *Early Histories*, 63.

7   French visitor Perrin du Lac described Ste. Genevieve's site in unflattering terms: "Its situation would have been more agreeable and healthy, if the houses, instead of being built at the foot of the hill, had been erected on the hill itself" (*Travels through the Two Louisianas*, 44). In Illinois, the town of Cahokia was repeatedly flooded. There, the devestation of the 1785 flood was so extreme that magistrates adopted procedures to protect cash-poor debtors from the seizure of their property, given "the unhappy conditions of the time, . . . and considering furthermore the loss of the cattle by the inundations and contagious disease" ("At a Court, October 1, 1785," *Cahokia Records, 1778-1790*, ed. Clarence Alvord, Virginia Series, vol. I, *Collections of the Illinois State Historical Library*, vol. II [Springfield: Illinois State Historical Library, 1907], 202-3).

8   Jacques Clamorgan to Zenon Trudeau, 1 April 1793, in *Before Lewis and Clark: Documents Illustrating the History of the Missouri, 1785-1804*, trans. and ed. A. P. Nasatir, vol. 1 (St. Louis: St. Louis Historical Documents Foundation, 1952), 1:170.

9   Philip Pittman, *Captain Philip Pittman's The present state of the European settlements on the Mississippi: with a geographical description of that river*, fascimile edition with an introduction and notes by John Francis McDermott (Memphis: Memphis State University Press, 1977), 51. Describing the countryside of the Missouri Indians in the 1720s, one explorer asserted it was the most beautiful in the world and full of wild animals. See Bourgmond, "Exacte déscription de la Louisiane, de ses ports, terres, et rivières, et noms des nations sauvage qui l'occupent et des comerce et avantages que l'on peut tirer dans l'établissement d'une colonie," in de Marc Villier, *La Decouverte du Missouri et L'histoire du Fort D'Orleans (1673-1728)* (Paris: Librairie Ancienne Honoréde France, 1925), 60-61.

10  Un Habitant des Kaskaskias, *Invitation Serieuse aux Habitants des Illinois* (Philadelphia, 1772), reprinted in facsimile with introduction by Clarence Alvord and Clarence Carter (Providence, Rhode Island: Club for Colonial Reprints, 1908), 9, 12-13. The author wrote that "le tabac fera un article bien considérable, & avantageux pour ceux qui voudront le cultiver sur les bords du Mississippi, car le terrain de la Virginie est presque usé, et ne peut pas continue longtem[p]s a produire" as before. For tobacco's role in profoundly shaping colonial society, see T. H. Breen, *Tobacco Culture: The Mentality of the Great Tidewater Planters on the Eve of the Revolution* (Princeton, N. J.: Princeton University Press, 1985).

11  Perrin du Lac, *Travels through the Two Louisianas*, 48.

12  Ibid.

13 Ibid.

14 Gilbert J. Garraghan, "Some Newly Discovered Missouri Maps," in *Missouri Historical Society Collections* 5, no. 3 (1928): 256-64, citation to 261.

15 Map script cited in Garraghan, "Some Newly Discovered Maps," 262.

16 Settlers in Jamestown died as a result of numerous causes, including malnutrition, a poor drinking water supply, and disease.

17 As Pittman noted, "The village of St. Louis is supplied with flour and other provisions from hence" (Pittman, *The Present State*, 50). In 1792, Trudeau reported a bad wheat harvest in St. Louis, adding that "if it were not for the harvest of maize in Ste. Genevieve being good, the inhabitants would not have had anything to live on all this year" (Zenon Trudeau to Seo's role in profoundly shaping colonial society, *Before Lewis and Clark*, ed. Nasatir, 160).

18 Chouteau, "Narrative," *Early Histories*, 49.

19 In the narrative, Laclede addressed the Missouris, recalling this description of their plight from the previous day's meeting. See Chouteau, "Narrative," *Early Histories*, 50.

20 Ibid.

21 Carolyn Merchant, *Ecological Revolutions: Nature, Gender, and Science in New England* (Chapel Hill: University of North Carolina Press, 1989), 44-48.

22 Pittman, *The Present State*, 51.

23 "Voyage fait par M. du Tisné en 1719, chez les Missouri pour aller aux Panioussas. Extrait de la Relation de Bernard de La Harpe," in Pierre Margry, *Découvertes et Etablissements des Francais dans l'ouest et dans le sud de l'Amerique Septentrionale, 1614-1754: Mémoires et Documents Originaux*, vol. 6 (Paris: Maisonneuve et Ch. Leclerc, 1888).

24 Grant Foreman, ed., "Notes of Auguste Chouteau on Boundaries of Various Indian Nations," in *Glimpses of the Past*, vol. 7 (St. Louis: Missouri Historical Society, 1940), 119-40, citation to 122.

25 For a discussion of colonists' changing attitudes toward Native Americans in terms of their degree of "civilization" and how they influenced English policies, see Gary Nash, "The Image of the Indian in the Southern Colonial Mind," in *William and Mary Quarterly*, 3d ser., vol. 29, no. 2 (1972): 197-230.

26 Foreman, ed., "Notes of Auguste Chouteau," 136.

27 Ibid.

28 Louis Houck, *A History of Missouri: From the Earliest Explorations and Settlements Until the Admission of the State Into the Union* (Chicago: R. R. Donnelly & Sons Company, 1908) 1:174.

29 Merchant, *Ecological Revolutions*, 48-50, 55.

30 On Cahokia, see William Iseminger, "Prehistoric Cultural and Environmental Interaction in the American Bottom and the Rise of Cahokia Mounds," in this volume.

31 Joseph Nicollet, "Sketch of the Early History of St. Louis," in *Early Histories*, 135.

32 See William Cronon, *Changes in the Land: Indians, Colonists, and the Ecology of New England* (New York: Hill and Wang, 1983).

33 Ibid. See also the testimony of Baptiste Riviere, 29 July 1825, *Hunt's Minutes*, vol. 2, Missouri Historical Society (hereafter MHS), 102.

34 Nicollet, "Sketch," *Early Histories*, 135-36.

35 "Letter of Father Gariel Marest, of the Society of Jesus to a Father of the same Society," 27 April 1699, *The Jesuit relations and allied documents: travels and explorations of the Jesuit missionaries in New France, 1610-1791*, ed. Reuben Gold Thwaites (Cleveland: Burrows, 1896), 65:83.

36 Pittman, *The Present State*, 48.

37 Perrin du Lac, *Travels through the Two Louisianas*, 44.

**38** Andre Michaux, "Travels into Kentucky, 1793-1795," in *Early Western Travels, 1748-1846*, ed. Reuben Gold Thwaites (Cleveland: Arthur H. Clark Company, 1904), 3:70.

**39** Chouteau, "Narrative," *Early Histories*, 50-51.

**40** Ibid.

**41** Louis St. Ange de Bellerive, 12 August 1764, *The Critical Period, 1763-1765*, ed. Clarence Alvord and Clarence Carter, British Series, vol. 1, Collections of the Illinois State Historical Library, vol. 10 (Springfield: Illinois State Historical Library, 1915), 292-93. The French were still in charge of the fort at this time because of Pontiac's rebellion, which delayed the English takeover of the Illinois Country; the post was transferred to the British in October 1765. See Paul M. Angle, ed. *Prairie State: Impressions of Illinois, 1673-1967, By Travelers and Other Observers* (Chicago: University of Chicago Press, 1968), 39.

**42** Archaeological findings confirm the location of the Missouri village. See Carl H. Chapman, "The Little Osage and Missouri Indian Village Sites, ca. 1727-1777 A.D.," in *The Missouri Archaeologist* 21, no. 1 (December 1959): 1-67. Chapman, relying on the work of Garraghan, stated that his "beginning date of 1727 has been assumed from the information that orders were given to abandon Fort Orleans in that year . . . , and abandonment of the fort may have been a stimulus for the move from the pinnacles where the Missouri and Little Osage sites were located in 1724," 2. For Bourgmont's experiences, see Frank Norall, *Bourgmont, Explorer of the Missouri, 1698-1725* (Lincoln: University of Nebraska Press, 1988).

**43** "Instructions données au sieur Bourgmont," 17 Janvier 1722, in Margry, *Découvertes et Etablissements des Francais*, 6:390.

**44** Chouteau, "Narrative," *Early Histories*, 51.

**45** Ibid. St. Louis and the Missouri village shared some basic topographical characteristics; both were located near the confluence of two rivers and upon the banks of the major one. Osage villages along the Osage and Missouri Rivers were similarly located on high river bluffs. Foley states the positions provided strategic vantage points (*History of Missouri*, 5).

**46** Chouteau, "Narrative," *Early Histories*, 52.

**47** Charles E. Peterson, *Colonial St. Louis: Building a Creole Capital* (St. Louis: Missouri Historical Society, 1949), 3, 5. See also Eric Sandweiss, "Construction and Community in South St. Louis, 1850-1910" (Ph.D. diss.: University of California, Berkeley, 1991), 9-14.

**48** Auguste Chouteau and William H. Lecompte testified that the fence was constructed in 1764, paid for and maintained collectively by the inhabitants. See Walter Lowrie, ed., *American State Papers: Public Lands* (Washington, D. C.: Printed by Duff Green, 1834), 2:549.

**49** Ibid., 54.

**50** Sebastian Louis Meurin to Bishop Briand, 23 March 1767, in *The New Regime, 1765-1767*, ed. Clarence Edwin Alvord and Clarence Walworth Carter, British Series, vol. 2, Collections of the Illinois State Historical Library, vol. XI (Springfield: Illinois State Historical Library, 1916), 523.

**51** "Journal of Captain H. Gordon 1766," in *New Regime*, ed. Alvord and Carter, 299.

**52** Auguste Chouteau, "Testimony before the Recorder of Land Titles, St. Louis, 1825," in *Early Histories*, 94. For this and related land matters, see *Hunt's Minutes*, MHS.

**53** Warfare decimated the tribe. According to N. Matson, after many of the tribe's warriors were killed or died at Starved Rock, the rest of the Peorias fled to the south and west. See Matson, *Pioneers of Illinois: Containing a Series of Sketches relating to Events that Occurred Previous to 1813* (Chicago: Knight & Leonard, Printers, 1882), 192.

**54** "Journal of Captain Gordon," *New Regime*, 300.

**55** Ibid., 301.

**56** Houck, *A History of Missouri*, 174.

**57** Nicollet, "Sketch," *Early Histories*, 146.

**58** Lieutenant Governor Sinclair to General Haldimand, 17 February 1780, reprinted in "Documents relating to the Attack upon St. Louis in 1780," Missouri Historical Society Collections 2, no. 6 (July 1906), 41. Apparently there was some confusion about the location of St. Louis, as one revolutionary war missive indicates. The author closed, "PS. We are as much at a loss to know where St. Louis is, as you can be, but suppose it to be where you mention" (John Page to Colonel George Morgan, 15 April 1777, [photocopy], Revolutionary War Collection, MHS, 1770-1957).

**59** Manuel Perez to Estevan Miro, 1 December 1788, in *Before Lewis and Clark*, ed. Nasatir, 129. In their contests for colonial empires, European powers distributed presents to their Indian allies and trading partners. In colonial St. Louis, Spanish authorities entertained many tribes, presenting them with a wide variety of gifts and festivities paid for by the crown. See William E. Foley and C. David Rice, *The First Chouteaus: River Barons of Early St. Louis* (Urbana: University of Illinois Press, 1983), 18.

**60** Sainte Ange, "Report of the various Indian tribes receiving presents in the district of Ylinoa or Illinois, 1769," *The Spanish Regime in Missouri*, ed. Louis Houck (Chicago: R. R. Donnelley and Sons Company, 1909), 1:44-45.

**61** Zenon Trudeau to Baron de Carondelet, 8 June 1794, in *Before Lewis and Clark*, ed. Nasatir, 232.

**62** Account of Auguste Chouteau, folio 4, letterbook no. 4, 1793-1794, Charles Gratiot Papers, MHS. By the 1790s, increased competition contributed to decreasing profits in the fur trade; profits fell from over 300 percent to 25 percent. See Foley and Rice, *The First Chouteaus*, 72.

**63** According to Auguste Chouteau, a late seventeenth-century band of Michegamias resided "on the right bank of the Mississipi at the spot where now stands the flourishing Town of St. Louis" (Grant Foreman, ed., "Notes of Auguste Chouteau on Boundaries of Various Indian Nations," in *Glimpses of the Past* 7 (St. Louis: Missouri Historical Society, 1940), 119-40, citation to 125. The exact location of the Jesuit mission site was determined by the discovery of some eighteenth-century maps. See Garraghan, "Some Newly Discovered Maps," 257.

**64** Houck, *A History of Missouri*, 1:243. Houck reports that the "supposed unhealthiness of the spot" prompted the departure of the settlers. Other accounts of this settlement simply describe the departure as "for reasons now obscure." See Angle, *Prairie State*, 37.

**65** George Morgan, "Voyage Down the Mississippi, November 21, 1766," in *New Regime*, 439.

**66** General Josiah Harmar, report to the Secretary of War, 24 November 1787, in *Prairie State*, ed. Angle. 48.

**67** One report declared that because of smallpox, tribes "numerous when the first Settlements were made on the Mississippi [were] now extinct & of the Kaskaskias, Peorias Missouries . . . there are only left a Sufficiency to inform us that Tribes of that name existed in times past." With a sense of inevitability about the widespread destruction that disease brought to the indigenous population, the author wrote that it seemed "that the Almighty [had] decreed the total extinction of the whole race" (Mackay's Notes on Indian Tribes [1797], box 2, William Clark Papers, MHS).

**68** The debate over the size of the indigenous population of North America during the colonial period is extensive. For a survey of the literature, see John D. Daniels, "The Indian Population of North America in 1492," in *William and Mary Quarterly*, 3d ser., vol. 49, no. 2, (April 1992): 298-320. Co-residence might be harmonious but not healthy. In 1712, Father Marest described the flare-up of disease in the Illinois mission village he moved to after leaving the Des Peres settlement: "a contagious disease desolated their Village, and carried off every day many Savages" (Marest, *Jesuit Relations*, ed. Thwaites, 66:239).

69 Father Gravier attributed the outbreak of disease among the indigenous people to divine will. Reporting that members of one tribe murdered the members of another tribe with whom they shared a village, he wrote, "The blood of so many Innocents cries for vengeance; consequently God is beginning to punish them by famine and disease" ("Relation or Journal of the voyage of Father Gravier," *Jesuit Relations*, ed. Thwaites, 65:157). Although it is not possible to determine what disease struck them, the newness and extent of the sickness suggest typical indicators of virgin soil epidemics. See Alfred W. Crosby, "Virgin Soil Epidemics as a Factor in the Aboriginal Depopulation in America," in *William and Mary Quarterly*, 3d ser., vol. 33, no. 2 (April 1976): 289-99.

70 Perrin du Lac, *Travels through the Two Louisianas*, 45. Not surprisingly, Auguste Chouteau concurred with this assessment of indigenous population decline, arguing that "the introduction of ardent Spirits among them . . . contributed to destroy both their phisical and moral capacity," leaving them vulnerable in the face of their enemies. See Chouteau, "Notes," in *Glimpses of the Past*, ed. Foreman, 125.

71 Houck, *A History of Missouri*, 1:173-74. According to Houck, more than two hundred Missouris were killed in a single battle.

72 Anonymous traveler's description of St. Louis, ca. 1798, folder "St. Louis—Early Days," box 1, St. Louis History Collection, MHS, 1762-1843.

73 "15 March 1778, before Cruzat," folder "St. Louis History 1770-1780," St. Louis History Collection, MHS.

74 Charles Gratiot described his life "in this country (which all strangers admit is the handsomest, the healthiest, and the most fertile of North America)." (Charles Gratiot to Collignon, 8 June 1794, letterbook no. 3, 1792-1797, trans. Frederick L. Billon, Charles Gratiot Papers, MHS). When a St. Louis resident reported to his brother that he had been ill and that the sickness "was a general thing throughout the country," he added that the "very sickly" state of the Missouri country was unprecedented "since the country was settled" (John Smith to David Smith, 12 December 1819, folder St. Louis History Papers, 1819-1827, box 1, St. Louis History Collection, MHS, 1762-1843).

## *F. Terry Norris,* Deforestation in the Mississippi Valley

1 William J. Peterson, *Steamboating on the Upper Mississippi* (Iowa City: State Historical Society of Iowa, 1968), 296; Henry Nash Smith, *Virgin Land: The American West as Symbol and Myth* (Cambridge, Mass.: Harvard University Press, 1950), 15-164; Frederick Jackson Turner, *The Frontier in American History* (New York: Henry Holt and Company, 1958).

2 Louis C. Hunter, *Steamboats on the Western Rivers* (Cambridge, Mass.: Harvard University Press, 1949), 43-52.

3 Ibid., 53.

4 Clarence Walworth Alvord, *The Illinois Country* (Springfield: Illinois Centennial Commission, 1920); Peterson, *Steamboating on the Upper Mississippi*.

5 Michael Williams, *Americans and Their Forests* (New York: Cambridge University Press, 1989), 146-57.

6 David S. Brose and Isaac Greber, "The Ringler Archaic Dugout from Savannah Lake, Ashland County, Ohio: With Speculations on Trade and Transformation in the Prehistory of the Eastern United States," in *Mid-Continent Journal of Archaeology* 7, no. 2 (1982).

7 Ibid., 248.

8 Ibid., 248-49.

9 Thomas Harriot, "A Brief Report of the Newfoundland of Virginia . . . ," facsimile reproduction of the Theodore de Bry edition (New York: Arno Press, 1972), 55.

10 Karen Magruder, "Channel Improvement Yields Buried Treasure," in *Uscoe Mainstem* 1, no. 90-91 (Vicksburg, Miss., 1989): 10-11.

11 Ibid., 10.

12 Robert C. Wheeler, *A Toast to the Fur Trade* (Saint Paul, Minn., 1985), 19-30.

13 Louis Hennepin, *A Description of Louisiana, by Father Louis Hennepin, Recollect Missionary*, trans. John Gilmary Shea (Iowa City: University of Iowa Press, 1966), 194; Louis Hennepin, *A New Discovery of a Vast Country in America by Father Louis Hennepin*, trans. Reuben Gold Thwaites (Chicago: A. C. McClurg & Co., 1903), 1:184.

14 Ibid., 645; Peterson, *Steamboating on the Upper Mississippi*, 31.

15 Peterson, *Steamboating on the Mississippi*, 50.

16 David D. Denman, "History of 'La Saline': Salt Manufacturing Site, 1675-1825," in *Missouri Historical Review* 73, no. 3 (1979): 311.

17 Jean-Babtiste Benard De La Harpe, *The Historical Journal of the Establishment of the French in Louisiana*, ed. Glen R. Conrad (Lafayette: Louisiana Historical Association, 1971), 200.

18 Peterson, *Steamboating on the Upper Mississippi*, 50; Wheeler, *A Toast to the Fur Trade*, 31-34.

19 Margaret Kimball Brown and Lawrie Cena Dean, *The French Colony in the Mid-Mississippi River Valley* (Carbondale: Southern Illinois University Press, 1995), 5.

20 Ibid., 6.

21 Carl J. Ekberg, *Colonial Ste. Genevieve: An Adventure on the Mississippi River Frontier* (St. Louis: Patrice Press, 1985), 460-68.

22 Peterson, *Steamboating on the Upper Mississippi*, 50-51.

23 Ibid., 51.

24 Ibid., 51-52.

25 Ibid.

26 Ibid., 52.

27 E. L. Jordan, *America: Glorious and Chaotic Land: Charles Sealsfield Discovers the Young United States* (New Jersey: Prentice Hall, 1969), 53, 76.

28 Leland D. Baldwin, *The Keelboat Age on the Western Waters* (Pittsburgh: University of Pittsburgh Press, 1980), 156.

29 Peterson, *Steamboating on the Upper Mississippi*, 58.

30 John Forbes, *Writings of General John Forbes Relating to His Service in North America* (New York: Arno Press, 1971), 262-63, 269.

31 Hunter, *Steamboats on the Western Rivers*, 12.

32 Peterson, *Steamboating on the Upper Mississippi*, 60, 65.

33 Ibid., 68.

34 James H. Lanman, "American Steam Navigation," in *Hunt's Merchant's Magazine and Commercial Review* (Louisville, Ken., 1841): 124.

35 Peterson, *Steamboating on the Upper Mississippi*, 343.

36 Hunter, *Steamboats on the Western Rivers*, 266-72.

37 Peterson, *Steamboating on the Upper Mississippi*, 64.

38 John C. Nelson, Anjela Redmond, and Richard Sparks, "Impacts of Settlement on Floodplain Vegetation at the Confluence of the Illinois and Mississippi Rivers," in *Transactions of the Illinois State Academy of Science* 87, nos. 3, 4 (Springfield: Illinois State Academy of Science, 1994), 117-33.

39 Michael Williams, "Products of the Forest: Mapping the Census of 1840," in *Journal of Forest History* (January 1980).

40 W. Havinghurst, *Voices on the River* (New York: MacMillan, 1964); F. Donovan, *Riverboats of America* (New York: Crowell, 1966); Nelson, et al., "Impacts of Settlement on Floodplain Vegetation," in *Transactions of the Illinois State Academy of Science*, 122-23; Ralph T. Ward, *Steamboats: A History of the Early Adventure* (Indianapolis, Ind.: Bobbs-Merrill Co., 1973).

41 Philip Gove Babcock, ed., *Webster's Third New International Dictionary* (Unabridged) (Springfield, Mass: G. & C. Merriam Co., 1981), 506.

42 Hunter, *Steamboats on the Western Rivers*, 33.

43 Ibid., 33.

44 Henry Lewis, *The Valley of the Mississippi Illustrated* (St. Paul: Minnesota Historical Society, 1967), 49.

45 Hunter, *Steamboats on the Western Rivers*, 266.

46 Peterson, *Steamboating on the Upper Mississippi*, 318.

47 Michael A. Stevens, Daryl Simons, and Stanley A. Schumm, "Man-Induced Changes of the Middle Mississippi River," in *Journal of the Waterways and Coastal Engineering Division*, American Society of Professional Engineers (Washington, D.C., 1975): 119-33.

48 Claude N. Strauser, "Army Engineers Restore the Middle Mississippi," Special Collections of the Morris Library, Southern Illinois University (Carbondale, Ill., 1988), 30.

49 Stevens, et al., "Man-Induced Changes," *Journal of the Waterways and Coastal Engineering Division*, 120.

50 Mark Twain, *Life On The Mississippi* (New York: Harper, 1944), 153.

51 Claude N. Strausser and Norbert C. Long, *Journal of the Waterways Harbors and Coastal Engineering Division: Proceedings of the American Society of Civil Engineers*, 102, no. WW2 (New York: Headquarters of the Society, 1976).

52 Ibid., 281.

53 Ibid.

54 Ibid.

55 James Swift, *Wrecks by River Mileage in the St. Louis District*, U.S. Army Corps Of Engineers (manuscript on file in the St. Louis district office, St. Louis, Missouri, 1995), 1-26.

56 Ibid.

57 F. Terry Norris, *St. Louis District Low Water Shipwreck Inventory*, U.S. Army Corps Of Engineers (manuscript on file in the St. Louis district office, St. Louis, Missouri, 1988), 1-12.

58 Daryl B. Simons, Stanley A Schumm, and Michael A. Stevens, *Geomorphology of the Middle Mississippi River* (Vicksburg: U.S. Army Engineer Waterways Experiment Station, 1975), 81-124.

59 David C. Hawley, *Treasures of the Steamboat Arabia* (Kansas City, Mo.: Arabia Steamboat Museum, 1995), 17, 20.

60 Charles J. Balesi, *The Time of the French in the Heart of North America* (Chicago: Alliance Francaise Chicago, 1991), 188-209.

61 Natalia M. Belting, "Kaskaskia under the French Regime," in *Illinois Studies in the Social Sciences* 29, no. 3 (Springfield: University of Illinois Press, 1948): 14; Ekberg, *Colonial Ste. Genevieve*, 126-27.

62 John Francis McDermott, *The French in the Mississippi Valley* (Urbana: University of Illinois Press, 1965), 81-92.

63 Paul Boyer and Steven Nissenbaum, *Salem Possessed: The Social Origins of Witchcraft* (Cambridge Mass.: Harvard University Press, 1974), ix-x; Jack P. Greene, *Pursuit Of Happiness* (Chapel Hill: University of North Carolina Press, 1988), xi-xv.

64 Belting, "Kaskaskia under the French Regime"; Margaret Kimball Brown and Lawrie Cena Dean, *The Village of Chartres in Colonial Illinois, 1720-1765* (New Orleans: Polyanthos, 1977); John Francis McDermott, *Old Cahokia* (St. Louis: St. Louis Historical Document Foundation, 1949); Charles E. Peterson, *Colonial St. Louis: Building a Creole Capital* (Tucson: Patrice Press, 1993).

65 Edward T. Safiran, "The Louvier Site at Prairie Du Rocher," in *French Colonial Archaeology* (Urbana: University of Illinois Press, 1991), 132.

66 Charles Dickens, *American Notes For General Circulation* (Baltimore: Johns Hopkins University Press, 1972), 215-16.

67 Robert W. Winks, ed., *The Historian as Detective* (New York, 1969), 3-23.

68 Carl L. Becker, "What Are Historical Facts," in *Ideas Of History* (New York: Dutton, 1969), 2:178-80; Edward Carr, *What Is History?* (New York: Knopf, 1961), 11-18; Walter W. Taylor, *A Study of Archaeology* (Carbondale: Southern Illinois Uiversity Press, 1967), 32, 35.

69 F. Terry Norris, "Old Cahokia, an Archaeological Site Model," in *Le Journal* 2 no. 1 (Prairie Du Rocher, Illinois, 1984): 1-21.

70 Ibid., 8-9.

71 Ibid., 21.

72 F. Terry Norris, "Ste. Genevieve, A French Colonial Village in the Illinois Country," in *French Colonial Archaeology* (Urbana: University of Illinois Press, 1991), 133-48.

## *Eric Sandweiss,* Paving St. Louis's Streets

1 For more on the colonial development of St. Louis and its context within French and Spanish planning practices elsewhere, see Dora P. Crouch, Daniel J. Garr, and Axel J. Mundigo, *Spanish City Planning in North America* (Cambridge, Mass.: M.I.T. Press, 1982); Charles E. Peterson, *Colonial St. Louis, Building a Creole Capital,* 2d ed. (St. Louis: Patrice Press, 1949); Michael Roark, ed., *French and Germans in the Mississippi Valley: Landscape and Cultural Traditions* (Cape Girardeau, Mo.: Center for Regional History and Cultural Heritage, 1988); and John R. Stilgoe, *Common Landscape of America, 1750 to 1845* (New Haven Conn.: Yale University Press, 1982).

2 Eric Sandweiss, "Construction and Community in South St. Louis, 1850-1910" (Ph.D. diss., University of California, Berkeley, 1991), 19.

3 James Parton, "The City of St. Louis," in *The Atlantic Monthly* 19 (1867): 657-58.

4 Samuel Curtis diary, 7 January 1851, Missouri Historical Society (hereafter cited as MHS) Archives.

5 See Clay McShane, "Transforming the Use of Urban Space: A Look at the Revolution in Street Pavements, 1880-1924," in *Journal of Urban History* 5 (1979): 279-307.

6 Curtis diary, 7 January 1851.

7 *Missouri Republican,* 2 March 1851.

8 "Report of the Street Commissioner," in *The Mayor's Message, with Accompanying Documents, to the City Council of the City of St. Louis* (hereafter cited as *Mayor's Message*) (St. Louis, 1872), 4; "Report of the Board of Public Improvements," in *Mayor's Message* (1881), 162; *Journal of the House of Delegates* (St. Louis, 1881), 87-88.

9 "Report of the City Engineer," in *Mayor's Message* (1872), 9, and (1874), 21, *Journal of the House of Delegates* (1881), 87-88.

10 "R.C." to "Mother," 9 May 1881, and anonymous diary entries, 13 and 14 January 1897, all in St. Louis History Papers, MHS Archives.

11 "Report of the City Engineer" in *Mayor's Message* (1871), table 1, and (1875), table 2; *Edwards's St. Louis Directory* (St. Louis, 1870, 1871); *Gould's St. Louis Directory* (St. Louis, 1874, 1875).

12 "Report of the Board of Public Improvements," in *Mayor's Message* (1878), 200-203.

13 "Report of the City Engineer," in *Mayor's Message* (1871), 155.

14 Ibid. (1875), 6.

15 "Abstracts of Damages and Judgments Awarded in Streets and Alley Openings," 18 April 1856, Microfilm C-3689, City of St. Louis Archival Library.

16 "Revised Charter of 1867," in *The Revised Ordinances of the City of St. Louis* (St. Louis: George Knapp & Co., 1871), 96

17 "Abstracts of Damages," c. 1871-1876, Microfilm Roll #C 3689, St. Louis City Archival Library.

18 See, for example, complaints lodged in *Journal of the Board of Public Improvements*, 3 June 1878 (n.p.); and *Journal of the House of Delegates of St. Louis, 1894-95*, 492.

19 Ordinance #6905, 14 June 1869.

20 Based on an examination of street opening and improvement ordinances listed in *Index—St. Louis City Ordinances from Incorporation to 1903* (St. Louis: William H. O'Brien, 1903) for those blocks included in the Benton Park neighborhood, as defined by the Landmarks Preservation Association of St. Louis. These blocks, which comprise the heart of the study area, have been the focus of historical research carried out by Landmarks; therefore, they provide a good basis on which to build further study.

21 *Scheme for the Separation and Re-Organization of the Governments of St. Louis City and County and Charter for the City of St. Louis* (hereafter cited as *Scheme and Charter*) (St. Louis: Woodward, Tiernan and Hale, 1877). The standard reference to the charter remains Thomas S. Barclay, *The St. Louis Home Rule Charter of 1876, Its Framing and Adoption* (Columbia: University of Missouri Press, 1962). See also Jon C. Teaford, *The Unheralded Triumph: City Government in America, 1870-1900* (Baltimore: Johns Hopkins University Press, 1948), 112-17.

22 *Scheme and Charter*, 78, 91-92, 95.

23 Ibid., 89.

24 See Christine Meisner Rosen, "Infrastructural Improvement in Nineteenth-Century Cities: A Conceptual Framework and Cases," in *Journal of Urban History* 12 (1986): 211-56; and Terrence J. McDonald, *The Parameters of Urban Fiscal Policy: Socioeconomic Change and Political Culture in San Francisco, 1860-1906* (Berkeley and Los Angeles: University of California Press, 1988), xi, for a fuller exploration of that fiscal philosophy as it related to public improvements. The broader implications of this developing complex of social and political attitudes in the late nineteenth century are discussed in Robert H. Wiebe, *The Search for Order* (New York: Hill and Wang, 1967), 133-35.

25 "Report of the Board of Public Improvements," in *Mayor's Message* (1878), 199.

26 "Report of the Street Commissioner," in *Mayor's Message* (1878), 248; "Report of the Board of Public Improvements," in *Mayor's Message* (1881), 160, and (1883), 166.

27 *Journal of the Board of Public Improvements*, October 1877-February 1880.

28 Ibid., 3 January 1878.

29 Ibid., 21 October 1879. The effects of landfill on streets already occupied by houses can still be seen on Lemp Avenue north of Cherokee Street, where the first stories of older buildings are entered below street level.

30 *Scheme and Charter*, 95.

31 "Report of the Board of Public Improvements," in *Mayor's Message* (1880), 175.

32 *Journal of the Board of Public Improvements*, 16 November 1877. The denial of this sidewalk petition was actually among those overturned by the subsequent pleadings before the Board of Councilman Nicholas Berg.

33 To some extent, portions of every American city suffered from this cycle of caution, neglect, and disrepair. A similar case is described in Carl V. Harris, *Political Power in Birmingham, 1871-1921* (Knoxville: University of Tennessee Press, 1977), 154-55.

34 "Report of the Board of Public Improvements," in *Mayor's Message* (1878), 207.

35 *Journal of the Board of Public Improvements*, 3 February 1880.

36 Walt Whitman, letter to "Lou" (Hannah Louise Whitman), 11 October 1879, MHS Archives. Whitman wrote to his sister while in St. Louis to visit his brother Jeff, a prominent engineer in the city.

37 "Report of the Street Commissioner," in *Mayor's Message* (1887), 266.

38 The only exception to this rule came in the following year, with the designation of the streets of the new Compton Heights Subdivision as boulevards. This subdivision is often assumed, wrongly, to be another of the private places.

39 For more on the dynamics of civic improvement in St. Louis, see "Fenced-Off Corners and Wider Settings: The Logic of Civic Improvement in Early Twentieth-Century St. Louis," in *Planning the American City since 1900*, ed. Mary Corbin Sies and Christopher Silver (Baltimore: Johns Hopkins University Press, 1996).

## *Katharine T. Corbett,* Politics of Sewers in St. Louis

1 Quoted in J. Thomas Scharf, *History of St. Louis City* (Philadelphia: Everet & Co., 1883), 656.

2 There is no comprehensive history of the St. Louis sewer system in the nineteenth century. Scharf's 1883 history of the city and William Hyde and Howard L. Conard, *Encyclopedia of the History of St. Louis: A Compendendium of History and Biography for Ready Reference* (New York, 1899) both include narrative descriptions of the system's development and rationale drawn largely from annual municipal reports. A more recent narrative that also relies heavily on sewer department reports is John P. Dietzler, "Sewage and Drainage in St. Louis, 1764-1954" (M.A. thesis, St. Louis University, 1954). Some of the most useful sources are the professional writings of Robert Moore and Robert McMath, cited elsewhere. Both men were St. Louis sewer commissioners and nationally prominent civil engineers. Frank E. Janson, Manager of Infrastructure for the Metropolitan St. Louis Sewer District, maintains the historical records of the former city sewer department and is the most authoritative source on its history.

3 For history and analysis of nineteenth-century sewerage the following are among the most useful: Joel A. Tarr, James McCurley, and Terry F. Yosie, "Development and Impact of Urban Wastewater Technology: Changing Concepts of Water Quality Control, 1850-1930," in *Pollution and Reform in American Cities, 1870-1930*, ed. Martin V. Melosie (Austin: University of Texas Press, 1980); Stanley K. Schultz and Clay McShane, "To Engineer the Metropolis: Sewers, Sanitation, and City Planning in Late-Nineteenth-Century America," in *Journal of American History*, (September 1978): 389-341; American Public Works Association, *History of Public Works in the United States*, ed. Ellis L. Armstrong, (Chicago: APWA, 1976); Joel A. Tarr and Josef W. Konvitz, "Patterns in the Development of the Urban Infrastructure," in *American Urbanism*, ed. Howard Gillette, Jr. and Zane I. Miller (New York: Greenwood Press, 1987); Ann Durkin Keating, *Invisible Networks: Exploring the History of Local Utilities and Public Works* (Malabar, Fla.: Kruger Publishing, 1994), 66-72 provides a guide to infrastructure research.

4 For further description of the area's nineteenth century karst topography and the location of ridges and major sinkholes see Scharf, *History of St. Louis City and County*, 773, and *Mayor's Message and Accompanying Documents, 1878* (St. Louis, 1878), 221-22. These volumes were published semi-annually or annually throughout the nineteenth century and included reports from the officials responsible for the city's sewer construction and maintenance, either the city engineer or, after 1877, the sewer commissioner.

5 James Neal Primm, *Lion of the Valley, St. Louis, Missouri*, 2d. ed. (Boulder, Col.: Pruett Publishing, 1990). Unless noted, all references to St. Louis population and area growth are taken from this volume, the most recent narrative history of the city.

6 Robert Moore, "Street Pavements in St. Louis," in *Journal of the Association of Engineering Societies (JAES)* 4, no. 6 (1885): 227; *St. Louis Ordinances, 1841-1843*, 200BCD.

7 Scharf, *History of St. Louis City and County*, 772-79.

8 See "Henry B. Kayser," *Encyclopedia of the History of St. Louis*, vol. 2, for a summary of Kayser's civil engineering career, and Andrew Hurley, "On the Waterfront: Railroad and Real Estate in Antebellum St. Louis," in *Gateway Heritage* (spring 1993): 4-17, for his later

involvement in local real estate ventures.

9  See Dietzer, *Sewerage and Drainage in St. Louis*, 8-14, for a description of Kayser's efforts to use sinkholes as natural sewers.

10 *Laws of the State of Missouri, Passed at the 1st Session of the 12th General Assembly, October 21, 1842 to February 8, 1843* (City of Jefferson, 1843), 127.

11 St. Louis Ordinances, 1841-1843, 666DE; Dietzer, *Sewerage and Drainage in St. Louis*, 20-21.

12 Primm, *Lion of the Valley*, 160-64.

13 Scharf, *History of St. Louis City and County*, 772.

14 Robert Moore, "Sewerage and Home Drainage in St. Louis," *JAES* 4, no. 4 (1885); *History of Public Works in the United States*, 400.

15 Walter B. Stevens, *History of St. Louis, The Fourth City, 1764-1909* (St. Louis, 1909): 134.

16 *Laws of the State of Missouri, 1849*, 519. In February the City Council had authorized drafting a plan for sewering the city and had petitioned the Missouri legislature for the enabling statute. See *St. Louis City Council, Journal of the Board of Delegates, 1849*, 35-43. Although Scharf (773-74) and others attribute the push for sewer construction to the cholera epidemic, Moore stated in 1885 that this was the culmination of years of debate. Cholera did not reach epidemic proportions until late summer. See Dietzer, *Sewerage and Drainage in St. Louis*, 26.

17 Dietzer, *Sewerage and Drainage in St. Louis*, 35-38.

18 *Mayor's Message, October 1851*, 9. See "The Journal of Samuel R. Curtis, 1850-52" (Missouri Historical Society) for Curtis's diary notes on the construction of the Biddle Street Sewer and "Samuel R. Curtis City Engineer (1850-1853);" *Pipeline, A Bi-monthly Newsletter to the Employees of the Metropolitan St. Louis Sewer District*, (May-June, 1993) 2, 6, for biographical information.

19 *Mayor's Message, October 1850*, 4-8.

20 Ibid., *May 1850*, 9.

21 *St. Louis Ordinances, 1849-50*, 1,434-1,434B.

22 *Mayor's Message, May 1851*, 6.

23 Dietzer, *Sewerage and Drainage*, 51-68, and passim. See also William Wise, "Mill Creek Sewer," *JAES* 4, no. 4 (1885): 263-274, for a detailed account by a longtime employee of the department of the construction of the Mill Creek Sewer. Wise concluded that while the design and construction of the sewer were not complex, dealing with the river, rock, and underfunding made the job slow and difficult.

24 *Mayor's Message, May 1860*, 10; *St. Louis Ordinances, 1859-61*, 3,001-3,003.

25 Primm, *Lion of the Valley*, 164, 198-201.

26 *Mayor's Message, May 1860*, 10.

27 Ibid., *May 1863*, 10.

28 Primm, *Lion of the Valley*, 163-64.

29 Tarr and Konvitz, "Patterns in the Development of the Urban Infrastructure."

30 Wise, "Mill Creek Sewer," 272; Scharf, *History of St. Louis City and County*, 776-79.

31 *Mayor's Message, May 1872*, 10-12; ibid., *November 1872*, 11.

32 Ibid., *May 1876*, 14; *ibid*., April 1877, 16.

33 William Cassella, "City-County Separation: The Great Divorce," in *Bulletin of the Missouri Historical Society* (*BMHS*) (January 1959).

34 *Mayor's Message, November 1873*, 7. The City Council spent twice as much on roads as on sewers and was more willing to incur debt for roads than sewers.

35 *Mayor's Message, November 1871*, 21.

36 Cassella, "City-County Separation" 85-104.

37 *Mayor's Message, 1878*, 221-25.

38 *Mayor's Message, 1879*, 2-3.

39 David T. Beito with Bruce Smith, "The Formation of Urban Infrastructure Through Nongovernmental Planning: The Private Places of St. Louis, 1869-1920," in *Journal of Urban History* 5 (1990).

40 Beito, "The Formation of the Urban Infrastructure," 271. Although St. Louis carried an average debt, the city, fourth in population, ranked eighth in per capita spending for municipal services in 1880 and ninth in 1890.

41 *St. Louis Ordinances, 1877-1878*, 973-75; see Schultz and McShane, "To Engineer the Metropolis," 399-403, for professionalization of sewer departments in this period. For a summary of Henry Flad's career see *German Engineers of Early St. Louis and their Works* (St. Louis, n.d.), 29-36.

42 *Mayor's Message, 1878*. Eighty-five percent of St. Louis sewers were brick compared to 37 percent of Chicago's. Clay pipe was not only cheaper, but its smooth surface made sewers more self-cleaning.

43 *Mayor's Message, 1880*, 245.

44 *Mayor's Message, 1879*, 5-7.

45 For a summary of Moore's career see his obituary, *St. Louis Globe-Democrat*, 26 July 1922. Moore gave a detailed description of his philosophy and reform efforts in Robert Moore, "Municipal Engineering in St. Louis," *JAES* 11, no. 3 (1892): 123-33.

46 *Mayor's Message, 1889*, 323-41, charts 13 and 14.

47 In 1880 sewer construction became a priority in the industrial area of Lowell to protect the purity of the water drawn for city use at Bissell's Point, just to the south, and to reduce "sickening odors" from factories, stockyards, and slaughter houses.

48 *Mayor's Message, 1880*, 34; ibid., 1883, 210.

49 *Mayor's Message, 1887*; 294-97; ibid., *1882*, 232; ibid., *1883*, 210-16. Most of the larger sewer outfalls were reconstructed by the early 1900s. See W. W. Horner and Leland Chives, "Mill Creek Sewer System in St. Louis, A $3,000,000 Pressure Tunnel Project" in *Engineering Record*, 3 and 10 October (1914): 368-406; and W. W. Horner, "Reconstruction and Relief of the Rocky Branch Sewer; St. Louis, Mo.," in *Engineering News*, 16 April (1914): 834-40.

50 *Mayor's Message, 1885*, 266; ibid, *1881*, 259-64; ibid., *1882*, 232.

51 J. P. Dietzer, "The Mill Creek Sewer Explosion, July 26, 1892," *BMHS* (January 1959); *Pipeline* (November-December 1989): 2.

52 *Mayor's Message, 1886*, 379; George Holman, *Sanitary Survey of St. Louis* (St. Louis, 1885), 15.

53 For a discussion of the controversy over separate and combined sewers see Joel A. Tarr, "The Separate vs. Combined Sewer Problem: A Case Study in Urban Technology Design Choice," in *Journal of Urban History* 5, no. 3 (1970): 308-39.

54 Moore, "Sewerage and House Drainage in St. Louis," 143; Robert Moore, "Combined Sewers vs. the Waring System—a Rejoinder," *JAES* 3, no. 9, (1884); Robert McMath, "Comparative Economy of Combined and Separate Sewers," *JAES* 3, no. 9 (1884).

55 Moore, "Sewerage and House Drainage," 18.

56 Beito, "The Formation of Urban Infrastructure." Beito found St. Louis to have the most private streets of any American city: ninety developed between 1870 and 1910. Although he acknowledges that the desire for land use restrictions and aggressive promotion by developers encouraged the growth of private subdivisions, Beito argues that the desire for control over infrastructure was the main reason for their popularity with wealthy St. Louisans. Some developers provided water tanks to flush private sewers into nearby watercourses. See especially pages 267, 271-74.

57 *Mayor's Message, 1887*, 292. A civil engineer for the War Department in the Civil War and later president of the Board of Public Improvement, McMath, like Robert Moore, wrote extensively on the engineering profession, sewer theory, and management for professional journals. See *St. Louis Globe-Democrat*, 1 June 1918.

**58** Beito, "The Formation of Urban Infrastructure," 281.

**59** *Mayor's Message, 1887*, 292, 297.

**60** For a full description of McMath's plan and his analysis of St. Louis's drainage problems see Robert E. McMath, "The Future Drainage of St. Louis," *JAES* 6, no. 4 (1887). See also "Topographical Map of the City of St. Louis," produced in 1889 and printed in 1895 by the sewer department. This planning tool provided topography and contours for areas of the city west of Grand Avenue and was used in planning both streets and sewers. Available in the MSD historical files.

**61** Horner, "Mill Creek Sewer," 369-70.

**62** *Mayor's Message, 1887*, xvi, 292, 297; ibid., *1891*, 301-2.

**63** *St.Louis Ordinances, April 1, 1887*, 16025.

**64** *Mayor's Message, 1889*, 325.

**65** *Mayor's Message, 1882*, 227; ibid., *1891*, 303; ibid., *1892*, 359.

**66** *Mayor's Message, 1887*, 292.

**67** Christine Meismer Rosen, "Infrastructure Improvement in Nineteenth-Century Cities: A Conceptual Framework and Cases," in *Journal of Urban History* 12, no. 3, (1986): 211-56. Rosen argues that the political economy of nineteenth-century American cities resulted in consumers unwilling or unable to pay costs involved in satisfying infrastructure needs. Difficulty and friction were unavoidable under existing urban economic, environmental, social, political, and cultural conditions.

**68** Primm, *Lion of the Valley*, 281-82.

**69** *Mayor's Message, 1894*, 425-27.

**70** *St. Louis Post-Dispatch*, 5 August 1894.

**71** *Mayor's Message, 1894*, 465.

**72** In 1896, a legal interpretation of the city charter that held the municipal government responsible for funding only sewers "along the principle courses of drainage" enabled the city to transfer more of the cost of construction to privately-funded sewer districts. See *The Republic*, 5 August 1896.

**73** *Mayor's Message, 1894*, 441.

**74** Primm, *Lion of the Valley*, 402; See Caroline Loughlin and Catherine Anderson, *Forest Park* (Columbia: University of Missouri Press, 1986), 54-55, 71-72, 85-86, 139-40, for information on the condition of the River des Peres in Forest Park before, during, and after the World's Fair. *Pipeline* (May-June, 1992), 2-3.

**75** Metropolitan Sewer District, *The River des Peres . . . A St. Louis Landmark* (St. Louis: MSD, c.1988), 3.

**76** See MSD, *The River des Peres*, for a history of the River des Peres Project. Frank Janson, MSD Manager of Infrastructure, provided much of the information for this report.

## *Mark Tebeau,* Fire Risk and Insurance in St. Louis

1   *The People's Organ*, 21 May 1849. Missouri Historical Society, St. Louis Veteran Volunteer Firemen's Collection (hereafter MHS, STLVVFC), box 1, folder 16, Newspaper Account, "The Great Fire," 1849.

2   MHS, SLVVFC, series I, vol 10, Missouri Fire Company Number Five, *Record of Fires*, 1846-1855.

3   These numbers were taken from two sources: MHS, STLVVFC, series I, vol. 10; Missouri Fire Company Number Five, *Record of Fires*, 1846-1855; and the National Board of Fire Underwriters (NBFU) publication *Safeguarding America Against Fire*, which began publication in 1920. *SAAF* kept yearly statistics on the amount of fire loss nationwide and tabulated the fires' origins.

4   The literature on urban conflagrations is vast. For two recent discussions of the Chicago fire and its aftermath see Christine Rosen, *The Limits of Power: Great Fires and the Process of City Growth in America* (New York: Cambridge University Press, 1986), or Karen Sawislak, "Smoldering City: Class, Ethnicity, and Politics in Chicago at the Time of the Great Fire, 1867-1874" (Ph.D. diss., Yale University, 1990).

5   David D. Dana, *The Fireman: The Fire Departments of the United States* (Boston, 1856), 358ff. Few scholars have systematically studied issues surrounding the suppression of fire. By far the best work dealing with how fire has been socially and culturally understood in American history is Stephen J. Pyne, *Fire in America: A Cultural History of Wildland and Rural Fire* (Princeton, N.J.: Princeton University Press, 1982); see too, Margaret Hindle Hazen and Robert M. Hazen, *Keepers of the Flame: The Role of Fire in American Culture, 1775-1925* (Princeton, N.J.: Princeton University Press, 1992). Less directly relevant are those studies which deal with fire in urban contexts—usually with the consequences of disasterous urban conflagrations. See, for instance, Carl Smith, *Urban Disorder and the Shape of Belief: The Great Chicago Fire, the Haymarket Bomb, and the Model Town of Pullman* (Chicago: University of Chicago Press, 1995); Christine Rosen, *The Limits of Power: Great Fires and the Process of City Growth in America* (New York: Cambridge University Press, 1986); Karen Sawislak, *Smoldering City: Chicagoans and the Great Fire, 1871-1874* (Chicago: University of Chicago Press, 1996).

6   *Mayor's Message, City of St. Louis, 1848*, 16; J. Thomas Scharf, *History of St. Louis City and County* (Philadelphia: Everts & Co., 1883), 819ff. For damage estimates, see *Missouri Republican*, 24 May 1849; MHS, STLVVFC, box 1, folder 16, "Great Fire of 1849; Recollections of Witnesses; News Clippings, 1849-1939"; MHS, STLVVFC, box 1, folder 17, "Official Accounts of the Great Fire, 1849-1902."

7   See, for instance, Glen Holt, "Volunteer Firefighting in St. Louis, 1818-1859," in *Gateway Heritage* 4, no 3, (1983-1984): 2-13; St. Louis City Ordinances, 1826.

8   MHS, STLVVFC, vol. 16, Firemen's Association, Minutes, 3.26.50.

9   A. W. Brayley, *A History of the Boston Fire Department* (Boston, 1878), 234.

10  On the National Board of Fire Underwriters, see A. L. Todd, *A Spark Lighted in Portland: The Record of the National Board of Fire Underwriters* (New York: McGraw-Hill, 1966); National Board of Fire Underwriters, *Pioneers of Progress* (1941).

11  Christine Rosen, *The Limits of Power: Great Fires and the Process of City Growth in America* (New York: Cambridge University Press, 1986).

12  Henry R. Gall and William R. Jordan, *One Hundred Years of Fire Insurance: Being a History of the Aetna Insurance Company, Hartford, Connecticut, 1819-1919* (Hartford, Conn.: Aetna Insurance Company, 1919).

13  Quoted in J. A. Fowler, *History of Insurance in Philadelphia for Two Centuries, 1683-1882* (Philadelphia: Review Publishing and Printing, 1888), 396. Binney's entire address may be found in *Centennial Meeting of the Philadelphia Contributionship for the Insurance of Houses from Loss by Fire* (Philadelphia: C. Sherman, 1852; corrected, 185).

14  CIGNA, Aetna Collection, RG 5/3: 1.4, *Instructions for the Use of Agents* (1857), 36ff. Hereafter, Aetna, *Instructions to Agents* (1857).

15  Aetna, *Instructions to Agents* (1857): 34-35.

16  CIGNA, Aetna Collection, RG 5/1: 19, "Classifications of Fire Risk," vol. 1, (1852-1872). See page 24 for the information on saloons and coffeehouses. The beginning pages offer an index, and the final pages offer summary information for every five-year period.

17  *Directions for the Use of Agents of the Aetna Fire Insurance Company* (Hartford, Conn.: Aetna Insurance Company, 1857), 4-5. This document can also be cited as CIGNA, Aetna Collection, RG 5/3: 1.3. Hereafter, Aetna, *Directions for Use . . .* (1857) Note, too, that Aetna published two guides for its agents dated "1857."

18 CIGNA, Aetna Collection, RG 5/1: 19 "Classifications of Fire Risk," vol. 1, (1852-1872); Aetna, *Instructions to Agents* (1857): 21ff.

19 Helena Wright, "Insurance Mapping and Industrial Archaeology," in *Industrial Archaeology: The Journal of the Society for Industrial Archaeology* 9, no. 1 (1993): 1-19. This article is the most thorough, though almost exclusively descriptive, discussion of fire insurance maps. See also R. P. Getty, "Insurance Surveying and Mapmaking," in *Cassier's Magazine: An Engineering Monthly* 39, no. 1 (November 1910): 19-25; Walter W. Ristow, "United States Fire Insurance and Underwriters' Maps, 1852-1968," in *The Quarterly Journal of the Library of Congress* 25, no. 3 (July 1968): 194-219; Sanborn Map Company, *Description and Utilization of The Sanborn Map* (New York: The Sanborn Map Company, 1953).

20 CIGNA Archives, INA Collection, Board of Directors Minutes, vol. 5, 1845-1860, 2 November 1852.

21 CIGNA Archives, Aetna Collection, RG 5/1, box 5, folder 21, "Dairies and Notebooks (7) of Special Agent A. A. Williams covering visits to Quebec, New England, and Mid-Atlantic States Agencies, 1855-1857," book 5, *Visit to Quebec* (1856). Hereafter cited as CIGNA, Aetna Collection, A. A. Williams, *Visit to Quebec* (1856).

22 Aetna, *Instructions to Agents* (1857).

23 On the early Perris Maps see W. J. Ristow, "U.S. Fire Insurance and Underwriters' Maps." Compare, for instance, Ernest Hexamer, *Maps of the City of Philadelphia Surveyed by Ernest Hexamer and William Locher, Civil Engineers and Surveyors, 1858; Volume 3, Comprising the 7th and 8th Wards* (Philadelphia: Ernest Hexamer and William Locher, 1858). The Map Division of the Library of Congress holds an extensive collection of nineteenth-century fire insurance maps, including the earliest such map of St. Louis. Bascome and Parr, *Insurance Map of St. Louis, MO: Western Bascome, Insurance Agent and Adjuster; John A. Parr, Surveyor and Draftsman* (St. Louis: 1859).

24 Hexamer, *Map of . . . Philadelphia* (1858).

25 See, for instance, Ernest Hexamer, *Insurance Maps of the City of Philadelphia, Surveyed and Drawn by Ernest Hexamer,* vol. 9 (Philadelphia: Ernest Hexamer, 1873; pasteovers to 1901).

26 Compare, for instance, the changes in Hexamer's maps in Hexamer, *Map of . . . Philadelphia* (1858); Hexamer, *Map of . . . Philadelphia* (1873); Hexamer, *Insurance Maps of Philadelphia* (1896).

27 See, for instance, Hexamer, *Map of Philadelphia* (1870); A. Whipple, *A. Whipple & Company's Insurance Map of St. Louis, Missouri* (1876). Of course, most map companies provided pasteovers which is evident when looking at an original, colored copy as opposed to black and white microfilm. See especially the 1876 Whipple map because the updates are listed on the front and back cover as well as on the frontspiece. Note, too, that not all maps have pasteovers. Those maps which were not used by underwriting companies, agents, or city governments may not have them.

28 See, for instance, *A. Whipple & Company's Insurance Map of St. Louis, Missouri* (1870), pages/plates 8, 11, 20; C. T. Aubin, *St. Louis Fire Insurance Maps, Surveyed and Drawn for the St. Louis Board of Fire Underwriters* (1874).

29 CIGNA, Aetna Collection, RG 5/1, box 5, folder 21, "Dairies and Notebooks (7) of Special Agent A. A. Williams covering visits to Quebec, New England, and Mid-Atlantic States Agencies, 1855-1857," Book 1, *Visit to New England* (1856). Hereafter cited as CIGNA, Aetna Collection, A. A. Williams, *Visit to New England* (1856). Both quotations from CIGNA, A. A. Williams, *Visit to Quebec* (1856).

30 CIGNA, Aetna Collection, A. A. Williams, *Visit to Quebec* (1856). This document is not paginated. Entries are listed according to block.

**31** CIGNA, Aetna Collection, A. A. Williams, *Visit to New England* (1856). Compare the drawings made by Williams with those that appear in both volumes of "instructions" published by Aetna in 1857; Aetna, *Instructions to Agents* (1857): sample diagram at the end of the volume; Aetna, *Directions for the Use of Agents of the Aetna Fire Insurance Company* (Hartford, Conn.: Aetna Insurance Company, 1857), 30-31. Fire insurance atlases contained similar "special hazards." For a fee surveyors drew maps of "special risks." As with other aspects of the map-making industry, these "General Surveys" as they were sometimes called complemented underwriting practice. Indeed, many companies recommended that their agents hire a surveyor to draw such a map at the client's expense. In fact, the Philadelphia Board of Fire Underwriters issued instructions in 1857 which listed drawing a map as one of the many requirements of good underwriting. As a result, Hexamer and other surveyors published maps of industrial risks as a service to their clients. In 1866, Ernest Hexamer published a map of "special risks" in Philadelphia for the first time; Whipple generated similar maps of St. Louis in 1872. See, for instance, A. Whipple, *A. Whipple and Company's Insurance Maps: 2nd series, Special Risks* (Revised Edition, 1872); CIGNA, A. A. Williams, *Visit to New England*, (1856), 6-9; Aetna, *Instructions. Rules & Rules* (Hartford, Conn.: Aetna Insurance Company, 1857). Sample diagram at the end of the volume.

**32** *Whipple's Daily Fire Reporter* 8, no. 17 (19 January 1883).

**33** Ibid.

**34** Ibid. 7, no. 212 (2 September 1882).

**35** Ibid. 8, no. 17 (19 January 1883); ibid. 7, no. 299 (13 December 1882).

**36** Ibid. 7, no. 21 (24 January 1882).

**37** See, for instance, ibid. 7, no. 130 (30 May 1882). Perusing notes of re-inspection reveals that approximately three-fourths of all properties inspected and found to contain risks removed those hazards.

**38** Ibid. 7, no. 9 (11 January 1882).

**39** Ibid.; the latter passage is taken from ibid. 7, no. 186 (3 August 1882).

**40** Ibid. 8, no. 17 (19 January 1883).

**41** For the aggregate causes of fires in 1882 see *Whipple's Daily Fire Reporter* 8, no. 17 (19 January 1883); ibid. 7, no. 120 (18 May 1882).

**42** Ibid. 7, no. 190 (24 January 1882).

**43** "Whipple's Annual Report for 1881," published in *Whipple's Daily Fire Reporter* 7, no. 21 (24 January 1882).

**44** *Whipple's Daily Fire Reporter* 7, no. 175 (21 July 1882).

**45** Ibid.

**46** Ibid. 7, no. 21 (24 January 1882).

**47** Ibid. 7, no. 213 (4 September 1882).

**48** Scholars have not carefully examined the fire insurance industry, though they have discussed fireproofing and "fire zones" as municipal regulations. See, for instance, Sawislak, *Smoldering City*, chapter 3; Christine Rosen, *The Limits of Power*, 95-108. On New England's textile manufacturers see Dane Yorke, *Able Men of Boston, the Remarkable Story of the First 100 Years of the Boston Manufacturers' Mutual Fire Insurance Company* (Boston, Mass.: Boston Manufacturers' Mutual Fire Insurance Company, 1950).

**49** Among other places, price competition is discussed in the *Proceedings of the National Board of Fire Underwriters* and Harry Brearly, *The History of the National Board of Fire Underwriters* (New York: Frederick Stokes and Company, 1916); see also Robert Riegel, *Fire Underwriters Associations in the United States* (New York: The Chronicle Company, 1916); Betsy W. Bahr, *New England Mill Engineering: Rationalization and Reform in Textile Mill Design*, 1790-1920 (Ph.D. diss., University of Delaware, 1988), especially chapter 4.

50 William Joseph Novak, "Salus Populi: The Roots of Regulation in America, 1787-1873" (Ph.D. diss., Brandeis University, 1992). In "Salus Populi," Novak argues that state authority over property was well established, especially in relation to fire danger prior to the Civil War. Even so, such intervention by the state, or the insurance industry, in building practice did not occur in a uniform fashion. By the twentieth century, building codes begin to show greater uniformity, in part because local municipalities applied the standards systematically developed by underwriters in the nineteenth century. For the story of the National Board of Fire Underwriters and the development of standards, see the *Proceedings of the National Board of Fire Underwriters*, 1866ff.

## *Andrew Hurley,* Regulation of Nuisance Trades In St. Louis

1   *St. Louis Globe-Democrat*, 19 July 1873.
2   Ibid., 15, 23 July 1873.
3   Ibid., 15 July 1873.
4   Ibid., 16 July 1873.
5   Ibid., 14 July, 1873.
6   Ibid., 19, 27 July 1873.
7   Martin V. Melosi, "Environmental Crisis in the City: The Relationship between Industrialization and Urban Pollution," in *Pollution and Reform in American Cities, 1870-1930* , ed. Melosi (Austin: University of Texas Press, 1980), 4-31; Craig Colten, "Industrial Wastes before 1940: A Neglected Dimension of the Hazardous Waste Issue," paper presented at Forests, Habitats, and Resources: A Conference in World Environmental History (Durham, North Carolina, 1987); Joseph M. Petulla, *American Environmental History*, 2d ed. (Columbus, Ohio: Merrill Publishing, 1988), 256-68.
8   Federal Census of Manufacturing, St. Louis, 1860, manuscript on microfilm, and Federal Census of Manufacturing, St. Louis, 1870, manuscript on microfilm, Missouri Historical Society Library, St. Louis, Missouri; Smoke Commission, City of St. Louis, *Smoke Abatement Ordinances and General Reports of the Smoke Commission, City of St. Louis* (St. Louis: Continental Print, 1893); James Neal Primm, *Lion of the Valley: St. Louis, Missouri* (Boulder, Col.: Pruett Publishing, 1981), 358-59; Lucius H. Cannon, *Smoke Abatement: A Study of the Police Power as Embodied in Laws, ordinances, and Court Decisions* (St. Louis: St. Louis Public Library, 1924), 210-17.
9   *Annual Report of the Health Commissioner, City of St. Louis, 1879-1880* (St. Louis: Woodward, Tiernan, and Hale, 1880), 43-50.
10  *Report of the Health Officer to the Board of Health of the City of Saint Louis* (St. Louis: St. Louis Times, 1872), 14; *Eighth Annual Report of the Board of Health of the City of St. Louis* (St. Louis: Woodward, Tiernan, and Hale, 1875), 14; *Annual Report of the Health Department, City of St. Louis, 1879*, 1-5; *Mayor's Message with Accompanying Documents to the Municipal Assembly of the City of St. Louis at Its Sessions, May, 1883* (St. Louis: A. Ungar and Co., 1883), 298; *The Mayor's Message with Accompanying Documents to the Municipal Assembly of the City of St. Louis at Its Sessions, May, 1884* (St. Louis: Woodward and Tiernan, 1884), 337. *Twelfth Annual Report of the Health Commissioner, City of St. Louis, Mo., 1888-1889* (St. Louis: Nixon-Jones Printing, 1889), 102.
11  *Missouri Republican*, 28 July 1893, George Homan scrapbook, Missouri Historical Society, 11.
12  *Missouri Republican*, 4 July 1893, George Homan scrapbook, 11.
13  *St. Louis Globe-Democrat*, 20 July 1873, 4.

**14** *Annual Report of the Health Department, City of St. Louis, 1879* (St. Louis: Times Printing House, 1879), 15-18. *Annual Report of the Health Commissioner, City of St. Louis, 1879-1880* (St. Louis: Woodward, Tiernan, and Hale, 1880), 46-51.

**15** *St. Louis Globe-Democrat*, 28 August 1878, 3.

**16** *St. Louis Globe-Democrat*, 29 August 1873, 4.

**17** Robert Moore, "Notes Upon the History of Cholera in St. Louis," in *A Sanitary Survey of St. Louis*, ed. George Homan (Concord, N.H.: Republican Press Association, 1885), 41-47; Patrick E. McLear, "The St. Louis Cholera Epidemic," in *Missouri Historical Review* 63 (January 1969): 171-81.

**18** Martin V. Melosi, "Hazardous Waste and Environmental Liablity: An Historical Perspective," in *Houston Law Review* 25 (July 1988): 762-68.

**19** John M. Krum, reviser, *The Revised Ordinances of the City of St. Louis* (St. Louis: Chambers & Knapp, 1850), 307; *The Ordinances of the City of St. Louis* (St. Louis: George Knapp & Co., 1861), 449, 458-60.

**20** *Mayor's Message and Accompanying Documents* (St. Louis: Dispatch Book and Job Office, 1866), 5-6.

**21** *First Annual Report of the Board of Health of the City of Saint Louis* (St. Louis: Missouri Democrat Printing, 1868), 6, 152-56.

**22** John D. Stevenson, "Organization of Health Department, Sanitary Legislation, and the Abatement of Nuisances," 12.

**23** *First Annual Report of the Board of Health of the City of Saint Louis*, 9-20, 129-30. *Report of the Health Officer to the Board of Health of the City of Saint Louis* (St. Louis: St. Louis Times, 1872), 1-12.

**24** *Missouri Republican*, 25 July 1873, 5; *St. Louis City Ordinance* 8981, 27 June 1874, Missouri Historical Society Library, St. Louis, Missouri.

**25** *First Annual Report of the Board of Health of the City of Saint Louis*, 21.

**26** *Annual Report of the Health Commissioner, City of Saint Louis, 1879-1880* (St. Louis: Woodward, Tiernan, and Hale, 1880), 28.

**27** *St. Louis Globe-Democrat*, 22 August 1873, 4.

**28** Ibid., 1 August 1873, 4.

**29** *First Annual Report of the Board of Health of the City of Saint Louis*, 20, 130-31; *Annual Report of the Health Department, City of St. Louis, 1879*, 5-8.

**30** *St. Louis Globe-Democrat*, 1 August 1873, 4.

**31** *Report of the Health Department, City of St. Louis, 1879*, 17.

**32** Simple housekeeping procedures were sometimes encoded into law. In 1882, for example, the city council mandated that all grease and offal carted through city streets be conveyed in containers with tight-fitting metallic or wooden lids. *St. Louis City Ordinance* 11,975, 30 March 1882, Missouri Historical Society Library, St. Louis, Missouri.

**33** *First Annual Report of the Board of Health of the City of Saint Louis*, 34-36. *Report of the Health Officer to the Board of Health of the City of Saint Louis* (St. Louis: St. Louis Times, 1872), 3.

**34** *Annual Report of the Health Commissioner, City of Saint Louis, 1879-1880*, 38.

**35** Ibid., 39.

**36** *St. Louis Globe-Democrat*, 5 August 1873, 4; *Annual Report of the Health Commissioner, City of Saint Louis, 1879-1880*, 39.

**37** *Annual Report of the Health Commissioner, City of Saint Louis, 1879-1880*, 39.

**38** Katharine T. Corbett and Howard S. Miller, *Saint Louis in the Gilded Age* (St. Louis: Missouri Historical Society Press, 1993), 47.

**39** *Annual Report of the Health Commissioner, City of Saint Louis, 1879-1880*, 47.

**40** Ibid., 46-47.

**41** Ibid., 39.

**42** *Report of the Health Officer to the Board of Health of the City of Saint Louis, 1872,* 11.

**43** *Report of the Health Department, City of St. Louis, 1879,* 12.

**44** Ibid. An analysis of census data reveals that the Lowell community consisted largely of households headed by manual laborers of Irish and German extraction in addition to a smaller number of African American families. "1880 Census of Population, City of St. Louis," Microfilm, Missouri Historical Society, Saint Louis, Missouri.

**45** *St. Louis Globe-Democrat,* 29 August 1873, 4.

**46** Ibid., 26 August 1878, 3.

**47** Ibid., 16 August 1878, 8; 26 August 1878, 3; 30 August 1878, 8.

**48** *Report of the Health Department, City of St. Louis, 1879,* 12-13.

**49** *Annual Report of the Health Commissioner, City of Saint Louis, 1879-1880,* 39.

**50** Ibid., 50.

**51** Whipple Fire Insurance Company, *Whipple's Fire Insurance Map of St. Louis, Missouri,* vol. 5, 2d ed. (1896), 277-84.

**52** Sidney Plotkin, *Keep Out: The Struggle for Land Use Control* (Berkeley: University of California Press, 1987), 103-9. The City Plan Commission of St. Louis, *Zoning For St. Louis: A Fundamental Part of the City Plan* (St. Louis: Nixon-Jones Printing, 1918); The City Plan Commission of St. Louis, *The Zone Plan* (St. Louis, 1919).

**53** The City Plan Commission of St. Louis, *Zoning For St. Louis: A Fundamental Part of the City Plan* (St. Louis: Nixon-Jones Printing, 1918); The City Plan Commission of St. Louis, *The Zone Plan* (St. Louis: Nixon-Jones Printing, 1919); St. Louis, Missouri Zoning Commission, *Use District Map* (December 1965). Other areas that were zoned unrestricted included the southern riverfront, much of the River des Peres floodplain, and a smaller area to the northwest of the intersection of Kingshighway Boulevard and Natural Bridge Road.

**54** City Plan Commission of St. Louis, *The Zone Plan.*

**55** City Plan Commission of St. Louis, *Comprehensive Plan, St. Louis: Zoning* (St. Louis, 1949), 3-4. Edward M. Bassett, *Zoning: The Laws, Administration, and Court Decisions During the First Twenty Years* (New York: Russell Sage Foundation, 1946).

## *Craig E. Colton,* Legal Response to Illinois Pollution

**1** H. D. Sexton, *East St. Louis: Past, Present, Future, 1890-1910,* manuscript of address delivered to the Commercial Club of St. Louis, 8 April 1909.

**2** For discussions of water pollution issues see Theodore Steinberg, *Nature Incorporated: Industrialization and the Waters of New England* (Amherst: University of Massachusetts Press, 1991); Craig E. Colten, "Illinois River Pollution Control, 1900-1970," in *The American Environment: Interpretations of Past Geographies,* ed. Larry M. Dilsaver and C. E. Colten (Lanham, Md.: Rowman & Littlefield, 1992), 193-214; Joel A. Tarr, "Searching for a 'Sink' for an Industrial Waste: Iron Making Fuels and the Environment," *Environmental History Review* 18 (1994): 9-34; and Andrew Hurley, "Creating Ecological Wastelands: Oil Pollution in New York City, 1870-1900," in *Journal of Urban History* 20 (1994): 340-64.

**3** Legal decisions favoring industrial interests are discussed in Morton J. Horwitz, *The Transformation of American Law, 1780-1860* (Cambridge, Mass.: Harvard University Press, 1977), 16-30; and the extension of such rulings into the twentieth century is treated by Jan G. Latios, "Legal Institutions and Pollution: Some Intersections between Law and History," in *Natural Resources Journal* 15 (1975): 423-51. Christine Rosen has challenged the traditional view that such decisions followed a consistent pattern. In a review of appellate court decisions, she discovered temporal and geographic differences. Toward the end of the nineteenth century, Rosen found that judges were more likely to render judgements that minimized human discomforts and imposed costs on the polluters. See Christine Rosen, "Differing Perceptions of the Value of Pollution Abatement across Time and Place: Balancing Doctrine in Pollution Nuisance Law, 1840-1906," in *Law and History Review* 11 (1993): 303-81.

4  Graham R. Taylor, *Satellite Cities: A Study of Industrial Suburbs* (New York: Appleton & Company, 1915).

5  See Lewis F. Thomas, *The Localization of Business Activities in Metropolitan St. Louis* (St. Louis: Washington University Studies in Social and Philosophical Sciences, Number 1, 1927); Robert A. Harper, *Metro-East Heavy Industry in the St. Louis Metropolitan Area* (Carbondale: Department of Geography, Southern Illinois University, 1965).

6  Taylor, *Satellite Cities*, 129-32; C. E. Colten, "Environmental Development in the East St. Louis Region," in *Environmental History Review* 14 (1990): 93-114.

7  See Thomas, *The Localization of Business Activities in Metropolitan St. Louis* , and Harper, *Metro-East Heavy Industry in the St. Louis Metropolitan Area.*

8  For example, East St. Louis prohibited the type of slaughtering and meat-packing activities carried out in the contiguous community of National City. Robert V. Gustin, comp., *Revised Municipal Code of East St. Louis* (East St. Louis: East St. Louis Publishing Company, 1908), 297. Although recognized at the time as a nuisance-causing activity, Granite City approved the operation of a coal-gas production facility in 1903. City of Granite City, *Revised Ordinances* (Granite City, Ill., 1906), 200-207.

9  See Colten, "Environmental Development in the East St. Louis Region."

10  See Joel A. Tarr in this volume and R. D. Grinder, "The Battle for Clean Air: The Smoke Problem in Post-Civil War America," in *Pollution and Reform in American Cities, 1870-1930*, ed. Martin V. Melosi (Austin: University of Texas Press, 1980), 83-103.

11  Colten, "Environmental Development."

12  The most complete treatment of this legal and scientific debate appears in M.O. Leighton, *Pollution of Illinois and Mississippi Rivers by Chicago Sewage*, 59th Cong., 2nd sess., 1907, H. Doc. 788. The U.S. Supreme Court decision, written by Justice Holmes, appears as *Missouri v. Illinois*, 200 U.S. 496 (1906).

13  G. H. Gehrmann (Medical Division, DuPont) to E.G. Robinson (General Manager, Organic Chemicals Department), Correspondence, 11 October 1935, accession 1813, box 20, file 4, W. P. Harrington Papers, Hagley Museum and Library Archives, Wilmington, Del.

14  H. G. Wood, *A Practical Treatise on the Law of Nuisance* (San Francisco: Bancroft-Whitney, 1893), 99.

15  Wood, *Law of Nuisance*, 581-82.

16  Edwin B. Goodell, *A Review of the Laws Forbidding Pollution of Inland Waters in the United States* (Washington: U.S. Geological Survey, Water-Supply and Irrigation Paper 152, 1905).

17  Stanley D. Montgomery and Earle B. Phelps, *Stream Pollution: A Digest of Judicial Decisions* (Washington: U.S. Public Health Service, Public Health Bulletin 87, 1918), 17-31. One notable exception was the case of *Pennsylvania Coal v. Sanderson* where the Pennsylvania courts recognized the use of a waterway to carry harmful discharges as reasonable.

18  *Hurd's Revised Statutes of Illinois* (Springfield: Illinois Journal, 1874), 386.

19  R. L. Kraft, "Locating the Chemical Plant," in *Chemical and Metallurgical Engineering* 34 (1927): 678; Fred D. Hartford, "Deciding on a Chemical Plant Location," in *Chemical and Metallurgical Engineering* 38 (1931): 72; and John H. Perry, ed. *Chemical Engineers Handbook* (New York: McGraw-Hill, 1934), 2408.

20  James A. Tobey, "Legal Aspects of the Industrial Waste Problem," in *Industrial and Engineering Chemistry* 31 (1939): 1321.

21 Paul Hansen, "Opinions Relative to Principles Governing Stream Pollution," in *Chemical and Biological Survey of the Waters of Illinois* (Urbana, Ill.: Water Survey Series No. 9, 1912), 65-66.

22 LeRoy K. Sherman, *Stream Pollution and Sewage Disposal in Illinois with Reference to Public Policy and Legislation* (Chicago: Illinois Rivers and Lakes Commission, Bulletin 16, 1915), 6.

23 Ibid.

24 Illinois Rivers and Lakes Commission, *Annual Report, 1913-1914* (Chicago, 1914), 18.

25 Ibid., (1915), 8-10.

26 Ibid., (1916), 7-13.

27 Ibid., (1913-16).

28 St. Clair Board of Supervisors, Minutes, 8 May 1904, 11.

29 East Side Levee and Sanitary District, *Proceedings of the Board of Trustees* (Granite City, Ill.: 5 May 1915), 1153.

30 Illinois Rivers and Lakes Commission, *Annual Report* (Chicago, 1916), 7.

31 "Engineering Work of the Small City," in *Engineering News-Record* 95 (13 August 1925): 260-61.

32 An Act to Establish a Sanitary Water Board, *Illinois Revised Statues* (Springfield, 1929), ch. 19, para. 129, 239.

33 "Abatement of Industrial Pollution in Illinois," in *Public Works* 67 (1936): 18.

34 Clarence Klassen, "Status of Sewerage and Industrial Wastes," unpublished manuscript, 1946, Illinois Environmental Protection Agency, Water Pollution Control Division, Sanitary Water Board Microfiche, Springfield, Ill., 6.

35 This survey of legal cases is based on a review of defendant indexes in the Madison and St. Clair counties court houses. I reviewed the cases involving major industries for the period from about 1910 to 1950, depending on the accessibility of the indexes. Where records were available, I obtained copies of briefs and other court records held by the county clerk. This was not an exhaustive search due to the relative inaccessibility of some records and the loss of some court documents. The cases discussed here reflect those with adequate court records to determine the issues at stake and the outcome.

36 *O'Connor v. Aluminum Ore Company*, 224 Ill. App. 613 (1922).

37 *Shelby Loan and Trust, et al., v. White Star Refining Co.*, 271 Ill. App. 266 (1933), and *Shelby Loan and Trust v. White Star Refining Co.*, Madison County Circuit Court, Injunction 5464, Chancery, 1932, Illinois State Archives, box 953, chancery roll 10, section 2, Springfield, Ill.

38 *Lillie Wheatly v. Monsanto Chemical Company*, St. Clair County Circuit Court, Case 3093, 1938; documents included the Amended Complaint, the Answer to the Amended Complaint, and a Notice of Appeal.

39 *Gardner et al. v. International Shoe Company*, 319 Ill. App. 416 (1943).

40 Ibid., 386 Ill. 418 (1944).

41 Ibid., 386 Ill. 426 (1944).

42 M. H. Kronenberg, "Investigation of Odor Complaint in Connection with the Settling Lagoon of International Shoe Tannery at Hartford, Ill.," unpublished report by the Division of Industrial Hygiene of the Illinois Sanitary Water Board, October 1941, Illinois Environmental Protection Agency, Water Pollution Control Division, Sanitary Water Board Microfiche, Hartford/International Shoe, Springfield, Ill. The staff detected that hydrogen sulfide at levels of 0.03 ppm and considered concentrations of 20 ppm safe, 7.

## *Jennefer Crets,* Urban Tourism and the Missouri Ozarks

1  "Outing in the Ozarks," in *Kansas City Star*, 4 August 1912, newsclipping, folder 77, Robert McClure Snyder, Jr. Papers, Western Historical Manuscript Collection, University of Missouri–Columbia (hereafter WHMC).

2  "De Luxe Camp No. 2, Rockaway Beach," advertisement, Lake Taneycomo and White River Country, The Vacation Paradise of the Ozarks, 1939, pamphlet, box 1, phase 1, Taney County, Lake Taneycomo Beach, Towns, and Resorts, Division of Historic Preservation, Department of Natural Resources, Jefferson City, Missouri (hereafter DHP/DNR), 10; Shore Acres Resort, (Hollister, Mo.) advertisement, Lake Taneycomo and White River Country, The Vacation Paradise of the Ozarks, 1939, pamphlet, box 1, phase 1, Taney County, Lake Taneycomo Beach, Towns, and Resorts, DHP/DNR, 13.

3  "Spend Your Sundays at the Beautiful Suburban Resorts on the Wabash Belt Railway," Railroad Papers, Wabash Belt Railway Flier, n.d. (before 1890), Archives, Missouri Historical Society, St. Louis, Missouri (hereafter MHS).

4  St. Louis County Scrapbook, vol. 3, Library, MHS, 135; Program, Independence Day, Creve Coeur Park, St. Louis History Papers, Archives, MHS.

5  Meramec Highlands brochure, Meramec Highlands Collection, Museum of Transportation, St. Louis, Missouri (hereafter MOT).

6  Carl O. Sauer, *Geography of the Ozark Highland of Missouri* (Chicago, Ill., 1920), 228.

7  Lynn Morrow, "Estate Builders in the Missouri Ozarks: Establishing a St. Louis Tradition," in *Gateway Heritage* 2 (winter 1981-82): 43; "Arcadia Country Club News," in *The Arcadian* 1 (May 1912): 18.

8  Morrow, "Estate Builders in the Missouri Ozarks," 43; "Valley Park Hotel Overlooking the Beautiful Meramec," brochure, folder 91, Robert McClure Snyder, Jr. Papers, WHMC.

9  Linda Myers-Phinney, "The Land of a Million Smiles: Tourism and Modernization in Taney County and Stone County, Missouri, 1900-1930" (Masters thesis, Southwest Missouri State University, 1989), 26-27.

10  A. Edward Fout, *Missouri State Automobile Directory and Guide* (St. Louis, 1911), 31.

11  *Third Biennial Report of the State Highway Commission of Missouri*, 1922, 234-35.

12  Warren James Belasco, *Americans on the Road: From Autocamp to Motel, 1910-1945* (Cambridge, Mass.: MIT Press, 1979), 19.

13  "Se-qui-o-ta Cave and Park at Sequiota, Missouri six miles from Springfield on the Frisco Lines" (St. Louis, Mo., [c. 1915]), 3.

14  "Weekend Tours," in *The St. Louis Times* (1918): 6.

15  Ibid.

16  Ibid., 2.

17  F. P. Rose, "'Ozark Trails Was a Mighty Predecessor," in *The Ozarks Mountaineer* (October 1953), box 1, phase I, Taney County, Lake Taneycomo Beach, Towns, and Resorts, DHP/DNR, 8.

18  E. L. Preston, "Missouri Notes Ten Year Gain in Highway Building," in *Missouriana* (May 1939): 23.

19  *Third Biennial Report of the State Highway Commission of Missouri*, 1922, 78.

20  U.S. Congress, *National Conference on Outdoor Recreation*, 68th Cong., S. Doc. 151, 1st sess., 1924, 27.

21  St. Louis & San Francisco Railway, *Feathers and Fins on the Frisco* (St. Louis, Mo., 1898).

22  Dona Brown, *Inventing New England: Regional Tourism in the Nineteenth Century* (Washington, D. C., 1995), 5.

23  Edith McCall, "Taney County's Aging Pioneer is a Bridge to the Past," in *The Ozarks Mountaineer* 42 (February 1994): 33.

24 *Feathers and Fins on the Frisco*, n.p.

25 Ibid.

26 "Hunting in the Ozarks," advertisement, *World's Fair Bulletin* 5, no. 5 (March 1904), back cover.

27 C. W. Orears, *Commercial and Architectural St. Louis* (St. Louis, Mo., 1891), 47.

28 See Brown, *Inventing New England*, 4.

29 Dr. D. R. Woolery, *The Grand Old Lady of the Ozarks* (Hominy, Okla.: Eagles' Nest Press, 1986), 21-22.

30 St. Louis & San Francisco Railway, *The Top of the Ozarks* (St. Louis, Mo., 1900), 27-28.

31 Milton D. Rafferty, *The Ozarks: Land and Life* (Norman, Okla., 1980), 199.

32 Woolery, *The Grand Old Lady of the Ozarks*, 18.

33 *Eureka Springs: A Pictorial History* (Eureka Springs, Ark., 1975), 27-28.

34 "One Night's Ride . . . from Saint Louis to Eureka Springs, Ark.," advertisement, *World's Fair Bulletin* 5 (November 1903), back cover.

35 *The Top of the Ozarks*, 26.

36 "Do You Get A Vacation?" advertisement, *The Arcadian* 1 (May 1912): 21.

37 St. Louis & San Francisco Railway, *Summer Homes in the Ozarks along the Frisco* (St. Louis, 1911), p. 9; "Do You Get A Vacation?" advertisement, 21.

38 Palace Bath House and European Hotel, 1908-1909, *Register*, Eureka Springs Historical Museum Collection, Eureka Springs, Arkansas.

39 Missouri–Pacific–Iron Mountain System, *The White River Country in Missouri and Arkansas* (St. Louis, n.d.), n.p.

40 *Pippin Place on the Gasconade in The Ozarks* (Waynesville, Mo., n.d.), Ozark Pamphlet box, MHS; Eden Letterhead, Stanley M. Riggs to Guy Park, 28 February 1934, folder 2115, Guy B. Park Papers, WHMC; E. Caisle, *St. Louis Houses, 1866-1916*, 124, Meramec Highlands Collection, MOT.

41 Lynn Morrow, ed., "Honeymooners' Romantic Experience in the Ozarks," in *White River Valley Historical Quarterly* (summer 1988): 13-14.

42 Report of the Missouri State Highway Board, *Third Biennial Report of the State Highway Commission of Missouri*, 1922, 54, Library, MHS.

43 See Myers-Phinney, "The Land of a Million Smiles," 48-57, for a full discussion of the early twentieth-century Arcadian literary genre and how it applied to the popularization of Ozark tourism.

44 Eleanor (Klouzek) Gallagher, *Rockaway Beach Vacation*, 1930 (Ellisville, Mo., 1994), 23.

45 See Belasco, *Americans on the Road*, for a discussion of the tensions between early automobile tourists and rural residents before the advent of highway-based overnight accommodations.

46 Ibid., 78.

47 Ozarks Playgrounds Association, *The Ozarks: "The Land of a Million Smiles."* (Joplin, Mo., [c. 1926]), box 1, phase 1, Taney County, Lake Taneycomo Beach, Towns, and Resorts, DHP/DNR.

48 Belasco, *Americans on the Road*, 113-15.

49 "Tourist Camps to be Standardized," in *Apropos* 5 (June 1925): 24.

50 "Cassville, Barry County Missouri, Gateway to the Roaring River Country," brochure, n.d., folder 170, Lucille Morris Upton Papers, WHMC.

51 Allen S. James, "'Travel' Camps in the Ozarks," in *National Petroleum News* (August 4, 1937): 38.

52 Brown, *Inventing New England*, 7.

53 Ibid., 7.

54 Gallagher, *Rockaway Beach Vacation*, 1, 7.

55 "Lake Taneycomo and White River Country, The Vacation Paradise of the Ozarks," 1939, pamphlet, box 1, phase 1, Taney County, Lake Taneycomo Beach, Towns, and Resorts, DHP/DNR, 12, 16.

56 Gallagher, *Rockaway Beach Vacation*, 16.

57 Lake Taneycomo's name was derived from its location, a combination of the words "TANEY COunty, MO (for Missouri)."

58 Elmo Ingenthron, *The Land of Taney: A History of an Ozark Commonwealth* (Point Lookout, MO, 1974), 290.

59 David M. Quick and Linda Myers-Phinney, "Historic Taneycomo Lakefront Tourism Resources of Branson, Taney County, Missouri," 3, Section E, Multiple Property Nomination Form, National Register of Historic Places, DHP/DNR, 3.

60 "St. Louis and San Francisco Railway," in *Saint Louis Magazine* 19, no. 114 (June 1880): 237; *The Ozarks: "The Land of a Million Smiles,"* brochure, c. 1926, box 1, phase 1, Taney County, Lake Taneycomo Beach, Towns, and Resorts, DHP/DNR, 8-9.

61 *The Ozarks: "The Land of a Million Smiles,"* brochure.

62 Roderick D. McKenzie, quoted in Michael L. Berger, *The Devil Wagon in God's Country: The Automobile and Social Change in Rural America, 1893-1929* (Hamden, Conn.: Archon Books, 1979), 79.

63 Venta Plummer, et al., *Seneca, Missouri, The Little Town on the Border*, vol. 2 (Seneca, Mo., 1982).

64 Map of Southwest Missouri and Northwest Arkansas, box 1, phase 1, Taney County, Lake Taneycomo Beach, Towns, and Resorts, DHP/DNR.

65 In 1924, an Ozark Playgrounds Association representative even addressed the National Conference on Outdoor Recreation "to tell . . . the story of community and regional building as applied to that portion of the Ozark country, which has been christened the land of a million smiles." U.S. Congress, National Conference on Outdoor Recreation, 113.

66 "Where to Go in the Ozarks," 1930, pamphlet, box 1, phase 1, Taney County, Lake Taneycomo Beach, Towns, and Resorts, DHP/DNR.

67 Gallagher, *Rockaway Beach Vacation*, 16.

68 "Osage Hills on Meramec Opens Formally Today," in *St. Louis Post-Dispatch*, 11 April 1926, Meramec Highlands Collection, MOT.

69 "Rockaway Beach, The Gem of the Ozarks," advertisement, "The Wonderland of the Ozarks," pamphlet, 1926, Rockaway Beach folder, box 1, phase 1, Taney County, Lake Taneycomo Beach, Towns, and Resorts, DHP/DNP.

70 David Quick, "Architectural and Landscape Context," in *An Overview and Survey of Lake Taneycomo Towns and Resorts*, phase II, DHP/DNP, 42.

71 Marguerite Mooers Marshall, "Vacations, Family Style Are an Investment in Happiness," in *Good Housekeeping* 96 (June 1933): 170.

72 Donald Powers, "Why Not Plan That Cabin Now?" in *Missouri Game and Fish News* (January 1930), box 1, phase 1, Taney County, Lake Taneycomo Beach, Towns, and Resorts, DHP/DNR, 5.

73 John R. Stilgoe, *Borderland: Origins of the American Suburb, 1820-1939* (New Haven, Conn.: Yale University Press, 1988), 305.

74 Charles Vaughn Boyd, "The Old Fashioned Log Cabin," in *Woman's Home Companion* 43 (May 1916): 46.

75 "What to Build in the Ozarks," Murphy Door Bed Co. advertisement, box 1, phase 1, Taney County, Lake Taneycomo Beach, Towns, and Resorts, DHP/DNR.

76 "Comfort and Color in Camp Decoration," in *Good Housekeeping* 97 (July 1933): 59.

77 John J. McCarthy and Robert Littell, "Three Hundred Thousand Shacks: The Arrival of a New American Industry," in *Harpers Monthly Magazine* 167 (July 1933): 184.

78 Ibid., p. 186.

79 David Quick, "A Summer Place at the Lake," in *Preservation Issues* 4 (July/August 1994): 5.

80 Gallagher, *Rockaway Beach Vacation*, 11.

81 Quick, "A Summer Place at the Lake," 5.

82 Ibid.

83 Ibid., 1.

84 Clifford Edward Clark, Jr., *The American Family Home, 1800-1960* (Chapel Hill: University of North Carolina Press, 1986), 113-14.

85 Belasco, *Americans on the Road*, 137.

86 "The Ozarks" (Joplin, Mo., [c. 1920s]), 8-9, Ozark Pamphlet Box, MHS.

87 Brown, *Inventing New England*, 13.

88 *The Ozarks: A Glimpse into the Playgrounds of America* (Joplin, Mo., [c. 1925]), 13-14.

89 Mary Ann Beecher, "The Motel in Builder's Literature and Architectural Publications," in *Roadside America: The Automobile in Design and Culture*, ed. Jan Jennings (Ames: Iowa State University Press, 1990), 116-17.

90 "Cedar Park, In the Heart of the Ozarks," c. 1915, brochure, box 1, phase 1, Taney County, Lake Taneycomo Beach, Towns, and Resorts, DHP/DNR.

91 Ingenthron, *The Land of Taney*, 288.

92 "Lake Taneycomo and The Shepherd of the Hills Country," 1926, pamphlet, Rockaway Beach folder, box 1, phase 1, Taney County, Lake Taneycomo Beach, Towns, and Resorts, DHP/DNR.

93 "Anchor Travel Village," advertisement, "Lake Taneycomo and White River Country, The Vacation Paradise of the Ozarks," 1939, pamphlet, box 1, phase 1, Taney County, Lake Taneycomo Beach, Towns, and Resorts, DHP/DNR, 10.

94 "Ozark Playground of Missouri" (Jefferson City, Mo., [1948]); "White River Country of Missouri" (Jefferson City, Mo., 1945).

95 Quick, "Architectural and Landscape Context," 49.

96 Brendan Gill and Dudley Witney, *Summer Places* (New York: Methuen, 1978), 40.

97 Advertisements, "Lake Taneycomo and White River Country, The Vacation Paradise of the Ozarks," 1939, pamphlet, box 1, phase 1, Taney County, Lake Taneycomo Beach, Towns, and Resorts, DHP/DNR, 16-17.

98 Gill and Witney, *Summer Places*, 40.

## *Joel A. Tarr and Carl Zimring,* Struggle for Smoke Control in St. Louis

1 See Stuart Galishoof, "Triumph and Failure: The American Response to the Urban Water Supply Problem, 1860-1923," and R. Dale Grinder, "The Battle for Clean Air: The Smoke Problem in Post-Civil War America," in *Pollution and Reform in American Cities, 1870-1930* ed. Martin V. Melosi, (Austin: University of Texas Press, 1980), 35-58, 83-104.

2 Henry Obermeyer, *Stop that Smoke!* (New York: Harper & Brothers, 1933), 27.

3 It is important to distinguish between the reduction of dense smoke and control of air pollution. The accomplishment of the first did not necessarily mean that the second was achieved.

4 In 1867, the great civil engineer James P. Kirkland planned St. Louis's first filtration plant, but it was never built. St. Louis's desire to impress visitors of the 1904 World's Fair provided the stimulus to build a plant to coagulate the water. See William B. Schoolroom and Don Marshall, "History of Water Supply in the St. Louis Area," an unpublished and undated ms. [but probably 1968] in the possession of the Water Division, St. Louis Department of Public Utilities; Jennifer Ann Crets, "'Water of Diamond Transparency': The Legacy of Chain of Rocks Waterworks Park," *Gateway Heritage* (summer 1994), 54-

57; James Neal Primm, *Lion of the Valley: St. Louis, Missouri* (Boulder, Col.: Pruett Publishing Co., 1981), 281-82, 400-401, 448-49.

5  Walter Schroeder, "Environmental Setting of the St. Louis Region," this volume. The four millions tons figure is from H. Cannon, *Smoke Abatement: A Study of the Police Power as Embodied in Laws, Ordinances and Court Decisions* (St. Louis: Public Library, August 1924), 222-23. Cannon was the Librarian of the St. Louis Municipal Reference Library.

6  St. Louis Community Development Agency, "1980 Environmental Review Record," St. Louis (November 1980), 18, 21; Grinder, "The Battle for Clean Air," 84; Primm, *Lion of the Valley*, 358, 474-75.

7  See "Annual Cost of Smoke Nuisance to St. Louis," Speakers Bulletin 13, Citizen's Smoke Abatement League, 1927; A. S. Langsdorf, "The Effect of Atmospheric Smoke Pollution: A Summary of Opinions from Current Literature," in *Transactions of the American Society of Mechanical Engineers* 50 (1927-28): 184-88. Langsdorf was Director of Industrial Engineering and Research at Washington University in St. Louis.

8  See "Damage to Greenhouse Plants at Garden Due to Smoke," in *Missouri Botanical Garden Bulletin* 5 (1917): 160-61; "Smoke Injury to Roses," ibid. 12 (1924): 132-33; "Thirty-Ninth Annual Report of the Director," ibid. 16 (January 1928): 1-4; "Effect of City Smoke on Plants," ibid. 20 (1932): 43 45. According to the St. Louis forester, in 1905-1906, smoke killed approximately one-third of the city's trees. Grinder, "The Battle for Clean Air," 87.

9  Langsdorf, "The Effect of Atmospheric Smoke Pollution," 184-88.

10  Paul Boyer, *Urban Masses and Moral Order in America, 1820-1930* (Cambridge: Harvard University Press, 1978), 220-51.

11  Obermeyer, *Stop that Smoke!*, 43.

12  For discussion of the "feminist perspective," see Harold L. Platt, "Invisible Gases: Smoke, Gender, and the Redefinition of Environmental Policy in Chicago, 1900-1920," *Planning Perspectives* 10 (January 1995): 70, 81-85; Maureen A. Flanagan, "Gender and Urban Political Reform: The City Club and the Women's City Club of Chicago in the Progressive Era," in *American Historical Review* 95 (1990): 1032-50; Suellen Hoy, "Municipal Housekeeping: The Role of Women in Improving Urban Sanitation Practices, 1880-1917," in *Pollution and Reform*, ed. Melosi, 173-98. In 1933, Henry Obermeyer argued that it was "natural that women should have been in the van of the battle against smoke" because they bore its costs, especially in regard to skin care, cleanliness, home furnishings, fashions, and children's health. See Obermeyer, *Stop that Smoke!*, 37-45.

13  Maureen A. Flanagan, "The City Profitable, The City Livable," in *Journal of Urban History* 22 (January 1996): 181. Flanagan also notes that the Chicago women reformers "stressed the absolute need for citizen participation in achieving this condition."

14  According to historian David Thelen, from the women's perspective attempts "to preserve growth with technological and educational alternatives to prosecution were an unacceptable compromise with the value of health." See David Thelen, *Paths of Resistance: Tradition and Democracy in Industrializing Missouri* (Columbia: University of Missouri Press, 1991, paperback ed.), 226-27; Robert Dale Grinder, "The War Against St. Louis's Smoke, 1891-1924," in *Missouri Historical Review* 69, no. 2 (January 1975): 192-97, 201; Cannon, *Smoke Abatement*, 223-25.

15  There were, however, overtones of class positions by spokespeople for some women's groups in 1940. See Oscar H. Allison, "Raymond R. Tucker: The Smoke Elimination Years, 1934-1950," (Ph.D. diss., St. Louis University, 1978), 68-69.

16  Ibid.; Grinder, "The War Against St. Louis's Smoke," 192 93.

17  See Allison, "Tucker: The Smoke Elimination Years," for a full discussion of Tucker's activities in regard to smoke control. While I have structured my own interpretation of

smoke control in St. Louis and of Tucker's activities, I am indebted to Dr. Allison for his detailed account of these years.

**18** Cannon, *Smoke Abatement*, 211-12. St. Louis had passed an ordinance requiring a minimum height for chimneys in 1867, reflecting complaints over smoke pollution. St. Louis possessed a number of private streets, and as early as the 1890s several of them had "enacted regulations prohibiting residents from burning bituminous coal." See David T. Beito with Bruce Smith, "The Formation of Urban Infrastructure through Nongovernmental Planning: The Private Places of St. Louis, 1869-1920," in *Journal of Urban History* 16 (May 1990): 276-77.

**19** Ibid., 213-15; Grinder, "The War Against St. Louis's Smoke," 194. David T. Day, U.S. Geological Survey, *Mineral Resources of the United States, 1893* (Washington, D.C.: GPO, 1894), 224-40, reported that the "best results in the suppression of smoke have been accomplished in Saint Louis."

**20** Cannon, *Smoke Abatement*, 216-17; Tucker, "St. Louis Smoke Ordinance," 2-3.

**21** "Report of Inspector of Boilers, Elevators and Smoke Abatement for Fiscal Year ending April 8, 1912," Missouri Historical Society, St. Louis.

**22** Grinder, "The War Against St. Louis's Smoke," 194-97; Cannon, *Smoke Abatement*, 224-25.

**23** Grinder, "The War Against St. Louis's Smoke," 197.

**24** Robert H. Karl to J. H. Gundlach, 14 November 1924, box 1, Papers of the Citizens'sSmoke Abatement League, Missouri Historical Society, St. Louis, Missouri. Gundlach was the chairman of the Smoke Abatement committee of the Chamber of Commerce.

**25** Karl to Gundlach, 14 November 1924. For a discussion of the technical component of the campaign, see Victor J. Azbe, "Smokeless and Efficient Firing of Domestic Furnaces: Parts I & II; *Transactions of the American Society of Mechanical Engineers* 50 (1927-28): 175-83, 223-38.

**26** Osborn Monnett, "The Smoke Problem of Cities," in *Proceedings of the International Conference on Bituminous Coal,* 15-18 November 1926 (Pittsburgh: Carnegie Institute of Technology, 1926), 614. Monnett was a mechanical engineer who was former chief of Chicago's Smoke Abatement Division. He played an important role in St. Louis. See also Obermeyer, *Stop that Smoke!*, 116-26; Raymond R. Tucker, "Smoke Elimination Program in St. Louis," paper given ca. 1940, 2, in Raymond R. Tucker Papers, Washington University, St. Louis.

**27** Victor J. Azbe, "Rationalizing Smoke Abatement," in *Proceedings of the Third International Conference on Bituminous Coal,* 16-21 November 1931, II (Pittsburgh: Carnegie Institute of Technology, 1931), 631-33. Azbe provides copies of some of the photographs.

**28** The ordinances are reprinted in Cannon, *Smoke Abatement*, 225-26; Primm, *Lion of the Valley*, 475; Obermeyer, *Stop that Smoke!*, 127, 143.

**29** Obermeyer, *Stop that Smoke!*, 208-9. Obermeyer reprints a list of percent reductions supposedly accomplished in the campaign.

**30** In the early 1930s, the exigencies of the depression caused the city council to reduce the number of smoke inspectors to one man, employed to control smoke emissions for more than 150,000 smoke stacks. See Tucker, "Smoke Elimination Program in St. Louis," 2.

**31** Tucker, "Smoke Abatement," The Engineers Club of Philadelphia, n.d., in Tucker Papers.

**32** Tucker, "Smoke Abatement: Its Past, Present, and Future in St. Louis," in *Mechanical Engineering* 60 (May 1938): 378.

**33** Tucker, "St. Louis Smoke Ordinance," 3.

**34** See Tucker, "A Smoke Elimination Program That Works," in *Heating, Piping and Air Conditioning* (hereafter *H/P/AC*) 17 (September 1945): 463; Azbe, "Rationalizing Smoke Abatement," II: 593-94.

**35** Tucker, "Smoke Abatement," The Engineers Club of Philadelphia, n.d., and "Address of Mr. Raymond R. Tucker . . . to the Engineers Club of St. Louis," 23 September 1937, in Tucker Papers. The smoke situation resembled a non-point rather than a point source pollution problem.

**36** Azbe, "Rationalizing Smoke Abatement," II: 629; Raymond R. Tucker, untitled speech before the National Association of Power Engineers, 9 September 1939, 2, Tucker Papers.

**37** Azbe, "Rationalizing Smoke Abatement," II: 594.

**38** Monnett, "The Smoke Problem of Cities," II: 613.

**39** Azbe, "Rationalizing Smoke Abatement," II: 604, 614-29; Osborn Monnett, "Smoke Ordinances," in *Industrial and Engineering Chemistry* 33 (July 1941): 839-40.

**40** Reported by Tucker in his remarks at the Illinois Coal Conference, Urbana, Illinois, 23 May 1939, manuscript in the Tucker Papers. Houses using room stoves for heating were much older than those with central heating.

**41** Azbe, "Rationalizing Smoke Control," II: 631-33.

**42** Raymond R. Tucker, "The Smoke Department in Operation," 29 September 1939, Tucker Papers, 6.

**43** Horace C. Porter, "The Economic Aspects of the Conversion of Coal into Smokeless Fuel," in *Proceedings of the International Conference on Bituminous Coal* (Pittsburgh: Carnegie Institute of Technology, 1926), 599-600; O. P. Hood, "Smokeless Fuel," ibid., 605-11; and, "Discussion," ibid., 615-33.

**44** Flad argued that the city should build experimental plants to test the coke-making processes, subsidizing the price to consumers if necessary. At a later time, he advocated that the city acquire the Laclede Gas Light Company plant that supplied the city with manufactured gas. Low carbonization coke operations, such as Flad advocated, were then being constructed for large utilities, while during the same period entrepreneurs were building merchant plants to produce foundry coke, domestic coke, and coke for making water gas, as well as producing gas to sell under contract to public utilities because of growing demand for these products. For Flad's plans, see Edward Flad to Thomas Bond, 10 October 1925; W. K. Kavanaugh to Victor J. Miller, mayor, 18 November 1925; Flad to Kavanaugh, 25 November 1926; Edward Flad, "A Proposed Solution of the Smoke Problem of the City of St. Louis, Mo.," St. Louis Section American Society of Civil Engineers, January 1927; and Edward Flad, "Proposed Solution of Our Smoke Problem," 3 January 1940 (a proposal to the Citizen's Committee on Smoke Pollution), all in Edward Flad Papers, Missouri Historical Society, St. Louis. For the coke industry and the domestic market, see F. G. Tryon, "Domestic Fuels Other Than Anthracite: Part I - Processed Coals," in *Transactions of the Fuel Conference, Vol. II, The Carbonisation Industry* (London: Percy Lund, Humphries & Co., 1928), 333-34. The Laclede Gas Light Company, which had a monopoly of the St. Louis gas distribution business, constructed byproduct coke plants in the 1930s, but they produced industrial not domestic grade coke.

**45** *Brown's Directory of American Gas Companies*, 1934, 145-46.

**46** "Natural Gas Finds Best Market Among Industrial Customers," in *Business Week* (13 August 1930): 18-19; Allison, "Tucker: The Smoke Elimination Years," 72-74; *Brown's Directory*, 1930, 202; Azbe, "Rationalizing Smoke Abatement," II: 624. One writer on natural gas history argues that limitations on natural gas supply kept the fuel out of the city until after World War II. See John H. Herbert, *Clean Cheap Heat: The Development of Residential Markets for Natural Gas in the United States* (New York: Praeger, 1992), 141, 167.

**47** Azbe, "Rationalizing Smoke Abatement," II: 623-24.

**48** Porter, "The Economic Aspects of the Conversion of Coal into Smokeless Fuel," 599-600.

**49** Tucker, "A Smoke Elimination Program That Works," 464; Allison, "Tucker: The Smoke Elimination Years," 9.

50 Ibid., 9-12.

51 Tucker, "Smoke Abatement," The Engineers Club of Philadelphia. See also "Address of Mayor Bernard F. Dickmann, Opening Convention of National Smoke Prevention Association, Hotel Statler, Tuesday, 21 May 1940, 2:00 p.m.," 72.

52 *New York Times*, 11 August 1940; Allison, "Tucker: The Smoke Elimination Years," 16-21.

53 Tucker, "A Smoke Elimination Program That Works," 464.

54 See the transcripts of Tucker's radio broadcasts, 1938-1940, in Tucker papers.

55 The money had actually been granted for a study by the Bureau of Mines, but the Bureau would not agree to make policy recommendations and recommended that the city hire a consultant. See, Tucker, "A Smoke Elimination Program That Works," 464.

56 Tucker, "Smoke Abatement," Engineers Club of Philadelphia, 4; Allison, "Tucker: The Smoke Elimination Years," 13-16.

57 Tucker, "St. Louis Smoke Ordinance," 4-5; Tucker, "A Smoke Elimination Program That Works," 464; Tucker, "Smoke Abatement: Its Past, Present, and Future in St. Louis," 379.

58 The *Post-Dispatch* editorially complained that the "washing-clause" provided a "fallacious solution" to the city's smoke problem. See *St. Louis Post-Dispatch*, 4, 5, 6 February 1937; Tucker, "A Smoke Elimination Program That Works," 465. Opponents immediately tested the ordinance in the federal courts, asking for an injunction against the city. But at a preliminary hearing the judge denied the motion, arguing that the police power provided a justification for the city to take any reasonable means to abate the smoke nuisance. The case was dropped and no further attempt was made to obtain an injunction against the ordinance. See Tucker, "A Smoke Elimination Program That Works," 465.

59 Tucker said he had originally refused the appointment because he was so involved in passage of the ordinance. The administration attempted to place the new division of smoke in the Health Department because of its broad police powers but this would have violated the city's charter. See Tucker, "A Smoke Elimination Program that Works," 465; Allison, "Tucker: The Smoke Elimination Years," 25-27.

60 Tucker, "A Smoke Elimination Program," 466; Tucker, "Smoke Abatement: Its Past, Present and Future," 379.

61 Tucker, "A Smoke Elimination Program That Works"; Tucker, "Smoke Elimination Program in St. Louis," 9.

62 Tucker, "Smoke Abatement: Its Past, Present and Future," 380.

63 Alternative figures were used in regard to the contribution of domestic smoke to the total smoke burden from over 60 percent to under 50 percent.

64 Tucker, "St. Louis Smoke Ordinance," 5.

65 The city experienced nine days of "thick" smoke in four weeks. *St. Louis Post-Dispatch*, 28 November 1939; Tucker "History of the Present Smoke Campaign," 7 March 1941, 1; Tucker, "St. Louis Smoke Ordinance," 6; Allison, "Tucker: The Smoke Elimination Years," 43-45. For excellent photographs of smoke conditions see "Speaking of Pictures . . . These Show How Smoke Blacks Out St. Louis," in *Life* (15 January 1940): 8-11.

66 Tucker to Bernard F. Dickmann, mayor, 22 November 1939, Tucker Papers; *St. Louis Post-Dispatch*, 23 November 1939.

67 Ibid., 26-27 November 1937.

68 Ibid., 27-30 November–1-2 December 1939; "Report of the St. Louis Committee on the Elimination of Smoke," 24 February 1940, 1; Allison, "Tucker: The Smoke Elimination Years," 49-54.

69 Tucker, "A Smoke Elimination Program That Works," 468. The "Minutes of Special Citizens' Committee with City Officials for consideration of the Smoke Elimination Program, held Tuesday, December 5, 1939," are in the Tucker Papers. No women were appointed to the committee even though women's groups had been active campaigners for smoke control.

70 Allison provides a full discussion of the committee's hearings. See Allison, "Tucker: The Smoke Elimination Years," 55-85; "Report of the St. Louis Committee on the Elimination of Smoke," 24 February 1940, 1-2.

71 Ibid., 2-3.

72 Ibid., 9-11.

73 Ibid., 3; "Should the City Provide a Subsidy Out of Tax Revenues to Make the Cost of This Fuel Even Less to the Domestic Consumers?" unpublished manuscript in the Tucker Papers, n.d.; "Memorandum," to Mayor Bernard F. Dickmann, from Joseph M. Darst, 16 October 1940, Tucker Papers; and, Allison, "Tucker: The Smoke Elimination Years," 77-79. It is possible that Tucker and Dickmann opposed formation of a municipal gas plant because they believed that it was politically unwise and would provoke opposition from business interests that would normally support the ordinance.

74 St. Louis had a district heating system in its downtown area that served a number of buildings. See National District Heating Association, *District Heating Handbook: A Manual of District Heating Practice, A Description of the District Heating Industry, A Guide to Modern Commercial Equipment* (Pittsburgh: NDHA, 3d ed., 1951), 11, 17.

75 Tucker rejected both district heating and natural gas as too expensive. He claimed that the "distribution of this gas presents a serious problem," although he did not explain what the problem was. See, Tucker to Oliver T. Remmers, undated letter in Tucker Papers. Tucker suggested to the mayor that the city purchase the gas generated by a byproduct plant that processed a smokeless fuel from Illinois coal and sell the gas to the Laclede Gas Light Company. Tucker to Bernard F. Dickmann, 2 December 1939, Tucker Papers. See also Allison, "Tucker: The Smoke Elimination Years," 75-77.

76 "Report of the St. Louis Committee on the Elimination of Smoke," 24 February 1940, 7.

77 Ibid., 12; Tucker, "A Smoke Elimination Program That Works," 402-3; and, Joel A. Tarr and Kenneth Koons, "Railroad Smoke Control: The Regulation of a Mobile Pollution Source," in *Energy and Transport: Historical Perspectives on Policy Issues,* ed. George H. Daniels and Mark H. Rose (Beverly Hills, Calif.: Sage Publications, 1982), 75.

78 *St. Louis Post-Dispatch,* 8 April 1940; Tucker, "Smoke Elimination Program in St. Louis," 9; Tucker, "A Smoke Elimination Program That Works," 469. A copy of the ordinance (Board Bill No. 361) is in the Tucker Papers. The Board of Aldermen attempted to pass a version of the bill that omitted railroads from the clean fuel requirement, but rescinded their action under pressure from the mayor and the press applied pressure. The Terminal Association claimed that the bill would add $800,000 a year to their fuel costs. The press blamed the Terminal Railroad Association for the bill. See also *St. Louis Post-Dispatch,* 10, 18 April 1940.

79 Tucker, "Smoke Elimination Program in St. Louis," 9; Tucker, "A Smoke Elimination Program That Works," 469.

80 Tucker, "A Smoke Elimination Program That Works," October-November 1945, 522.

81 James L. Ford, Jr. to Joseph B. Eastman, 19 April 1940, Tucker Papers. Ford and Tucker were old friends. Ford also sent a telegram to the president of eight eastern railroads asking for their support of the $2.00 rate. The chair of the Traffic Executive Association - Eastern Territory, representative of the roads, wrote back that while the roads "sympathize with the efforts being made to ameliorate the smoke problem of St. Louis . . . , the rate proposed presents a very serious situation to our lines . . . "; the association filed a protest with the ICC. See memo to "Miss Bott," signed by Bernard F. Dickmann, mayor, Thom. N. Dysart, President, Chamber of Commerce, and James L. Ford, Jr., 28 May 1940; Tucker Papers, and D. T. Lawrence, chairman, to Dickman [*sic*], Dysart, and Ford, 5 June 1940, Tucker Papers.

82 C. H. Uhlinger [general manager, City Coal Company and treasurer, Brotherhood of Stationary Engineers], to Hubert A. Hoeflinger [chair, Public Safety Committee, Board of Aldermen] 28 March 1940, Tucker Papers.

83 V. M. W. [*sic*] to Mr. Dickman [*sic*], 18 August 1940; Joseph M. Darst to Mayor Bernard F. Dickmann, 16 October 1940; R. R. Tucker to John B. Sullivan, secretary to the mayor, 7 November 1940; Kendall J. Wentz to William Dee Becker, mayor of St. Louis, 19 June 1941, all in Tucker Papers.

84 "Newspaper Release, Dec. 1, 1940," and "Press release, Aug. 29, 1941," Tucker Papers.

85 The citizens committee had recommended that a provision be put in the ordinance permitting the city to declare an emergency if smokeless fuel could not be found at a reasonable price. The ordinance approved an appropriation of $300,000 to purchase smokeless fuel if necessary and to distribute it. A summary of opinion on the smoke control plan from different St. Louis labor unions is in the *Cincinnati Post*, 20 November 1946. See untitled "Speech—Cincinnati, Ohio, Oct. 7, 1946," in Tucker papers. The chair of the Pittsburgh Smoke Commission, Abraham Wolk, also claimed that the St. Louis poor had not been adversely affected by smoke control. See "Proceedings of the Fifth Meeting of the Pittsburgh Smoke Commission," 31 March 1941, 70-72, Pittsburgh City Council Records. See Allison, "Tucker: The Smoke Elimination Years," 123-25.

86 The smoke ordinance was challenged in court and went to the Missouri Supreme Court. In the case of *Ex Parte Ballentine v. Nester* (164 S.W. (2) 378), the court upheld the ordinance's validity.

87 A useful summary of division activities is in the Department of Public Safety, Division of Smoke Regulation, *Annual Report for Year 1942-1943*; "Highlights of St. Louis Smoke Elimination Program," July 1944, Division of Smoke Regulation.

88 These results are reported in the *Annual Reports* of the Division of Public Safety, Division of Smoke Regulation, from 1941-1947. See also Walter J. Moxom, "Observation of Smoke Conditions in the City of St. Louis, MO," in Smoke Prevention Association of America, Inc., *Manual of Ordinances and Requirements In the Interest of Air Pollution, Smoke Elimination, Fuel Combustion* (Chicago, 1941), 98-101.

89 J. H. Carter [Commissioner of Smoke Regulation, St. Louis, Missouri], "Does Smoke Abatement Pay?" *H/P/AC* (April 1946), 80-84.

90 *St. Louis Post-Dispatch*, 26 February 1941; "Requests for information concerning the St. Louis Smoke Ordinance," memo dated 17 October 1944, Dept. of Public Safety, Division of Smoke Regulations, Tucker Papers.

91 Tucker's consulting activities are examined in detail in Allison, "Tucker: The Smoke Elimination Years," 134-79; Joel A. Tarr and Bill C. Lamperes, "Changing Fuel Use Behavior and Energy Transitions: The Pittsburgh Smoke Control Movement, 1940-1950," in *Journal of Social History* 14 (summer 1981): 561-88.

92 H. H. Carter to Tucker, 14 November 1950, Tucker Papers; *Brown's Directory of American Gas Companies*, 1949-50 (New York: Moore Publishing Co., 1950), 211-12; H. A. Eddins, "Strong Civic Appreciation Marks Laclede Conversion," in *American Gas Journal* 172 (May 1950): 22-23; Primm, *Lion of the Valley*, 477. By 1947, the price of natural gas was approximately the same as bituminous coal per heating unit, and by 1948 it was cheaper. See Herbert, *Clean Heat*, 101.

93 Tucker resigned as Smoke Commissioner in 1941. He had been re-appointed by newly elected Republican mayor, William Dee Becker, but left to head the Mechanical Engineering Department at Washington University. At his resignation, Mayor Becker had Tucker prepare a statement for him to issue declaring his fidelity to Tucker's smoke control program, indicating what broad support the program had. For the mayor's statement about smoke control, see Tucker to Hon. William Dee Becker, 29 August 1941, Tucker Papers. The smoke control issue was obviously influential but does not appear to have been the major issue in the mayoralty campaign. See radio address by Tucker, 15 March 1941, in Tucker Papers; Allison, "Tucker: The Smoke Elimination Years," 128. In 1953, Tucker himself was elected St. Louis mayor.

**94** By 1960, the percentage of consumers using natural gas for house heating nationally was 68.4 percent, while the number of coal-burning steam locomotives had decreased from 30,344 in 1949 to 374 in 1960. See Joel A. Tarr, "The Search for the Ultimate Sink: Urban Air, Land, and Water Pollution in Historical Perspective," in *Records of the Columbia Historical Society of Washington, D.C.* 51 (Charlottesville: University Press of Virginia, 1984), 13.

## Rosemary Feurer, St. Louis Labor and the MVA

**1** This comment was made to the author by an activist involved in the campaign opposing the Calloway plant.

**2** James Bellamy Foster, *The Limits of Environmentalism Without Class: Lessons From the Ancient Forest Struggle of the Pacific Northwest* (New York: Monthly Review Press, 1993).

**3** See especially Rexford G. Tugwell and E. C. Banfield, "Grass-Roots Democracy—Myth or Reality," in *Public Administration Review* 10 (winter 1950): 47-55; Edwin C. Hargrove and Paul K. Conkin, ed. *TVA: Fifty Years of Grass-Roots Bureaucracy* (Urbana: University of Illinois Press, 1983); Walter L. Creese, *TVA's Public Planning: The Vision, The Reality* (Knoxville: The University of Tennessee Press, 1990). Actually, the TVA perfectly reflected two tendencies that contested for the soul of liberalism in the 1930s and '40s—the first espoused technocratic solutions to political problems and the other sought to democratize American life. Recent histories have questioned—justifiably I think—whether TVA deserves the democratic merits attributed to it. The transfer of power to technocratic experts at the local level, with few mechanisms to include local residents in the planning process, held grave consequences for local residents, many of whom were forcibly displaced with little recourse, by TVA projects. See William Bruce Wheeler and Michael J. McDonald, *TVA and the Tellico Dam, 1936-1979: A Bureaucratic Crisis in Post-Industrial America* (Knoxville: University of Tennessee Press, 1986). Recent critics have criticized TVA nuclear power projects as mocking TVA claims to environmental stewardship. See William U. Chandler, *The Myth of the TVA: Conservation and Development in the Tennessee Valley, 1933-1983* (Cambridge, Mass.: Ballinger Publishing Co., 1984).

**4** "Memo: Re: M.V.A.," series 2, box 1, folder 1, William Sentner Papers, Washington University, St. Louis (hereafter Sentner Papers); Marion Clawson, *New Deal Planning: the National Resources Planning Board* (Baltimore: Johns Hopkins University Press, 1981).

**5** *New York Times*, 24 May 1944; Henry Hart, *The Dark Missouri* (Madison: University of Wisconsin Press, 1957), 120.

**6** *St. Louis Post-Dispatch*, 17 July 1951; John T. Farrell, *Heartland Engineers: A History* (Kansas City, Mo.: Army Corps of Engineers, 1993).

**7** Donald Worster, *Rivers of Empire: Water, Aridity, and the Growth of the American West* (New York: Pantheon, 1985), 268-69; Paul Scheele, "Resource Development Politics in the Missouri Basin: Federal Power, Navigation, and Reservoir Operation Policies, 1944-1968" (Ph.D diss., University of Nebraska, 1969), 35, 41, 45, 49. Scheele points out that Pick did not bother to explain why any of his proposed "features were necessary either at their proposed size, cost, or location."

**8** *St. Louis Post-Dispatch*, 14 May 1944.

**9** Rosemary Feurer, "William Sentner, the UE, and Civic Unionism in St. Louis," in *The CIO's Left-Led Unions*, ed. Steven Rosswurm (New Brunswick, N.J.: Rutgers University Press, 1992).

10 Gerald T. White, *Billions for Defense* (Tuscaloosa: University of Alabama Press, 1980), 48; Paul Koistinen, "The Hammer and the Sword: Labor, the Military, and Industrial Mobilization, 1920-1945" (Ph.D. diss., University of California, Berkeley, 1964), 664. Steve Fraser, *Labor Will Rule: Sidney Hillman and the Rise of American Labor* (New York: Free Press, 1991), 649, fn 83.

11 Nelson Lichtenstein, *Labor's War at Home: The CIO in World War II* (New York: Cambridge University Press, 1987), 41; Steve Fraser, *Labor Will Rule*; James Matles to John L. Lewis, 22 July 1940, Sentner Papers.

12 William Sentner to James Matles, 6 August 1941, D8/67, United Electrical Workers Archives, University of Pittsburgh (hereafter UEA); James Payne to Julius Emspak, 12 August 1941, and attachments: Resolution and Petition, O/1081, UEA. Payne to JM, 18 August 1941, O/1081; *Evansville Courier*, 28 August 1941—2 September 1941; *UE News*, 20 September 1941; William Sentner, Report on Midwest Emergency Conference on Unemployment Due to Priorities, O/1321, UEA; James Payne to James Matles, 10 September 1941, O/1082, UEA; *Evansville Courier*, 28 August—2 September 1941.

13 Lyle Dowling to Sentner, October 1941, UE National Office Correspondence, Sentner Papers.

14 See Rosemary Feurer, "Left Unionism in the Heartland: St. Louis District Eight, United Electrical Workers-CIO," (Ph.D. diss., Washington University, St. Louis), chapter 6.

15 William Sentner to Harry S. Truman, 29 May 1944, D/8-88, UEA.

16 William Sentner to William McClellan, 30 August 1944, D/8-89, UEA.

17 *UE News*, 11 March 1944, 14 April 1944.

18 *St. Louis Globe-Democrat*, 7 September 1942, in Morgue files, Mercantile Library, St. Louis; *St. Louis Globe-Democrat*, 12 July 1942; District Executive Board Report, 30 January 1945; *St. Louis American*, 2 April 1943.

19 DeSoto Post-War Planning Conference, 30 July 1944, series 5, box 5, folder 1, Sentner Papers.

20 District Executive Board, "MVA Report," series 2, box 2, folder 17, Sentner Papers; NR Press Release, 21 March 1944, series 2 box 1, folder 2.

21 "Correspondence, One River, One Plan," series 2, box 1, folder 3; "Post War Planning and the Missouri River Valley Basin," 13 July 1944, series 2, box 1, folder 2, Sentner Papers; District Executive Board, "MVA Report," August 1944; Untitled fact sheet, series 2, box 2, folder 17, Sentner Papers.

22 Naomi Ring to Bill McMurphy, 26 September 1944, series 2, box 1, folder 1; William McMurphy to Naomi Ring, 6 October 1944, series 2, box 1, folder 1; see also, William Sentner to Jerry O'Connal, 26 September 1944, all in Sentner Papers.

23 Worster, *Rivers of Empire*, 249-50; Walter E. Packard to William Sentner, 29 July 1944; Paul G. Pinsky to William Sentner, 18 July 1944; William Sentner to Walter Packard, 22 July 1944, all in Sentner Papers, series 2, box 1, folder 2, Sentner Papers.

24 See letters "Correspondence, One River, One Plan"; William Sentner in *The Worker Magazine*, 8 October 1944, series 2, box 1, folder 1, both in Sentner Papers; "Statement by James A. Davis before Congress," undated, folder 798, James Davis Papers, Collection 3666, Western Historical Manuscripts Collection-University of Missouri, Columbia.

25 "UE Role on M.V.A.," series 2, box 1, folder 1, Sentner Papers.

26 H. E. Klinefelter to William Sentner, 21 July 1944, series 2, box 1, folder 2, Sentner Papers.

27 *St. Louis Star-Times*, 18 October 1944.

28 *St. Louis Post-Dispatch*, 11 September 1944; "Patton Urges Farm Union to Stand Firm for MVA," series 2, box 1, folder 4, Sentner Papers; Glenn Talbott to Naomi Ring, 31 August 1944, series 2, box 1, folder 2, Sentner Papers.

29 Naomi Ring to Kenneth Simons, *Bismarck Tribune* (North Dakota), 31 August 1944, Sentner Papers.

**30** Naomi Ring to Glenn Talbott, 5 September 1944, reply to Talbott's letter of 31 August 1944; William Sentner to A. M. Piper, 1 September 1944; H. E. Klinefelter to 10 August 1944, all in Sentner Papers.

**31** Naomi Ring to William Sentner, 18 August 1944, series 2, box 5, folder 1, Sentner Papers.

**32** William Sentner to Francis Saylor, 29 July 1944, series 2, box 1, folder 2, Sentner Papers. In this letter, Sentner describes the drafting of the legislation. Donald E. Spritzer, in "One River, One Problem: James Murray and the Missouri Valley Authority," in *Montana and the West: Essays in Honor of K. Ross Tool*, ed. Rex. C. Myers and Harry W. Fritz (Boulder, Col.: Pruett Publishing Co., 1984), 125, asserts that the bill was written by Murray and his staff with the assistance of David Lilienthal. Murray, however, tended to underplay any role of organized labor in strategizing for the bill. Sentner's letter to Saylor is too detailed to controvert his version of the writing of the bill.

**33** *St. Louis Post-Dispatch*, 18 August 1944.

**34** *St. Louis Star-Times*, 16 November 1944.

**35** "MVA Report," September 1944, series 2, box 2, folder 17, Sentner Papers; William Sentner to Glen Talbott, 12 October 1944; William Sentner, "Speech on the Missouri Valley Authority," series 2, box 2, folder 6, Sentner Papers.

**36** *St. Louis Post-Dispatch*, 14-16 October 1944; "Patton Urges Farm Union to Stand Firm For MVA," unidentified newspaper article, 21 November 1944, series 2, box 1, folder 4, Sentner Papers; Spritzer, "One River, One Problem," 127.

**37** *St. Louis Post-Dispatch*, 18 November 1944; Spritzer, "One River, One Problem," 128; *St. Louis Post-Dispatch*, 30 November 1944; Walter Packard to Thomas Blaisdell, 6 December 1944.

**38** Spritzer, "One River, One Problem"; Walter Packard to James Patton, 6 December 1944; 21 November 1944, series 2, box 1, folder 4; *St. Louis Post-Dispatch*, 29 November 1944; *Star-Times*, 16 November 1944; *St. Louis Post-Dispatch*, 29, 15 November 1944.

**39** *Missouri Farmer*, December 1944.

**40** William Sentner to William Chambers, 12 December 1944, series 2, box 2, folder 17, Sentner Papers.

**41** "Program for the Development of the Campaign," attached to William Sentner to Bill Chambers, 12 December 1944; William Chambers to H. E. Klinefelter, 27 December 1944, Sentner Papers.

**42** William Chambers to Clifford McEvoy, 21 December 1944, series 2, box 1, folder 1; William Sentner to Glenn Talbott, series 2, box 1, folder 2; St. Louis Committee for an MVA, "Statement of Principles," 10 January 1945, folder 794, James Davis Papers; *St. Louis Post-Dispatch*, 21 January 1945; William Chambers, "Memorandum" to Bill Sentner and Jack Becker, 18 January 1945, series 2, box 2, folder 17.

**43** "Program for the Development of the Campaign," 12/12/44 WS to Bill Chambers; William Chambers to H. E. Klinefelter, 27 December 1944; Naomi Ring to Bill McMurphy, 26 September 1944, series 2, box 1, folder 1; Carleton Ball, "What the M.V.A. Proposal Promises for America," in *Social Action*, folder 795, James Davis Papers.

**44** William Sentner to Francis Saylor, 31 March 1945, William Chambers to William Sentner, 10 January 1945, both in series 2, box 2, folder 17, Sentner Papers; *St. Louis Post-Dispatch*, 20 February 1945.

**45** William Sentner to Francis Sayler, 31 March 1945, series 2, box 2, folder 16, Sentner Papers; Smith, 67.

**46** "Basic Information for Speakers on MVA," January 1945, D8/MVA, United Electrical Workers Archives; *St. Louis Post-Dispatch*, 20 February 1945.

**47** *St. Louis Post-Dispatch*, 22 March 1945; Walter Packard to Jerry McConnell.

**48** Press release, Missouri Conference on MVA, 16 April 1945; Raymond Tucker to James A. Davis, 30 April 1945; in folder 794, James Davis Papers.

49 "Regional Conference on MVA, 6-7 July 1945," Davis Papers, folder 795; "Special to Farm and Labor Press," 30 June 1945, series 2, box 1, folder 8, Sentner Papers; "Sponsors of Regional Conference on MVA," D8/MVA, United Electrical Workers Archives, Pittsburgh, Pennsylvania; Spritzer, "One River, One Problem," 133.

50 "Political Significance of the MVA Movement," series 2, box 2, folder 1, Sentner Papers.

51 *St. Louis Post-Dispatch*, 20 February 1945; *Star-Times*, 17 February 1945; Larry Allen Whiteside, "Harry S. Truman and James E. Murray: The Missouri Valley Authority Proposal," (Master's Thesis, Central Missouri State University, 1970), 77; Spritzer, "One River, One Problem," 129. William Sentner to Jack Becker, 21 May 1945, series 2, box 1, folder 8, Sentner Papers.

52 Spritzer, "One River, One Problem," 131.

53 *St. Louis Post-Dispatch*, 29 November 1944, 4 August 1945; Sentner, "Political Significance of the MVA Movement," series 2, box 2, folder 1; Spritzer, "One River, One Problem," 132; Scheele, 41-43.

54 Jack (Becker) to William Sentner, 13 October 1945, series 2, box 1, folder 7, Sentner Papers; *St. Louis Post-Dispatch*, 24 October 1945.

55 Spritzer, "One River, One Problem," 132; Scheele, 41-43; Marian Ridgeway, *The Missouri Basin's Pick-Sloan Plan: A Case Study in Congressional Determination* (Urbana: University of Illinois Press, 1955), 215; Sentner, "Political Significance of the MVA Movement"; *Fairfield Iowa Ledger*, 18 September 1945, in series 2, box 1, folder 7, Sentner Papers; *Kansas City Star*, 8 July 1945, series 2, box 1, folder 8, Sentner Papers. For pro-MVA forces' arguments that the MVA was a clear step toward decentralized government, see Patton quoted in unidentified newspaper article, 21 November 1944, series 2, box 1, folder 4, Sentner Papers, and William Sentner to A. M. Piper, 1 September 1944, series 2, box 1, folder 2, Sentner Papers.

56 Statement by James A. Davis before Congress, undated, folder 798; Press Release, 21 September 1945, folder 800, both in James Davis Papers.

57 "Political Significance of the MVA movement," series 2, box 2, folder 1, Sentner Papers; William Sentner to C. B. Baldwin, 3 November 1945, series 2, box 2, folder 10, Sentner Papers.

58 On the way that internal divisions and red-baiting affected the CIO's participation in MVA and on centralization of CIO's activities in Washington, D.C., see Francis Saylor to William Sentner, 12 February 1945, series 2 box 2, folder 10; Neil Brant to William Sentner, 15 February 1945, William Sentner to Neil Brant, 17 February 1945, Francis Saylor to William Sentner, 1 March 1945, series 2, box 2 folder 10; William Sentner to Julius Emspak, 9 July 1945, D-8/92, UEA; Jack Becker to Phil Murray, 23 July 1945, series 2, box 1, folder 8; Albert Fitzgerald to John Brophy, 24 July 1945, William Sentner to Reid Robinson, 8 August 1945, series 2 box 1, folder 7; *St. Louis Post-Dispatch*, 20 March 1945; Ruth Roemer to William Sentner, 14 July 1947, Ruth Roemer to Robert Logsdon, 19 July 1945, Robert Logsdon to Morris L. Cooke, 21 July 1947, series 2, box 1, folder 10, Sentner Papers; John Brophy to James A. Davis, 1 April 1948, folder 819, James Davis Papers.

59 Spritzer, "One River, One Problem," 132-36; Benton Stong to Members, 30 November 1948.

60 Morris Cooke, "Plain Talk About MVA," in *Iowa Law Review*, Davis Papers; F. V. Heinkle, Pres. Missouri Farmers Association, Valley Authority Conference, 17-18 July 1947, 84, folder 808, James Davis Papers.

61 CIO committee on Regional Development and Conservation, folder 821, James Davis Papers.

62 *St. Louis Post-Dispatch*, 17 July 1951; Scheele, 56, 80-82, 102.

## Andrew Hurley, Environmental Hazards Since World War II

1 This relationship between wealth and immunity does not hold to the same degree for earthquakes, largely because stone masonry construction tends to be more vulnerable than wood frames. When massive earthquakes along the New Madrid fault shook St. Louis in 1811, brick chimneys toppled and stone houses cracked while cheaper wooden homes remained unscathed. James Lal Penick, Jr., *The New Madrid Earthquakes*, revised edition (Columbia: University of Missouri Press, 1981), 111.

2 Martin Green, *The Great Tornado at St. Louis* (St. Louis: Graf Engraving Co., 1896); Southern Age, *Pictured Story of the Tornado* (St. Louis: Great Western Printing Co., ca. 1896); Julian Cruzon, *The Great Cyclone at St. Louis and East St. Louis, May 27, 1896* (St. Louis: Cyclone Publishing Co., 1896), 21-55, 75-211.

3 *St. Louis Post-Dispatch*, 21 May 1943, 3D.

4 By the 1970s, two-thirds of the metropolitan floodplain had been developed, an unusually high amount for urban areas. William J. Schneider and James E. Goddard, "Extent and Development of Urban Flood Plains," in *Geology in the Urban Environment*, ed. R. O. Utgard, G. D. McKenzie, and D. Foley (Minneapolis: Burgess Publishing Co., 1978), 38-39.

5 Lewis F. Thomas, *The Localization of Business Activities in Metropolitan St. Louis* (St. Louis: Washington University, 1927), 6, 12.

6 Carolyn Hewes Toft, ed., *Carondelet: the Ethnic Heritage of an Urban Neighborhood* (St. Louis: Washington University, 1975), 17.

7 *St. Louis Post-Dispatch*, 7 June 1903, 4-5.

8 Newspaper clipping, "Floods in St. Louis Vicinity," 2, (scrapbook), Missouri Historical Society Library.

9 U.S. Secretary of War, "Harbor and Approaches to St. Louis," U.S. House of Representatives Document no. 772, 59th Cong., 1st Sess., 4 May 1906, 3-20; *St. Louis Post-Dispatch*, 5 June 1903, 2; 7 June 1903, 5. On flood control developments in the vicinity of East St. Louis, see Craig Colten, "Environmental Development in the East St. Louis Region, 1890-1970," in *Environmental History Review* 14 (spring/summer 1990): 96-101.

10 Fredrick J. Dobney, *River Engineers on the Middle Mississippi: A History of the St. Louis District, U.S. Army Corps of Engineers* (Washington, D.C.: Government Printing Office, 1978), 77.

11 U.S. Army Corps of Engineers, *Mississippi River at St. Louis, Missouri* (Washington, D.C.: U.S. Government Printing Office, 1954), 19.

12 Anne Whiston Spirn, *The Granite Garden: Urban Nature and Human Design* (New York: Basic Books, 1984), 131.

13 *St. Louis Post-Dispatch*, 28 May, 1948, 9A: *St. Louis Globe-Democrat*, 9 December 1948, 3A; Malcolm Elliot, "Statement Concerning Character and Extent of Improvement for Flood Control Desired in the City of St. Louis and Need and Advisability of their Execution," 8 December 1948; U.S. Army Corps of Engineers, *Mississippi River at St. Louis, Missouri*, 5-6; City Plan Commission, *River Des Peres Plan* (St. Louis: A. R. Fleming, 1916); W. W. Horner, "Constructing River des Peres Drainage Canal in Earth-II," in *Engineering News-Record*, 31 July 1930, 176-80.

14 C. D. Stelzer, "The River Bottom Line," in *Riverfront Times*, 4-10 August 1993, 14-16; U.S. Army Corps of Engineers, *Mississippi River at St. Louis, Missouri*, 1-10, 25, 50, 63-64.

15 Subcommittee of the Committee on Public Works, U.S. Senate, *Flood Control—River and Harbor Projects* (Washington, D.C.: U.S. Government Printing Office, 1955), 97-101, 116.

16 Dobney, *River Engineers on the Middle Mississippi*, 134. *St. Louis Globe-Democrat*, 18 October 1964, magazine section, 1.

17 Subcommittee of the Committee on Public Works, U.S. Senate, *Flood Control—River and Harbor Projects*, 89. U.S. Army Corps of Engineers, *Mississippi River at St. Louis, Missouri*, 9.

18 C. D. Stelzer, "The River Bottom Line," 14-16; *St. Louis Post-Dispatch*, 31 July 1994, 4B.

19 George Gaylord Simpson, "A Fossil Deposit Cave in St. Louis," in *American Museum Novitates* (4 February 1949): 1-11.

20 Forest Stevens, "The City as Habitat for Wildlife and Man," in *Urbanization and Environment: The Physical Geography of the City*, ed. Thomas R. Detwyler and Melvin G. Marcus (Belmont, Calif.: Duxbury Press, 1972), 261-77; Steven D. Garber, *The Urban Naturalist* (New York: John Wiley & Sons, 1987), 52-208; Don Gill and Penelope Bonnett, *Nature in the Urban Landscape: A Study of City Ecosystems* (Baltimore: York Press, 1973).

21 Clay McShane and Joel A. Tarr, "The Centrality of the Horse to the Nineteenth Century American City," in *The Making of Urban America*, 2nd edition, ed. Raymond Mohl (Wilmington: Scholarly Resources, forthcoming); U.S. Census Office, "Report of the Social Statistics of Cities, Part II" (Washington, D.C.: U.S. Government Printing Office, 1887), 581.

22 Sterling P. Jones, *Migratory and Permanent Resident Birds* (St. Louis: The St. Louis Bird Club, 1947), 6-9; Garber, *The Urban Naturalist*, 143-45.

23 Garber, *The Urban Naturalist*, 182-85; *St. Louis Globe-Democrat*, 10 February 1946, 6E; 5 February 1955, 6A; Department of Health and Hospitals, City of St. Louis, Health Division, "Rat Control Project Evaluation Report," September 1980, 1-2; League of Women Voters of St. Louis, "Rat Control" in *Journal of the Board of Aldermen of the City of St. Louis*, Regular Session, 1945-1946, no. 9, 1 June 1945, 68-69, box 56, folder 737; League of Women Voters of St. Louis (1919), Addenda, 1916-1977, Western Historical Manuscripts Collection, University of Missouri-St. Louis, St. Louis, Missouri.

24 Sam Bass Warner, Jr., *The Way We Really Live* (Boston Public Library, 1978), 57.

25 *Journal of the Board of Aldermen of the City of St. Louis*, 1 June 1945, 70.

26 *St. Louis Star-Times*, 23 July 1945, box 56, folder 737, League of Women Voters Addenda. League of Women Voters of St. Louis, "Rat Control," ca. 1945, box 56, folder 737, League of Women Voters Addenda.

27 *St. Louis Star-Times*, 23 July 1945; *Journal of the Board of Aldermen*, 1 June 1945, 67-74; *St. Louis Globe-Democrat*, 4 February 1955, 1; Department of Health and Hospitals, *Rat Control Project Evaluation Report*, 1-3; St. Louis Health Division, "Project Rat Countdown," (1968), 72-74; Community Program Development Corporation, "Tandy-Sherman Neighborhood, Neighborhood Development Strategies Report," draft, ca. 1989, Community Development Agency of St. Louis library, St. Louis, 25, 40-41. "Community Development Needs Analysis, District 12," ca. 1976, Community Development Agency of St. Louis library, 4-14.

28 *Journal of the Board of Aldermen*, 1 June 1945, 70-72.

29 Census records reports reveal that roughly 90 percent of housing in the Mill Creek Valley was composed of rental units. U.S. Bureau of the Census, *U.S. Census of the Population: 1950. Volume III, Census Tract Statistics*, chap. 47, (Washington, D.C.: U.S. Government Publications Office, 1952), 54-55.

30 *St. Louis Globe-Democrat*, 4 February 1955, 1; 5 February 1955, 6A.

31 *St. Louis Star-Times*, 23 July 1945; St. Louis Health Division, "Project Rat Countdown," 21-26.

32 Department of Health and Hospitals, City of St. Louis, "Rat Control Project Evaluation Report," 2.

33 *St. Louis Globe-Democrat*, 5 February 1955, 6A; St. Louis Health Division, "Project Rat Countdown," 21-22.

34 *St. Louis Globe-Democrat*, 6 February 1955, 4A; 21 February 1955, 10A.

35 Teamsters Local 688, "The People Must Act," ca. 1955, "Labor Organizations" folder, series 1, box 15, Raymond Tucker Papers, Washington University Archives, St. Louis, Missouri.

36 *St. Louis Globe-Democrat,* 18 June 1964, 3A; St. Louis Health Division, "Project Rat Countdown," 28, 69, 70.

37 Department of Health and Hospitals, City of St. Louis, *Rat Control Project Evaluation Report.*

38 United Church of Christ Commission for Racial Justice and Public Data Access, Inc., *Toxic Wastes and Race in the United States: A National Report on the Racial and Socioeconomic Characteristics of Communities with Hazardous Waste Sites* (New York, 1987); Follow-up studies include: Paul Mohai and Bunyan Bryant, "Environmental Racism: Reviewing the Evidence," in *Race and the Incidence of Environmental Hazard: A Time for Discourse,* ed. Bunyan Bryant and Paul Mohai (Boulder, Col.: Westview Press, 1992), 169-76; Douglas L. Anderton, Andy B. Anderson, Peter H. Rossi, John Michael Oakes, Michael R. Fraser, Eleanor W. Weber, and Edward J. Calabrese, "Hazardous Waste Facilities: 'Environmental Equity' Issues in Metropolitan Areas," in *Evaluation Review* 18 (April 1994), 123-40; John A. Hird, *Superfund: The Political Economy of Environmental Risk* (Baltimore: Johns Hopkins University Press, 1994): 130-37; Benjamin A. Goldman and Laura Fitton, *Toxic Wastes and Race Revisited: An Update of the 1987 Report on the Racial and Socioeconomic Characteristics of Communities With Hazardous Waste Sites* (Washington, D.C.: Center for Policy Alternatives, 1994). With the exception of Anderton, et al., the above studies confirmed the conclusions of the UCC report.

39 J.A. Dacus and James W. Buel, *A Tour of St. Louis; Or, The Inside Life of a Great City* (St. Louis: Western Publishing Co., 1878), 243-46.

40 "Explanation of Significant Differences for the NL Industries/Taracorp Site, Granite City, Illinois, February 1993, Taracorp folder, Bureau of Land Pollution files, Illinois Environmental Protection Agency" (henceforth cited as IEPA), Springfield, Illinois. Missouri Department of Natural Resources, Division of Environmental Quality, *Confirmed Abandoned or Uncontrolled Hazardous Waste Disposal Sites in Missouri and Hazardous Waste Remedial Fund Statement of Revenues, Expenditures, and Changes in Fund Balance* (Jefferson City: Missouri Department of Natural Resources, 1994), 197.

41 George Lipsitz, *A Life in the Struggle: Ivory Perry and the Culture of Opposition,* rev. ed. (Philadelphia: Temple University Press, 1988), 173-97.

42 Missouri Department of Natural Resources, *Confirmed Abandoned or Uncontrolled Hazardous Waste,* 21; Roy Weston, Inc. "Formerly Utilized Sites Remedial Action Program, St. Louis Airport Storage Site (SLAPSS), Technical Series," vol. 1, no. 1, January 1982, FUSRAP Administrative Record files, St. Louis Public Library, St. Louis, Missouri, 3-1 through 3-4; *Federal Register,* 9 January 1992, 887-89.

43 Samuel S. Epstein, Lester O. Brown, and Carl Pope, *Hazardous Waste in America* (San Francisco: Sierra Club Books, 1982), 11-12, 20-30. Harold C. Barnett, *Toxic Debts and the Superfund Dilemma* (Chapel Hill: University of North Carolina Press, 1994), 14-16.

44 Craig E. Colten and Peter N. Skinner, *The Road to Love Canal: Managing Industrial Waste Before EPA* (Austin: University of Texas Press, 1996), 69-95.

45 NEPACCO entered into a waste disposal contract with Independent Petrochemical Company which then subcontracted the work to Bliss.

46 Hearing "Before the Hazardous Waste Management Commission, State of Missouri," 24 July 1985, transcript, 12-15, Hammill Transfer, Technical, folder, Hazardous Waste Program files, Missouri Department of Natural Resources, Jefferson City, Missouri.

47 Epstein, Brown, and Pope, *Hazardous Waste in America,* 135-40; Missouri Department of Natural Resources, *Confirmed, Abandoned, or Uncontrolled Hazardous Waste,* 22, 35-41, 58-60, 83-85, 142-46, 149-58; *Kansas City Star,* 23 August 1981, A1.

**48** U.S. EPA, "Superfund Fact Sheet, Lanson Chemical Company Site, East St. Louis, Illinois," September 1992, Lanson Chemical Company SF, Technical, folder, Bureau of Land Management files, IEPA; *St. Louis Post-Dispatch*, 15 July 1993, 3B.

**49** "ACF Site, St. Louis, Missouri, Clean-Up Assessment," 10 August 1984, ACF folder, Hazardous Waste Management files, Missouri Department of Natural Resources, Sunset Hills, Missouri. Missouri Department of Natural Resources, *Confirmed, Abandoned, or Uncontrolled Hazardous Waste Disposal Sites in Missouri*, 173-75.

**50** Memorandum form Timothy Murphy to Alan Altur, 20 February 1992, Sauget Sites folder, IEPA; *St. Louis Post-Dispatch*, 7 October, 1991, 1A.

**51** Richard J. Compton and Camille N. Dry, *Pictorial St. Louis: A Topological Survey Drawn in Perspective* (St. Louis: Compton and Company, 1876), 137.

**52** "Final Report, Acme Battery Manufacturing, Inc.," 27 March 1989, U.S. EPA Administrative Record files, St. Louis Public Library, Grand Avenue, St. Louis, Missouri.

**53** *St. Louis Post-Dispatch*, 12 February 1985, 4.

**54** *St. Louis Post-Dispatch*, 30 October 1987, 3A; "Sites Recommended for Sampling for Possible Dioxin Contamination," 1 September 1983, Arkansas Best Freight, Technical, folder, Hazardous Waste Program files, Missouri Department of Natural Resources, Jefferson City; *Potential Hazardous Waste Site, EPA Site Inspection Report*, 31 January 1984, Hammill Transfer Company, Technical, folder, Missouri Department of Natural Resources, Jefferson City.

**55** Thomas Lambert and Christopher Boerner, *Environmental Inequity: Economic Causes, Economic Solutions*, Policy Study no. 125 (St. Louis: Center for the Study of American Business, Washington University, 1995), 8; Andrew Hurley, *Toxic Waste and Race in St. Louis* (St. Louis: Public Policy Research Centers, University of Missouri–St. Louis, 1995). One recent study has found similar patterns of inequality with regard to exposure from toxic air emissions. Kevin L. Brown, "Environmental Discrimination: Myth or Reality," unpublished research paper, Washington University School of Law, St. Louis, Missouri, 29 March 1991, photocopy in author's possession.

**56** Lambert and Boerner, *Environmental Inequity*, 8-13.

**57** Katharine T. Corbett and Mary E. Seematter, "No Crystal Stair: Black St. Louis, 1920-1940" in *Gateway Heritage* 8 (fall 1987): 9.

**58** Interview with Lee Demba, Demba Realty Corporation, University City, Missouri, 28 November 1994; U.S. Bureau of the Census, *U.S. Census of Population and Housing: 1960; Census Tracts*, Final Report PHC (1)-131 (Washington, D.C.: U.S. Government Printing Office, 1962), 32, 119; U.S. Bureau of the Census, *U.S. Census of Population and Housing: 1970; Census Tracts*, Final Report PHC (1)-181, St. Louis, Mo.-Ill. SMSA (Washington, D.C.: U.S. Government Printing Office, 1972), P20, P29-P35; U.S. Bureau of the Census, *U.S. Census of Population and Housing: 1980; Census Tracts*, Final Report PHC80-2-313, St. Louis, Mo.-Ill. SMSA (Washington, D.C., U.S. Government Printing Office, 1983), P155-P157.

**59** East-West Coordinating Council, *Transportation Redefined: A Plan for the Region's Future* (St. Louis, 1994), 90.

# Acknowledgments

Many thanks are due to the Missouri Historical Society, not only for doing a wonderful job publishing this collection of essays, but also for granting me a research exchange fellowship in the fall of 1995 for the purposes of executing the project. Several individuals at the Society deserve special mention. Lee Ann Sandweiss, director of publications, remained steadfast in her enthusiastic support. The prose benefited from the skillful editorial guidance of Ben Cawthra and Tim Fox. Duane Sneddeker provided invaluable assistance with the illustrations, all of which are housed in the Missouri Historical Society's collections unless otherwise noted. I would also like to thank all of the contributors for responding promptly and thoughtfully to my requests for revisions. I owe a special debt of gratitude to Patricia Cleary, Craig Colten, and Eric Sandweiss for critiquing drafts of my chapters. Finally, Eric Sandweiss deserves the credit from coming up with the book's title.

# Index